Praise for *Think Perl 6*

Perl 6 from a fresh and interesting perspective.

—*brian d foy, author of* Mastering Perl

Think Perl 6 will teach you programming in a way that is optimized for fun. Starting from basic concepts, you are taken along toward being able to design, build, and maintain your own programming projects in the style of your choosing: be it procedural, functional or object-oriented, or any mix of them. Because Perl 6 allows you to program in the way you think!

—*Elizabeth Mattijsen, Perl 6 core contributor*

Think Perl 6 is a solid introduction to both programming and Perl 6. I couldn't be happier about it.

—*Moritz Lenz, Perl 6 core contributor*

In my 30+ years as a student of computer languages, this is the most engaging and well-written technology book I have read. The author is undoubtedly well-versed in Perl 6 and knows how to present the material in both a highly readable and informative manner. The book includes an impressive amount of example code and thorough and engaging exercises for each topic. If you want to become proficient in Perl 6 in the minimum amount of time, and enjoy the process, this is the book for you.

—*Allen Hardesty, Software Developer*

Think Perl 6

How to Think Like a Computer Scientist

Laurent Rosenfeld, with Allen B. Downey

Beijing · Boston · Farnham · Sebastopol · Tokyo

Think Perl 6

by Laurent Rosenfeld, with Allen B. Downey

Copyright © 2017 Allen Downey, Laurent Rosenfeld. All rights reserved.

Printed in the United States of America.

Published by O'Reilly Media, Inc., 1005 Gravenstein Highway North, Sebastopol, CA 95472.

Editors: Dawn Schanafelt and Brian Foster
Production Editor: Kristen Brown
Copyeditor: Charles Roumeliotis
Proofreader: Molly Ives Brower

Indexer: Laurent Rosenfeld and Allen B. Downey
Interior Designer: David Futato
Cover Designer: Karen Montgomery
Illustrator: Rebecca Demarest

May 2017:   First Edition

Revision History for the First Edition
2017-05-05:   First Release

See *http://oreilly.com/catalog/errata.csp?isbn=9781491980552* for release details.

978-1-491-98055-2

[LSI]

Table of Contents

Preface. xiii

Part I. Starting with the Basics

1. The Way of the Program. 3
What Is a Program?   3
Running Perl 6   4
The First Program   6
Arithmetic Operators   6
Values and Types   7
Formal and Natural Languages   10
Debugging   11
Glossary   12
Exercises   14

2. Variables, Expressions, and Statements. 15
Assignment Statements   15
Variable Names   17
Expressions and Statements   19
Script Mode   21
One-Liner Mode   22
Order of Operations   23
String Operations   24
Comments   25
Debugging   25
Glossary   26
Exercises   28

3. Functions. **31**

Function Calls   31
Functions and Methods   34
Math Functions   34
Composition   36
Adding New Functions (a.k.a. Subroutines)   37
Definitions and Uses   39
Flow of Execution   39
Parameters and Arguments   40
Variables and Parameters Are Local   41
Stack Diagrams   42
Fruitful Functions and Void Functions   42
Function Signatures   44
Immutable and Mutable Parameters   46
Functions and Subroutines as First-Class Citizens   47
Why Functions and Subroutines?   49
Debugging   50
Glossary   50
Exercises   53

4. Loops, Conditionals, and Recursion. **55**

Integer Division and Modulo   55
Boolean expressions   56
Logical Operators   58
Conditional Execution   60
Alternative Execution   61
Chained Conditionals   61
Nested Conditionals   62
if Conditionals as Statement Modifiers   63
Unless Conditional Statement   63
for Loops   64
Recursion   66
Stack Diagrams for Recursive Subroutines   67
Infinite Recursion   68
Keyboard Input   68
Program Arguments and the MAIN Subroutine   69
Debugging   70
Glossary   71
Exercises   73

5. Fruitful Subroutines. **77**

Return Values   77

Incremental Development   79
Composition   81
Boolean Functions   82
A Complete Programming Language   83
More Recursion   84
Leap of Faith   86
One More Example   87
Checking Types   87
Multi Subroutines   89
Debugging   90
Glossary   91
Exercises   92

6. Iteration. 95
Assignment Versus Equality   95
Reassignment   96
Updating Variables   96
The while Statement   97
Local Variables and Variable Scoping   99
Control Flow Statements (last, next, etc.)   102
Square Roots   104
Algorithms   106
Debugging   106
Glossary   107
Exercises   107

7. Strings. 109
A String Is a Sequence   109
Common String Operators   110
    String Length   110
    Searching for a Substring Within the String   111
    Extracting a Substring from a String   111
    A Few Other Useful String Functions or Methods   112
String Traversal with a while or for Loop   115
Looping and Counting   116
Regular Expressions (Regexes)   116
Using Regexes   118
Building your Regex Patterns   119
    Literal Matching   119
    Wildcards and Character Classes   120
    Quantifiers   121
    Anchors and Assertions   122

Alternation	124
Grouping and Capturing	124
Adverbs (a.k.a. Modifiers)	125
Exercises on Regexes	126
Putting It All Together	127
Extracting Dates	127
Extracting an IP Address	128
Substitutions	130
The subst Method	130
The s/search/replace/ Construct	130
Using Captures	131
Adverbs	131
Debugging	131
Glossary	134
Exercises	135

8. Case Study: Word Play. **139**

Reading from and Writing to Files	139
Reading Word Lists	141
Exercises	142
Search	143
Words Longer Than 20 Characters (Solution)	143
Words with No "e" (Solution)	144
Avoiding Other Letters (Solution)	145
Using Only Some Letters (Solution)	146
Using All Letters of a List (Solution)	147
Alphabetic Order (Solution)	147
Another Example of Reduction to a Previously Solved Problem	148
Debugging	149
Glossary	149
Exercises	150

9. Arrays and Lists. **153**

Lists and Arrays Are Sequences	153
Arrays Are Mutable	155
Adding New Elements to an Array or Removing Some	158
Stacks and Queues	159
Other Ways to Modify an Array	160
Traversing a List	162
New Looping Constructs	164
Map, Filter, and Reduce	165
Reducing a List to a Value	165

    The Reduction Metaoperator 166
    Mapping a List to Another List 167
    Filtering the Elements of a List 168
    Higher-Order Functions and Functional Programming 169
  Fixed-Size, Typed, and Shaped Arrays 170
  Multidimensional Arrays 171
  Sorting Arrays or Lists 172
  More Advanced Sorting Techniques 173
  Debugging 176
  Glossary 177
  Exercises 178

10. Hashes. **183**
  A Hash Is a Mapping 183
  Common Operations on Hashes 186
  Hash as a Collection of Counters 187
  Looping and Hashes 188
  Reverse Lookup 189
  Testing for Existence 190
  Hash Keys Are Unique 192
  Hashes and Arrays 193
  Memos 195
  Hashes as Dispatch Tables 197
  Global Variables 198
  Debugging 199
  Glossary 200
  Exercises 201

11. Case Study: Data Structure Selection. **203**
  The Ternary Conditional Operator 203
  The given ... when "Switch" Statement 204
  Subroutine Named and Optional Parameters 206
    Named Parameters 206
    Optional Parameters 207
  Word Frequency Analysis 208
  Random Numbers 208
  Word Histogram 210
  Most Common Words 212
  Optional Parameters 213
  Hash Subtraction 214
  Constructing New Operators 214
  Sets, Bags, and Mixes 215

Random Words   217
Markov Analysis   219
Data Structures   221
Building Your Own Data Structures   222
    Linked Lists   223
    Trees   224
    Binary Heaps   224
Debugging   227
Glossary   229
Exercises: Huffman Coding   230
    Variable-Length Codes   230
    The Frequency Table   231
    Building the Huffman Code   231

Part II.   Moving Forward

12. Classes and Objects. **237**
Objects, Methods, and Object-Oriented Programming   237
Programmer-Defined Types   239
Attributes   240
Creating Methods   242
Rectangles and Object Composition   245
Instances as Return Values   247
Inheritance   247
    The Pixel Class   248
    The MovablePoint Class   250
    Multiple Inheritance: Attractive, but Is It Wise?   251
Roles and Composition   252
    Classes and Roles: An Example   253
    Role Composition and Code Reuse   255
    Roles, Classes, Objects, and Types   256
Method Delegation   256
Polymorphism   258
Encapsulation   259
    Private Methods   260
    Constructing Objects with Private Attributes   261
Interface and Implementation   264
Object-Oriented Programming: A Tale   264
    The Fable of the Shepherd   265
    The Moral   265
Debugging   266

The Perl 6 Debugger   266
Getting Some Help   267
Stepping Through the Code   267
Stopping at the Right Place with Breakpoints   268
Logging Information with Trace Points   268
Stepping Through a Regex Match   269
Glossary   270

13. Regexes and Grammars. **273**
A Brief Refresher   273
Declarative Programming   275
Captures   275
Named Rules (a.k.a. Subrules)   276
Grammars   279
Grammar Inheritance   281
Actions Objects   282
A Grammar for Parsing JSON   284
The JSON Format   284
Our JSON Sample   284
Writing the JSON Grammar Step by Step   285
The JSON Grammar   287
Adding Actions   289
Inheritance and Mutable Grammars   291
Debugging   291
Glossary   293
Exercise: A Grammar for an Arithmetic Calculator   294

14. Functional Programming in Perl. **297**
Higher-Order Functions   297
A Refresher on Functions as First-Class Objects   297
Anonymous Subroutines and Lambdas   299
Closures   300
List Processing and Pipeline Programming   302
Feed and Backward Feed Operators   303
The Reduction Metaoperator   304
The Hyperoperator   304
The Cross (X) and Zip (Z) Operators   305
List Operators: A Summary   306
Creating New Operators   307
Creating Your Own Map-Like Functions   310
Custom versions of map, grep, etc.   310
Our Own Version of a Sort Function   311

       An Iterator Version of map   313
       An Iterator Version of grep   314
     The gather and take Construct   316
     Lazy Lists and the Sequence Operator   319
       The Sequence Operator   319
       Infinite Lists   320
       Using an Explicit Generator   320
     Currying and the Whatever Operator   322
       Creating a Curried Subroutine   323
       Currying an Existing Subroutine with the assuming Method   323
       Currying with the Whatever Star Parameter   324
     Using a Functional Programming Style   325
       The Merge Sort Algorithm   325
       A Nonfunctional Implementation of Merge Sort   326
       A Functional Implementation of Merge Sort   328
     Debugging   329
     Glossary   333
     Exercise: Quick Sort   334

15. Some Final Advice. **337**
     Make It Clear, Keep It Simple   337
     Dos and Don'ts   338
     Use Idioms   340
     What's Next?   343

A. Solutions to the Exercises. **345**

Index. **427**

Preface

Welcome to the art of computer programming and to the new Perl 6 language. This will probably be the first published book using Perl 6 (or one of the first), a powerful, expressive, malleable, and highly extensible programming language. But this book is less about Perl 6, and more about learning how to write programs for computers.

This book is intended for beginners and does not require any prior programming knowledge, but it is my hope that even those of you with programming experience will benefit from reading it.

The Aim of This Book

This aim of this book is not primarily to teach Perl 6, but instead to teach the art of programming, using the Perl 6 language. After having completed this book, you should hopefully be able to write programs to solve relatively difficult problems in Perl 6, but my main aim is to teach computer science, software programming, and problem solving rather than solely to teach the Perl 6 language itself.

This means that I will not cover every aspect of Perl 6, but only a (relatively large, but yet incomplete) subset of it. By no means is this book intended to be a reference on the language.

It is not possible to learn programming or to learn a new programming language by just reading a book; practicing is essential. This book contains a lot of exercises. You are strongly encouraged to make a real effort to do them. And, whether successful or not in solving the exercises, you should take a look at the solutions in the Appendix, as, very often, several solutions are suggested with further discussion on the subject and the issues involved. Sometimes, the solution section of the Appendix also introduces examples of topics that will be covered in the next chapter—and sometimes even things that are not covered elsewhere in the book. So, to get the most out of the book, I suggest you try to solve the exercises as well as review the solutions and attempt them.

There are more than one thousand code examples in this book; study them, make sure to understand them, and run them. When possible, try to change them and see what happens. You're likely to learn a lot from this process.

The History of This Book

In the course of the last three to four years, I have translated or adapted to French a number of tutorials and articles on Perl 6, and I've also written a few entirely new ones in French.[1] Together, these documents represented by the end of 2015 somewhere between 250 and 300 pages of material on Perl 6. By that time, I had probably made public more material on Perl 6 in French than all other authors taken together.

In late 2015, I began to feel that a Perl 6 document for beginners was something missing that I was willing to undertake. I looked around and found that it did not seem to exist in English either. I came to the idea that, after all, it might be more useful to write such a document initially in English, to give it a broader audience. I started contemplating writing a beginner introduction to Perl 6 programming. My idea at the time was something like a 50- to 70-page tutorial and I started to gather material and ideas in this direction.

Then, something happened that changed my plans.

In December 2015, friends of mine were contemplating translating into French Allen B. Downey's *Think Python, Second Edition*.[2] I had read an earlier edition of that book and fully supported the idea of translating it.[3] As it turned out, I ended up being a co-translator and the technical editor of the French translation of that book.[4]

While working on the French translation of Allen's Python book, the idea came to me that, rather than writing a tutorial on Perl 6, it might be more useful to make a "Perl 6 translation" of *Think Python*. Since I was in contact with Allen in the context of the French translation, I suggested this to Allen, who warmly welcomed the idea. This is how I started to write this book late January 2016, just after having completed the work on the French translation of his Python book.

This book is thus largely derived on Allen's *Think Python*, but adapted to Perl 6. As it happened, it is also much more than just a "Perl 6 translation" of Allen's book: with quite a lot of new material, it has become a brand new book, largely indebted to

---

1 See, for example, *http://perl.developpez.com/cours/#TutorielsPerl6*.

2 See *http://greenteapress.com/wp/think-python-2e/*.

3 I know, it's about Python, not Perl. But I don't believe in engaging in "language wars" and think that we all have to learn from other languages; to me, Perl's motto, "there is more than one way to do it," also means that doing it in Python (or some other language) is truly an acceptable possibility.

4 See *http://allen-downey.developpez.com/livres/python/pensez-python/*.

Allen's book, but yet a new book for which I take all responsibility. Any errors are my own, not Allen's.

My hope is that this will be useful to the Perl 6 community, and more broadly to the open source and general computer programming communities. In an interview with *LinuxVoice* (July 2015), Larry Wall, the creator of Perl 6, said: "We do think that Perl 6 will be learnable as a first language." Hopefully this book will contribute to making this happen.

Conventions Used in This Book

The following typographical conventions are used in this book:

Italic
Indicates new terms, URLs, email addresses, filenames, and file extensions.

`Constant width`
Used for program listings, as well as within paragraphs to refer to program elements such as variable or function names, databases, data types, environment variables, statements, and keywords.

`Constant width bold`
Shows commands or other text that should be typed literally by the user.

`Constant width italic`
Shows text that should be replaced with user-supplied values or by values determined by context.

This element signifies a tip or suggestion.

This element signifies a general note.

This element indicates a warning or caution.

Using Code Examples

Supplemental material (code examples, exercises, etc.) is available for download at *https://github.com/LaurentRosenfeld/thinkperl6/*.

This book is here to help you get your job done. In general, if example code is offered with this book, you may use it in your programs and documentation. You do not need to contact us for permission unless you're reproducing a significant portion of the code. For example, writing a program that uses several chunks of code from this book does not require permission. Selling or distributing a CD-ROM of examples from O'Reilly books does require permission. Answering a question by citing this book and quoting example code does not require permission. Incorporating a significant amount of example code from this book into your product's documentation does require permission.

We appreciate, but do not require, attribution. An attribution usually includes the title, author, publisher, and ISBN. For example: "*Think Perl 6* by Laurent Rosenfeld with Allen B. Downey (O'Reilly). Copyright 2017 Allen Downey, Laurent Rosenfeld, 978-1-491-98055-2."

If you feel your use of code examples falls outside fair use or the permission given above, feel free to contact us at *permissions@oreilly.com*.

O'Reilly Safari

 Safari (formerly Safari Books Online) is a membership-based training and reference platform for enterprise, government, educators, and individuals.

Members have access to thousands of books, training videos, Learning Paths, interactive tutorials, and curated playlists from over 250 publishers, including O'Reilly Media, Harvard Business Review, Prentice Hall Professional, Addison-Wesley Professional, Microsoft Press, Sams, Que, Peachpit Press, Adobe, Focal Press, Cisco Press, John Wiley & Sons, Syngress, Morgan Kaufmann, IBM Redbooks, Packt, Adobe Press, FT Press, Apress, Manning, New Riders, McGraw-Hill, Jones & Bartlett, and Course Technology, among others.

For more information, please visit *http://oreilly.com/safari*.

How to Contact Us

Please address comments and questions concerning this book to the publisher:

O'Reilly Media, Inc.
1005 Gravenstein Highway North
Sebastopol, CA 95472
800-998-9938 (in the United States or Canada)
707-829-0515 (international or local)
707-829-0104 (fax)

We have a web page for this book, where we list errata, examples, and any additional information. You can access this page at *http://bit.ly/thinkPerl6*.

To comment or ask technical questions about this book, send email to *bookquestions@oreilly.com*.

For more information about our books, courses, conferences, and news, see our website at *http://www.oreilly.com*.

Find us on Facebook: *http://facebook.com/oreilly*

Follow us on Twitter: *http://twitter.com/oreillymedia*

Watch us on YouTube: *http://www.youtube.com/oreillymedia*

Acknowledgments

I just don't know how I could thank Larry Wall to the level of gratitude he deserves for having created Perl in the first place, and Perl 6 more recently. Be blessed for eternity, Larry, for all of that.

And thank you to all of you who took part in this adventure (in no particular order), Tom, Damian, chromatic, Nathan, brian, Jan, Jarkko, John, Johan, Randall, Mark Jason, Ovid, Nick, Tim, Andy, Chip, Matt, Michael, Tatsuhiko, Dave, Rafael, Chris, Stevan, Saraty, Malcolm, Graham, Leon, Ricardo, Gurusamy, Scott, and too many others to name.

All my thanks also to those who believed in this Perl 6 project and made it happen, including those who quit at one point or another but contributed for some time; I know that this wasn't always easy.

Many thanks to Allen Downey, who very kindly supported my idea of adapting his book to Perl 6 and helped me in many respects, but also refrained from interfering into what I was putting in this new book.

I very warmly thank the people at O'Reilly who accepted the idea of this book and suggested many corrections or improvements. I want to thank especially Dawn Schanafelt, my editor at O'Reilly, whose advice has truly contributed to making this a better book. I also want to thank Kristen Brown for her helpful comments and work on publishing this book, and Charles Roumeliotis and Molly Ives Brower for their constructive review and edits.

Thanks a lot in advance to readers who will offer comments or submit suggestions or corrections, as well as encouragement.

If you see anything that needs to be corrected or that could be improved, please kindly send your comments to *think.perl6@gmail.com*.

Contributor List

I would like to thank especially Moritz Lenz and Elizabeth Mattijsen, who reviewed in detail drafts of this book and suggested quite a number of improvements and corrections. Liz spent a lot of time on a detailed review of the full content of this book and I am especially grateful to her for her numerous and very useful comments. Thanks also to Timo Paulssen and ryanschoppe who also reviewed early drafts and provided some useful suggestions. Many thanks also to Uri Guttman, who reviewed this book and suggested a number of small corrections and improvements shortly before publication.

Starting with the Basics

This book has been divided into two parts. The main reason for that is that I wanted to make a distinction between, on the one hand, relatively basic notions that are really necessary for any programmer using Perl 6; and on the other hand, more advanced concepts that a good programmer needs to know but are possibly used less often in day-to-day development work.

The first eleven chapters (a bit more than 200 pages) that make up this first part are meant to teach the concepts that every programmer should know: variables, expressions, statements, functions, conditionals, recursion, operator precedence, and loops, as well as commonly used basic data structures and the most useful algorithms. These chapters can, I believe, be the basis for a one-semester introductory course on programming.

Of course, the professor or teacher who wishes to use this material is entirely free to skip some details from Part I (and also to include sections from Part II), but, at least, I have provided some guidelines on how I think this book could be used to teach programming with the Perl 6 language.

Part II focuses on different programming paradigms and more advanced programming techniques that are (in my opinion) of paramount importance, but should probably be studied in the context of a second, more advanced, semester.

For now, let's get down to the basics. It is my hope that you will enjoy the trip.

## CHAPTER 1

The Way of the Program

The goal of this book is to teach you to think like a computer scientist. This way of thinking combines some of the best features of mathematics, engineering, and natural science. Like mathematicians, computer scientists use formal languages to denote ideas (specifically computations). Like engineers, they design things, assembling components into systems and evaluating tradeoffs among alternatives. Like scientists, they observe the behavior of complex systems, form hypotheses, and test predictions.

The single most important skill for a computer scientist is *problem solving*. Problem solving means the ability to formulate problems, think creatively about solutions, and express a solution clearly and accurately. As it turns out, the process of learning to program is an excellent opportunity to practice problem-solving skills. That's why this chapter is called, "The Way of the Program."

On one level, you will be learning to program, a useful skill by itself. On another level, you will use programming as a means to an end. As we go along, that end will become clearer.

What Is a Program?

A *program* is a sequence of instructions that specifies how to perform a computation. The computation might be something mathematical, such as solving a system of equations or finding the roots of a polynomial, but it can also be a symbolic computation, such as searching and replacing text in a document, or something graphical, like processing an image or playing a video.

The details look different in different languages, but a few basic instructions appear in just about every language:

Input

Get data from the keyboard, a file, the network, a sensor, a GPS chip, or some other device.

Output

Display data on the screen, save it in a file, send it over the network, act on a mechanical device, etc.

Math

Perform basic mathematical operations like addition and multiplication.

Conditional execution

Check for certain conditions and run the appropriate code.

Repetition

Perform some action repeatedly, usually with some variation.

Believe it or not, that's pretty much all there is to it. Every program you've ever used, no matter how complicated, is made up of instructions that look pretty much like these. So you can think of programming as the process of breaking a large, complex task into smaller and smaller subtasks until the subtasks are simple enough to be performed with one of these basic instructions.

Using or calling these subtasks makes it possible to create various levels of *abstraction*. You have probably been told that computers only use 0's and 1's at the lowest level; but we usually don't have to worry about that. When we use a word processor to write a letter or a report, we are interested in files containing text and some formatting instructions, and with commands to change the file or to print it; fortunately, we don't have to care about the underlying 0's and 1's; the word-processing program offers us a much higher view (files, commands, etc.) that hides the gory underlying details.

Similarly, when we write a program, we usually use and/or create several layers of abstraction, so that, for example, once we have created a subtask that queries a database and stores the relevant data in memory, we no longer have to worry about the technical details of the subtask. We can use it as a sort of black box that will perform the desired operation for us. The essence of programming is to a large extent this art of creating these successive layers of abstraction so that performing the higher level tasks becomes relatively easy.

Running Perl 6

One of the challenges of getting started with Perl 6 is that you might have to install Perl 6 and related software on your computer. If you are familiar with your operating system, and especially if you are comfortable with the shell or command-line interface, you will have no trouble installing Perl 6. But for beginners, it can be painful to learn about system administration and programming at the same time.

To avoid that problem, you can start out running Perl 6 in a web browser. You might want to use a search engine to find such a site. Currently, the easiest is probably to connect to the glot.io site (*https://glot.io/new/perl6*), where you can type some Perl 6 code in the main window, run it, and see the result in the output window below.

Sooner or later, however, you will really need to install Perl 6 on your computer.

The easiest way to install Perl 6 on your system is to download Rakudo Star (a distribution of Perl 6 that contains the Rakudo Perl 6 *compiler*, documentation and useful modules): follow the instructions for your operating system at the Rakudo (*http://rakudo.org/how-to-get-rakudo/*) and Perl 6 (*https://perl6.org/downloads/*) websites.

As of this writing, the most recent specification of the language is Perl 6 version 6c (v6.c), and the most recent release available for download is Rakudo Star 2016.07;[1] the examples in this book should all run with this version. You can find out the installed version by issuing the following command at the operating system prompt:

```
$ perl6 -v
This is Rakudo version 2016.07.1 built on MoarVM version 2016.07
implementing Perl 6.c.
```

However, you should probably download and install the most recent version you can find. The output (warnings, error messages, etc.) you'll get from your version of Perl might in some cases slightly differ from what is printed in this book, but these possible differences should essentially be only cosmetic.

Compared to Perl 5, Perl 6 is not just a new version of Perl. It is more like a new little sister of Perl 5. It does not aim to replace Perl 5. Perl 6 is really a new programming language, with a syntax that is similar to earlier versions of Perl (such as Perl 5), but still markedly different. Unless stated otherwise, this book is about Perl 6 only, not about Perl 5 and preceding versions of the Perl programming language. From now on, whenever we speak about *Perl* with no further qualification, we mean Perl 6.

The Perl 6 *interpreter* is a program that reads and executes Perl 6 code. It is sometimes called REPL (for "read, evaluate, print, loop"). Depending on your environment, you might start the interpreter by clicking on an icon, or by typing perl6 on a command line.

When it starts, you should see output like this:

```
To exit type 'exit' or '^D'
(Possibly some information about Perl and related software)
>
```

---

1 As we go to press, the latest version is 2017.01.

The last line with > is a *prompt* that indicates that the REPL is ready for you to enter code. If you type a line of code and hit Enter, the interpreter displays the result:

```
> 1 + 1
2
>
```

You can type exit at the REPL prompt to exit the REPL.

Now you're ready to get started. From here on, we assume that you know how to start the Perl 6 REPL and run code.

The First Program

Traditionally, the first program you write in a new language is called "Hello, World" because all it does is display the words "Hello, World". In Perl 6, it looks like this:

```
> say "Hello, World";
Hello, World
>
```

This is an example of what is usually called a *print statement*, although it doesn't actually print anything on paper and doesn't even use the print keyword[2] (keywords are words which have a special meaning to the language and are used by the interpreter to recognize the structure of the program). The print statement displays a result on the screen. In this case, the result is the words Hello, World. The quotation marks in the program indicate the beginning and end of the text to be displayed; they don't appear in the result.

The semicolon (";") at the end of the line indicates that this is the end of the current statement. Although a semicolon is technically not needed when running simple code directly under the REPL, it is usually necessary when writing a program with several lines of code, so you might as well just get into the habit of ending code instructions with a semicolon.

Many other programming languages would require parentheses around the sentence to be displayed, but this is usually not necessary in Perl 6.

Arithmetic Operators

After "Hello, World," the next step is arithmetic. Perl 6 provides *operators*, which are special symbols that represent computations like addition and multiplication.

---

2 Perl also has a print function, but the say built-in function is used here because it adds a newline character to the output.

The operators +, -, *, and / perform addition, subtraction, multiplication, and division, as in the following examples under the REPL:

```
> 40 + 2
42
> 43 - 1
42
> 6 * 7
42
> 84 / 2
42
```

Since we use the REPL, we don't need an explicit print statement in these examples, as the REPL automatically prints out the result of the statements for us. In a real program, you would need a print statement to display the result, as we'll see later. Similarly, if you run Perl statements in the web browser mentioned in "Running Perl 6" on page 4, you will need a print statement to display the result of these operations. For example:

```
say 40 + 2;   # -> 42
```

Finally, the operator ** performs exponentiation; that is, it raises a number to a power:

```
> 6**2 + 6
42
```

In some other languages, the caret ("^") or circumflex accent is used for exponentiation, but in Perl 6 it is used for some other purposes.

Values and Types

A *value* is one of the basic things a program works with, like a letter or a number. Some values we have seen so far are 2, 42, and "Hello, World".

These values belong to different *types*: 2 is an *integer*, 40 + 2 is also an integer, 84/2 is a *rational number*, and "Hello, World" is a *string*, so called because the characters it contains are strung together.

If you are not sure what type a value has, Perl can tell you:

```
> say 42.WHAT;
(Int)
> say (40 + 2).WHAT;
(Int)
> say (84 / 2).WHAT;
(Rat)
> say (42.0).WHAT
(Rat)
> say ("Hello, World").WHAT;
```

```
(Str)
>
```

In these instructions, .WHAT is known as an *introspection method*; that is, a kind of method which will tell you *what* (of which type) the preceding expression is. 42.WHAT is an example of the dot syntax used for method invocation: it calls the .WHAT built-in on the "42" expression (the *invocant*) and provides to the say function the result of this invocation, which in this case is the type of the expression.

Not surprisingly, integers belong to the type Int, strings belong to Str, and rational numbers belong to Rat.

Although 40 + 2 and 84 / 2 seem to yield the same result (42), the first expression returns an integer (Int) and the second a rational number (Rat). The number 42.0 is also a rational.

The rational type is somewhat uncommon in most programming languages. Internally, these numbers are stored as two integers representing the numerator and the denominator (in their simplest terms). For example, the number 17.3 might be stored as two integers, 173 and 10, meaning that Perl is really storing something meaning the $\frac{173}{10}$ fraction. Although this is usually not needed (except for introspection or debugging), you might access these two integers with the following methods:

```
> my $num = 17.3;
17.3
> say $num.WHAT;
(Rat)
> say $num.numerator, " ", $num.denominator; # say can print a list
173 10
> say $num.nude;          # "nude" stands for numerator-denominator
(173 10)
```

This may seem anecdotal, but, for reasons which are beyond the scope of this book, this makes it possible for Perl 6 to perform arithmetical operations on rational numbers with a much higher accuracy than most common programming languages. For example, if you try to perform the arithmetical operation 0.3 - 0.2 - 0.1 with most general purpose programming languages (and depending on your machine architecture), you might obtain a result such as –2.77555756156289e-17 (in Perl 5), –2.775558e-17 (in C under GCC), or –2.7755575615628914e-17 (Java, Python 3, Ruby, TCL). Don't worry about these values if you don't understand them; let us just say that they are extremely small but they are not 0, whereas, obviously, the result should really be zero. In Perl 6, the result is 0 (even to the fiftieth decimal digit):

```
> my $result-should-be-zero = 0.3 - 0.2 - 0.1;
0
> printf "%.50f", $result-should-be-zero; # prints 50 decimal digits
0.00000000000000000000000000000000000000000000000000
```

In Perl 6, you might even compare the result of the operation with 0:

```
> say $result-should-be-zero == 0;
True
```

Don't do such a comparison with most common programming languages; you're very likely to get a wrong result.

What about values like "2" and "42.0"? They look like numbers, but they are in quotation marks like strings.

```
> say '2'.perl; # perl returns a Perlish representation of the invocant
"2"
> say "2".WHAT;
(Str)
> say '42'.WHAT;
(Str)
```

They're strings because they are defined within quotes. Although Perl will often perform the necessary conversions for you, it is generally a good practice not to use quotation marks if your value is intended to be a number.

When you type a large integer, you might be tempted to use commas between groups of digits, as in 1,234,567. This is not a legal *integer* in Perl 6, but it is a legal expression:

```
> 1,234,567
(1 234 567)
>
```

That's actually a list of three different integer numbers, and not what we expected at all!

```
> say (1,234,567).WHAT
(List)
```

Perl 6 interprets 1,234,567 as a comma-separated sequence of three integers. As we will see later, the comma is a separator used for constructing lists.

You can, however, separate groups of digits with the underscore character ("_") for better legibility and obtain a proper integer:

```
> 1_234_567
1234567
> say 1_234_567.WHAT
(Int)
>
```

Formal and Natural Languages

Natural languages are the languages people speak, such as English, Spanish, and French. They were not designed by people (although people try to impose some order on them); they evolved naturally.

Formal languages are languages that are designed by people for specific applications. For example, the notation that mathematicians use is a formal language that is particularly good at denoting relationships among numbers and symbols. Chemists use a formal language to represent the chemical structure of molecules. And most importantly:

> *Programming languages are formal languages that have been designed to express computations.*

Formal languages tend to have strict *syntax* rules that govern the structure of statements. For example, in mathematics the statement 3 + 3 = 6 has correct syntax, but not 3 + = 3$6. In chemistry H_2O is a syntactically correct formula, but $_2Zz$ is not.

Syntax rules come in two flavors, pertaining to *tokens* and *structure*. Tokens are the basic elements of the language, such as words, numbers, and chemical elements. One of the problems with 3 + = 3$6 is that $ is not a legal token in mathematics (at least as far as I know). Similarly, $_2Zz$ is not legal because there is no chemical element with the abbreviation Zz.

The second type of syntax rule, structure, pertains to the way tokens are combined. The equation 3 + = 3 is illegal in mathematics because even though + and = are legal tokens, you can't have one right after the other. Similarly, in a chemical formula, the subscript representing the number of atoms in a chemical compound comes after the element name, not before.

This is @ well-structured Engli$h sentence with invalid t*kens in it. This sentence all valid tokens has, but invalid structure with.

When you read a sentence in English or a statement in a formal language, you have to figure out the structure (although in a natural language you do this subconsciously). This process is called *parsing*.

Although formal and natural languages have many features in common—tokens, structure, and syntax—there are some differences:

Ambiguity
  Natural languages are full of ambiguity, which people deal with by using contextual clues and other information. Formal languages are designed to be nearly or completely unambiguous, which means that any statement has exactly one meaning.

Redundancy

In order to make up for ambiguity and reduce misunderstandings, natural languages employ lots of redundancy. As a result, they are often verbose. Formal languages are less redundant and more concise.

Literalness

Natural languages are full of idiom and metaphor. If we say, "The penny dropped," there is probably no penny and nothing dropping (this idiom means that someone understood something after a period of confusion). Formal languages mean exactly what they say.

Because we all grow up speaking natural languages, it is sometimes hard to adjust to formal languages. The difference between formal and natural language is like the difference between poetry and prose, but more so:

Poetry

Words are used for their sounds as well as for their meaning, and the whole poem together creates an effect or emotional response. Ambiguity is not only common but often deliberate.

Prose

The literal meaning of words is more important, and the structure contributes more meaning. Prose is more amenable to analysis than poetry but still often ambiguous.

Programs

The meaning of a computer program is unambiguous and literal, and can be understood entirely by analysis of the tokens and structure.

Formal languages are more dense than natural languages, so it takes longer to read them. Also, the structure is important, so it is not always best to read from top to bottom, left to right. Instead, learn to parse the program in your head, identifying the tokens and interpreting the structure. Finally, the details matter. Small errors in spelling and punctuation, which you can get away with in natural languages, can make a big difference in a formal language.

Debugging

Programmers make mistakes. Programming errors are called *bugs* and the process of tracking them down is called *debugging*.

Programming, and especially debugging, sometimes brings out strong emotions. If you are struggling with a difficult bug, you might feel angry, despondent, or embarrassed.

There is evidence that people naturally respond to computers as if they were people. When they work well, we think of them as teammates, and when they are obstinate or rude, we respond to them the same way we respond to rude, obstinate people[3].

Preparing for these reactions might help you deal with them. One approach is to think of the computer as an employee with certain strengths, like speed and precision, and particular weaknesses, like lack of empathy and inability to grasp the big picture.

Your job is to be a good manager: find ways to take advantage of the strengths and mitigate the weaknesses. And find ways to use your emotions to engage with the problem, without letting your reactions interfere with your ability to work effectively.

Learning to debug can be frustrating, but it is a valuable skill that is useful for many activities beyond programming. At the end of each chapter there is a section, like this one, with our suggestions for debugging. I hope they help!

Glossary

abstraction
> A way of providing a high-level view of a task and hiding the underlying technical details so that this task becomes easy.

bug
> An error in a program.

compiler
> A program that reads another program and transforms it into executable computer code; there used to be a strong difference between interpreted and compiled languages, but this distinction has become blurred over the last two decades or so.

debugging
> The process of finding and correcting bugs.

formal language
> Any one of the languages that people have designed for specific purposes, such as representing mathematical ideas or computer programs; all programming languages are formal languages.

integer
> A type that represents whole numbers.

---

3 Byron Reeves and Clifford Nass, *The Media Equation: How People Treat Computers, Television, and New Media Like Real People and Places* (Center for the Study of Language and Information, 2003)

interpreter
  A program that reads another program and executes it.

natural language
  Any one of the languages that people speak that evolved naturally.

operator
  A special symbol that represents a simple computation like addition, multiplication, or string concatenation.

parse
  To examine a program and analyze the syntactic structure.

print statement
  An instruction that causes the Perl 6 interpreter to display a value on the screen.

problem solving
  The process of formulating a problem, finding a solution, and expressing it.

program
  A set of instructions that specifies a computation.

prompt
  Characters displayed by the interpreter to indicate that it is ready to take input from the user.

rational
  A type that represents numbers with fractional parts. Internally, Perl stores a rational as two integers representing respectively the numerator and the denominator of the fractional number.

string
  A type that represents sequences of characters.

syntax
  The rules that govern the structure of a program.

token
  One of the basic elements of the syntactic structure of a program, analogous to a word in a natural language.

type
  A category of values. The types we have seen so far are integers (type `Int`), rational numbers (type `Rat`), and strings (type `Str`).

value
  One of the basic units of data, like a number or string, that a program manipulates.

Exercises

Exercise 1-1.

It is a good idea to read this book in front of a computer so you can try out the examples as you go.

Whenever you are experimenting with a new feature, you should try to make mistakes. For example, in the "Hello, world!" program, what happens if you leave out one of the quotation marks? What if you leave out both? What if you spell say wrong?

This kind of experiment helps you remember what you read; it also helps when you are programming, because you get to know what the error messages mean. It is better to make mistakes now and on purpose than later and accidentally.

Please note that most exercises in this book are provided with a solution in the appendix. However, the exercises in this chapter and in the next chapter are not intended to let you solve an actual problem but are designed to simply let you experiment with the Perl interpreter; there is no good solution, just try out what is proposed to get a feeling on how it works.

1. If you are trying to print a string, what happens if you leave out one of the quotation marks, or both?

2. You can use a minus sign to make a negative number like -2. What happens if you put a plus sign before a number? What about 2++2?

3. In math notation, leading zeros are OK, as in 02. What happens if you try this in Perl?

4. What happens if you have two values with no operator between them, such as say 2 2;?

Exercise 1-2.

Start the Perl 6 REPL interpreter and use it as a calculator.

1. How many seconds are there in 42 minutes, 42 seconds?

2. How many miles are there in 10 kilometers? Hint: there are 1.61 kilometers in a mile.

3. If you run a 10-kilometer race in 42 minutes, 42 seconds, what is your average pace (time per mile in minutes and seconds)? What is your average speed in miles per hour?

## CHAPTER 2

Variables, Expressions, and Statements

One of the most powerful features of a programming language is the ability to manipulate *variables*. Broadly speaking, a variable is a name that refers to a value. It might be more accurate to say that a variable is a container that has a name and holds a value.

Assignment Statements

An *assignment statement* uses the equals sign (=) and gives a value to a variable, but, before you can assign a value to a variable, you first need to create the variable by declaring it (if it does not already exist):

```
> my $message;            # variable declaration, no value yet
> $message = 'And now for something completely different';
And now for something completely different
> my $number = 42;        # variable declaration and assignment
42
> $number = 17;           # new assignment
17
> my $phi = 1.618033988;
1.618033988
>
```

This example makes four assignment statements. The first assigns a string to a new variable named $message, the second assigns the integer 42 to $number, the third reassigns the integer 17 to $number, and the fourth assigns the (approximate) value of the golden ratio to $phi.

There are two important syntax features to understand here.

First, in Perl, variable names start with a so-called *sigil*, i.e., a special non-alphanumeric character such as $, @, %, &, and some others. This special character tells us and the Perl compiler (the program that reads the code of our program and transforms it into computer instructions) which kind of variable it is. For example, the $ character indicates that the variables above are all *scalar variables*, which means that they can contain only one value at any given time. We'll see later other types of variables that may contain more than one value.

Second, notice that all three variables above are first introduced by the keyword my, which is a way of declaring a new variable. Whenever you create a new variable in Perl, you need to *declare* it, i.e., tell Perl that you're going to use that new variable; this is most commonly done with the my keyword, which declares a *lexical* variable. We will explain later what a lexical variable is; let's just say for the time being that it enables you to make your variable local to a limited part of your code. One of the good consequences of the requirement to declare variables before you use them is that, if you accidentally make a typo when writing a variable name, the compiler will usually be able to tell you that you are using a variable that has not been declared previously and thus help you find your error. This has other far-reaching implications, which we will examine later.

When we wrote at the beginning of this section that a variable has to be declared before it is used (or just when it is used), it plainly means that the declaration has to be before (or at the point of) the variable's first use in the text file containing the program. We will see later that programs don't necessarily run from top to bottom in the order in which the lines or code appear in the program file; still, the variable declaration must be before its use in the text file containing the program.

If you neglect to declare a variable, you get a syntax error:

```
> $number = 5;
===SORRY!=== Error while compiling <unknown file>
Variable '$number' is not declared
at <unknown file>:1
------> <BOL><HERE>$number = 5;
>
```

Please remember that you may obtain slightly different error messages depending on the version of Rakudo you run. The above message was obtained in February 2016; with a newer version (October 2016), the same error is now displayed somewhat more cleanly as:

```
>
> $number = 5;
===SORRY!=== Error while compiling:
Variable '$number' is not declared
at line 2
------> <BOL><HERE>$number = 5;
>
```

A common way to represent variables on paper is to write the name with an arrow pointing to its value. This kind of figure is called a *state diagram* because it shows what state each of the variables is in (think of it as the variable's state of mind). Figure 2-1 shows the result of the previous example.

```
$message  ────▶ 'And now for something completely different'
$number   ────▶ 17
   $phi   ────▶ 1.618033988
```

Figure 2-1. State diagram

Variable Names

Programmers generally choose names for their variables that are meaningful—they document what the variable is used for.

Variable names can be as long as you like. They can contain both letters and numbers, but user-defined variable names can't begin with a number. Variable names are case-sensitive, i.e., $message is not the same variable as $Message or $MESSAGE. It is legal to use uppercase letters, but it is conventional to use only lowercase for most variables names. Some people nonetheless like to use $TitleCase for their variables or even pure $UPPERCASE for some special variables.

Unlike most other programming languages, Perl 6 does not require the letters and digits used in variable names to be plain ASCII. You can use all kinds of Unicode letters, i.e., letters from almost any language in the world, so that, for example, $brücke, $payé, or $niño are valid variable names, which can be useful for non-English programmers (provided that these Unicode characters are handled correctly by your text editor and your screen configuration). Similarly, instead of using $phi for the name of the golden ratio variable, we might have used the Greek small letter phi, φ (Unicode code point U+03C6), just as we could have used the Greek small letter pi, π, for the well-known circle circumference-to-diameter ratio:

```
> my $φ = (5 ** .5 + 1)/2;      # golden ratio
1.61803398874989
> say 'Variable $φ = ', $φ;
Variable $φ = 1.61803398874989
> my $π = 4 * atan 1;
3.14159265358979
> # you could also use the pi or π built-in constant:
> pi
3.14159265358979
```

The underscore character, _, can appear anywhere in a variable name. It is often used in names with multiple words, such as $your_name or $airspeed_of_unladen_swallow.

You may even use dashes to create so-called "kebab case"[1] and name those variables $your-name or $airspeed-of-unladen-swallow, and this might make them slightly easier to read: a dash is valid in variable names provided it is immediately followed by an alphabetical character and preceded by an alphanumerical character. For example, $double-click or $la-niña are legitimate variable names. Similarly, you can use an apostrophe ' (or single quote) between letters, so $isn't or $o'brien's-age are valid identifiers.

If you give a variable an illegal name, you get a syntax error:

```
> my $76trombones = 'big parade'
===SORRY!=== Error while compiling <unknown file>
Cannot declare a numeric variable
at <unknown file>:1
------> my $76<HERE>trombones = "big parade";
>
> my $more§ = 100000;
===SORRY!=== Error while compiling <unknown file>
Bogus postfix
at <unknown file>:1
------> my $more<HERE>§ = 100000;
(...)
```

$76trombones is illegal because it begins with a number. $more§ is illegal because it contains an illegal character, §.

If you've ever used another programming language and stumbled across a terse message such as "SyntaxError: invalid syntax", you will notice that the Perl designers have made quite a bit of effort to provide detailed, useful, and meaningful error messages.

Many programming languages have *keywords* or *reserved words* that are part of the syntax, such as if, while, or for, and thus cannot be used for identifying variables because this would create ambiguity. There is no such problem in Perl: since variable names start with a sigil, the compiler is always able to tell the difference between a keyword and a variable. Names such as $if or $while are syntactically valid variable identifiers in Perl (whether such names make sense is a different matter).

---

1 Because the words appear to be skewered like pieces of food prepared for a barbecue.

Expressions and Statements

An *expression* is a combination of terms and operators. Terms may be variables or literals, i.e., constant values such as a number or a string. A value all by itself is considered an expression, and so is a variable, so the following are all legal expressions:

```
> 42
42
> my $n = 17;
17
> $n;
17
> $n + 25;
42
>
```

When you type an expression at the prompt, the interpreter *evaluates* it, which means that it finds the value of the expression. In this example, $n has the value 17 and $n + 25 has the value 42.

A *statement* is a unit of code that has an effect, like creating a variable or displaying a value, and usually needs to end with a semicolon ; (but the semicolon can sometimes be omitted, as we will see later):

```
> my $n = 17;
17
> say $n;
17
```

The first line is an assignment statement that gives a value to $n. The second line is a print statement that displays the value of $n.

When you type a statement and then press Enter, the interpreter *executes* it, which means that it does whatever the statement says.

An assignment can be combined with expressions using arithmetic operators. For example, you might write:

```
> my $answer = 17 + 25;
42
> say $answer;
42
```

The + symbol is obviously the addition operator and, after the assignment statement, the $answer variable contains the result of the addition. The terms on each side of the operator (here 17 and 25) are sometimes called the *operands* of the operation (an addition in this case).

Note that the REPL actually displays the result of the assignment (the first line with "42"), so the print statement was not really necessary in this example *under the REPL*;

from now on, for the sake of brevity, we will generally omit the print statements in the examples where the REPL displays the result.

In some cases, you want to add something to a variable and assign the result to that same variable. This could be written:

```
> my $answer = 17;
17
> $answer = $answer + 25;
42
```

Here, $answer is first declared with a value of 17. The next statement assigns to $answer the current value of $answer (i.e., 17) + 25. This is such a common operation that Perl, like many other programming languages, has a shortcut for this:

```
> my $answer = 17;
17
> $answer += 25;
42
```

The += operator combines the arithmetic addition operator and the assignment operator to modify a value and apply the result to a variable in one go, so that $n += 2 means take the current value of $n, add 2, and assign the result to $n. This syntax works with all other arithmetic operators. For example, -= similarly performs a subtraction and an assignment, *= a multiplication and an assignment, etc. It can even be used with operators other than arithmetic operators, such as the string concatenation operator that we will see later.

Adding 1 to a variable is a very common version of this, so that there is a shortcut to the shortcut, the *increment* operator, which increments its argument by one, and returns the incremented value:

```
> my $n = 17;
17
> ++$n;
18
> say $n;
18
```

This is called the prefix increment operator, because the ++ operator is placed before the variable to be incremented. There is also a postfix version, $n++, which first returns the current value and then increments the variable by one. It would not make a difference in the code snippet above, but the result can be very different in slightly more complex expressions.

There is also a decrement operator --, which decrements its argument by one and also exists in a prefix and a postfix form.

Script Mode

So far we have run Perl in *interactive mode*, which means that you interact directly with the interpreter (the REPL). Interactive mode is a good way to get started, but if you are working with more than a few lines of code, it can be clumsy and even tedious.

The alternative is to use a text editor and save code in a file called a *script* and then run the interpreter in *script mode* to execute the script. By convention, Perl 6 scripts have names that end with .pl, .p6, or .pl6.

Please make sure that you're really using a *text editor* and not a *word-processing program* (such as MS Word, OpenOffice, or LibreOffice Writer). There is a very large number of text editors available for free. On Linux, you might use vi (or vim), emacs, gEdit, or nano. On Windows, you may use notepad (very limited) or notepad++. There are also many cross-platform editors or integrated development environments (IDEs) providing text editor functionality, including padre, eclipse, or atom. Many of these provide various syntax highlighting capabilities, which might help you use correct syntax (and find some syntax errors).

Once you've saved your code in a file (say, for example, *my_script.pl6*), you can run the program by issuing the following command at the operating system prompt (for example in a Linux console or in a cmd window under Windows):

```
perl6 my_script.pl6
```

Because Perl provides both modes, you can test bits of code in interactive mode before you put them in a script. But there are differences between interactive mode and script mode that can be confusing.

For example, if you are using Perl 6 as a calculator, you might type:

```
> my $miles = 26.2;
26.2
> $miles * 1.61;
42.182
```

The first line assigns a value to $miles and displays that value. The second line is an expression, so the interpreter evaluates it and displays the result. It turns out that a marathon is about 42 kilometers.

But if you type the same code into a script and run it, you get no output at all. In script mode, an expression, all by itself, has no visible effect. Perl actually evaluates the expression, but it doesn't display the value unless you tell it to:

```
my $miles = 26.2;
say $miles * 1.61;
```

This behavior can be confusing at first. Let's examine why.

A script usually contains a sequence of statements. If there is more than one statement, the results appear one at a time as the print statements execute.

For example, consider the following script:

```
say 1;
my $x = 2;
say $x;
```

It produces the following output:

```
1
2
```

The assignment statement produces no output.

To check your understanding, type the following statements in the Perl interpreter and see what they do:

```
5;
my $x = 5;
$x + 1;
```

Now put the same statements in a script and run it. What is the output? Modify the script by transforming each expression into a print statement and then run it again.

One-Liner Mode

Perl also has a *one-liner mode*, which enables you to type directly a very short script at the operating system prompt. Under Windows, it might look like this:

```
C:\Users\Laurent>perl6 -e "my $value = 42; say 'The answer is ', $value;"
The answer is 42
```

The -e option tells the compiler that the script to be run is not saved in a file but instead typed at the prompt between quotation marks immediately after this option.

Under Unix and Linux, you would replace double quotation marks with apostrophes (or single quotes) and apostrophes with double quotation marks:

```
$ perl6 -e 'my $value = 42; say "The answer is $value";'
The answer is 42
```

The one-liner above may not seem to be very useful, but throwaway one-liners can be very practical to perform simple one-off operations, such as quickly modifying a file not properly formatted, without having to save a script in a separate file before running it.

We will not give any additional details about the one-liner mode here, but will give some more useful examples later in this book, for example, "Words Longer Than 20 Characters (Solution)" on page 143, "Exercise 7-3: Caesar's Cipher" on page 375 (solving the "rot-13" exercise), or "Exercise 8-7: Consecutive Double Letters" on page 376 (solving the exercise on consecutive double letters).

Order of Operations

When an expression contains more than one operator, the order of evaluation depends on the *order of operations* or *operator precedence*. For mathematical operators, Perl follows mathematical convention. The acronym *PEMDAS*[2] is a useful way to remember the rules:

- *Parentheses* have the highest (or tightest) precedence and can be used to force an expression to evaluate in the order you want. Since expressions in parentheses are evaluated first, `2 * (3-1)` is 4, and `(1+1)**(5-2)` is 8. You can also use parentheses to make an expression easier to read, as in `($minute * 100) / 60`, even if it doesn't change the result.

- *Exponentiation* has the next highest precedence, so `1 + 2**3` is 9 $(1 + 8)$, not 27, and `2 * 3**2` is 18, not 36.

- *Multiplication* and *Division* have higher precedence than *Addition* and *Subtraction*. So `2*3-1` is 5, not 4, and `6+4/2` is 8, not 5.

- Operators with the same precedence are usually evaluated from left to right (except exponentiation). So in the expression `$degrees / 2 * pi`, the division happens first and the result is multiplied by `pi`, which is not the expected result. (Note that `pi` is not a variable, but a predefined constant in Perl 6, and therefore does not require a sigil.) To divide by 2π, you can use parentheses:

      my $result = $degrees / (2 * pi);

  or write `$degrees / 2 / pi` or `$degrees / 2/`π, which will divide `$degrees` by 2, and then divide the result of that operation by π (which is equivalent `$degrees` by 2π.

I don't work very hard to remember the precedence of operators. If I can't tell by looking at the expression, I use parentheses to make it obvious. If I don't know for sure which of two operators has the higher precedence, then the next person reading or maintaining the code may also not know.

---

2 US students are sometimes taught to use the "Please Excuse My Dear Aunt Sally" mnemonic to remember the right order of the letters in the acronym

String Operations

In general, you can't perform mathematical operations on strings, unless the strings look so much like numbers that Perl can transform or *coerce* them into numbers and still make sense, so the following are illegal:

```
'2'-'1a'    'eggs'/'easy'    'third'*'a charm'
```

For example, this produces an error:

```
> '2'-'1a'
Cannot convert string to number: trailing characters after number
in '1?a' (indicated by ?)
  in block <unit> at <unknown file>:1
```

But the following expressions are valid because these strings can be coerced to numbers without any ambiguity:

```
> '2'-'1'
1
> '3'/'4'
0.75
```

The ~ operator performs *string concatenation*, which means it joins the strings by linking them end-to-end. For example:

```
> my $first = 'throat'
throat
> my $second = 'warbler'
warbler
> $first ~ $second
throatwarbler
```

The x operator also works on strings; it performs repetition. For example:

```
> 'ab' x 3;
ababab
> 42 x 3
424242
> 3 x 42
333333333333333333333333333333333333333333
```

Notice that, although the x operator somewhat looks like the multiplication operator when we write it by hand, x is obviously not commutative, contrary to the * multiplication operator. The first operator is a string or is *coerced* to a string (i.e., transformed into a string: 42 is coerced to '42'), and the second operator has to be a number or something that can be transformed into a number.

Comments

As programs get bigger and more complicated, they get more difficult to read. Formal languages are dense, and it is often difficult to look at a piece of code and figure out what it is doing, or why.

For this reason, it is a good idea to add notes to your programs to explain in natural language what the program is doing. These notes are called *comments*, and they start with the # symbol:

```
# compute the percentage of the hour that has elapsed
my $percentage = ($minute * 100) / 60;
```

In this case, the comment appears on a line by itself. You can also put comments at the end of a line:

```
$percentage = ($minute * 100) / 60;     # percentage of an hour
```

Everything from the # to the end of the line is ignored—it has no effect on the execution of the program.

Comments are most useful when they document nonobvious features of the code. It is reasonable to assume that the reader can figure out *what* the code does; it is more useful to explain *why*.

This comment is redundant with the code and useless:

```
my $value = 5;          # assign 5 to $value
```

This comment, by contrast, contains useful information that is not in the code:

```
my $velocity = 5;       # velocity in meters/second.
```

Good variable names can reduce the need for comments, but long names can make complex expressions hard to read, so there is a tradeoff.

Debugging

Three kinds of errors can occur in a program: syntax errors, runtime errors, and semantic errors. It is useful to distinguish between them in order to track them down more quickly.

Syntax error

> *Syntax* refers to the structure of a program and the rules about that structure. For example, parentheses have to come in matching pairs, so (1 + 2) is legal, but 8) is a syntax error.[3]

> If there is a syntax error anywhere in your program, Perl displays an error message and quits without even starting to run your program, and you will obviously not be able to run the program. During the first few weeks of your programming career, you might spend a lot of time tracking down syntax errors. As you gain experience, you will make fewer errors and find them faster.

Runtime error

> The second type of error is a *runtime error*, so called because the error does not appear until after the program has started running. These errors are also called *exceptions* because they usually indicate that something exceptional (and bad) has happened.

> Runtime errors are rare in the simple programs you will see in the first few chapters, so it might be a while before you encounter one. We have seen one example of such errors, though, at the beginning of "String Operations" on page 24 , when we tried to subtract '2'-'1a'.

Semantic error

> The third type of error is *semantic*, which means related to meaning. If there is a semantic error in your program, it will run without generating error messages, but it will not do the right thing. It will do something else. Specifically, it will do what you *told* it to do, but not what you *intended* it to do.

> Identifying semantic errors can be tricky because it requires you to work backward by looking at the output of the program and trying to figure out what it is doing.

Glossary

assignment

> A statement that assigns a value to a variable.

comment

> Information in a program that is meant for other programmers (or anyone reading the source code) and has no effect on the execution of the program.

---

3 We are using "syntax error" here as a quasi-synonym for "compile-time error"; they are not exactly the same thing (you may in theory have syntax errors that are not compile-time errors and the other way around), but they can be deemed to be the same for practical purposes here. In Perl 6, compile-time errors have the "===SORRY!===" string at the beginning of the error message.

concatenate
> To join two string operands end-to-end.

evaluate
> To simplify an expression by performing the operations in order to yield a single value.

exception
> An error that is detected while the program is running.

execute
> To run a statement and do what it says.

expression
> A combination of operators and terms that represents a single result.

interactive mode (or interpreter mode)
> A way of using the Perl interpreter by typing code at the prompt.

keyword
> A reserved word that is used to parse a program; in many languages, you cannot use keywords like `if`, `for`, and `while` as variable names. This problem usually does not occur in Perl because variable names begin with a *sigil*.

one-liner mode
> A way of using the Perl interpreter to read code passed at the operating system prompt and run it.

operand
> One of the values used by an operator.

order of operations
> Rules governing the order in which expressions involving multiple operators and operands are evaluated. It is also called operator precedence.

script
> A program stored in a file.

script mode
> A way of using the Perl interpreter to read code from a script and run it.

semantic error
> An error in a program that makes it do something other than what the programmer intended.

semantics
> The meaning of a program.

state diagram
  A graphical representation of a set of variables and the values they refer to.

statement
  A section of code that represents a command or action. So far, the statements we have seen are assignments and print statements. Statements usually end with a semicolon.

syntax error
  An error in a program that makes it impossible to parse (and therefore impossible to compile and to run).

term
  A variable or a literal value.

variable
  Informally, a name that refers to a value. More accurately, a variable is a container that has a name and holds a value.

Exercises

Exercise 2-1.

Repeating our advice from the previous chapter, whenever you learn a new feature, you should try it out in interactive mode (under the REPL) and make errors on purpose to see what goes wrong.

- We've seen that $n = 42 is legal. What about 42 = $n?
- How about $x = $y = 1? (Hint: note that you will have to declare both variables, for example with a statement such as my $x; my $y; or possibly my ($x, $y);, before you can run the above.)
- In some languages, statements don't have to end with a semicolon, ;. What happens in script mode if you omit a semicolon at the end of a Perl statement?
- What if you put a period at the end of a statement?
- In math notation you can multiply *x* and *y* like this: *xy*. What happens if you try that in Perl?

Exercise 2-2.

Practice using the Perl interpreter as a calculator:

1. The volume of a sphere with radius r is $\frac{4}{3}\pi r^3$. What is the volume of a sphere with radius 5?

2. Suppose the cover price of a book is $24.95, but bookstores get a 40% discount. Shipping costs $3 for the first copy and 75 cents for each additional copy. What is the total wholesale cost for 60 copies?

3. If I leave my house at 6:52 a.m. and run 1 mile at an easy pace (8:15 per mile), then 3 miles at tempo (7:12 per mile) and 1 mile at easy pace again, what time is it when I complete my running exercise?

## CHAPTER 3

Functions

In the context of programming, a *function* is usually a named sequence of statements that performs a computation. In Perl, functions are often also called *subroutines*, and the two terms can (for now) be considered more or less equivalent. When you define a function, you specify the name and the sequence of statements. Later, when you want to perform a computation, you can "call" the function by name and this will run the sequence of statements contained in the *function definition*.

Perl comes with many built-in functions that are quite handy. You've already seen some of them: for example, say is a built-in function, and we will see many more in the course of this book. And if Perl doesn't already have a function that does what you want, you can build your own. This teaches you the basics of functions and how to build new ones.

Function Calls

We have already seen examples of *function calls*:

```
> say 42;
42
```

The name of the function is say. The expression following the function name is called the *argument* of the function. The say function causes the argument to be displayed on the screen. If you need to pass several values to a function, then just separate the arguments with commas:

```
> say "The answer to the ultimate question is ", 42;
The answer to the ultimate question is 42
```

Many programming languages require the arguments of a function to be inserted between parentheses. This is not required (and usually not recommended) in Perl 6 for most built-in functions (except when needed for precedence), but if you do use parentheses, you should make sure to avoid inserting spaces between the function name and the opening parenthesis. For example, the round function usually takes two arguments: the value to be rounded and the unit or scale. You may call it in any of the following ways:

```
> round 42.45, 1;
42
> round 42.45, .1;
42.5
> round(42.45, .1);      # But not: round (42.45, .1);
42.5
> round( 42.45, .1);     # Space is OK *after* the opening paren
42.5
```

Experienced Perl programmers usually prefer to omit the parentheses when they can. Doing so makes it possible to chain several functions with a visually cleaner syntax. Consider for example the differences between these two calls:

```
> say round 42.45, 1;
42
> say(round(42.45, 1));
42
```

The second statement is explicitly saying what is going on, but the accumulation of parentheses actually makes things not very clear. By contrast, the first statement can be seen as a pipeline to be read from right to left: the last function on the right, round, is taking two arguments, 42.45, 1, and the value produced by round is passed as an argument to say.

It is common to say that a function "takes" one or several arguments and "returns" a result. The result is also called the *return value*.

Perl provides functions that convert values from one type to another. When called with only one argument, the round function takes any value and converts it to an integer, if it can, or complains otherwise:

```
> round 42.3;
42
> round "yes"
Cannot convert string to number: base-10 number must begin with valid
digits or '.' in '<HERE>yes' (indicated by <HERE>)
  in block <unit> at <unknown file> line 1
```

Note that, in Perl 6, many built-in functions can also use a *method invocation* syntax with the so-called *dot notation*. The following statements display the same result:

```
> round 42.7;    # Function call syntax
43
> 42.7.round;    # Method invocation syntax
43
```

The round function can round off rational and floating-point values to integers. There is an Int method that can also convert noninteger numerical values into integers, but it doesn't round off; it chops off the fraction part:

```
> round 42.7
43
> 42.7.Int
42
```

We'll come back to methods in the next section.

The Rat built-in function converts integers and strings to rational numbers (if possible):

```
> say 4.Rat;
4
> say 4.Rat.WHAT;
(Rat)
> say Rat(4).WHAT
(Rat)
> say Rat(4).nude
(4 1)
> say Rat('3.14159')
3.14159
> say Rat('3.14159').nude
(314159 100000)
```

(As you might remember, the nude method displays the *nu*merator and *de*nominator of a rational number.)

Finally, Str converts its argument to a string:

```
> say 42.Str.WHAT
(Str)
> say Str(42).WHAT;
(Str)
```

Note that these type conversion functions often don't need to be called explicitly, as Perl will in many cases try to do the right thing for you. For example, if you have a string that looks like an integer number, Perl will coerce the string to an integer for you if you try to apply an arithmetic operation on it:

```
> say "21" * "2";
42
```

Similarly, integers will be coerced to strings if you apply the string concatenation operator to them:

```
> say 4 ~ 2;
42
> say (4 ~ 2).WHAT;
(Str)
```

The coercion can even happen twice within the same expression if needed:

```
> say (4 ~ 1) + 1;
42
> say ((4 ~ 1) + 1).WHAT;
(Int)
```

Functions and Methods

A method is similar to a function—it takes arguments and returns a value—but the calling syntax is different. With a function, you specify the name of the function followed by its arguments. A method, by contrast, uses the dot notation: you specify the name of the object on which the method is called, followed by a dot and the name of the method (and possibly additional arguments).

A method call is often called an *invocation*. The deeper differences between functions and methods will become apparent much later, when studying object-oriented programming (in Chapter 12).

For the time being, we can consider that the difference is essentially a matter of a different calling syntax when using Perl's built-ins. Most Perl built-ins accept both a function call syntax and a method invocation syntax. For example, the following statements are equivalent:

```
> say 42;           # function call syntax
42
> 42.say;           # method invocation syntax
42
```

You can also chain built-in routines with both syntactic forms:

```
> 42.WHAT.say;      # method syntax
(Int)
> say WHAT 42;      # function syntax
(Int)
> say 42.WHAT;      # mixed syntax
(Int)
```

It is up to you to decide whether you prefer one form or the other, but we will use both forms, if only to get you used to both of them.

Math Functions

Perl provides most of the familiar mathematical functions.

For some less common functions, you might need to use a specialized module such as `Math::Matrix` or `Math::Trig`. A *module* is a file that contains a collection of related functions.

Before we can use the functions in a module, we have to import it with a *use statement*:

```
use Math::Trig;
```

This statement will import a number of functions that you will then be able to use as if you had defined them in your main source file, for example deg2rad to perform conversion of angular values from degrees to radians, or rad2deg to perform the opposite conversion.

For most common mathematical functions, however, you don't need any math module, as they are included in the core of the language:

```
> my $noise-power = 5.5;
5.5
> my $signal-power = 125.6;
125.6
> my $decibels = 10 * log10 $signal-power / $noise-power;
13.5862694990693
```

This example uses log10 (common logarithm) to compute a signal-to-noise ratio in decibels (assuming that signal-power and noise-power are defined in the proper units). Perl also provides a log function which, when receiving one argument, computes logarithm base e of the argument, and, when receiving two arguments, computes the logarithm of the first argument to the base of the second argument:

```
> say e;                 # e is predefined as Euler's constant
2.71828182845905
> my $val = e ** e;
15.1542622414793
> say log $val;          # natural logarithm
2.71828182845905
> say log $val, e;       # logarithm base e or natural logarithm
2.71828182845905
> say log 1024, 2;       # binary logarithm or logarithm base 2
10
```

Perl also provides most common trigonometric functions:

```
> my $radians = 0.7;
0.7
> my $height = sin $radians;
0.644217687237691
```

This example finds the sine of $radians. The name of the variable is a hint that sin and the other trigonometric functions (cos, tan, etc.) take arguments in radians. To convert from degrees to radians, you may use the deg2rad function of the Math::Trig module, or simply divide by 180 and multiply by π:

```
> my $degrees = 45;
45
> my $radians = $degrees / 180.0 * pi;    # pi, predefined constant
0.785398163397448
> say sin $radians;       # should be square root of 2 divided by 2
0.707106781186547
```

The expression `pi` is a predefined constant for an approximation of π, accurate to about 14 digits.

If you know trigonometry, you can check the previous result by comparing it to the square root of two divided by two:

```
> say sqrt(2) / 2;
0.707106781186548
```

Composition

So far, we have looked at the elements of a program—variables, expressions, and statements—in isolation, without talking about how to combine them.

One of the most useful features of programming languages is their ability to take small building blocks and *compose* them, i.e., to combine them in such a way that the result of one is the input of another one. For example, the argument of a function can be any kind of expression, including arithmetic operations:

```
> my $degrees = 45;
45
> my $height = sin($degrees / 360.0 * 2 * pi);
0.707106781186547
```

Here, we have used parentheses for the argument to the `sin` function to clarify that all the arithmetic operations within the parentheses are completed before the `sin` function is actually called, so that it will use the result of these operations as its argument.

You can also compose function calls:

```
> my $x = 10;
10
>   $x = exp log($x+1)
11
```

Almost anywhere you can put a value, you can put an arbitrary expression, with one exception: the left side of an assignment statement has to be a variable name, possibly along with its declaration. Almost any other expression on the left side is a syntax error (we will see rare exceptions to this rule later):

```
> my $hours = 1;
1
> my $minutes = 0;
0
```

```
> $minutes = $hours * 60;        # right
60
> $hours * 60 = $minutes;        # wrong !!
Cannot modify an immutable Int
  in block <unit> at <unknown file> line 1
```

Adding New Functions (a.k.a. Subroutines)

So far, we have only been using the functions that come with Perl, but it is also possible to add new functions. In Perl, user-defined functions are often called subroutines, but you might choose either word for them.

A *function definition* starts with the sub keyword (for subroutine) and specifies the name of a new subroutine and the sequence of statements that run when the function is called.

Here is an example of a subroutine quoting Martin Luther King's famous "I Have a Dream" speech at the Lincoln Memorial in Washington (1963):

```
sub print-speech() {
    say "Let freedom ring from the prodigious hilltops of New Hampshire.";
    say "Let freedom ring from the mighty mountains of New York.";
}
```

sub is a keyword that indicates that this is a subroutine definition. The name of the function is print-speech. The rules for subroutine names are the same as for variable names: letters, numbers, and underscores are legal, as well as a dash or an apostrophe between letters, but the first character must be a letter or an underscore. You shouldn't use a language keyword (such as if or while) as the name of a function (in some cases, it might actually work, but it would be very confusing, at least for the human reader).

The empty parentheses after the name indicate that this function doesn't take any arguments. They are optional in that case, but are required when parameters need to be defined for the subroutine.

The first line of the subroutine definition is sometimes called the *header*; the rest is called the *body*. The body has to be a code block placed between curly braces and it can contain any number of statements. Although there is no requirement to do so, it is good practice (and highly recommended) to indent body statements by a few leading spaces, since it makes it easier to figure out visually where the function body starts and ends.

Please note that you cannot use a method-invocation syntax for subroutines (such as print-speech) that you write: you must call them with a function call syntax.

The strings in the print statements are enclosed in double quotes. In this specific case, single quotes could have been used instead to do the same thing, but there are many cases where they wouldn't do the same thing, so you'll have to choose one or the other depending on the circumstances.

Most people use double quotes in cases where a single quote (which is also an apostrophe) appears in the string:

```
say "And so we've come here today to dramatize a shameful condition.";
```

Conversely, you might use single quotes when double quotes appear in the string:

```
say 'America has given the Negro people a bad check,
    a check which has come back marked "insufficient funds."';
```

There is, however, a more important difference between single quotes and double quotes: double quotes allow *variable interpolation*, and single quotes don't. Variable interpolation means that if a variable name appears within the double-quoted string, this variable name will be replaced by the variable value; within a single-quoted string, the variable name will appear verbatim. For example:

```
my $var = 42;
say "His age is $var.";        # -> His age is 42.
say 'Her age is $var.';        # -> Her age is $var.
```

The reason is not that the lady's age should be kept secret. In the first string, $var is simply replaced within the string by its value, 42, because the string is quoted with double quotes; in the second one, it isn't because single quotes are meant to provide a more verbatim type of quoting mechanism. There are other quoting constructs offering finer control over the way variables and special characters are displayed in the output, but simple and double quotes are the most useful ones.

The syntax for calling the new subroutine is the same as for built-in functions:

```
> print-speech();
Let freedom ring from the prodigious hilltops of New Hampshire.
Let freedom ring from the mighty mountains of New York.
```

However, you cannot use the method-invocation syntax with such subroutines. We will see much later in this book (Chapter 12) how to create methods. For the time being, we'll stick to the function-call syntax.

Once you have defined a subroutine, you can use it inside another subroutine. For example, to repeat the previous excerpts of King's address, we could write a subroutine called repeat-speech:

```
sub repeat-speech() {
    print-speech();
    print-speech();
}
```

And then call `repeat-speech`:

```
> repeat-speech();
Let freedom ring from the prodigious hilltops of New Hampshire.
Let freedom ring from the mighty mountains of New York.
Let freedom ring from the prodigious hilltops of New Hampshire.
Let freedom ring from the mighty mountains of New York.
```

But that's not really how the speech goes.

Definitions and Uses

Pulling together the code fragments from the previous section, the whole program looks like this:

```
sub print-speech () {
    say "let freedom ring from the prodigious hilltops of New Hampshire.";
    say "Let freedom ring from the mighty mountains of New York.";
}
sub repeat-speech () {
    print-speech();
    print-speech();
}
repeat-speech();
```

This program contains two subroutine definitions: `print-speech` and `repeat-speech`. Function definitions get executed just like other statements, but the effect is to create the function. The statements inside the function do not run until the function is called, and the function definition generates no output.

You don't have to create a subroutine before you can run it; the function definition may come after its call:

```
repeat-speech;
sub repeat-speech() {
    print-speech;
    print-speech;
}
sub print-speech() {
    # ...
}
```

Flow of Execution

To ensure, for example, that a variable is defined (i.e., populated) before its first use, you have to know the order statements run in, which is called the *flow of execution*.

Execution always begins at the first statement of the program (well, really *almost* always, but let's say always for the time being). Statements are run one at a time, in order from top to bottom.

Subroutine definitions do not alter the flow of execution of the program, but remember that statements inside a function don't run until the function is called.

A function call is like a detour in the flow of execution. Instead of going to the next statement, the flow jumps to the body of the function, runs the statements there, and then comes back to pick up where it left off.

That sounds simple enough, until you remember that one function can call another. While in the middle of one function, the program might have to run the statements in another function. Then, while running that new function, the program might have to run yet another function!

Fortunately, Perl is good at keeping track of where it is, so each time a function completes, the program picks up where it left off in the function that called it. When it gets to the end of the program, it terminates.

In summary, when you read a program, you don't always want to read from top to bottom. Sometimes it makes more sense if you follow the flow of execution.

Parameters and Arguments

Some of the functions we have seen require arguments. For example, when you call sin you pass a number as an argument. Some functions take more than one argument: for example the round function seen at the beginning of this chapter took two, the number to be rounded and the scale (although the round function may accept a single argument, in which case the scale is defaulted to 1).

Inside the subroutine, the arguments are assigned to variables called *parameters*. Here is a definition for a subroutine that takes a single argument:

```
sub print-twice($value) {
    say $value;
    say $value
}
```

This subroutine assigns the argument to a parameter named $value. Another common way to say it is that the subroutine binds the parameter defined in its header to the argument with which it was called. When the above subroutine is called, it prints the content of the parameter (whatever it is) twice.

This function works with any argument value that can be printed:

```
> print-twice("Let freedom ring")
Let freedom ring
Let freedom ring
> print-twice(42)
42
42
> print-twice(pi)
```

```
3.14159265358979
3.14159265358979
```

The same rules of composition that apply to built-in functions also apply to programmer-defined subroutines, so we can use any kind of expression as an argument for print-twice:

```
> print-twice('Let freedom ring! ' x 2)
Let freedom ring! Let freedom ring!
Let freedom ring! Let freedom ring!
> print-twice(cos pi)
-1
-1
```

The argument is evaluated before the function is called, so in the examples the expressions 'Let freedom ring! ' x 2 and cos pi are only evaluated once.

You can also use a variable as an argument:

```
> my $declaration = 'When in the Course of human events, ...'
> print-twice($declaration)
When in the Course of human events, ...
When in the Course of human events, ...
```

The name of the variable we pass as an argument ($declaration) has nothing to do with the name of the parameter ($value). It doesn't matter what the variable was called back home (in the caller); here, within print-twice, we call the parameter $value, irrespective of the name or content of the argument passed to the subroutine.

Variables and Parameters Are Local

When you create a variable inside a subroutine with the my keyword, it is *local*, or, more accurately, *lexically scoped*, to the function block, which means that it only exists inside the function. For example:

```
sub concat_twice($part1, $part2) {
    my $concatenation = $part1 ~ $part2;
    print-twice($concatenation);
}
```

This function takes two arguments, concatenates them, and prints the result twice. Here is an example that uses it:

```
> my $start = 'Let freedom ring from ';
> my $end = 'the mighty mountains of New York.';
> concat_twice($start, $end);
Let freedom ring from the mighty mountains of New York.
Let freedom ring from the mighty mountains of New York.
```

When concat_twice terminates, the variable $concatenation is destroyed. If we try to print it, we get an exception:

```
> say $concatenation;
===SORRY!=== Error while compiling <unknown file>
Variable '$concatenation' is not declared
at <unknown file>:1
------> say <HERE>$concatenation;
```

Parameters are also scoped to the subroutine. For example, outside print-twice, there is no such thing as $value.

Stack Diagrams

To keep track of which variables can be used where, it is sometimes useful to draw a *stack diagram*. Like state diagrams, stack diagrams show the value of each variable, but they also show the function each variable belongs to.

Each function is represented graphically by a *frame*. A frame is a box with the name of a function beside it and the parameters and variables of the function inside it. The stack diagram for the previous example is shown in Figure 3-1.

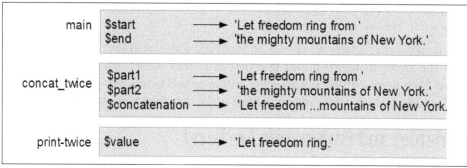

Figure 3-1. Stack diagram

The frames are arranged in a stack that indicates which function called which, and so on. In this example, print-twice was called by concat_twice, and concat_twice was called by main, which is a special name for the topmost frame. When you create a variable outside of any function, it belongs to main.

Each parameter refers to the same value as its corresponding argument. So, $part1 has the same value as $start, $part2 has the same value as $end, and $value has the same value as $concatenation.

Fruitful Functions and Void Functions

Some of the functions we have used, such as the math functions, return results and are useful only insofar we use that return value; for lack of a better name, we may call them *fruitful functions*. Other functions, like print-twice, perform an action but don't appear to return a value (it does in fact return a value, True, but we don't care about it). They are sometimes called empty or *void functions* in some other programming languages.

In some programming languages, such as Pascal or Ada, there is a strong distinction between a *function* (which returns a value) and a *procedure* (which doesn't); they are even defined with different keywords. This distinction does not apply to Perl and to most modern programming languages.

In fact, from a pure syntactic standpoint, Perl functions always return a result. So the distinction between "fruitful" and "void" functions does not really exist syntactically, but only semantically, i.e., from the standpoint of the meaning of the program: maybe we need to use the return value, or maybe we don't.

Another distinction commonly made is between functions and mutators: functions do not change the initial state of the arguments they were called on, and mutators do modify it. We will not use this distinction here, but it is useful to keep it in mind.

When you call a fruitful function, you almost always want to do something with the result; for example, you might assign it to a variable or use it as part of an expression:

```
my $height = sin $radians;
my $golden = (sqrt(5) + 1) / 2;
```

When you call a function in interactive mode (under the REPL), Perl usually displays the result:

```
> sqrt 5;
2.23606797749979
```

But in a script, if you call a fruitful function all by itself, the return value is lost forever! In some cases, the compiler will be able to warn you, but not always. For example, consider the following program:

```
my $five = 5;
sqrt $five;
say $five;
```

It produces the following warning:

```
WARNINGS for /home/Laurent/perl6_tests/sqrt.pl6:
Useless use of "sqrt $five" in expression "sqrt $five" in sink context (line 2)
5
```

This script computes the square root of 5, but since it doesn't store or display the result, it is not very useful.

Void functions might display something on the screen, save some data to a file, modify a variable or an object, or have some other effect, but they generally don't have a return value, or at least not a useful one. If you assign the result to a variable, you may get the return value of the subroutine, the value of the last expression which was evaluated in the function, or a special value such as Any, which essentially means something that has not been defined, or Nil.

The subroutines we have written so far were essentially printing things to the screen. In that case, they usually return True, at least when the printing was successful. Although they return a true value, what they return isn't very useful and we can consider them all void for our practical purposes.

The following is an example of a very simple fruitful subroutine:

```
> sub square($number) { return $number ** 2 }
sub square ($number) { #`(Sub|118134416) ... }
> say square 5;
25
```

The Sub|118134416 message displayed by the REPL is just an internal identifier for the subroutine we've just defined.

The return statement instructs the function to terminate the execution of the function at this statement and to return the value of the following expression to the caller. In such a simple case where the program is in fact running the last statement of a function, the return keyword can be omitted since the function will return the value of the last evaluated statement, so that the square subroutine could be written this way:

```
sub square($number) {
    $number ** 2
}
```

We will be using fruitful functions more intensively in a few chapters.

Function Signatures

When a function receives arguments, which are stored into parameters, the part of the function definition describing the parameters between parentheses is called the *function signature*. The function signatures we have seen so far are very simple and consist only of one parameter or possibly a parameter list.

Signatures can provide a lot more information about the parameters used by a function. First, you may define the type of the parameters. Some functions make sense only if their parameters are numeric and should probably raise an error if they get a string that cannot be converted to a numeric value. For example, if you define a function half that computes a value equal to its argument divided by 2, it does not make sense to try to compute half of a string that is not numeric. It could be written as follows:

```
sub half(Int $number) {
    return $number / 2
}
say half 84; # -> 42
```

If this function is called with a string, we get the following error:

```
> say half "Douglas Adams"
===SORRY!=== Error while compiling <unknown file>
Calling half(Str) will never work with declared signature (Int $number)
at <unknown file>:1
------> say <HERE>half "Douglas Adams"
```

The `Int` type included in the function signature is a type constraint that can help prevent subtle bugs. In some cases, it can also be an annoyance. Consider this code snippet:

```
sub half(Int $number) {  $number / 2 }
say half "84"; # -> ERROR
```

Because the argument to the `half` subroutine is "84", i.e., a string, this code will fail with a type error. If we had not included the `Int` type in the signature, the script would have converted (or coerced) the "84" string to a number, divided it by two, and printed out the expected result:

```
sub half( $number) { $number / 2 }
say half "84"; # -> 42
```

In some cases, you want this conversion to occur, in others you don't. It is up to you to decide whether you want strict typing or not, depending on the specific situation and needs. It is probably helpful to use parameter typing in many cases, but it can also become a straitjacket in some situations. Perl 6 lets you decide how strict you want to be about these things.

Our original `half` subroutine has another limitation: it can work only on integers. But a function halving its argument should presumably be useful for rational or even other numbers. You can use the `Real` or `Numeric` types to make the function more general (the difference between the two types is that the `Numeric` type will accept not only `Real` but also `Complex` numbers). As it turns out that this `half` function will also work correctly with complex numbers,[1] choosing a `Numeric` type opens more possibilities:

```
sub half(Numeric $number) { $number / 2 }
say half(3+4i); # -> 1.5+2i
```

---

1 Complex numbers are numbers in the form "$a + bi$," where a and b are real numbers, and i an imaginary number such that i^2 equals -1.

The following table sums up and illustrates some of the various types we have seen so far:

Type	Example
String	`"A string", 'Another string', "42"`
Integer	`-3, -2, 0, 2, 42`
Rational	`1/2, 0.5, 3,14159, 22/7, 42.0`
Real	$π$, pi, $\sqrt{2}$, e, log 42, sin 0.7
Complex	$5.4 + 3i$

Immutable and Mutable Parameters

By default, subroutine parameters are *immutable* aliases for the arguments passed to the subroutine. In other words, they cannot be changed within the function and you cannot accidentally modify the argument in the caller:

```
sub plus-three(Int $number) { $number += 3}
my $value = 5;
say plus-three $value; # ERROR: Cannot assign to an immutable value
```

In some other languages, this behavior is named a "call by value" semantic: loosely speaking, the subroutine receives (by default) a value rather than a variable, and the parameter therefore cannot be modified.

If you want to change the value of the parameter within the subroutine (but without changing the argument in the caller) you can add the `is copy` *trait* to the signature:

```
sub plus-three(Int $number is copy) { $number += 3}
my $value = 5;
say plus-three $value;   # 8
say $value;              # 5 (unchanged)
```

A trait is a property of the parameter defined at compile time. Here, the `$number` parameter is modified within the subroutine and the incremented value is returned to the caller and printed as 8, but, within the caller, the variable used as an argument to the function, `$value`, is not modified (it is still 5).

Although this can sometimes be dangerous, you may also want to write a subroutine that modifies its argument at the caller side. For this, you can use the `is rw` trait in the signature:

```
sub plus-three(Int $number is rw) { $number += 3}
my $value = 5;
say plus-three $value;   # 8
say $value;              # 8 ($value modified)
```

With the `is rw` trait, the $number parameter is now *bound* to the $value argument, so that any change made using $number within the subroutine will immediately be applied to $value at the caller side, because $number and $value are just different names for the same thing (they both refer to the same memory location). The argument is now fully *mutable*.

In some other languages, this is named a "call by reference" parameter passing mechanism, because, in those languages, if you pass a reference (or a pointer) to a variable to a function, then it is possible for the function to modify the variable referred to by the reference.

Functions and Subroutines as First-Class Citizens

Subroutines and other code objects can be passed around as values, just like any variable, literal, or object. Functions are said to be *first-class objects* or sometimes first-class citizens or higher-order functions. This means that a Perl function (its code, not the value returned by it) is a value you can assign to a variable or pass around as an argument. For example, `do-twice` is a subroutine that takes a function as an argument and calls it twice:

```
sub do-twice($code) {
    $code();
    $code();
}
```

Here, the $code parameter refers to a function or some other callable code object. This is an example that uses `do-twice` to call a function named `greet` twice:

```
sub greet {
    say "Hello World!";
}
do-twice &greet;
```

This will print:

```
Hello World!
Hello World!
```

The & sigil placed before the subroutine name in the argument list tells Perl that you are passing around a subroutine or some other callable code object (and not calling the subroutine at the moment).

In fact, it would be more idiomatic to also use the & sigil in the `do-twice` subroutine definition, to better specify that the parameter is a callable code object:

```
sub do-twice(&code) {
    &code();
    &code();
}
```

or even:

```
sub do-twice(&code) {
    code();
    code();
}
```

The syntax with the & sigil has the benefit that it will provide a better error message if you make a mistake and pass something noncallable to do-twice.

All the functions we have seen so far had a name, but a function does not need to have a name and can be *anonymous*. For example, it may be stored directly in a scalar variable:

```
my $greet = sub {
    say "Hello World!";
};
$greet();               # prints "Hello World"
do-twice $greet;        # prints "Hello World" twice
```

It could be argued that the above $greet subroutine is not really anonymous, since it is stored in a scalar variable that could in a certain way be considered its name. But the subroutine really has no name; it just happens to be assigned to a scalar variable. Just to show that the subroutine can really have no name at all, consider this:

```
do-twice(sub {say "Hello World!"} );
```

It will happily print "Hello World" twice. If the $do-twice function was declared earlier, you can even simplify the syntax and omit the parentheses:

```
do-twice sub {say "Hello World!"};
```

For such a simple case where there is no need to pass an argument or return a value; you can even omit the sub keyword and pass a code block directly to the function:

```
do-twice {say "Hello World!"};
do-twice {say "what's up doc"};
```

As you can see, do-twice is a *generic* subroutine in charge of just performing twice any function or code block passed to it, without any knowledge about what this function or code block is doing. This is a powerful concept for some relatively advanced programming techniques that we will cover later in this book.

Subroutines may also be passed as return values from other subroutines:

```
> sub create-func ($person) { return sub { say "Hello $person!"}}
# Creating two greeting functions
sub create-func ($person) { #`(Sub|176738440) ... }
> my $greet_world = create-func "World";
sub () { #`(Sub|176738592) ... }
> my $greet_friend = create-func "dear friend";
sub () { #`(Sub|176739048) ... }
# Using the greet functions
```

```
> $greet_world();
Hello World!
> $greet_friend();
Hello dear friend!
```

Here, `create-func` returns a subroutine greeting someone. It is called twice with two different arguments in order to create two different functions at runtime, `$greet_world` and `$greet_friend`. A function such as `create-func` is sometimes a *function factory* because you may create as many functions as you like by just calling `create-func`. This example may seem to be a slightly complicated way of doing something quite simple. At this point, it is just a bit too early to give really useful examples, but this is also a very powerful programming technique.

We'll come back to these techniques in various places in this book and even devote an entire chapter (Chapter 14) to this subject and related topics.

Why Functions and Subroutines?

It may not be clear why it is worth the trouble to divide a program into functions or subroutines. There are several reasons:

- Creating a new subroutine gives you an opportunity to name a group of statements, which makes your program easier to read and debug. Subroutines also help make the flow of execution clearer to the reader.

- Subroutines can make a program smaller by eliminating repetitive code. Later, if you make a change, you only have to make it in one place.

- Dividing a long program into subroutines allows you to debug the parts one at a time and then assemble them into a working whole.

- Well-designed subroutines are often useful for many programs. Once you write and debug one, you can reuse it.

- Creating subroutines is one of the major ways to break up a difficult problem into smaller easier subtasks and to create successive layers of abstraction, which are the key to solve complex problems.

- Writing good subroutines lets you create black boxes, with a known input and a known output. So you don't have to think about them anymore when you're working on something else. They've become a tool. Once you've assembled an electric screwdriver, you don't need to think about how it works internally when you use it to build or repair something.

- In the current open source world, chances are that your code will have to be understood, maintained, or enhanced by people other than you. Coding has become much more of a social activity than before. Breaking up your code into small subroutines whose purpose is easy to understand will make their work easier. And you'll be even more delighted when the person having to maintain or refactor your code is...you.

Debugging

One of the most important programming skills you will acquire is debugging. Although it can sometimes be frustrating, debugging is one of the most intellectually rich, challenging, and interesting parts of programming.

In some ways debugging is like detective work. You are confronted with clues and you have to infer the processes and events that led to the results you see.

Debugging is also like an experimental science. Once you have an idea about what is going wrong, you modify your program and try again. If your hypothesis was correct, you can predict the result of the modification, and you take a step closer to a working program. If your hypothesis was wrong, you have to come up with a new one. As Sherlock Holmes pointed out, "...When you have eliminated the impossible, whatever remains, however improbable, must be the truth" (A. Conan Doyle, *The Sign of Four*).

In cases where you are not able to come up with a hypothesis on what's wrong, you can try to introduce code that you expect to create a certain type of error, a "negative hypothesis" if you will. Sometimes you can learn a lot from the fact that it didn't create the error that was expected. Making a hypothesis does not necessarily mean you have an idea about how to make the code work; it could also be a hypothesis on how it should break.

For some people, programming and debugging are the same thing. That is, programming is the process of gradually debugging a program until it does what you want. The idea is that you should start with a working program and make small modifications, debugging them as you go.

For example, Linux is an operating system that contains millions of lines of code, but it started out as a simple program Linus Torvalds used to explore the Intel 80386 chip. According to Larry Greenfield, "One of Linus's earlier projects was a program that would switch between printing AAAA and BBBB. This later evolved to Linux." (*The Linux Users' Guide* Beta Version 1).

Glossary

anonymous function
    A function that has no name.

Any

   A special value typically found in variables that haven't been assigned a value. It is also a special value returned by some functions that we have called "void" (because they return something generally useless such as "Any").

argument

   A value provided to a function when the function is called. This value is assigned to the corresponding parameter in the function.

body

   The sequence of statements inside a function definition, usually in a code block delimited by braces.

composition

   Using an expression as part of a larger expression, or a statement as part of a larger statement.

first-class object

   Perl's subroutines are said to be higher order objects or first-class objects, because they can be passed around as other subroutines' arguments or return values, just as any other objects.

flow of execution

   The order in which statements run.

frame

   A box in a stack diagram that represents a subroutine call. It contains the local variables and parameters of the subroutine.

fruitful function

   A function or subroutine that returns a useful value.

function

   A named sequence of statements that performs some useful operation. Functions may or may not take arguments and may or may not produce a result. Perl comes with many built-in functions, and you can also create your own. In Perl, user-defined functions are often called subroutines.

function call

   A statement that runs a function. It consists of the function name followed by an argument list, which may or may not be enclosed within parentheses.

function definition

   A statement that creates a new function, specifying its name, parameters, and the statements it contains.

function factory
> A function that produces other functions as return values.

function signature
> The part of the definition of a function (usually between parentheses) that defines its parameters and possibly their types and other properties.

header
> The first line of a function definition.

immutable parameter
> A function or subroutine parameter that cannot be changed within the function body. By default, subroutine parameters are immutable.

lexical variable
> A variable defined inside a subroutine or a code block. A lexical variable defined within a function can only be used inside that function.

module
> A file that contains a collection of related functions and other definitions.

Nil
> A special value sometimes returned by some "void" subroutines.

parameter
> A name used inside a subroutine to refer to the value passed as an argument.

return value
> The result of a function. If a function call is used as an expression, the return value is the value of the expression.

stack diagram
> A graphical representation of a stack of subroutines, their variables, and the values they refer to.

trait
> A property of a function or subroutine parameter that is defined at compile time.

use statement
> A statement that reads a module file and usually imports some functions.

void function
> A function or subroutine that does not return a useful value.

Exercises

Exercise 3-1.

Write a subroutine named `right-justify` that takes a string named `$input-string` as a parameter and prints the string with enough leading spaces so that the last letter of the string is in column 70 of the display.

```
> right-justify('Larry Wall')
                                                              Larry Wall
```

Hint: use string concatenation and repetition. Also, Perl provides a built-in function called `chars` that returns the length of a string, so the value of `chars 'Larry Wall'` or `'Larry Wall'.chars` is 10. Solution: "Exercise 3-1: Subroutine right-justify" on page 345.

Exercise 3-2.

We have seen that functions and other code objects can be passed around as values, just like any object. Functions are said to be *first-class objects*. For example, `do-twice` is a function that takes a function as an argument and calls it twice:

```
sub do-twice($code) {
    $code();
    $code();
}
sub greet {
    say "Hello World!";
}
do-twice(&greet);
```

1. Type this example into a script and test it.
2. Modify `do-twice` so that it takes two arguments, a function and a value, and calls the function twice, passing the value as an argument.
3. Copy the definition of `print-twice` from earlier in this chapter to your script.
4. Use the modified version of `do-twice` to call `print-twice` twice, passing "What's up doc" as an argument.
5. Define a new function called `do-four` that takes a function and a value and calls the function four times, passing the value as a parameter. There should be only two statements in the body of this function, not four.

Solution: "Exercise 3-2: Subroutine do-twice" on page 347.

Exercise 3-3.

Note: this exercise should be done using only the statements and other features we have learned so far.

1. Write a subroutine that draws a grid like the following:

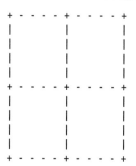

   Hint: to print more than one value on a line, you can print a comma-separated sequence of values:

   ```
   say '+', '-';
   ```

   The say function prints its arguments with a newline at the end (it advances to the next line). If you don't want to go to the next line, use the print function instead:

   ```
   print '+', ' ';
   print '-';
   ```

   The output of these statements is "+ -".

   A say statement with an empty string argument ends the current line and goes to the next line.

2. Write a subroutine that draws a similar grid with four rows and four columns.

Solution: "Exercise 3-3: Subroutine print-grid" on page 348.

Credit: this exercise is based on an exercise in *Practical C Programming, 3rd Edition*, by Steve Oualline (O'Reilly, 1997).

## CHAPTER 4

Loops, Conditionals, and Recursion

The main topic of this chapter is the `if` statement, which executes different code depending on the state of the program. But first I want to introduce two new operators: integer division and modulo.

Integer Division and Modulo

The *integer division* operator, `div`, divides two numbers and rounds down to an integer. For example, suppose the runtime of a movie is 105 minutes. You might want to know how long that is in hours. In Perl, conventional division returns a rational number (in many languages, it returns a floating-point number, which is another kind of internal representation for noninteger numbers):

```
> my $minutes = 105;
> $minutes / 60;
1.75
```

But we don't normally write hours with decimal points. Integer division returns the integer number of hours, dropping the fraction part:

```
> my $minutes = 105;
> my $hours = $minutes div 60;
1
```

In arithmetic, integer division is sometimes called *Euclidean division*, which computes a quotient and a remainder.

To get the remainder, you could subtract off one hour in minutes:

```
> my $remainder = $minutes - $hours * 60;
45
```

An alternative is to use the *modulo operator*, %, which divides two numbers and returns the remainder:

```
> my $remainder = minutes % 60;
45
```

The modulo operator is very common in programming languages and is more useful than it seems. For example, you can check whether one number is divisible by another—if $dividend % $divisor is zero, then $dividend is divisible by $divisor. This is commonly used, for example, with a divisor equal to 2 in order to determine whether an integer is even or odd. We will see an example of that later in this chapter (see "Alternative Execution" on page 61).

To tell the truth, Perl 6 also has a specific operator for divisibility, %%. The $dividend %% $divisor expression returns a true value if $dividend % $divisor is equal to 0, that is if $dividend is divisible by $divisor (and false otherwise).

Also, you can extract the rightmost digit or digits from a number with the modulo operator. For example, $x % 10 yields the rightmost digit of $x (in base 10). Similarly, $x % 100 yields the last two digits:

```
> 642 % 100;
42
```

Boolean expressions

A *Boolean expression* is an expression that is either true or false. The following examples use the operator ==, which compares two numeric operands and produces True if they are equal and False otherwise:

```
> 5 == 5;
True
> 5 == 6;
False
```

True and False are special values that belong to the type Bool; they are not strings:

```
> say True.WHAT
(Bool)
> say False.WHAT
(Bool)
```

The == operator is one of the *numeric relational operators* and checks whether the operands are equal; the others are:

```
$x != $y        # $x is not numerically equal to $y
$x > $y         # $x is numerically greater than $y
$x < $y         # $x is numerically less than $y
$x >= $y        # $x is numerically greater than or equal to $y
```

```
$x <= $y          # $x is numerically less than or equal to $y
$x === $y         # $x and $y are truly identical
```

Although these operations are probably familiar to you, the Perl symbols are different from the mathematical symbols. A common error is to use a single equals sign (=) instead of a double equals sign (==). Remember that = is an assignment operator and == is a relational operator. There is no such thing as =<, and there exists a => operator, but it is not a relational operator, but something completely different (it is, as we'll see later, a pair constructor).

The difference between == and === is that the former operator checks whether the values of the operands are equal and the latter checks whether the operands are truly identical. As an example, consider this:

```
say 42 ==  42;        # True
say 42 ==  42.0;      # True
say 42 === 42;        # True
say 42 === 42.0;      # False
```

These relational operators can only compare numeric values (numbers or variables containing numbers) or values that can be coerced to numeric values, such as, for example, the string "42" which, if used with these operators (except ===), will be coerced to the number 42.

For comparing strings (in a lexicographic or "pseudo-alphabetic" type of comparison), you need to use the *string relational operators*:

```
$x eq $y          # $x is string-wise equal to $y
$x ne $y          # $x is string-wise not equal to $y
$x gt $y          # $x is greater than $y (alphabetically after)
$x lt $y          # $x is less than $y (alphabetically before)
$x ge $y          # $x is greater than or equal to $y
$x le $y          # $x is less than or equal to $y
$x eqv $y         # $x is truly equivalent to $y
```

For example, you may compare (alphabetically) two former US presidents:

```
> 'FDR' eq 'JFK';
False
> 'FDR' lt 'JFK';      # alphabetical comparison
True
```

Unlike most other programming languages, Perl 6 allows you to chain relational operators transitively, just as in mathematical notation:

```
say 4 < 7 < 12;      # True
say 4 < 7 < 5;       # False
```

It may be useful to point out that numeric relational operators and string relational operators don't work the same way (and that's a good reason for having different operators), because they don't have the same idea of what is *greater than* or *less than*.

When comparing two positive integers, a number with four digits is always greater than a number with only two or three digits. For example, 1110 is greater than 886.

String comparisons, in contrast, basically follow (pseudo) alphabetical rules: "b" is greater than "aaa" because the commonly accepted rule for string comparisons is to start by comparing the first letter of each string: which string is greater is known if the two letters are different, irrespective of what character comes next; you need to proceed to comparing the second letter of each word only if comparing the first letter of each string led to a draw, and so on. Thus, any word starting with "a" is less than any word starting with "b," irrespective of the length of these words. You may think that this is nitpicking, but this becomes essential when you start sorting items: you really have to think about which type of order (numeric or alphabetical) you want to use.

There are also some so-called "three-way" relational operators, cmp, <=>, and leg, but we'll come back to them when we study how to sort the items in a list. Similarly, we need to learn quite a few other things about Perl before we can do justice to the incredibly powerful and expressive smart match operator, ~~.

A final point to be noted about string comparisons is that uppercase letters are always deemed smaller than lowercase letters. So "A," "B," "BB," and "C" are *all* less than "a," "b," "bb," and "c." We will not go into the details here, but this becomes more complicated (and sometimes confusing) when the strings to be compared contain nonalphabetical characters (or non-ASCII Unicode letters).

Logical Operators

There are three main pairs of *logical operators*:

- logical *and*: "and" and &&
- logical *or*: "or" and ||
- logical *not*: "not" and !

The semantics (meaning) of these operators is similar to their meaning in English. For example, $x > 0 and $x < 10 is true only if $x is greater than 0 *and* less than 10.

$n % 2 == 0 and $n % 3 == 0 is true if *both* conditions are true, that is, if the number is divisible by 2 *and* by 3, i.e., is in fact divisible by 6 (which could be better written as: $n % 6 == 0 or $n %% 6).

$n % 2 == 0 or $n % 3 == 0 is true if *either or both* of the conditions is true, that is, if the number is divisible by 2 *or* by 3 (or both).

Finally, the not operator negates a Boolean expression, so not (x > y) is true if x > y is false, that is, if x is less than or equal to y.

The &&, ||, and ! operators have the same meanings, respectively, as and, or, and not, but they have a tighter precedence, which means that when they stand in an expression with some other operators, they have a higher priority of execution. We will come back to precedence later, but let's say for the time being that, in most common cases, the and, or, and not operators will usually do what you want.

Strictly speaking, the operands of the logical operators should be Boolean expressions, but Perl, just like many languages partly derived from C, is not very strict on that. The numbers 0 and 0.0 are false; and any nonzero number or nonempty string is interpreted as True:

```
> 42 and True;
True
```

This flexibility can be very useful, but there are some subtleties to it that might be confusing. You might want to avoid it unless you know what you are doing.

The so built-in function returns a Boolean evaluation of its argument:

```
> say so (0 and True);
False
```

Here, the expression (0 and True) is false because 0 is false and the expression could be true only if both arguments of the and operator were true.

When several Boolean conditions are linked with some logical operator, Perl will only perform the comparisons that are strictly necessary to figure out the final result, starting with those on the left. For example, if you write:

```
> False and $number > 0;
False
```

there is no need to evaluate the second Boolean expression to know that the overall expression will be false. In this case, Perl does not try to check whether the number is positive or even whether it is defined. It is sometimes said that these operators "short circuit" unnecessary conditions.

Similarly, in the following code, the compute-pension subroutine will not even be called if the person's age is less than 65:

```
$age >= 65 and compute-pension();
```

The same goes with the or operator, but the other way around: if the first Boolean expression of an or statement is true, then the next expression will not be evaluated. The following code is thus equivalent to the previous one:

```
$age < 65 or compute-pension();
```

This *can* be a way of running the compute-pension subroutine conditionally, depending on the value of the age, and this is sometimes used, notably in idiomatic constructs such as:

```
do-something() or die "could not do something";
```

which aborts the program if do-something returns a false value, meaning that it was not able to do something so essential that it would not make sense to try to continue running it.

We will examine now clearer and much more common ways of running conditional code.

Conditional Execution

In order to write useful programs, we almost always need the ability to check conditions and change the behavior of the program accordingly. *Conditional statements* give us this ability. The simplest form is the if statement:

```
if $number > 0 {
    say '$number is positive';
}
```

The Boolean expression after if is called the *condition*. If it is true, the subsequent block of code runs. If not, nothing happens. The block of code may contain any number of statements.

It is conventional and highly recommended (although not strictly mandatory from the standpoint of the compiler) to indent the statements in the block, in order to help visualize the *control flow* of the program, i.e., its structure of execution: with such indentation, we can see much better that the statements within the conditional block will run only if the condition is true.

The condition may be a compound Boolean expression:

```
if $n > 0 and $n < 20 and $n %% 2 {
    say '$n is an even and positive number smaller than 20'
}
```

Note that in the print statement above, the final semicolon has been omitted. When a statement is the last code line of a block, immediately before the curly brace } closing that code block, the final semicolon is optional and may be omitted, though it might be considered good form to include it.

In theory, the overall code snippet above is itself a statement and should also end with a semicolon after the closing brace. But a closing curly brace followed by a newline character implies a statement separator, so you don't need a semicolon here and it is generally omitted.

Alternative Execution

A second form of the `if` statement is "alternative execution," in which there are two possibilities and the condition determines which one runs. Given a `$number` variable containing an integer, the following code displays two different messages depending on whether the value of the integer is even or odd:

```
if $number % 2 == 0 {
    say 'Variable $number is even'
} else {
    say 'Variable $number is odd'
}
```

If the remainder when `$number` is divided by 2 is 0, then we know that `$number` is even, and the program displays an appropriate message. If the condition is false, the second set of statements runs. Since the condition must be true or false, exactly one of the alternatives will run. The alternatives are called *branches*, because they are branches in the flow of execution.

Note that if `$number` is evenly divisible by two, this code will print:

```
Variable $number is even
```

The `$number` variable value is not interpolated, because we used single quotes for the purpose of printing out the variable name rather than its value. We would have to use double quotes if we wanted to display the variable's value instead of its name.

Chained Conditionals

Sometimes there are more than two possibilities and we need more than two branches. One way to express a computation like that is a *chained conditional*:

```
if $x < $y {
    say 'Variable $x is less than variable $y'
} elsif $x > $y {
    say 'Variable $x is greater than variable  $y'
} else {
    say 'Variables $x and $y are equal'
}
```

The `elsif` keyword is an abbreviation of "else if" that has the advantage of avoiding nesting of blocks. Again, exactly one branch will run. There is no limit on the number of `elsif` statements.

If there is an `else` clause, it has to be at the end, but there doesn't have to be one:

```
if $choice eq 'a' {
    draw_a()
} elsif $choice eq 'b' {
    draw_b()
```

```
} elsif $choice eq 'c' {
    draw_c()
}
```

Each condition is checked in order. If the first is false, the next is checked, and so on. If one of them is true, the corresponding branch runs and the statement ends. Even if more than one condition is true, only the first true branch runs.

Nested Conditionals

One conditional can also be nested within another. We could have written the example in the previous section like this:

```
if $x == $y {
    say 'Variables $x and $y are equal'
} else {
    if $x < $y {
        say 'Variable $x is less than variable $y'
    } else {
        say 'Variable $x is greater than variable $y'
    }
}
```

The outer conditional contains two branches. The first branch contains a simple statement. The second branch contains another if statement, which has two branches of its own. Those two branches are both simple statements, although they could have been conditional statements as well. The if $x < $y conditional is said to be nested within the else branch of the outer conditional.

Such nested conditionals show how critical it is for your own comprehension to properly indent conditional statements, as it would be very difficult here to visually grasp the structure without the help of correct indentation.

Although the indentation of the statements helps make the structure apparent, *nested conditionals* become difficult to read very quickly. It is a good idea to avoid them when you can. Logical operators often provide a way to simplify nested conditional statements. For example, consider the following code (which assumes $x to be an integer):

```
my Int $x;
# ... $x = ...;
if 0 < $x {
    if $x < 10 {
        say 'Value of $x is a positive single-digit number.'
    }
}
```

The say statement runs only if we make it past both conditionals, so we can get the same effect with the and Boolean operator, and the code can be rewritten using a single conditional:

```
if 0 < $x and $x < 10 {
    say '$x is a positive single-digit number.'
}
```

For this kind of condition, Perl 6 provides a more concise option using the chained relational operators described earlier:

```
if 0 < $x < 10 {
    say '$x is a positive single-digit number.'
}
```

if Conditionals as Statement Modifiers

There is also a form of if called a *statement modifier* (or sometimes "postfix conditional") form when there is only one conditional statement. In this case, the if and the condition come after the code you want to run conditionally. Note that the condition is still always evaluated first:

```
say '$number is negative.' if $number < 0;
```

This is equivalent to:

```
if $number < 0 {
    say '$number is negative.'
}
```

This syntactic form is more concise as it takes only one code line instead of three. The advantage is that you can see more of your program code on one screen, without having to scroll up and down. However, this syntax is neat and clean only when both the condition and the statement are short and simple, so it is probably best used only in these cases.

The statement modifier form does not allow else and elsif statements.

Unless Conditional Statement

If you don't like having to write negative conditions in a conditional if statement such as:

```
if not $number >= 0 {
    say '$number is negative.'
}
```

you may write this instead:

```
unless $number >= 0 {
    say '$number is negative.'
}
```

This *unless* keyword does exactly what the English says: it will display the sentence "$number is negative." *unless* the number is greater than or equal to 0.

You cannot use `else` or `elsif` statements with `unless`, because that would end up getting confusing.

The `unless` conditional is most commonly used in its statement modifier (or postfix notation) form:

```
say '$number is negative.' unless $number >= 0;
```

for Loops

Suppose you need to compute and print the product of the first five positive digits (1 to 5). This product is known in mathematics as the *factorial* of 5 and is sometimes written as 5!. You could write this program:

```
my $product = 1 * 2 * 3 * 4 * 5;
say $product;          # prints 120
```

You could make it slightly simpler:

```
say 2 * 3 * 4 * 5;     # prints 120
```

The problem is that this syntactic construct does not scale well and becomes tedious for the product of the first 10 integers (or factorial 10). And it becomes almost a nightmare for factorial 100. Calculating the factorial of a number is a fairly common computation in mathematics (especially in the fields of combinatorics and probability) and in computer science. We need to automatize it, and using a `for` loop is one of the most obvious ways of doing that:

```
my $product = 1;
for 1..5 {
    $product *= $_
}
say $product;          # prints 120
```

Now, if you need to compute factorial 100, you just need to replace the 5 in the code above with 100. Beware, though, the factorial function is known to grow extremely rapidly, and you'll get a truly huge number, with 158 digits (i.e., a number much larger than the estimated total number of atoms in the known universe).

In this script, `1..5` is the range operator, which is used here to generate a list of consecutive numbers between 1 and 5. The `for` keyword is used to iterate over that list, and `$_` is a special variable that takes each successive value of this list: first 1, then 2, etc. until 5. In the code block forming the body of the loop, the `$product` variable is multiplied successively by each value of $_. The loop ends with 5 and the result, 120, is printed on the last line.

This is a simple use of the for statement, but probably not the most commonly used in Perl 6; we will see more below. We will also see other types of loops. But that should be enough for now to let you write some loops. Loops are found everywhere in computer programming.

The $_ special variable is known as the *topical variable* or simply the *topic*. It does not need to be declared and many syntactic constructs assign a value to it without explicitly mentioning it. Also, $_ is an implicit argument to methods called without an explicit invocant. For example, to print the first five integers, you might write:

```
for 1..5 {.say};  # prints numbers 1 to 5, each on its line
```

Here .say is a syntax shorthand equivalent to $_.say. And since, as we saw, $_ takes each successive value of the range introduced by the for keyword, this very short code line prints each number between 1 and 5, each on a different line. This is a typical example of the $_ topical variable being used without even being explicitly mentioned. We will see many other uses of the $_ special variable.

Sometimes, you don't use the $_ loop variable within the loop, for example if you just want to do something five times but don't care each time through the loop at which iteration you have arrived. A subroutine that prints a message *n* times might look like this:

```
sub print-n-times (Int $n, Str $message) {
    for 1..$n { say $message }
}
```

The for loop also has a statement modifier or postfix form, used here to compute again the factorial of 5:

```
my $product = 1;
$product *= $_ for 1..5;
say $product;            # prints 120
```

There is another syntax for the for loop, using an explicit loop variable:

```
sub factorial (Int $num) {
    my $product = 1;
    for 1..$num -> $x {
        $product *= $x
    }
    return $product
}
say factorial 10;    # 3628800
```

The `for` loop in this subroutine is using what is called a "pointy block" syntax. It is essentially the same idea as the previous `for` loops, except that, instead of using the `$_` topical variable, we now declare an explicit `$x` loop variable with the `1..$num -> $x` syntax to iterate over the range of values. Using an explicit loop variable can make your code clearer when things get more complicated, for example when you need to nest several `for` loops. We will see more examples of that later.

We will also see several other ways of computing the factorial of a number in this book.

Recursion

It is legal for one function or subroutine to call another; it is also legal for a subroutine to call itself. It may not be obvious why that is a good thing, but it turns out to be one of the most magical things a program can do. For example, look at the following subroutine:

```
sub countdown(Int $time-left) {
    if $time-left <= 0 {
        say 'Blastoff!';
    } else {
        say $time-left;
        countdown($time-left - 1);
    }
}
```

If `$n` is 0 or negative, it outputs the word "Blastoff!" Otherwise, it outputs `$time-left` and then calls a subroutine named `countdown`—itself— passing `$n-1` as an argument.

What happens if we call the subroutine like this?

```
countdown(3);
```

The execution of `countdown` begins with `$time-left = 3`, and since `$time-left` is greater than 0, it outputs the value 3, and then calls itself...

> The execution of `countdown` begins with `$time-left = 2`, and since `$time-left` is greater than 0, it outputs the value 2, and then calls itself...

>> The execution of `countdown` begins with `$time-left = 1`, and since `$time-left` is greater than 0, it outputs the value 1, and then calls itself...

>>> The execution of `countdown` begins with `$time-left = 0`, and since `$time-left` is not greater than 0, it outputs the word "Blastoff!" and then returns.

>> The countdown that got `$time-left = 1` returns.

> The countdown that got `$time-left = 2` returns.

The countdown that got $time-left = 3 returns.

And then you're back in the main program. So, the total output looks like this:

```
3
2
1
Blastoff!
```

A subroutine that calls itself is *recursive*; the process of executing it is called *recursion*.

As another example, we can write a subroutine that prints a string $n times:

```
sub print-n-times(Str $sentence, Int $n) {
    return if $n <= 0;
    say $sentence;
    print-n-times($sentence, $n - 1);
}
```

If $n <= 0, the *return statement* exits the subroutine. The flow of execution immediately returns to the caller, and the remaining lines of the subroutine don't run. This illustrates a feature of the return subroutine that we have not seen before: it is used here for flow control, i.e., to stop the execution of the subroutine and pass control back to the caller. Note also that here the return statement does not return any value to the caller; print-n-times is a void function.

The rest of the subroutine is similar to countdown: it displays $sentence and then calls itself to display $sentence $n − 1 additional times. So the number of lines of output is 1 + ($n - 1), which adds up to $n.

For simple examples like this, it may seem easier to use a for loop. But we will see examples later that are hard to write with a for loop and easy to write with recursion, so it is good to start early.

Stack Diagrams for Recursive Subroutines

In "Stack Diagrams" on page 42, we used a stack diagram to represent the state of a program during a subroutine call. The same kind of diagram can help interpret a recursive subroutine.

Every time a subroutine gets called, Perl creates a frame to contain the subroutine's local variables and parameters. For a recursive subroutine, there might be more than one frame on the stack at the same time.

Figure 4-1 shows a stack diagram for countdown called with n = 3.

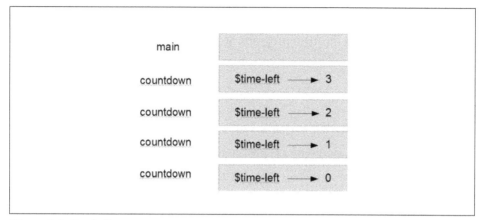

Figure 4-1. Stack diagram

As usual, the top of the stack is the frame for the main program. It is empty because we did not create any variables in it or pass any arguments to it.

The four countdown frames have different values for the parameter $time-left. The bottom of the stack, where $time-left = 0, is called the *base case*. It does not make a recursive call, so there are no more frames.

As an exercise, draw a stack diagram for print-n-times called with $sentence = 'Hello' and $n = 2. Then write a function called do-n-times that takes a function and a number, $num, as arguments, and that calls the given function $num times. Solution: see "Exercises of Chapter 4: Conditionals and Recursion" on page 350.

Infinite Recursion

If a recursion never reaches a base case, it goes on making recursive calls forever, and the program never terminates. This is known as *infinite recursion*, and it is generally not a good idea. In fact, your program will not actually execute forever but will die at some point when the computer runs out of memory or some other critical resource.

You have to be careful when writing recursive subroutines. Make sure that you have a base case, and make sure that you are guaranteed to reach it. Actually, although this is not absolutely required by the language, I would advise you to make a habit of treating the base case first.

Keyboard Input

The programs we have written so far accept no input from the user. They just do the same thing every time. Perl provides built-in functions that stop the program and wait for the user to type something.

For example, the prompt function prompts the user with a question or an instruction. When the user presses Return or Enter, the program resumes and prompt returns what the user typed as a string (without the newline character corresponding to the Return key typed by the user):

```
my $user = prompt "Please type in your name: ";
say "Hello $user";
```

This is probably one of the most common ways to obtain interactive user input, because it is usually a good idea to tell the user what is expected.

Another possibility is to use the get method (which reads a single line) on standard input:

```
say "Please type in your name: ";
my $user = $*IN.get;
say "Hello $user";
```

or the get function, which reads a line from standard input by default:

```
say "Please type in your name: ";
my $user = get;
say "Hello $user";
```

Program Arguments and the MAIN Subroutine

There is another (and often better) way to have a program use varying input defined by the user, which is to pass command-line arguments to the program, just as we have passed arguments to our subroutines.

The easiest way to retrieve arguments passed to a program is to use a special subroutine named MAIN. A program that has a defined MAIN subroutine will usually start its execution with that subroutine and the command-line arguments supplied to the program will be passed as arguments to MAIN. The MAIN signature will thus enable you to retrieve the arguments provided in the command line and possibly also check their validity.

For example, the *greet.pl6* program might look like this:

```
sub MAIN (Str $name) {
    say "Hello $name";
}
```

You may call this program twice with different command-line arguments as follows:

```
$ perl6 greet.pl6 Larry
Hello Larry

$ perl6 greet.pl6 world
Hello world
```

It is very easy to change the argument, since all you need to do under the operating system command line is use the up arrow and edit the end of the previous command line.

If you forget to supply the argument (or provide the wrong number of arguments, or arguments not matching the signature), the program will die and Perl 6 will nicely generate and display a usage method:

```
$ perl6 greet.pl6
Usage:
  greet.pl6 <name>
```

Debugging

When a syntax or runtime error occurs, the error message contains a lot of information, but it can be overwhelming. The most useful parts are usually:

- What kind of error it was
- Where it occurred

Syntax errors are usually easy to find, but there are a few gotchas. In general, error messages indicate where the problem was discovered, but the actual error might be earlier in the code, sometimes on a previous line or even many lines before.

For example, the goal of the following code was to display the multiplication tables:

```
sub multiplication-tables {
    for 1..10 -> $x {
    for 1..10 -> $y {
        say "$x x $y\t= ", $x * $y;
      say "";
      }
}

multiplication-tables();
```

It failed at compilation with the following error:

```
$ perl6 mult_table.pl6
===SORRY!=== Error while compiling /home/Laurent/mult_table.pl6
Missing block (taken by some undeclared routine?)
at /home/Laurent/mult_table.pl6:9
------> multiplication-tables();<HERE><EOL>
```

The error message reports an error on line 9 of the program (the last line of the code), at the end of the line, but the actual error is a missing closing brace after line 4 and before line 5. The reason for this is that while the programmer made the mistake on line 4, the Perl interpreter could not detect this error before it reached the end of the program. The correct program for displaying multiplication tables might be:

```
sub multiplication-tables {
    for 1..10 -> $x {
        for 1..10 -> $y {
            say "$x x $y\t= ", $x * $y;
        }
        say "";
    }
}
multiplication-tables();
```

When an error is reported on the last line of a program, it is quite commonly due to a missing closing parenthesis, bracket, brace, or quotation mark several lines earlier. An editor with syntax highlighting can sometimes help you.

The same is true of runtime errors. Consider this program aimed at computing 360 degrees divided successively by the integers between 2 and 5:

```
my ($a, $b, $c, $d) = 2, 3, 5;
my $value = 360;
$value /= $_ for $a, $b, $c, $d;
say $value;
```

This program compiles correctly but displays a warning and then an exception on runtime:

```
Use of uninitialized value of type Any in numeric context
in block  at product.pl6 line 3
Attempt to divide 12 by zero using div
  in block <unit> at product.pl6 line 4
```

The error message indicates a "division by zero" exception on line 4, but there is nothing wrong with that line. The warning on line 3 might give us a clue that the script attempts to use an undefined value, but the real error is on the first line of the script, where one of the four necessary integers (4) was omitted by mistake from the list assignment.

You should take the time to read error messages carefully, but don't assume they point to the root cause of the exception; they often point to subsequent problems.

Glossary

base case
> A conditional branch in a recursive function that does not make a recursive call.

Boolean expression
> An expression whose value is either True or False.

branch
> One of the alternative sequences of statements in a conditional statement.

chained conditional
    A conditional statement with a series of alternative branches.

condition
    The Boolean expression in a conditional statement that determines which branch runs.

conditional statement
    A statement that controls the flow of execution depending on some condition.

infinite recursion
    A recursion that doesn't have a base case, or never reaches it. Eventually, an infinite recursion causes a runtime error, for which you may not want to wait because it may take a long time.

integer division
    An operation, denoted div, that divides two numbers and rounds down (toward zero) the result to an integer.

logical operator
    One of the operators that combines Boolean expressions: and, or, and not. The equivalent higher-precedence operators are &&, ||, and !.

modulo operator
    An operator, denoted with a percent sign (%), that works on integers and returns the remainder when one number is divided by another.

nested conditional
    A conditional statement that appears in one of the branches of another conditional statement.

recursion
    The process of calling the function that is currently executing.

relational operator
    One of the operators that compares its operands. The most common numeric relational operators are ==, !=, >, <, >=, and <=. The equivalent string relational operators are eq, ne, gt, lt, ge, and le.

return statement
    A statement that causes a function to end immediately and return to the caller.

statement modifier
    A postfix conditional expression, i.e., a conditional expression (using for example if, unless, or for) that is placed after the statement the execution of which it controls. It can also refer to a postfix looping expression.

Exercises

Exercise 4-1.

Using the integer division and the modulo operators:

1. Write a subroutine that computes how many days, hours, minutes, and seconds there are in the number of seconds passed as an argument to the subroutine.
2. Write a script that computes how many days, hours, minutes, and seconds there are in 240,000 seconds.
3. Change your script to compute the number of days, hours, minutes, and seconds there are in a number of seconds entered by the script user when prompted to give a number of seconds.

Solution: "Exercise 4-1: Days, Hours, Minutes, and Seconds" on page 350.

Exercise 4-2.

Fermat's Last Theorem says that there are no positive integers a, b, and c such that

$$a^n + b^n = c^n$$

for any values of n greater than 2.

1. Write a function named check-fermat that takes four parameters—a, b, c, and n —and checks to see if Fermat's theorem holds. If n is greater than 2 and

$$a^n + b^n = c^n$$

the program should print, "Holy smokes, Fermat was wrong!" Otherwise the program should print, "No, that doesn't work."

2. Write a function that prompts the user to input values for a, b, c, and n, converts them to integers, and uses check-fermat to check whether they violate Fermat's theorem.

Solution: "Exercise 4-2: Fermat's Theorem" on page 352.

Exercise 4-3.

If you are given three sticks, you may or may not be able to arrange them in a triangle. For example, if one of the sticks is 12 inches long and the other two are 1 inch long, you will not be able to get the short sticks to meet in the middle. For any three lengths, there is a simple test to see if it is possible to form a triangle:

> If any of the three lengths is greater than the sum of the other two, then you cannot form a triangle. Otherwise, you can. (If the sum of two lengths equals the third, they form what is called a "degenerate" triangle.)

1. Write a function named is-triangle that takes three positive numbers as arguments, and that prints either "Yes" or "No," depending on whether you can form a triangle from sticks with the given lengths.

2. Write a function that prompts the user to input three stick lengths and uses is-triangle to check whether sticks with the given lengths can form a triangle.

Solution: "Exercise 4-3: Is It a Triangle?" on page 352.

Exercise 4-4.

The Fibonacci numbers were invented by Leonardo Fibonacci (a.k.a. Leonardo of Pisa or simply Fibonacci), an Italian mathematician of the thirteenth century.

The Fibonacci numbers are a sequence of numbers such as

> 1, 1, 2, 3, 5, 8, 13, 21, 34, ...

in which the first two numbers are equal to 1 and each subsequent number of the sequence is defined as the sum of the previous two (for example, 5 = 2 + 3, 8 = 3 + 5, etc.).

In mathematical notation, the Fibonacci numbers could be defined by recurrence as follows:

$$F_1 = 1, \ F_2 = 1, \text{ and } F_n = F_{n-1} + F_{n-2}$$

1. Write a program using a for loop that prints on screen the first 20 Fibonacci numbers.

2. Write a program which prompts the user to enter a number n and, using a for loop, computes and displays the nth Fibonacci number.

Solution: "Exercise 4-4: The Fibonacci Numbers" on page 353.

Exercise 4-5.

What is the output of the following program? Draw a stack diagram that shows the state of the program when it prints the result.

```
sub recurse($n, $s) {
    if ($n == 0) {
        say $s;
    } else {
        recurse $n - 1, $n + $s;
    }
}
recurse 3, 0;
```

1. What would happen if you called the function like this: `recurse(-1, 0)`?

2. Write a documentation comment (maybe in the form of a multiline comment) that explains everything someone would need to know in order to use this function (and nothing else).

Solution: "Exercise 4-5: The recurse Subroutine" on page 354.

## CHAPTER 5

Fruitful Subroutines

Most of the Perl functions we have used, such as the math functions, produce return values. But most of the subroutines we've written so far are void: they have an effect, like printing a value, but they don't have a return value. In this chapter you will learn to write fruitful functions.

Return Values

Calling a fruitful function generates a return value, which we usually assign to a variable or use as part of an expression:

```
my $pi = 4 * atan 1;
my $height = $radius * sin $radians;
```

Many of the subroutines we have written so far are void. Speaking casually, they have no usable return value; more precisely, their return value may be Any, (), or True.

In this chapter, we are (finally) going to write fruitful subroutines. The first example is area, which returns the area of a circle with the given radius:

```
sub area($radius) {
    my $circular_area = pi * $radius**2;
    return $circular_area;
}
```

We have seen the return statement before, but in a fruitful function the return statement includes an expression. This statement means: "Return immediately from this function and use the following expression as a return value." The expression can be arbitrarily complicated, so we could have written this function more concisely:

```
sub area($radius) {
    return pi * $radius**2;
}
```

On the other hand, *temporary variables* like `$circular_area` can make debugging easier. They may also help document what is going on.

Sometimes it is useful to have multiple `return` statements, for example one in each branch of a conditional:

```
sub absolute_value($num){
    if $num < 0 {
        return -$num;
    } else {
        return $num;
    }
}
```

Since these `return` statements are in an alternative conditional, only one runs.

This could also be written more concisely using the statement modifier syntax:

```
sub absolute_value($num){
    return -$num if $num < 0;
    return $num;
}
```

Here again, only one of the `return` statements runs: if the number is negative, the first `return` statement is executed and the subroutine execution stops there; if the number is positive or zero, then only the second `return` statement is executed.

As soon as a `return` statement runs, the function terminates without executing any subsequent statements. Code that appears after an unconditional `return` statement, or any other place the flow of execution can never reach, is called *dead code*.

In a fruitful function, it is a good idea to ensure that every possible path through the program hits a `return` statement. For example:

```
sub absolute_value($num){
    if $num < 0 {
        return -$num;
    }
    if $num > 0 {
        return $num;
    }
}
```

This subroutine is incorrect because if $num happens to be 0, neither condition is true, and the subroutine ends without hitting a `return` statement. If the flow of execution gets to the end of a function, the return value is (), which basically means "not defined" and is clearly not the absolute value of 0:

```
> absolute_value(0)
()
```

By the way, Perl provides a built-in function called `abs` that computes absolute values.

As an exercise, write a compare subroutine that takes two numbers, $x and $y, and returns 1 if $x > $y, 0 if $x == $y, and -1 if $x < $y. Solution: "Exercise: Compare" on page 356.

Incremental Development

As you write larger functions, you might find yourself spending more time debugging.

To deal with increasingly complex programs, you might want to try a process called *incremental development*. The goal of incremental development is to avoid long debugging sessions by adding and testing only a small amount of code at a time.

As an example, suppose you want to find the distance between two points, given by the Cartesian or rectangular coordinates (x_1, y_1) and (x_2, y_2). By the Pythagorean theorem, the distance is:

$$distance = \sqrt{(x_2 - x_1)^2 + (y_2 - y_1)^2}$$

The first step is to consider what a distance function should look like in Perl. In other words, what are the inputs (parameters) and what is the output (return value)?

In this case, the inputs are two points, which you can represent using four numbers. The return value is the distance represented by a numeric value.

Immediately you can write an outline of the function:

```
sub distance($x1, $y1, $x2, $y2) {
    return 0.0;
}
```

Obviously, this version doesn't compute distances; it always returns zero. But it is syntactically correct, and it runs, which means that you can test it before you make it more complicated.

To test the new function, call it with sample arguments:

```
> distance(1, 2, 4, 6);
0.0
```

I chose these values so that the horizontal distance is 3 and the vertical distance is 4; that way, the result is 5, the hypotenuse of a 3-4-5 triangle. When testing a function, it is useful to know the right answer.

At this point we have confirmed that the function is syntactically correct, and we can start adding code to the body. A reasonable next step is to find the differences $x_2 - x_1$

and $y_2 - y_1$. The next version stores those values in temporary variables and prints them:

```
sub distance($x1, $y1, $x2, $y2) {
    my $dx = $x2 - $x1;
    my $dy = $y2 - $y1;
    say '$dx is', $dx;
    say '$dy is', $dy;
    return 0.0;
}
```

If the function is working, it should display $dx is 3 and $dy is 4 (and still return 0.0). If so, we know that the function is getting the right arguments and performing the first computation correctly. If not, there are only a few lines to check.

Next we compute the sum of squares of $dx and $dy:

```
sub distance($x1, $y1, $x2, $y2) {
    my $dx = $x2 - $x1;
    my $dy = $y2 - $y1;
    my $dsquared = $dx**2 + $dy**2;
    say '$dsquared is: ', $dsquared;
    return 0.0;
}
```

Again, you would run the program at this stage and check the output (which should be 25). Finally, you can use the sqrt built-in function to compute and return the result:

```
sub distance($x1, $y1, $x2, $y2) {
    my $dx = $x2 - $x1;
    my $dy = $y2 - $y1;
    my $dsquared = $dx**2 + $dy**2;
    my $result = sqrt $dsquared;
    return $result;
}
```

If that works correctly, you are done. Otherwise, you might want to print the value of $result before the return statement.

The final version of the subroutine doesn't display anything when it runs; it only returns a value. The print statements we wrote are useful for debugging, but once you get the function working, you should remove them. Code like that is sometimes called *scaffolding* because it is helpful for building the program but is not part of the final product.

When you start programming, you should add only a line or two of code at a time. As you gain more experience, you might find yourself writing and debugging bigger chunks. Either way, incremental development can save you a lot of debugging time.

The key aspects of the process are:

1. Start with a working program and make small incremental changes. At any point, if there is an error, you should have a good idea where it is.

2. Use variables to hold intermediate values so you can display and check them.

3. Once the program is working, you might want to remove some of the scaffolding or consolidate multiple statements into compound expressions, but only if doing so does not make the program difficult to read.

Note that, at least for relatively simple cases, you can also use the REPL to test expressions and even multiline statements or subroutines in interactive mode before you commit them to your program code. This is usually fast and can save you some time.

As an exercise, use incremental development to write a function called hypotenuse that returns the length of the hypotenuse of a right triangle given the lengths of the other two legs as arguments. Record each stage of the development process as you go. Solution: "Exercise: Hypotenuse" on page 356.

Composition

As you should expect by now, you can call one function from within another. As an example, we'll write a function that takes two points, the center of the circle and a point on the perimeter, and computes the area of the circle.

Assume that the center point is stored in the variables $x-c and $y-c, and the perimeter point is in $x-p and $y-p. The first step is to find the radius of the circle, which is the distance between the two points. We just wrote a function, distance, that does that:

```
my $radius = distance($x-c, $y-c, $x-p, $y-p);
```

The next step is to find the area of a circle with that radius; we just wrote that, too:

```
my $result = area($radius);
```

Encapsulating these steps in a function, we get:

```
sub circle-area($x-c, $y-c, $x-p, $y-p) {
    my $radius = distance($x-c, $y-c, $x-p, $y-p);
    my $result = area($radius)
    return $result;
}
```

The temporary variables $radius and $result are useful for development and debugging, but once the program is working, we can make it more concise by composing the function calls:

```
sub circle-area($x-c, $y-c, $x-p, $y-p) {
    return area distance($x-c, $y-c, $x-p, $y-p);
}
```

The last line of the previous example now works like a data pipeline from right to left: the distance function takes the four arguments and returns a distance (the radius) which is fed as an argument to the area; with this argument, area is now able to return the area, which is then returned by circle-area to the caller code. We'll come back later to this very expressive data pipeline model.

Boolean Functions

Functions can return Boolean values, which is often convenient for hiding complicated tests inside functions. For example:

```
sub is-divisible(Int $x, Int $y) {
    if $x % $y == 0 {
        return True;
    } else {
        return False;
    {
}
```

It is common to give Boolean functions names that sound like yes/no questions; is-divisible, for instance, returns either True or False to indicate whether x is divisible by y.

Here is an example:

```
> is-divisible(6, 4);
False
> is-divisible(6, 3);
True
```

The result of the == operator is a Boolean value, so we can write the subroutine more concisely by returning it directly:

```
sub is-divisible(Int $x, Int $y) {
    return $x % $y == 0
}
```

If there is no return statement, a Perl subroutine returns the value of expression on the last code line of the subroutine (provided the last code line is an expression that gets evaluated), so that the return statement is not required here. In addition, since 0 is a false value and any other integer a true value, this could be further rewritten as follows:

```
sub is-divisible(Int $x, Int $y) {
    not $x % $y
}
```

The Int type declarations in the subroutine signatures above are not necessary. The subroutine would work without them, but they can provide some form of protection against using this subroutine with faulty arguments.

Boolean functions are often used in statement modifiers:

```
say "$x is divisible by $y" if is-divisible($x, $y);
```

It might be tempting to write something like:

```
say "$x is divisible by $y" if is-divisible($x, $y) == True;
```

But the extra comparison is unnecessary: is-divisible returns a Boolean value that can be interpreted directly by the if conditional.

As an exercise, write a function is-between(x, y, z) that returns True if $x \le y \le z$ or False otherwise. Solution: "Exercise: Chained Relational Operators" on page 357.

A Complete Programming Language

We've seen in the section above several ways of writing a subroutine to check the divisibility of two integers.

In fact, Perl 6 has a "is divisible" operator, %%, which returns True if the number on the left is divisible by the one on the right:

```
> 9 %% 3
True
> 9 %% 4
False
```

So there was no need to write the is-divisible subroutine. But don't worry, that's alright if you did not know that. Speakers of natural languages are allowed to have different skill levels, to learn as they go and to put the language to good use before they know the whole language. The same is true with Perl. You (and I) don't know all about Perl 6 yet, just as we don't know all of English. But it is in fact "Officially Okay in Perl Culture" to use the subset of the language that you know. You are in fact encouraged to use what is sometimes called "baby Perl" to write programs, even if they are somewhat clumsy at the beginning. That's the best way of learning Perl, just as using "baby talk" is the right way for a child to learn English.

The number of different ways of accomplishing a given task, such as checking whether one number is divisible by another, is an example of one of Perl's mottos: *there is more than one way to do it*, oft abbreviated TIMTOWTDI. Some ways may be more concise or more efficient than others, but, in the Perl philosophy, you are perfectly entitled to do it your way, especially if you're a beginner, provided you find the correct result.

We have only covered a small subset of Perl 6 so far, but you might be interested to know that this subset is a *complete* programming language, which means that essentially anything that can be computed can be expressed in this language. Any program ever written could be rewritten using only the language features you have learned so far (actually, you would need a few commands to control devices like the mouse, disks, networks, etc., but that's all).

Proving that claim is a nontrivial exercise first accomplished by Alan Turing, one of the first computer scientists (some would argue that he was a mathematician, but a lot of early computer scientists started as mathematicians). Accordingly, it is known as the Turing Thesis. For a more complete (and accurate) discussion of the Turing Thesis, I recommend Michael Sipser's book *Introduction to the Theory of Computation* (Cengage Learning).

More Recursion

To give you an idea of what you can do with the tools you have learned so far, we'll evaluate a few recursively defined mathematical functions. A recursive definition is similar to a circular definition, in the sense that the definition contains a reference to the thing being defined. A truly circular definition is not very useful:

vorpal
    An adjective used to describe something that is vorpal.

If you saw that definition in the dictionary, you might be annoyed. On the other hand, if you looked up the definition of the factorial function, denoted with the symbol !, you might get something like this:

$$0! = 1$$
$$n! = n(n-1)!$$

This definition says that the factorial of 0 is 1, and the factorial of any other (positive integer) value, n, is n multiplied by the factorial of $n - 1$.

So 3! is 3 times 2!, which is 2 times 1!, which is 1 times 0!. Putting it all together, 3! equals 3 times 2 times 1 times 1, which is 6.

If you can write a recursive definition of something, you can write a Perl program to evaluate it. The first step is to decide what the parameters should be. In this case it should be clear that `factorial` takes a number:[1]

```
sub factorial($n){
}
```

If the argument happens to be 0, all we have to do is return 1:

---

1 It should really be an integer, but we'll get back to that later in this chapter.

```
sub factorial($n){
    if $n == 0 {
        return 1;
    }
}
```

Otherwise, and this is the interesting part, we have to make a recursive call to find the factorial of *n* − 1 and then multiply it by *n*:

```
sub factorial($n){
    if $n == 0 {
        return 1;
    } else {
        my $recurse = factorial($n-1);
        my $result = $n * $recurse;
        return $result;
    }
}
```

The flow of execution for this program is similar to the flow of countdown in "Recursion" on page 66. If we call factorial with the value 3:

Since 3 is not 0, we take the second branch and calculate the factorial of $n-1...

    Since 2 is not 0, we take the second branch and calculate the factorial of $n-1...

        Since 1 is not 0, we take the second branch and calculate the factorial of $n-1...

            Since 0 equals 0, we take the first branch and return 1 without making any more recursive calls.

        The return value, 1, is multiplied by $n, which is 1, and the result is returned.

    The return value, 1, is multiplied by $n, which is 2, and the result is returned.

The return value, 2, is multiplied by $n, which is 3, and the result, 6, becomes the return value of the subroutine call that started the whole process.

Figure 5-1 shows what the stack diagram looks like for this sequence of function calls.

The return values are shown being passed back up the stack. In each frame, the return value is the value of result, which is the product of n and recurse.

In the last frame, the local variables recurse and result do not exist, because the branch that creates them does not run.

```
```

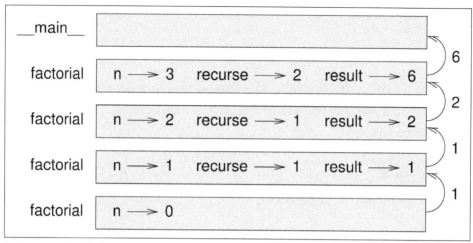

Figure 5-1. Stack diagram

A seasoned Perl programmer might write a more concise or more idiomatic subroutine:[2]

```
sub factorial($n){
    return 1 if $n == 0;
    return $n * factorial $n-1;
}
```

This is not better than our initial version, and will probably not run significantly faster, but this is arguably clearer, at least once you get used to this type of syntax.

Leap of Faith

Following the flow of execution is one way to read programs, but it can quickly become overwhelming. An alternative is what may be called the "leap of faith." When you come to a subroutine call, instead of following the flow of execution, you *assume* that the subroutine works correctly and returns the right result.

In fact, you are already practicing this leap of faith when you use built-in functions. When you call math functions such as cos or sqrt, you don't examine the bodies of those functions. You just assume that they work because the people who wrote the built-in functions were likely to be good programmers (and because you can safely assume that they have been thoroughly tested).

The same is true when you call one of your own subroutines. For example, in "Boolean Functions" on page 82, we wrote a subroutine called is-divisible that

---

2 We will see later even more idiomatic ways of computing the factorial of a number.

determines whether one number is divisible by another. Once we have convinced ourselves that this subroutine is correct—by examining the code and testing—we can use the subroutine without looking at the body again.

The same is true of recursive programs. When you get to the recursive call, instead of following the flow of execution, you should assume that the recursive call works (returns the correct result) and then ask yourself, "Assuming that I can find the factorial of $n-1$, can I compute the factorial of n?" It is clear that you can, by multiplying by $n.

Of course, it's a bit strange to assume that the subroutine works correctly when you haven't finished writing it, but that's why it's called a leap of faith!

One More Example

After `factorial`, the most common example of a recursively defined mathematical function is `fibonacci`, which has the following definition (see also the Wikipedia entry (*http://en.wikipedia.org/wiki/Fibonacci_number*)):

$$\text{fibonacci}(0) = 1$$
$$\text{fibonacci}(1) = 1$$
$$\text{fibonacci}(n) = \text{fibonacci}(n-1) + \text{fibonacci}(n-2)$$

In plain English, a Fibonacci sequence is a sequence of numbers such as:

```
1, 1, 2, 3, 5, 8, 13, 21, ...
```

where the two first terms are equal to 1 and any other term is the sum of the two preceding ones.

We briefly covered the Fibonacci sequence in Exercise 4-4 and implemented it with a for loop. Let's now translate the recursive definition into Perl. It looks like this:

```
sub fibonacci ($n) {
    return 1 if $n == 0 or $n == 1;
    return fibonacci($n-1) + fibonacci($n-2);
}
```

If you try to follow the flow of execution here, even for fairly small values of $n, your head explodes. But according to the leap of faith, if you assume that the two recursive calls work correctly, then it is clear that you get the right result by adding them together.

Checking Types

What happens if we call `factorial` and give it 1.5 as an argument?

It seems that we get an infinite recursion. How can that be? The subroutine has a base case—when $n == 0. But if $n is not an integer, we can *miss* the base case and recurse forever.

In the first recursive call, the value of $n is 0.5. In the next, it is –0.5. From there, it gets smaller (more negative), but it will never be 0.

We have two choices. We can try to generalize the `factorial` function to work with noninteger numbers, or we can make `factorial` check its argument. The first option is called the *gamma function*, and it's a little beyond the scope of this book. So we'll go for the second.

We have already seen examples of subroutines using the signature to verify the type of the argument. So we can add the `Int` type to the parameter in the signature. While we're at it, we can also make sure the argument is positive or zero.

```
sub factorial(Int $n where $n >= 0){
    return 1 if $n == 0;
    return $n * factorial $n-1;
}
```

The `Int` type checking in the signature handles nonintegers; this is not new. The `where $n >= 0` part is a parameter constraint: if the parameter is negative, the subroutine should fail. Technically, the constraint is implemented here within the signature using a syntax feature called a *trait*, a property imposed on the parameter at compile time. If the argument passed to the function is not an integer or if it is negative, the program prints an error message to indicate that something went wrong:

```
> say factorial 1.5
Type check failed in binding $n; expected Int but got Rat
  in sub factorial at <unknown file> line 1
  in block <unit> at <unknown file> line 1

> say factorial -3
Constraint type check failed for parameter '$n'
> say factorial "Fred"
Type check failed in binding $n; expected Int but got Str
  in sub factorial at <unknown file> line 1
  in block <unit> at <unknown file> line 1
```

If we get past both checks, we know that $n is an integer and that it is positive or zero, so we can prove that the recursion terminates.

Another way to achieve a similar result is to define your own subset of the built-in types. For example, you can create an `Even-int` subset of integers and then use it more or less as if it were a new type for declaring your variables or typing your subroutine parameters:

```
subset Even-int of Int where { $_ %% 2 } # or : … where { $_ % 2 == 0 }
# Even-int can now be used as a type
```

```
my Even-int $x = 2; # OK
my Even-int $y = 3; # Type mismatch error
```

Similarly, in the case of the `factorial` subroutine, we can create a *nonnegative integer* subset and use it for checking the parameter passed to the subroutine:

```
subset Non-neg-int of Int where { $_ >= 0}
# ...

sub factorial(Non-neg-int $n){
    return 1 if $n == 0;
    return $n * factorial $n-1;
}
```

If we pass a negative integer to the subroutine, we get a similar error as before:

```
Constraint type check failed for parameter '$n'...
```

This program demonstrates a pattern sometimes called a *guardian*. The signature acts as a guardian, protecting the code that follows from values that might cause an error. The guardians make it possible to prove the correctness of the code.

Multi Subroutines

It is possible to write multiple versions of a subroutine with the same name but with different signatures, for example a different *arity* (a fancy word for the number of arguments) or different argument types, using the `multi` keyword. In this case, the interpreter will pick the version of the subroutine whose signature matches (or best matches) the argument list.

For example, we could rewrite the factorial function as follows:

```
multi sub fact(0) { 1 };
multi sub fact(Int $n where $n > 0) {
    $n * fact $n - 1;
}
say fact 0;   # -> 1
say fact 10;  # -> 3628800
```

Here, we don't enter into infinite recursion because, when the parameter passed to `fact` is 0, it is the first version of the multi subroutine that is called and it returns an integer value (1), and this ends the recursion.

Similarly, the Fibonacci function can be rewritten with multi subroutines:

```
multi fibonacci(0) { 0 }
multi fibonacci(1) { 1 }
multi fibonacci(Int $n where $n > 1) {
    fibonacci($n - 2) + fibonacci($n - 1)
}
say fibonacci 10;  # -> 55
```

Many built-in functions and most operators of Perl 6 are written as multi subroutines.

Debugging

Breaking a large program into smaller functions or subroutines creates natural checkpoints for debugging. If a subroutine is not working, there are three possibilities to consider:

- There is something wrong with the arguments the subroutine is getting; a precondition is violated.
- There is something wrong with the subroutine; a postcondition is violated.
- There is something wrong with the return value or the way it is being used.

To rule out the first possibility, you can add a print statement at the beginning of the function and display the values of the parameters (and maybe their types). Or you can write code that checks the preconditions explicitly.

For the purpose of debugging, it is often useful to print the content of a variable or of a parameter within a string with surrounding characters, so that you may visualize characters that are otherwise invisible, such as spaces or newlines. For example, you think that the $var should contain "two," and run the following test:

```
if $var eq "two" {
    do-something()
}
```

But it fails and the do-something subroutine is never called.

Perhaps you want to use a print statement that will ascertain the content of $var:

```
say "[$var]";
if $var eq "two" {
    do-something()
}
```

This might print:

```
[two ]
```

or:

```
[two
]
```

Now, you know that the equality test fails because $var contains a trailing character (space or newline) that might otherwise be difficult to detect.

If the parameters look good, add a print statement before each return statement and display the return value. If possible, check the result by hand. Consider calling the function with values that make it easy to check the result (as in "Incremental Development" on page 79).

If the function seems to be working, look at the function call to make sure the return value is being used correctly (or used at all!).

Adding print statements at the beginning and end of a function can help make the flow of execution more visible. For example, here is a version of factorial with print statements:

```
sub factorial(Int $n) {
    my $space = ' ' x (4 * $n);
    say $space, 'factorial ', $n;
    if $n == 0 {
        say $space, 'returning 1';
        return 1;
    } else {
        my $result = $n * factorial $n-1;
        say $space, 'returning ', $result;
        return $result;
    }
}
```

The $space variable is a string of space characters that controls the indentation of the output. Here is the result of factorial(4) :

```
                factorial 4
            factorial 3
        factorial 2
    factorial 1
factorial 0
returning 1
    returning 1
        returning 2
            returning 6
                returning 24
```

If you are confused about the flow of execution, this kind of output can be helpful. It takes some time to develop effective scaffolding, but a bit of scaffolding can save a lot of debugging.

Glossary

dead code
Part of a program that can never run, often because it appears after a return statement.

guardian
A programming pattern that uses a conditional statement to check for and handle circumstances that might cause an error.

incremental development
    A program development plan intended to avoid debugging by adding and testing
    only a small amount of code at a time.

scaffolding
    Code that is used during program development but is not part of the final ver-
    sion.

temporary variable
    A variable used to store an intermediate value in a complex calculation.

Exercises

Exercise 5-1.

Draw a stack diagram for the following program. What does the program print?
Please try to answer these questions before trying to run the program.

```
sub b(Int $z) {
    my $prod = a($z, $z);
    say $z, " ", $prod;
    return $prod;
}
sub a(Int $x is copy, Int $y) {
    $x++;
    return $x * $y;
}
sub c(Int $x, Int $y, Int $z) {
    my $total = $x + $y + $z;
    my $square = b($total) ** 2;
    return $square;
}

my $x = 1;
my $y = $x + 1;
say c($x, $y + 3, $x + $y);
```

Exercise 5-2.

The Ackermann function, $A(m, n)$, is defined as follows:

$$A(m, n) = \begin{cases} n + 1 & \text{if } m = 0 \\ A(m - 1, 1) & \text{if } m > 0 \text{ and } n = 0 \\ A(m - 1, A(m, n - 1)) & \text{if } m > 0 \text{ and } n > 0 \end{cases}$$

See *http://en.wikipedia.org/wiki/Ackermann_function*. Write a subroutine named ack that evaluates the Ackermann function. Use your subroutine to evaluate ack(3, 4), which should be 125. What happens for larger values of m and n? Solution: "Exercise 5-2: The Ackermann Function" on page 358.

Exercise 5-3.

A palindrome is a word that is spelled the same backward and forward, like "noon" and "redivider." Recursively, a word is a palindrome if the first and last letters are the same and the middle is a palindrome.

The following are subroutines that take a string argument and return the first, last, and middle letters:

```
sub first_l(Str $word){
    return substr $word, 0, 1;
}

sub last_l(Str $word){
    return substr $word, *-1, 1;
}

sub middle_l(Str $word){
    return substr $word, 1, *-1;
}
```

Don't worry about how they work for the time being; we will see that in Chapter 7 on strings. For now:

1. Type these subroutines into a file named palindrome.pl6 and test them out. What happens if you call middle_l with a string with two letters? One letter? What about the empty string, which is written ' ' and contains no letters? Given that the .chars method returns the length of a string, how could you add a signature constraint to reject invalid input?

2. Write a subroutine called is-palindrome that takes a string argument and returns True if it is a palindrome and False otherwise. Remember that you can use the built-in method .chars to check the length of a string.

Solution: "Exercise 5-3: Palindromes" on page 358.

Exercise 5-4.

An integer number, *a*, is a power of *b* if it is divisible by *b* and *a*/*b* is a power of *b*. Write a function called is-power-of that takes parameters a and b and returns True if a is a power of b. Note: you will have to think about the base case.

Solution: "Exercise 5-4: Powers" on page 359

Exercise 5-5.

The greatest common divisor (GCD) of a and b is the largest number that divides both of them with no remainder.

One way to find the GCD of two numbers is based on the observation that if r is the remainder when a is divided by b, then $gcd(a, b) = gcd(b, r)$. As a base case, we can use $gcd(a, 0) = a$.

Write a function called gcd that takes parameters a and b and returns their greatest common divisor.

Credit: this exercise is based on an example from Abelson and Sussman's *Structure and Interpretation of Computer Programs* (MIT Press).

Solution: "Exercise 5-5: Finding the GCD of Two Numbers" on page 360.

## CHAPTER 6

Iteration

This chapter is about iteration, which is the ability to run a block of statements repeatedly. We saw a kind of iteration, using recursion, in "Recursion" on page 66. We saw another kind, using a `for` loop, in "for Loops" on page 64. In this chapter we'll see yet another kind, using a `while` statement. But first I want to say a little more about variable assignment.

Assignment Versus Equality

Before going further, I want to address a common source of confusion. Because Perl uses the equals sign (=) for assignment, it is tempting to interpret a statement like $a = $b as a mathematical proposition of equality, that is, the claim that $a and $b are equal. But this interpretation is wrong.

First, equality is a symmetric relationship and assignment is not. For example, in mathematics, if $a = 7$ then $7 = a$. But in Perl, the statement $a = 7 is legal and 7 = $a is not.

Also, in mathematics, a proposition of equality is either true or false for all time. If $a = b$ now, then a will always equal b. In Perl, an assignment statement can make two variables equal, but they don't have to stay that way:

```
> my $a = 5;
5
> my $b = $a;      # $a and $b are now equal
5
> $a = 3;          # $a and $b are no longer equal
3
> say $b;
5
```

The third line changes the value of $a but does not change the value of $b, so they are no longer equal.

In brief, remember that = is an assignment operator and not an equality operator; the operators for testing equality between two terms are == for numbers and eq for strings.

Reassignment

As you may have discovered, it is legal to make more than one assignment to the same variable. A new assignment makes an existing variable refer to a new value (and stop referring to the old value):

```
> my $x = 5;
5
> say $x;
5
> $x = 7;
7
> say $x
7
```

The first time we display $x, its value is 5; the second time, its value is 7.

Figure 6-1 shows what *reassignment* looks like in a state diagram.

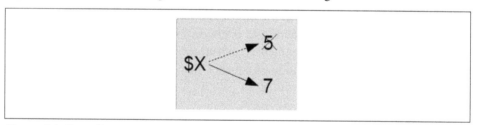

Figure 6-1. State diagram

Reassigning variables is often useful, but you should use this feature with some caution. If the values of variables change frequently, it can make the code difficult to read and debug.

Updating Variables

A common kind of reassignment is an *update*, where the new value of the variable depends on the old:

```
> $x = $x + 1;
```

This means "get the current value of $x, add one, and then update $x with the new value."

If you try to update a variable that has not been given a value, you get a warning, because Perl evaluates the right side of the assignment statement before it assigns a value to $x:

```
> my $x;
> $x = $x + 1;
Use of uninitialized value of type Any in numeric context
  in block <unit> at <unknown file> line 1
```

Before you can update a variable, you have to declare it and *initialize* it, usually with an assignment:

```
> my $x = 0;
> $x = $x + 1;
```

Updating a variable by adding 1 is called an *increment*; subtracting 1 is called a *decrement*.

As mentioned earlier in "Expressions and Statements" on page 19, Perl has some shortcuts for increment and decrement:

```
$x += 1; # equivalent to $x = $x + 1
$x++;    # also equivalent

$x -= 1; # equivalent to $x = $x - 1
$x--;    # also equivalent
```

The while Statement

Computers are often used to automate repetitive tasks. Repeating identical or similar tasks without making errors is something that computers do well and people do poorly. In a computer program, repetition is also called *iteration*.

We have already seen two functions, countdown and print-n-times, that iterate using recursion (see "Recursion" on page 66). Because iteration is so common, most programming languages including Perl provide language features to make it easier. One is the for statement we saw in "for Loops" on page 64. We'll get back to that later.

Another is the while statement. Here is a version of countdown that uses a while statement:

```
sub countdown(Int $n is copy) {
    while $n > 0 {
        say $n;
        $n--;
    }
    say 'Blastoff!';
}
```

You can almost read the while statement as if it were English. It means, "While $n is greater than 0, display the value of n and then decrement $n. When you get to 0, display the word Blastoff!"

More formally, here is the flow of execution for a while statement:

1. Determine whether the condition is true or false.

2. If false, exit the while statement and continue execution at the next statement.

3. If the condition is true, run the body and then go back to step 1.

This type of flow is called a loop because the third step loops back around to the top.

The body of the loop should change the value of one or more variables so that the condition becomes false eventually and the loop terminates. Otherwise, the loop will repeat forever, which is called an *infinite loop*. An endless source of amusement for computer scientists is the observation that the directions on shampoo, "Lather, rinse, repeat," are an infinite loop.

In the case of countdown, we can prove that the loop terminates: if $n is zero or negative, the loop never runs. Otherwise, $n gets smaller each time through the loop, so eventually we have to get to 0.

For some other loops, it is not so easy to tell whether the loop terminates. For example:

```
sub sequence($n is copy) {
    while $n != 1 {
        say $n;
        if $n %% 2 {        # $n is even
            $n = $n / 2;
        } else {            # $n is odd
            $n = $n*3 + 1
        }
    }
    return $n;
}
```

The condition for this loop is $n != 1, so the loop will continue until $n is 1, which makes the condition false.

Each time through the loop, the program outputs the value of $n and then checks whether it is even or odd. If it is even, $n is divided by 2. If it is odd, the value of $n is replaced with $n*3 + 1. For example, if the argument passed to sequence is 42, the resulting values of n are 42, 21, 64, 32, 16, 8, 4, 2, 1.

Since $n sometimes increases and sometimes decreases, there is no obvious proof that $n will ever reach 1, or that the program terminates. For some particular values of n, we can prove termination. For example, if the starting value is a power of two, n will be even every time through the loop until it reaches 1. The previous example ends with such a sequence of powers of two, starting with 64.

The hard question is whether we can prove that this program terminates for *all* positive values of n. So far, no one has been able to prove it *or* disprove it! (See *http://en.wikipedia.org/wiki/Collatz_conjecture.*)

As an exercise, you might want to rewrite the function print-n-times from "Recursion" on page 66 using iteration instead of recursion.

The while statement can also be used as a statement modifier (or postfix syntax):

```
my $val = 5;
print "$val " while $val-- > 0;   # prints 4 3 2 1 0
print "\n";
```

The while loop statement executes the block as long as its condition is true. There is also an until loop statement, which executes the block as long as its condition is false:

```
my $val = 1;
until $val > 5 {
    print $val++;              # prints 12345
}
print "\n";
```

Local Variables and Variable Scoping

We have seen in "Variables and Parameters Are Local" on page 41 that variables created within a subroutine (with the my keyword) are *local* to that subroutine. The my keyword if often called a *declarator*, because it is used for declaring a new variable (or other identifier). It is by far the most common declarator. Other declarators include our or state, briefly described later in this chapter.

Similarly, subroutine parameters are also usually *local* to the subroutine in the signature of which they are declared.

We briefly mentioned that the term *lexically scoped* is probably more accurate than local, but it was too early at that point to really explain what this means.

Declaring a variable with my gives it *lexical scope*. This means it only exists within the current block. Loosely speaking, a block is a piece of Perl code within curly brackets or braces. For example, the body of a subroutine and the code of a while or for loop or of an if conditional statement are code blocks. Any variable created with the my declarator exists and is available for use only between the place where it is declared and the end of the enclosing code block.

For example, this code:

```
if $condition eq True {
    my $foo = "bar";
    say $foo;  # prints "bar"
}
say $foo;       # ERROR: "Variable '$foo' is not declared ..."
```

will fail on the second print statement, because the say function call is not in the lexical scope of the $foo variable, which ends with the closing brace of the condition block. If we want this variable to be accessible after the end of the condition, then we would need to declare it before the if statement. For example:

```
my $foo;
if $condition eq True {
    $foo = "bar";
    say $foo;  # prints "bar"
} else {
    $foo = "baz";
}
say $foo;       # prints "bar" or "baz" depending on $condition
```

If a lexical variable is not declared within a block, its scope will extend until the end of the file (this is sometimes called a static or a global variable, although these terms are somewhat inaccurate). For example, in the last code snippet above, the scope of the $foo variable will extend until the end of the file, which may or may not be a good thing, depending on how you intend to use it. It is often better to reduce the scope of variables as much as possible, because this helps reduce dependencies between various parts of the code and limits the risk of subtle bugs. In the code above, if we want to limit the scope of $foo, we could add braces to create an enclosing block for the sole purpose of limiting the scope:

```
{
    my $foo;
    if $condition eq True {
        $foo = "bar";
        say $foo; # prints "bar"
    } else {
        $foo = "baz";
    }
    say $foo;       # prints "bar" or "baz" depending on $condition
}
```

Now, the outer braces create an enclosing block limiting the scope of $foo to where we need it. This may seem to be a somewhat contrived example, but it is not uncommon to add braces only for the purpose of precisely defining the scope of something.

Lexical scoping also means that variables with the same names can be temporarily redefined in a new scope:

```
my $location = "outside";
sub outer {
    say $location;
```

```
    }
    sub inner {
        my $location = "inside";
        say $location;
    }
    say $location;    # -> outside
    outer();          # -> outside
    inner();          # -> inside
    say $location;    # -> outside
```

We have in effect two variables with the same name, $location, but different scopes. One is valid only within the inner subroutine where it has been redefined, and the other anywhere else.

If we add a new subroutine:

```
    sub nowhere {
        my $location = "nowhere";
        outer();
    }
    nowhere();        # -> outside
```

this will still print "outside," because the outer subroutine knows about the "outside" version of the $location variable, which existed when outer was defined. In other words, the outer code that referenced to the outer variable ("outside") knows about the variable that existed when it was created, but not about the variable existing where it was called. This is how *lexical* variables work. This behavior is the basis for building *closures*, a form of subroutine with some special properties that we will study later in this book, but is in fact implicitly present everywhere in Perl 6.

While having different variables with the same name can give you a lot of expressive power, we would advise you to avoid creating different variables with the same name and different scopes, at least until you really understand these concepts well enough to know what you are doing, as this can be quite tricky.

By far, most variables used in Perl are lexical variables, declared with the my declarator. Although they are not declared with my, parameters declared in the signature of subroutines and parameters of pointy blocks also have a lexical scope limited to the body of the subroutine or the pointy block.

There are other declarators, such as our, which creates a package-scoped variable, and state, which creates a lexically scoped variable but with a persistent value. They are relatively rarely used.

One last point: although they are usually not declared with a my declarator, subroutines themselves also have by default a lexical scope. If they are defined within a block, they will be seen only within that block. An example of this has been given at the end of the solution to the GCD exercise of the previous chapter (see "Exercise 5-5:

Finding the GCD of Two Numbers" on page 360). That being said, you *can* declare a subroutine with a my declarator if you wish:

```
my sub frobnicate {
    # ...
}
```

This technique might add some consistency or some form of self-documenting feature, but you won't buy very much added functionality with that.

Control Flow Statements (last, next, etc.)

Sometimes you don't know it's time to end a loop until you get halfway through the body. In that case, you can use a control flow statement such as last to jump out of the loop.

For example, suppose you want to take input from the user until they type done. You could write:

```
while True {
    my $line = prompt "Enter something ('done' for exiting)\n";
    last if $line eq "done";
    say $line;
}
say 'Done!';
```

The loop condition is True, which is always true, so the loop runs until it hits the last statement.

Each time through, it prompts the user to type something. If the user types done, the last statement exits the loop. Otherwise, the program echoes whatever the user types and goes back to the top of the loop. Here's a sample run:

```
$ perl6 while_done.pl6
Enter something ('done' for exiting)
Not done
Not done
Enter something ('done' for exiting)
done
Done!
```

This way of writing while loops is common because you can check the condition anywhere in the loop (not just at the top) and you can express the stop condition affirmatively ("stop when this happens") rather than negatively ("keep going until that happens").

Using a while loop with a condition that is always true is a quite natural way of writing an infinite loop, i.e., a loop that will run forever until something else in the code (such as the last statement used above) forces the program to break out of the loop. This is commonly used in many programming languages, and this works well in Perl.

There is, however, another common and more idiomatic way of constructing infinite loops in Perl 6: using the `loop` statement, which we will study in "New Looping Constructs" on page 164. For now, we'll use the `while True` statement, which is fairly legitimate.

Sometimes, rather than simply breaking out of the `while` loop as with the `last` control statement, you need to start the body of the loop at the beginning. For example, you may want to check whether the user input is correct with some (unspecified) `is-valid` subroutine before processing the data, and ask the user to try again if the input was not correct. In this case, the `next` control statement lets you start at the top the loop body again:

```
while True {
    my $line = prompt "Enter something ('done' for exiting)\n";
    last if $line eq "done";
    next unless is-valid($line);
    # further processing of $line;
}
print('Done!')
```

Here, the loop terminates if the user types "done." If not, the user input is checked by the `is-valid` subroutine; if the subroutine returns a true value, the processing continues forward; if it returns a false value, then the control flow starts again at the beginning of the body of the loop, so the user is prompted again to submit a valid input.

The `last` and `next` control statements also work in `for` loops. For example, the following `for` loop iterates in theory on a range of integer numbers between 1 and 20, but discards odd numbers by virtue of a `next` statement and breaks out of the loop with a `last` statement as soon as the loop variable is greater than $max (i.e., 10 in this example):

```
my $max = 10;
for 1..20 -> $i {
    next unless $i %% 2; # keeps only even values
    last if $i > $max;   # stops loop if $i is greater than $max
    say $i;              # prints 2 4 6 8 10
}
```

You may have as many `last` and `next` statements as you like, just as you may have as many `return` statements as you like in a subroutine. Using such control flow statements is not considered poor practice. During the early days of structured programming, some people insisted that loops and subroutines have only one entry and one exit. The one-entry notion is still a good idea, but the one-exit notion has led people to bend over backward and write a lot of unnatural code. Much of programming consists of traversing decision trees. A decision tree naturally starts with a single trunk but ends with many leaves. Write your code with the number of loop controls (and subroutine exits) that is natural to the problem you're trying to solve. If you've declared your variables with reasonable scopes, everything gets automatically cleaned up at the appropriate moment, no matter how you leave the block.

Square Roots

Loops are often used in programs that compute numerical results by starting with an approximate answer and iteratively improving it.

For example, one way of computing square roots is Newton's method (also known as the Newton–Raphson method). Suppose that you want to know the square root of a. If you start with almost any estimate, x, you can compute a better estimate y with the following formula:

$$y = \frac{x + a/x}{2}$$

For example, if a is 4 and x is 3:

```
> my $a = 4;
4
> my $x = 3;
3
> my $y = ($x + $a/$x)/2;
2.166667
```

The result is closer than 3 to the correct answer ($\sqrt{4} = 2$) . If we repeat the process with the new estimate, it gets even closer:

```
> $x = $y;
2.166667
> $y = ($x + $a/$x)/2;
2.006410
```

After a few more updates, the estimate is almost exact:

```
> $x = $y;
2.006410
> $y = ($x + $a/$x)/2;
2.000010
> $x = $y;
2.000010
> $y = ($x + $a/$x)/2;
2.000000000026
```

In general we don't know ahead of time how many steps it takes to get to the right answer, but we know when we get there because the estimate stops changing:

```
> $x = $y;
2.000000000026
> $y = ($x + $a/$x)/2;
2
> $x = $y;
2
> $y = ($x + $a/$x)/2;
2
```

When $y == $x, we can stop. Here is a loop that starts with an initial estimate, x, and improves it until it stops changing:

```
my ($a, $x) = (4, 3);
while True {
    say "-- Intermediate value: $x";
    my $y = ($x + $a/$x) / 2;
    last if $y == $x;
    $x = $y;
}
say "Final result is $x";
```

This will print:

```
-- Intermediate value: 3
-- Intermediate value: 2.166667
-- Intermediate value: 2.006410
-- Intermediate value: 2.000010
-- Intermediate value: 2.000000000026
-- Intermediate value: 2
Final result is 2
```

For most values of $a this works fine, but there are a couple of caveats with this approach. First, in most programming languages, it is dangerous to test float equality, because floating-point values are only approximately right. We do not have this problem with Perl 6, because, as we have already mentioned, it is using a better representation of rational numbers than most generalist programming languages. (You may want to keep this in mind if you are using some other languages.) Even if we don't have this problem with Perl, there may also be some problems with algorithms that do not behave as well as Newton's algorithm. For example, some algorithms might not converge as fast and as neatly as Newton's algorithm but might instead produce alternate values above and below the accurate result.

Rather than checking whether $x and $y are exactly equal, it is safer to use the built-in function abs to compute the absolute value, or magnitude, of the difference between them:

```
last if abs($y - $x) < $epsilon:
```

where epsilon has a very small value like 0.0000001 that determines how close is close enough.

Algorithms

Newton's method is an example of an *algorithm*: it is a mechanical process for solving a category of problems (in this case, computing square roots).

To understand what an algorithm is, it might help to start with something that is not an algorithm. When you learned to multiply single-digit numbers, you probably memorized the multiplication table. In effect, you memorized 100 specific solutions. That kind of knowledge is not algorithmic.

But if you were "lazy," you might have learned a few tricks. For example, to find the product of n and 9, you can write $n - 1$ as the first digit and $10 - n$ as the second digit. (For example, to figure out $9 * 7$, $n - 1$ is 6 and $10 - n$ is 3, so the product $9 * 7$ is 63.) This trick is a general solution for multiplying any single-digit number by 9. That's an algorithm!

Similarly, the techniques you learned in school for addition (with carrying), subtraction (with borrowing), and long division are all algorithms. One of the characteristics of algorithms is that they do not require any intelligence to carry out. They are mechanical processes where each step follows from the last according to a simple set of rules.

Executing algorithms is boring, but designing them is interesting, intellectually challenging, and a central part of computer science.

Some of the things that people do naturally, without difficulty or conscious thought, are the hardest to express algorithmically. Understanding natural language is a good example. We all do it, but so far no one has been able to explain *how* we do it, at least not in the form of an algorithm.

Debugging

As you start writing bigger programs, you might find yourself spending more time debugging. More code means more chances to make an error and more places for bugs to hide.

One way to cut your debugging time is "debugging by bisection." For example, if there are 100 lines in your program and you check them one at a time, it would take 100 steps.

Instead, try to break the problem in half. Look at the middle of the program, or near it, for an intermediate value you can check. Add a `say` statement (or something else that has a verifiable effect) and run the program.

If the midpoint check is incorrect, there must be a problem in the first half of the program. If it is correct, the problem is in the second half.

Every time you perform a check like this, you halve the number of lines you have to search. After six steps (which is fewer than 100), you would be down to one or two lines of code, at least in theory.

In practice it is not always clear what the "middle of the program" is and not always possible to check it. It doesn't make sense to count lines and find the exact midpoint. Instead, think about places in the program where there might be errors and places where it is easy to put a check. Then choose a spot where you think the chances are about the same that the bug is before or after the check.

Glossary

algorithm
    A general process for solving a category of problems.

decrement
    An update that decreases the value of a variable.

increment
    An update that increases the value of a variable (often by one).

infinite loop
    A loop in which the terminating condition is never satisfied.

initialization
    An assignment that gives an initial value to a variable that may later be updated.

iteration
    Repeated execution of a set of statements using either a recursive function call or a loop.

reassignment
    Assigning a new value to a variable that already exists.

update
    An assignment where the new value of the variable depends on the old.

Exercises

Exercise 6-1.

Copy the loop from "Square Roots" on page 104 and encapsulate it in a subroutine called my-sqrt that takes $a as a parameter, chooses a reasonable value of $x, and returns an estimate of the square root of $a.

To test it, write a function named test-square-root that prints a table like this:

```
a  mysqrt(a)        sqrt(a)          diff
1  1.0000000000000  1.0000000000000  1.110223e-15
2  1.4142135623747  1.4142135623731  1.594724e-12
3  1.7320508075689  1.7320508075689  0.000000e+00
4  2.0000000000000  2.0000000000000  0.000000e+00
5  2.2360679774998  2.2360679774998  0.000000e+00
6  2.4494897427832  2.4494897427832  8.881784e-16
7  2.6457513110647  2.6457513110646  1.025846e-13
8  2.8284271247494  2.8284271247462  3.189449e-12
9  3.0000000000000  3.0000000000000  0.000000e+00
```

The first column is a number, *a*; the second column is the square root of *a* computed with my-sqrt; the third column is the square root computed by the sqrt built-in function of Perl; and the fourth column is the absolute value of the difference between the two estimates. Don't worry too much about obtaining clean tabular formatting; we haven't seen the built-in functions to do that. Solution: "Exercise 6-1: Square Root" on page 363.

Exercise 6-2.

The mathematician Srinivasa Ramanujan found an infinite series that can be used to generate a numerical approximation of $1/\pi$:

$$\frac{1}{\pi} = \frac{2\sqrt{2}}{9801} \sum_{k=0}^{\infty} \frac{(4k)!(1103 + 26390k)}{(k!)^4 396^{4k}}$$

Write a function called estimate-pi that uses this formula to compute and return an estimate of π. It should use a while loop to compute terms of the summation until the last term is smaller than 1e-15 (which is Perl notation for 10^{-15}). You can check the result by comparing it to the built-in constant pi. Solution: "Exercise 6-2: Pi Estimate" on page 364.

## CHAPTER 7

Strings

Strings are not like integers, rationals, and Booleans. A string is a *sequence* of characters, which means it is an ordered collection of other values, and you sometimes need to access to some of these individual values. In this chapter you'll see how to analyze, handle, and modify strings, and you'll learn about some of the methods strings provide. You will also start to learn about a very powerful tool for manipulating text data: regular expressions, a.k.a. *regexes*.

A String Is a Sequence

A string is primarily a piece of textual data, but it is technically an ordered sequence of characters.

Many programming languages allow you to access individual characters of a string with an index between brackets. This is not directly possible in Perl, but you still can access the characters one at a time using the `comb` built-in method and the bracket operator:

```
> my $string = "banana";
banana
> my $st = $string.comb;
(b a n a n a)
> say $st[1];
a
> say $st[2];
n
```

The `comb` in the second statement splits the string into a list of characters that you can then access individually with square brackets.

The expression in brackets is called an *index* (it is sometimes also called a subscript). The index indicates which character in the sequence you want (hence the name). But this may not be what you expected: the *item* with index 1 is the second letter of the word. For computer scientists, the index is usually an offset from the beginning. The offset of the first letter ("b") is zero, and the offset of the first "a" is 1, not 2, and so on.

You could also retrieve a *slice* of several characters in one go using the range operator within the brackets:

```
> say $st[2..5]
(n a n a)
```

Again, the "nana" substring starts on the third letter of 'banana', but this letter is indexed 2, and the sixth letter is index 5.

But, even if all this might be useful at times, this is not the way you would usually handle strings in Perl, which has higher level tools that are more powerful and more expressive, so that you seldom need to use indexes or subscripts to access individual characters.

Also, if there is a real need to access and manipulate individual letters, it would make more sense to store them in an array, but we haven't covered arrays yet, so we'll have to come back to that later.

Common String Operators

Perl provides a number of operators and functions to handle strings. Let's review some of the most popular ones.

String Length

The first thing we might want to know about a string is its length. The chars built-in returns the number of characters in a string and can be used with either a method or a function syntax:

```
> say "banana".chars;    # method invocation syntax
6
> say chars "banana";    # function call syntax
6
```

Note that, with the advent of Unicode, the notion of string length has become more complicated than it used to be in the era of ASCII-only strings. Today, a character may be made of one, two, or more bytes. The chars routine returns the number of characters (in the sense of Unicode graphemes, which is more or less what humans perceive as characters) within the string, even if some of these characters require an encoding over 2, 3, or 4 bytes.

A string with a length of zero (i.e., no characters) is called an *empty string*.

Searching for a Substring Within the String

The `index` built-in usually takes two arguments, a string and a substring (sometimes called the "haystack" and the "needle"), searches for the substring in the string, and returns the position where the substring is found (or an undefined value if it is not found):

```
> say index "banana", "na";
2
> say index "banana", "ni";
Nil
```

Here again, the index is an offset from the beginning of the string, so that the index of the first letter ("b") is zero, and the offset of the first "n" is 2, not 3.

You may also call `index` with a method syntax:

```
> say "banana".index("na");
2
```

The `index` function can take a third optional argument, an integer indicating where to start the *search* (thus ignoring in the search any characters before the start position):

```
> say index "banana", "na", 3;
4
```

Here, the `index` function started the search on the middle "a" and thus found the position of the second occurrence of the "na" substring.

There is also a `rindex` function, which searches the string backwards from the end and returns the last position of the substring within the string:

```
> say rindex "banana", "na";
4
```

Note that even though the `rindex` function searches the string backwards (from the end), it returns a position computed from the start of the string.

Extracting a Substring from a String

The opposite of the `index` function is the `substr` function or method, which, given a start position and a length, extracts a substring from a string:

```
> say substr "I have a dream", 0, 6;
I have
> say "I have a dream".substr(9, 5)
dream
```

Note that, just as for the `chars` function, the length is expressed in characters (or Unicode graphemes), not in bytes. Also, as you can see, spaces separating words within the string obviously count as characters. The length argument is optional; if it is not provided, the substr function returns the substring starting on the start position to the end of the string:

```
> say "I have a dream".substr(7)
a dream
```

Similarly, if the length value is too large for the substring starting on the start position, the substr function will return the substring starting on the start position to the end of the string:

```
> say substr "banana", 2, 10;
nana
```

Of course, the start position and length parameters need not be hardcoded numbers as in the examples above; you may use a variable instead (or even an expression or a function returning a numeric value), provided the variable or value can be coerced into an integer. But the start position must be within the string range, failing which you would obtain a Start argument to substr out of range ... error; so you may have to verify it against the length of the string beforehand.

You can also start counting backwards from the end of the string with the following syntax:

```
> say "I have a dream".substr(*-5)
dream
> say substr "I have a dream", *-5;
dream
```

Here, the star (*) may be thought as representing the total size of the string; *-5 is therefore the position in the string five characters before the end of the string. So, substr(*-5) returns the characters from that position to the end of the string (i.e., the last five characters of the string).

A Few Other Useful String Functions or Methods

This may not be obvious yet, but we will see soon that the combination of the above string functions gives you already a lot of power to manipulate strings way beyond what you may think possible at this point.

Let us just mention very briefly a few additional functions that may prove useful at times.

flip

The flip function or method reverses a string:

```
> say flip "banana";
ananab
```

---

split

The `split` function or method splits a string into substrings, based on delimiters found in the string:

```
> say $_ for split "-", "25-12-2016";
25
12
2016
> for "25-12-2016".split("-") -> $val {say $val};
25
12
2016
```

The delimiter can be a single quoted character as in the examples above or a string of several characters, such as a comma and a space in the example below:

```
> .say for split  ", ", "Jan, Feb, Mar";
Jan
Feb
Mar
```

Remember that `.say` is a shortcut for `$_.say`.

By default, the delimiters don't appear in the output produced by the `split` function or method, but this behavior can be changed with the use of an appropriate *adverb*. An adverb is basically a named argument to a function that modifies the way the function behaves. For example, the `:v` (values) adverb tells `split` to also output the value of the delimiters:

```
> .perl.say for split  ', ', "Jan, Feb, Mar", :v;
"Jan"
", "
"Feb"
", "
"Mar"
```

The other adverbs that can be used in this context are `:k` (keys), `:kv` (keys and values), and `:p` (pairs). Their detailed meaning can be found in the documentation for `split` (*https://docs.perl6.org/routine/split*). The `skip-empty` adverb removes empty chunks from the result list.

The `split` function can also use a regular expression *pattern* as delimiter, and this can make it much more powerful. We will study regular expressions later in this chapter.

String concatenation

The ~ operator concatenates two strings into one:

```
> say "ban" ~ "ana";
banana
```

You may chain several occurrences of this operator to concatenate more than two strings:

```
> say "ba" ~ "na" ~ "na";
banana
```

Used as a unary prefix operator, ~ "stringifies" (i.e., transforms into a string) its argument:

```
> say (~42).WHAT;
(Str)
```

Splitting on words

The words function returns a list of words that make up the string:

```
> say "I have a dream".words.perl;
("I", "have", "a", "dream").Seq
> .say for "I have a dream".words;
I
have
a
dream
```

join

The join function takes a separator argument and a list of strings as arguments; it interleaves them with the separator, concatenates everything into a single string, and returns the resulting string.

This example illustrates the chained use of the words and join functions or methods:

```
say 'I have a dream'.words.join('|');    # -> I|have|a|dream
say join ";", words "I have a dream";    # -> I;have;a;dream
```

In both cases, words first splits the original string into a list of words, and join stitches the items of this list back into a new string interleaved with the separator.

Changing the case

The lc and uc routines return respectively a lowercase and an uppercase version of their arguments. There is also a tc function or method returning its argument with the first letter converted to title case or uppercase:

```
say lc "April";    # -> april
say "April".lc;    # -> april
say uc "april";    # -> APRIL
say tc "april";    # -> April
```

Remember also that the eq operator checks the equality of two strings.

String Traversal with a while or for Loop

A lot of computations involve processing a string one character at a time. Often they start at the beginning, select each character in turn, do something to it or with it, and continue until the end. This pattern of processing is called a *traversal*. One way to write a traversal is with a while loop and the index function:

```
my $index = 0;
my $fruit = "banana";
while $index < $fruit.chars {
    my $letter = substr $fruit, $index, 1;
    say $letter;
    $index++;
}
```

This will output each letter, one at a time:

```
b
a
n
a
n
a
```

This loop traverses the string and displays each letter on a line by itself. The loop condition is $index < $fruit.chars, so when $index is equal to the length of the string, the condition is false, and the body of the loop doesn't run. In other words, the loop stops when $index is the length of the string minus one, which corresponds to the last character of the string.

As an exercise, write a function that takes a string as an argument and displays the letters backward, one per line. Do it at least once without using the flip function. Solution: "Exercise: String Traversal" on page 365.

Another way to write a traversal is with a for loop:

```
my $fruit = "banana";
for $fruit.comb -> $letter {
    say $letter
}
```

Each time through the loop, the next character in the string is assigned to the variable $letter. The loop continues until no characters are left.

The loop could also use the substr function:

```
for 0..$fruit.chars - 1 -> $index {
    say substr $fruit, $index, 1;
}
```

The following example shows how to use concatenation and a `for` loop to generate an abecedarian series (that is, in alphabetical order). In Robert McCloskey's book *Make Way for Ducklings*, the names of the ducklings are Jack, Kack, Lack, Mack, Nack, Ouack, Pack, and Quack. This loop outputs these names in order:

```
my $suffix = 'ack';
for 'J'..'Q' -> $letter {
    say $letter ~ $suffix;
}
```

The output is:

```
Jack
Kack
Lack
Mack
Nack
Oack
Pack
Qack
```

Of course, that's not quite right because "Ouack" and "Quack" are misspelled. As an exercise, modify the program to fix this error. Solution: "Exercise: The Ducklings" on page 366.

Looping and Counting

The following program counts the number of times the letter "a" appears in a string:

```
my $word = 'banana';
my $count = 0;
for $word.comb -> $letter {
    $count++ if $letter eq 'a';
}
say $count;                 # -> 3
```

This program demonstrates another pattern of computation called a *counter*. The variable `$count` is initialized to 0 and then incremented each time an "a" is found. When the loop exits, `$count` contains the result—the total number of occurrences of letter "a".

As an exercise, encapsulate this code in a subroutine named `count`, and generalize it so that it accepts the string and the searched letter as arguments. Solution: "Exercise: Counting the Letters of a String" on page 367.

Regular Expressions (Regexes)

The string functions and methods we have seen so far are quite powerful, and can be used for a number of string manipulation operations. But suppose you want to extract from the string "yellow submarine" any letter that is immediately preceded by the letter "l" and followed by the letter "w". This kind of "fuzzy search" can be done in a loop, but this is somewhat unpractical. You may try to do it as an exercise if you wish, but you should be warned: it is quite tricky and difficult. Even if you don't do it, the solution may be of some interest to you: see "Exercise: Simulating a Regex with a Loop" on page 367.

If you add some further condition, for example that this letter should be captured (i.e., saved for later use) only if the rest of the string contains the substring "rin", this starts to be really tedious. Also, any change to the requirements leads to a substantial rewrite or even complete refactoring of the code.

For this type of work, *regular expressions* or *regexes* are a much more powerful and expressive tool. Here's one way to extract letters using the criteria described above:

```
> my $string = "yellow submarine";
yellow submarine
> say ~$0 if $string ~~ / l (.) w .*? rin /;
o
```

Don't worry if you don't understand this example; hopefully it will be clear very soon.

The ~~ operator is called the smart match operator. It is a very powerful relational operator that can be used for many advanced comparison tasks. In this case, it checks whether the $string variable on its left "matches" the funny expression on its right, i.e., as a first approximation, whether the expression on the right describes the string (or part of it).

The / l (.) w .*? rin / part is called a regex pattern and means: the letter "l", followed by any single character (the dot) to be captured (thanks to the parentheses), followed by the letter "w", followed by an unspecified number of characters, followed by the substring "rin". Phew! All this in one single code line! Quite powerful, isn't it? If the string matches the pattern, then the match will return a true value and $0 will be populated with the character to be captured—the letter "o" in this case.

Unless specified otherwise (we will see more detail later), whitespace is not significant within a regex pattern. You can add spaces within a pattern to separate its pieces and make your intentions clearer.

Most of the rest of this chapter will cover the basics of constructing such regex patterns and using them. But the concept of regexes is so crucial in Perl that we will also devote a full chapter to this subject and some related matters (Chapter 13).

The notion of regular expressions is originally a concept stemming from the theory of formal languages. The first uses of regular expressions in computing came from Unix utilities, some of which are still in wide use today, such as grep, created by Ken Thomson in 1973, sed (ca. 1974), and awk, developed a few years later (in 1977) by

Aho, Weinberger, and Kernighan. Earlier versions of the Perl language in the 1980s included an extended version of regular expressions that has since been imitated by many other recent languages. The difference, though, is that regular expressions are deeply rooted within the core of the Perl language, whereas most other languages have adopted them as an add-on or a plug-in, often based or derived on a library known as Perl Compatible Regular Expressions (PCRE).

The Perl regular expressions have extended these notions so much that they have little to do with the original language theory concept, so that it has been deemed appropriate to stop calling them *regular expressions* and to speak about *regexes*, i.e., a sort of sublanguage that works similarly to regular expressions.

Using Regexes

A simple way to use a regex is to use the smart match operator ~~:

```
say "Matched" if "abcdef" ~~ / bc.e /;      # -> Matched
```

Here, the smart match operator compares the "abcdef" string with the /*bc.e*/ pattern and report a success, since, in this case, the "bc" in the string matches the *bc* part of the pattern, the dot in the pattern matches any character in the string (and matches in this case *d*) and, finally, the *e* of the string matches the *e* in the pattern.

The part of the string that was matched is contained in the $/ variable representing the match *object*, which we can stringify with the ~ operator. We can make good use of this to better visualize the part of the string that was matched by the regex pattern:

```
say ~$/ if "abcdef" ~~ / bc.e /;           # -> bcde
```

The matching process might be described as follows (but please note that this is a rough simplification): look in the string (from left to right) for a character matching the first atom (i.e., the first matchable item) of the pattern; when found, see whether the second character can match the second atom of the pattern, and so on. If the entire pattern is used, then the regex is successful. If it fails during the process, start again from the position immediately after the initial match point. (This is called *backtracking*.) And repeat that until one of the following occurs:

- There is a successful match, in which case the process ends and success is reported.
- The string has been exhausted without finding a match, in which case the regex failed.

Let us examine an example of backtracking:

```
say "Matched" if "abcabcdef" ~~ / bc.e /;  # -> Matched
```

Here, the regex engine starts by matching "bca" with *bc*., but that initial match attempt fails, because the next letter in the string, "b", does not match the "e" of the pattern. The regex engine backtracks and starts the search again from the third letter ("c") of the string. It starts a new match on the fifth letter of the string (the second "b"), manages to match successfully "bcde", and exits with a successful status (without even looking for any further match).

If the string to be analyzed is contained in the $_ topical variable, then the smart match operator is implicit and the syntax is even simpler:

```
for 'abcdef' {                          # $_ now contains 'abcdef'
    say "Matched" if / cd.f /;          # -> Matched
}
```

You might also use a method invocation syntax:

```
say "Matched" if "abcdef".match(/ b.d.f /); # -> Matched
```

In all cases we have seen so far, we directly used a pattern within a pair of / slash delimiters. We can use other delimiters if we prefix our pattern with the letter "m":

```
say "Matched" if "abcdef" ~~ m{ bc.e };      # -> Matched
```

or:

```
say "Matched" if "abcdef" ~~ m! bc.e !;      # -> Matched
```

The "m" operator does not alter the way a regex works; it only makes it possible to use delimiters other than slashes. Said differently, the "m" prefix is the standard way to introduce a pattern, but it is implicit and can be omitted when the pattern is delimited with slashes. It is probably best to use slashes (because that's what people commonly use and immediately recognize), and to use other delimiters only when the regex pattern itself contains slashes.

A pattern may also be stored in a variable (or, more accurately, in a regex object), using the rx// operator:

```
my $regex = rx/c..f/;
say "Matched" if 'abcdef' ~~ $regex;        # -> Matched
```

Building your Regex Patterns

It is now time to study the basic building blocks of a regex pattern.

Literal Matching

As you have probably figured out by now, the simplest case of a regex pattern is a constant string. Matching a string against such a regex is more or less equivalent to searching for that string with the index function:

```
my $string = "superlative";
say "$string contains 'perl'." if $string ~~ /perl/;
                            # -> superlative contains 'perl'.
```

Note however that, for such literal matches, the `index` function discussed earlier is likely to be slightly more efficient than a regex on large strings. The `contains` method, which returns `True` if its argument is a substring of its invocant, is also likely to be faster.

Alphanumeric characters and the underscore (_) are literal matches. All other characters must either be escaped with a backslash (for example, `\?` to match a question mark), or included in quotes:

```
say "Success" if 'name@company.uk' ~~ / name@co /; # Fails to compile
say "Success" if 'name@company.uk' ~~ / 'name@co' /;   # -> Success
say "Success" if 'name@company.uk' ~~ / name\@co/ ;    # -> Success
say "Success" if 'name@company.uk' ~~ / name '@' co /; # -> Success
```

Wildcards and Character Classes

Regexes wouldn't be very useful if they could only do literal matching. We are now getting to the more interesting parts.

In a regex pattern, some symbols can match not a specific character, but a whole family of characters, such as letters, digits, etc. They are called character classes.

We have already seen that the dot is a sort of wildcard matching any single character of the target string:

```
my $string = "superlative";
say "$string contains 'pe.l'." if $string ~~ / pe . l /;
                        # -> superlative contains 'pe.l'.
```

The example above illustrates another feature of regexes: whitespace is usually not significant within regex patterns (unless specified otherwise with the :s or :*sigspace* adverb, as we will see later).

There are predefined character classes of the form \w. Its negation is written with an uppercase letter, \W. \w ("word character") matches one single alphanumeric character (i.e., among alphabetical characters, digits, and the _ character). \W will match any other character. Note however that Perl is Unicode-compliant and that, for example, letters of the Greek or Cyrillic alphabets or Thai digits will be matched by \w:

```
say "Matched" if 'abcδ' ~~ / ab\w\w /;  # -> Matched
```

Here, the string was matched because, according to the Unicode standard, δ (Greek small letter delta) is a letter and it therefore belongs to the \w character class.

Other common character classes include:

- \d (digits) and \D (non-digits)
- \s (whitespace) and \S (non-whitespace)
- \n (newline) and \N (non-newline)

```
say ~$/ if 'Bond 007' ~~ /\w\D\s\d\d\d/;  # -> "nd 007"
```

Here, we've matched "nd 007" because we have found one word character (n), followed by a nondigit ("d"), followed by a space, followed by three digits.

You can also specify your own character classes by inserting between <[ ]> any number of single characters and ranges of characters (expressed with two dots between the end points), with or without whitespace. For example, a character class for a hexadecimal digit might be:

```
<[0..9 a..f A..F]>
```

You can negate such a character class by inserting a "-" after the opening angle bracket. For example, a string is not a valid hexadecimal integer if it contains any character not in <[0..9a..fA..F]>, i.e., any character matched by the negated hexadecimal character class:

```
say "Not an hex number" if $string ~~ /<-[0..9 a..f A..F]>/;
```

Please note that you generally don't need to escape nonalphanumeric characters in your character classes:

```
say ~$/  if "-17.5" ~~ /(<[\d.-]>+)/; # -> -17.5
```

In this example, we use the "+" quantifier that we'll discuss in the next section, but the point here is that you don't need to escape the dot and the dash within the character class definition.

Quantifiers

A quantifier makes a preceding atom[1] match not exactly once, but rather a specified or variable number of times. For example, a+ matches one or more "a" characters. In the following code, the \d+ matches one or more digits (three digits in this case):

```
say ~$/ if 'Bond 007' ~~ /\w\D\s\d\+/;  # -> "nd 007"
```

The predefined quantifiers include:

- +: one or more times

---

1 The word *atom* means a single character, or several characters or other atoms, grouped together with a set of parentheses or square brackets.

- *: zero or more times

- ?: zero or one match

The + and * quantifiers are said to be *greedy*, which means that they match as many characters as they can. For example:

```
say ~$/ if 'aabaababa' ~~ / .+ b /;      # -> aabaabab
```

Here, the .+ matches as much as it possibly can of the string, while still being able to match the final "b". This is often what you want, but not always. Perhaps your intention was to match all letters until the first "b". In such cases, you would use the *frugal* (nongreedy) versions of those quantifiers, which are obtained by suffixing them with a question mark: +? and * ?. A frugal quantifier will match as much as it has to for the overall regex to succeed, but not more than that. To match all letters until the first *b*, you could use:

```
say ~$/ if 'aabaababa' ~~ / .+? b /;      # -> aab
```

You can also specify a range (min..max) for the number of times an atom may be matched. For example, to match an integer smaller than 1,000:

```
say 'Is a number < 1,000' if $string ~~ / ^ \d ** 1..3 $ /;
```

This matches one to three digits. The ^ and $ characters are anchors representing the beginning and the end of the string; they will be covered in the next section.

For matching an exact number of times, just replace the range with a single number:

```
say 'Is a 3-digit number' if $num ~~ / ^ \d ** 3 $ /;
```

Anchors and Assertions

Sometimes, matching a substring is not good enough; you want to match the whole string, or you want the match to occur at the beginning or at the end of the string, or at some other specific place within the string. Anchors and assertions make it possible to specify where the match should occur. They need to match successfully in order for the whole regex to succeed, but they do not use up characters while matching.

Anchors

The most commonly used anchors are the ^ start of string and $ end of string anchors:

```
my $string = "superlative";
say "$string starts with 'perl'" if $string ~~ /^perl/; # (No output)
say "$string ends with 'perl'" if $string ~~ /perl$/;   # (No output)
say "$string equals 'perl'" if $string ~~ /^perl$/;     # (No output)
```

All three regexes fail because, even though $string contains the "perl" substring, the substring is neither at the start, nor at the end of the string.

In the event that you are handling multiline strings, you might also use the ^^ start of line and $$ end of line anchors.

There are some other useful anchors, such as the << start of word (or word left boundary) and >> end of word (or word right boundary) anchors.

Look-around assertions

Look-around assertions make it possible to specify more complex rules: for example, match "foo", but only if preceded (or followed) by "bar" (or not preceded or not followed by "bar"):

```
say "foobar" ~~ /foo <?before bar>/; # -> foo (lookahead assertion)
say "foobaz" ~~ /foo <?before bar>/; # -> Nil (regex failed)
say "foobar" ~~ /<?after foo> bar/;  # -> bar (lookbehind assertion)
```

Using an exclamation mark instead of a question mark transforms these look-around assertion into negative assertions. For example:

```
say "foobar" ~~ /foo <!before baz>/; # -> foo
say "foobar" ~~ /<!after foo> bar/;  # -> Nil (regex failed)
```

I assume that the examples above are rather clear; look into the documentation (*http://bit.ly/2q9WDcf*) if you need further details.

Code assertions

You can also include a code assertion <?{...}>, which will match if the code block returns a true value:

```
> say ~$/ if /\d\d <?{$/ == 42}>/ for <A12 B34 C42 D50>;
42
```

A negative code assertion <!{...}> will match unless the code block returns a true value:

```
> say ~$/ if /\d\d <!{$/ == 42}>/ for <A12 B34 C42 D50>
12
34
50
```

Code assertions are useful to specify conditions that cannot easily be expressed as regexes.

They can also be used to display something, for example for the purpose of debugging a regex by printing out information about partial matches:

```
> say "Matched $/" if "A12B34D50" ~~ /(\D) <?{ say ~$0}> \d\d$/;
A
```

```
B
D
Matched D50
```

The output shows the various attempted matches that failed ("A" and "B") before the backtracking process ultimately led to success ("D50" at the end of the string).

However, code assertions are in fact rarely needed for such simple cases, because you can very often just add a simple code block for the same purpose:

```
> say "Matched $/" if "A12B34D50" ~~ /(\D) { say ~$0} \d\d$/;
```

This code produces the same output, and there is no need to worry about whether the block returns a true value.

Alternation

Alternations are used to match one of several alternatives.

For example, to check whether a string represents one of the three base image colors (in JPEG and some other image formats), you might use:

```
say 'Is a JPEG color' if $string ~~ /^ [ red | green | blue ] $/;
```

There are two forms of alternations. First-match alternation uses the || operator and stops on the first alternative that matches the pattern:

```
say ~$/ if "abcdef" ~~ /ab || abcde/;        # -> ab
```

Here, the pattern matches "ab", without trying to match any further, although there would be an arguably "better" (i.e., longer) match with the other alternative. When using this type of alternation, you have to think carefully about the order in which you put the various alternatives, depending on what you need to do.

The longest-match alternation uses the | operator and will try all the alternatives and match the longest one:

```
say ~$/ if "abcdef" ~~ /ab | abcde/;         # -> abcde
```

Beware, though, that this will work as explained only if the alternative matches all start on the same position within the string:

```
say ~$/ if "abcdef" ~~ /ab | bcde/;          # -> ab
```

Here, the match on the leftmost position wins (this is a general rule with regexes).

Grouping and Capturing

Parentheses and square brackets can be used to group things together or to override precedence:

```
/ a || bc /      # matches 'a' or 'bc'
/ ( a || b ) c / # matches 'ac' or 'bc'
```

```
/ [ a || b ] c /  # Same: matches 'ac' or 'bc', non-capturing grouping
/ a b+ /          # Matches an 'a' followed by one or more 'b's
/ (a b)+ /        # Matches one or more sequences of 'ab'
/ [a b]+ /        # Matches one or more sequences of 'ab', non-capturing
/ (a || b)+ /     # Matches a sequence of 'a's and 'b's (at least one)
```

The difference between parentheses and square brackets is that parentheses don't just group things together, they also capture data: they make the string matched within the parentheses available as a special variable (and also as an element of the resulting match object):

```
my $str = 'number 42';
say "The number is $0" if $str ~~ /number\s+ (\d+) /;  # -> The number is 42
```

Here, the pattern matched the $str string and the part of the pattern within parentheses was captured into the $0 special variable. Where there are several parenthesized groups, they are captured into variables named $0, $1, $2, etc. (from left to right, counting the opening parentheses):

```
say "$0 $1 $2" if "abcde" ~~ /(a) b (c) d (e)/;        # -> a c e
# or: say "$/[0..2]" if "abcde" ~~ /(a) b (c) d (e)/;  # -> a c e
```

The $0, $1, etc. variables are actually a shorthand for $/[0], $/[1], the first and second items of the matched object in list context, so that printing "The number is $/[0]" would have had the same effect.

As noted, the parentheses perform two roles in regexes: they group regex elements and they capture what is matched by the subregex within parentheses. If you want only the grouping behavior, use square brackets [...] instead:

```
say ~$0 if 'cacbcd' ~~ / [a||b] (c.) /;  # -> cb
```

Using square brackets when there is no need to capture text has the advantage of not cluttering the $0, $1, $2, etc. variables, and it is likely to be slightly faster.

Adverbs (a.k.a. Modifiers)

Adverbs modify the way the regex engine works. They often have a long form and a shorthand form.

For example, the :ignorecase (or :i) adverb tells the compiler to ignore the distinction between uppercase and lowercase:

```
> say so 'AB' ~~ /ab/;
False
> say so 'AB' ~~ /:i ab/;
True
```

The so built-in used here coerces its argument (i.e., the value returned by the regex match expression) into a Boolean value.

If placed before the pattern, an adverb applies to the whole pattern:

```
> say so 'AB' ~~ m:i/ ab/;
True
```

The adverb may also be placed later in the pattern and affects in this case only the part of the regex that comes afterwards:

```
> say so 'AB' ~~ /a :i b/;
False
> say so 'aB' ~~ /a :i b/;
True
```

I said earlier that whitespace is usually not significant in regex patterns. The :sig space or :s adverb makes whitespace significant in a regex:

```
> say so 'ab' ~~ /a+ b/;
True
> say so 'ab' ~~ /:s a+ b/;
False
> say so 'ab' ~~ /:s a+b/;
True
```

Instead of searching for just one match and returning a match object, the :global or :g adverb tells the compiler to search for every nonoverlapping match and return them in a list:

```
> say "Word count = ", $/.elems if "I have a dream" ~~ m:g/ \w+/;
Word count = 4
> say ~$/[3];
dream
```

These are the most commonly used adverbs. Another adverb, :ratchet or :r, tells the regex engine not to backtrack and is very important for some specific uses, but we will come back to it in a later chapter.

Exercises on Regexes

As a simple exercise, write some regexes to match and capture:

- A succession of 10 digits within a longer string
- A valid octal number (octal numbers use only digits 0 to 7)
- The first word at the start of a string (for the purpose of these small exercises, the word separator may be deemed to be a space, but you might do it without this assumption)
- The first word of a string starting with an "a"
- The first word of a string starting with a lowercase vowel

- A French mobile telephone number (in France, mobile phone numbers have 10 digits and start with "06" or "07"); assume the digits are consecutive (no spaces)
- The first word of a string starting with a vowel in either upper- or lowercase
- The first occurrence of a double letter (the same letter twice in a row)
- The second occurrence of a double letter

Solution: "Exercise: Regex Exercises" on page 369.

Putting It All Together

This section gives a few examples that combine several of the regex features we have seen, in order to solve practical problems.

Extracting Dates

Assume we have a string containing somewhere a date in the YYYY-MM-DD format.

```
my $string = "Christmas : 2016-12-25.";
```

As mentioned earlier, one of the mottos in Perl is, "There is more than one way to do it" (TIMTOWTDI). The various examples below should illustrate that principle quite well by showing several different ways to retrieve the date in the string:

- Using a character class (digits and dash):

    ```
    say ~$0 if $string ~~ /(<[\d-]>+)/;        # -> 2016-12-25
    ```

- Using a character class and a quantifier to avoid matching some small numbers elsewhere in the string if any:

    ```
    say ~$0 if $string ~~ /(<[\d-]> ** 10)/;   # -> 2016-12-25
    ```

- Using a more detailed description of the date format:

    ```
    say ~$/ if $string ~~ /(\d ** 4 \- \d\d \- \d\d)/;
    ```

- The same regex, but using an additional grouping to avoid repetition of the \- \d\d subpattern:

    ```
    say ~$/[0] if $string ~~ /(\d ** 4 [\- \d\d] ** 2 )/;
    ```

- Capturing the individual elements of the date:

    ```
    $string ~~ /(\d ** 4) \- (\d\d) \- (\d\d)/;
    my ($year, $month, $day) = ~$0, ~$1, ~$2;
    ```

Note that using the tilde as a prefix above leads $year, $month, and $day to be populated with strings. Assuming you want these variables to contain integers instead, you might numify them, i.e., coerce them to numeric values using the prefix + operator:

```
$string ~~ /(\d ** 4) \- (\d\d) \- (\d\d)/;
my ($year, $month, $day) = +$0, +$1, +$2;
```

- Using subpatterns as building blocks:

```
my $y = rx/\d ** 4/;
my $m = rx/\d ** 2/;
my $d = rx/\d ** 2/;
$string ~~ /(<$y>) \- (<$m>) \- (<$d>)/;
my ($year, $month, $day) = ~$0, ~$1, ~$2;
```

Using subpatterns as building blocks is a quite efficient way of constructing step-by-step complicated regexes, but we will see in Chapter 13 even better ways of doing this type of thing.

- We could improve the $m (month) subpattern so that it matches only "01" to "12" and thus verify that it matches a valid month number:

```
my $m = rx {    1 <[0..2]>    # 10 to 12
             || 0 <[1..9]>    # 01 to 09
           };
```

As you can see, using comments and whitespace helps make the regex's intent clearer.

Another way of achieving the same goal is to use a code assertion to check that the value is numerically between 1 and 12:

```
my $m = rx /\d ** 2 <?{ 1 <= $/ <= 12 }> /;
```

As an exercise, you could try to validate that the $d (day) subpattern falls within the 01 to 31 range. Try to use both validation techniques outlined just above.

The $/ match object has the `prematch` and `postmatch` methods for extracting what comes before and after the matched part of the string:

```
$string ~~ /(\d ** 4) \- (\d\d) \- (\d\d)/;
say $/.prematch;              # -> "Christmas : "
say $/.postmatch;             # -> "."
```

As an exercise, try to adapt the above regexes for various other date formats (such as DD/MM/YYYY or YYYY MM, DD) and test them. If you're trying with the YYYY MM, DD format, please remember that spaces are usually not significant in a regex pattern, so you may need either to specify explicit spaces (using for example the \s character class) or the :s adverb to make whitespace significant.

Extracting an IP Address

Assume we have a string containing an IP-v4 address somewhere. IP addresses are most often written in the dot-decimal notation, which consists of four octets of the address expressed individually in decimal numbers and separated by periods, for example 17.125.246.28.

For the purpose of these examples, our sample target string will be as follows:

```
my $string = "IP address: 17.125.246.28;";
```

Let's now try a few different ways to capture the IP address in that string, in the same way as we just did for the dates:

- Using a character class:

  ```
  say ~$0 if $string ~~ /(<[\d.]>+)/;        # -> 17.125.246.28
  ```

- Using a character class and a quantifier (note that each octet may have 1 to 3 digits, so the total number of characters may vary from 7 to 15):

  ```
  say ~$0 if $string ~~ /(<[\d.]> ** 7..15)/;
  ```

- Using a more detailed description of the IP format:

  ```
  say ~$/ if $string ~~ /([\d ** 1..3 \.] ** 3 \d ** 1..3 )/;
  ```

- Using subpatterns as building blocks:

  ```
  my $octet = rx/\d ** 1..3/;
  say ~$/ if $string ~~ /([<$octet> \.] ** 3 <$octet>)/;
  ```

- The maximal value of an octet is 255. We can refine somewhat the definition of the $octet subpattern:

  ```
  my $octet = rx/<[1..2]>? \d ** 1..2/;
  say ~$/ if $string ~~ /([<$octet> \.] ** 3 <$octet>)/;
  ```

  With this definition of the $octet pattern, the regex would match any number of one or two digits, or a three-digit number starting with digits 1 to 2.

- But that is not good enough if we really want to check that the IP address is valid (for example, it would erroneously accept 276 as a valid octet). The definition of the $octet subpattern can be further refined to really match only authorized values:

  ```
  my $octet = rx { (     25 <[0..5]>      # 250 to 255
                   || 2  <[0..4]> \d      # 200 to 249
                   || 1  \d ** 2          # 100 to 199
                   || \d ** 1..2          # 0 to 99
                 )
            };
  say ~$/ if $string ~~ /([<$octet> \.] ** 3 <$octet>)/;
  ```

This definition of $octet illustrates once more how the abundant use of whitespace and comments can help make the intent clearer.

- We could also use a code assertion to limit the value of an $octet to the 0..255 range:

```
my $octet = = rx{(\d ** 1..3) <?{0 <= $0 <= 255 }> };
say ~$/ if $string ~~ /([<$octet> \.] ** 3 <$octet>)/;
```

Substitutions

Replacing part of a string with some other substring is a very frequent requirement in string handling. This might be needed for spelling corrections, data reformatting, removal of personal information from data, etc.

The subst Method

Perl has a subst method which can replace some text with some other text:

```
my $string = "abcdefg";
$string = $string.subst("cd", "DC");          # -> abDCefg
```

The first argument to this method is the search part, and can be a literal string, as in the example above, or a regex:

```
my $string = "abcdefg";
$string = $string.subst(/c \w+ f/, "SUBST");  # -> abSUBSTg
```

The s/search/replace/ Construct

The most common way to perform text substitution in Perl is the s/search/replace construct, which is quite concise, plays well within the general regex syntax, and has the advantage of enabling in-place substitution.

This is an example of the standard syntax for this type of substitution:

```
my $string = "abcdefg";
$string ~~ s/ c \w+ f /SUBST/;                # -> abSUBSTg
```

Here, the search part is a regex and the replacement part is a simple string (no quotation marks needed).

If the string is contained in the $_ topical variable, you don't need to use the smart-match operator:

```
$_ = "abcdefg";
s/c \w+ f/SUBST/;                             # -> abSUBSTg
```

The delimiters don't need to be slashes (and this can be quite useful if either the search or the replacement contain slashes):

```
my $str = "<c>foo</c> <a>foo</a>";
$str ~~ s!'<a>foo</a>'!<a>bar</a>!;           # -> <c>foo</c> <a>bar</a>
```

Unless specified otherwise (with an adverb), the substitution is done only once, which helps to prevent unexpected results:

```
$_ = 'There can be twly two';
s/tw/on/;                       # Replace 'tw' with 'on' once
.say;                           # There can be only two
```

If the substitution were done throughout the string, "two" would have been replaced by "ono", clearly not the expected result.

Using Captures

If the regex on the lefthand side contains captures, the replacement part on the right-hand side can use the $0, $1, and $2 variables on the right side to insert captured substrings in the replacement text. A typical example of that is date reformatting:

```
my $string = "Xmas = 2016-12-25";
$string ~~ s/(\d ** 4) \- (\d\d) \- (\d\d)/$2-$1-$0/;
                        # $string is now: Xmas = 25-12-2016
```

Adverbs

The adverbs discussed above ("Adverbs (a.k.a. Modifiers)" on page 125) can be used with the substitution operator.

The modifiers most commonly used in substitutions are the :ignorecase (or :i) and :global (or :g) adverbs. They work just as described when we were discussing regexes and matching in "Adverbs (a.k.a. Modifiers)" on page 125.

The one specific point to be made here is that substitutions are usually done only once. But with the :global (or :g) adverb, they will be done throughout the whole string:

```
my $string = "foo bar bar foo bar";
$string ~~ s:g/bar/baz/;  # string is now "foo baz baz foo baz"
```

Debugging

When you use indices to traverse the values in a sequence, it is tricky to get the beginning and end of the traversal right. Here is a subroutine that is supposed to compare two words and return True if one of the words is the reverse of the other, but it contains two errors:

```
# ATTENTION, watch out: code with errors
sub is-reverse(Str $word1, Str $word2) {
    return False if $word1.chars != $word2.chars;

    my $i = 0;
```

```
    my $j = $word2.chars;

    while $j > 0 {
        return False if substr($word1, $i, 1) ne substr($word1, $j, 1);
        $i++; $j--;
    }
    return True;
}
say is-reverse "pots", "stop";
```

The first postfix `if` statement checks whether the words are the same length. If not, we can return `False` immediately. Otherwise, for the rest of the subroutine, we can assume that the words are the same length. This is an example of the guardian pattern described in "Checking Types" on page 87 .

`$i` and `$j` are indices: `$i` traverses `$word1` forward while `$j` traverses `$word2` backward. If we find two letters that don't match, we can return `False` immediately. If we get through the whole loop and all the letters match, we return `True`.

If we test this function with the words "stop" and "pots", we expect the return value `True`, but we get `False` instead. So, what's wrong here?

With this kind of code, the usual suspect is a possible blunder in the management of indices (especially perhaps an off-by-one error). For debugging this kind of error, the first move might be to print the values of the indices immediately before the line where they are used:

```
sub is-reverse(Str $word1, Str $word2) {
    return False if $word1.chars != $word2.chars;

    my $i = 0;
    my $j = $word2.chars;

    while $j > 0 {
        say '$i = ', $i, ' $j = ', $j;
        return False if substr($word1, $i, 1) ne substr($word1, $j, 1);
        $i++; $j--;
    }
    return True;
}
```

Now when we run the program again, we get more information:

```
$i = 0 $j = 4
False
```

The first time through the loop, the value of `$j` is 4, which is out of range for the string `'pots'`. The index of the last character is 3, so the initial value for `$j` should be `$word2.chars - 1`.

Note that in the event that this was still not enough for us to spot the out-of-range error, we could have gone one step further and printed the letters themselves, and we would have seen that we did not get the last letter of the second word.

If we fix that error and run the program again, we get:

```
$i = 0 $j = 3
$i = 1 $j = 2
$i = 2 $j = 1
True
```

This time we get the right answer, but it looks like the loop only ran three times, which is suspicious: it seems that the program did not compare the last letter of the first word (indexed $i = 3$) with the last letter of the second word (indexed $j = 0$).

We can confirm this by running the subroutine with the following arguments: "stop" and "lots", which displays:

```
$i = 0 $j = 3
$i = 1 $j = 2
$i = 2 $j = 1
True
```

This is obviously wrong, as "lots" is not the reverse of "stop"; the subroutine should return False. So we have another bug here.

To get a better idea of what is happening, it is useful to draw a state diagram. During the first iteration, the frame for is_reverse is shown in Figure 7-1.

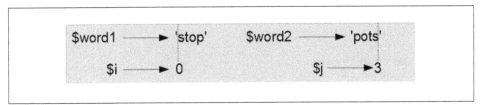

Figure 7-1. State diagram

We took some license by arranging the variables in the frame and adding dotted lines to show that the values of $i and $j indicate characters in $word1 and $word2.

Starting with this diagram, run the program on paper, changing the values of $i and $j during each iteration. Find and fix the second error in this function. (Solution: "Exercise: is-reverse Subroutine" on page 372.)

Glossary

atom

> In a regex pattern, a single character, or several characters grouped together by parentheses or square brackets.

adverb

> An argument to a function or to a regex that modifies the way the function or the regex engine behaves.

backtracking

> The process by which when a given attempt to match a string fails, the regex engine abandons part of the current match attempt, goes back into the string, and tries to see if it can find another route to a successful match. The backtracking process eventually stops as soon as a successful match succeeds, or ultimately when all possible match possibilities have failed.

counter

> A variable used to count something, usually initialized to zero and then incremented.

empty string

> A string with no characters and length 0, represented by two quotation marks.

index

> An integer value used to select an item in a sequence, such as a character in a string. In Perl indices start from 0.

item

> One of the values in a sequence.

object

> Something a variable can store. For now, you can use "object" and "value" interchangeably.

pattern

> A sequence of characters using a special syntax to describe from left to right the content that is intended to be matched within a target string.

regexes

> A pattern-matching sublanguage of Perl 6 derived from regular expressions.

regular expressions

> A pattern-matching sublanguage derived from formal language theory.

search

> A pattern of traversal that stops when it finds what it is looking for.

sequence
>An ordered collection of values where each value is identified by an integer index.

slice
>A part of a string specified by a range of indices.

traverse
>To iterate through the items in a sequence, performing a similar operation on each.

Exercises

Exercise 7-1.

Write a subroutine that uses the `index` function in a loop to count the number of "a" characters in `'banana'`, as we did in "Looping and Counting" on page 116. Modify it to count any letter in any word passed as arguments to the subroutine.

Write another subroutine counting a given letter in a given word using the `substr` function.

Solution: "Exercise 7-1: Counting Letters" on page 372.

Exercise 7-2.

The `<[a..z]>` character class matches any lowercase character (only plain ASCII lowercase characters, not Unicode characters). The following subroutine:

```
sub is-lower (Str $input) {
    return so $char ~~ /^<[a..z]>$/
}
```

should return `True` if its argument is an ASCII lowercase letter and `False` otherwise. Test that it works as expected (and amend it if needed). The `so` function coerces the result of the regex match into a Boolean value.

The following subroutines use the `is-lower` subroutine and are all *intended* to check whether a string contains any lowercase letters, but at least some of them are wrong. Analyze each subroutine by hand, determine whether it is correct, and describe what it actually does (assuming that the parameter is a string). Then test them with various input strings to check whether your analysis was correct.

```
# ATTENTION: some of the subroutines below are wrong

sub any_lowercase1(Str $string){
    for $string.comb -> $char {
```

```
            if is-lower $char {
                return True;
            } else {
                return False;
            }
        }
    }

    sub any_lowercase2(Str $string){
        for $string.comb -> $char {
            if is-lower "char" {
                return True;
            } else {
                return False;
            }
        }
    }

    sub any_lowercase3(Str $string){
        my $flag;
        for $string.comb -> $char {
            $flag =  is-lower $char;
        }
        return $flag;
    }

    sub any_lowercase4(Str $string){
        my $flag = False;
        for $string.comb -> $char {
            $flag = $flag or is-lower $char;
        }
        return $flag;
    }

    sub any_lowercase5(Str $string){
        my $flag = False;
        for $string.comb -> $char {
            if is-lower $char {
                $flag = True;
            }
        }
        return $flag;
    }

    sub any_lowercase6(Str $string){
        for $string.comb -> $char {
            if is-lower $char {
                return 'True';
            }
        }
        return 'False';
    }
```

```
sub any_lowercase7(Str $string){
    for $string.comb -> $char {
        return True if is-lower $char;
    }
    return False;
}

sub any_lowercase8(Str $string){
    for $string.comb -> $char {
        return False unless is-lower $char;
    }
    return True;
}

sub any_lowercase9(Str $string){
    for $string.comb -> $char {
        if not is-lower $char {
            return False;
        }
    return True;
    }
}
```

Solution: "Exercise 7-2: Lowercase Letters" on page 373.

Exercise 7-3.

A Caesar cipher is a weak form of encryption that involves "rotating" each letter by a fixed number of places. To rotate a letter means to shift it through the alphabet, wrapping around to the beginning if necessary, so "A" rotated by 3 is "D" and "Z" rotated by 1 is "A".

To rotate a word, rotate each letter by the same amount. For example, "cheer" rotated by 7 is "jolly" and "melon" rotated by –10 is "cubed." In the movie *2001: A Space Odyssey*, the ship's computer is called HAL, which is IBM rotated by –1.

Write a function called `rotate-word` that takes a string and an integer as parameters, and returns a new string that contains the letters from the original string rotated by the given amount.

You might want to use the built-in functions `ord`, which converts a character to a numeric code (Unicode code point), and `chr`, which converts such numeric codes back to characters:

```
> say 'c'.ord;
99
> say chr 99
c
```

Letters of the alphabet are encoded in alphabetical order, so for example:

```
> ord('c') - ord('a')
2
```

because `'c'` is the second letter after `'a'` in the alphabet. But beware: the numeric codes for uppercase letters are different.

Potentially offensive jokes on the internet are sometimes encoded in ROT13, which is a Caesar cipher with rotation 13. Since 13 is half the number of letters in our alphabet, applying rotation 13 twice returns the original word, so that the same procedure can be used for both encoding and decoding in rotation 13. If you are not easily offended, find and decode some of these jokes. (ROT13 is also used for other purposes, such as weakly hiding the solution to a puzzle.) Solution: "Exercise 7-3: Caesar's Cipher" on page 375.

CHAPTER 8

Case Study: Word Play

This chapter is intended to let you practice and consolidate the knowledge you have acquired so far, rather than introducing new concepts. To help you gain experience with programming, we will cover a case study that involves solving word puzzles by searching for words that have certain properties. For example, we'll find the longest palindromes in English and search for words whose letters appear in alphabetical order. And I will present another program development plan: reduction to a previously solved problem.

Reading from and Writing to Files

For the exercises in this chapter, we will need our programs to read text from files. In many programming languages, this often means that we need a statement to open a file, then a statement or group of statements to read the file's content, and finally a statement to close the file (although this last operation may be performed automatically in some circumstances).

We are interested here in text files that are usually made of lines separated by logical newline characters; depending on your operating system, such logical newline characters consist of either one (Linux, Mac) or two (Windows) physical characters (bytes).

The Perl built-in function open takes the path and name of the file as a parameter and returns a *file handle* (IO::Handle object) which you can use to read the file (or to write to it):

```
my $fh = open("path/to/myfile.txt", :r);
my $data = $fh.slurp-rest;
$fh.close;
```

The :r option is the file mode (read). $fh is a common name for a file handle. The *file object* provides methods for reading, such as slurp-rest, which returns the full content of the file from the current position to the end (and the entire content of the file if we've just opened it).

This is the traditional way of opening and reading files in most languages.

However, Perl's IO role (in simple terms, a role is a collection of related methods) offers simpler methods which can open a file and read it all in one single instruction (i.e., without having to first open a file handle and then close it):

```
my $text = slurp "path/to/myfile.txt";
# or:
my $text = "path/to/myfile.txt".IO.slurp;
```

slurp takes care of opening and closing the file for you.

We can also read the file line by line, which is very practical if each line contains a logical entity such as a record, and is especially useful for very large files that might not fit into memory:

```
for 'path/to/hugefile.txt'.IO.lines -> $line {
    # Do something with $line
}
```

By default, the .lines method will remove the trailing newline characters from each line, so that you don't have to worry about them.

We haven't studied arrays yet, but you can also read all lines of a file into an array, with each line of the file becoming an array item. For example, you can load the *myfile.txt* file into the @lines array:

```
my @lines = "myfile.txt".IO.lines;
```

Accessing any line can then be done with the bracket operator and an index. For example, to print the first and the seventh line:

```
say @lines[0];
say @lines[6];
```

To write data to a file, it is possible to open a file just as when wanting to read from it, except that the :w (write) option should be used:

```
my $fh = open("path/to/myfile.txt", :w);
$fh.say("line to be written to the file");
$fh.close;
```

If the file already existed, any existing content will be clobbered. So be careful when you want to open a file in write mode.

It is also possible to open the file in append mode, using the :a option. New data will then be added after the existing content.

Writing to a file can be simplified using the `spurt` function, which opens the file, writes the data to it, and closes it:

```
spurt "path/to/myfile.txt", "line to be written to the file\n";
```

Used this way, `spurt` will clobber any existing content in the file. It may also be used in append mode with the `:append` option:

```
spurt "path/to/myfile.txt", "line to be added\n", :append;
```

Reading Word Lists

For the exercises in this chapter we need a list of English words. There are lots of word lists available on the web, but one of the most suitable for our purpose is one of the word lists collected and contributed to the public domain by Grady Ward as part of the Moby lexicon project (*http://wikipedia.org/wiki/Moby_Project*). It is a list of 113,809 official crosswords; that is, words that are considered valid in crossword puzzles and other word games. In the Moby collection, the filename is *113809of.fic*; you can download a copy, with the simpler name *words.txt*, from *http://thinkpython2.com/code/words.txt*.

This file is in plain text (with each word of the list on its own line), so you can open it with a text editor, but you can also read it from Perl. Let's do so in the interactive mode (with the REPL):

```
> my $fh = open("words.txt", :r);
IO::Handle<words.txt>(opened, at octet 0)
> my $line = get $fh;
aa
> say "<<$line>>";
<<aa>>
```

The `get` function reads one line from the file handle.

The first word in this particular list is "aa" (a kind of lava).

Printing the `$line` variable between angle brackets within a string shows us that the `get` function removed implicitly the trailing newline characters, in this case a \r\n (carriage return and newline) character combination, since this file was apparently prepared under Windows.

The file handle keeps track of what has been read from the file and what it should read next, so if you call `get` again, you obtain the next line:

```
> my $line = get $fh;
aah
```

The next word is "aah," which is a perfectly legitimate word, so stop looking at me like that.

This is good and fine if we want to explore the first few lines of the *words.txt* file, but we are not going to read the 113,809 lines of the file this way.

We need a loop to do it for us. We could insert the above `get` instruction into a `while` loop, but earlier we discussed an easier and more efficient way of doing this with a `for` loop and the `IO.lines` method, without the hassle of having to open or close the file:

```
for 'words.txt'.IO.lines -> $line {
    say $line;
}
```

This code reads the file line by line, and prints each line to the screen. We'll soon do more interesting things than just displaying the lines on the screen.

Exercises

This case study consists mainly of exercises and solutions to them within the body of the chapter because solving the exercises is the main teaching material of this chapter. Therefore, solutions to these exercises are in the following sections of this chapter, not in the appendix. You should at least attempt each one before you read the solutions.

Exercise 8-1.

Write a program that reads *words.txt* and prints only the words with more than 20 characters.

Exercise 8-2.

In 1939 Ernest Vincent Wright published a 50,000-word novel called *Gadsby* that does not contain the letter "e". Since "e" is the most common letter in English, that's not easy to do. In fact, it is difficult to construct a solitary thought without using that most common letter. Such a writing in which one letter is avoided is sometimes called a *lipogram*.

Write a subroutine called `has-no-e` that returns `True` if the given word doesn't have the letter "e" in it.

Modify your program from the previous exercise to print only the words that have no "e" and compute the percentage of the words in the list that have no "e".

(The word dictionary we are using, *words.txt*, is entirely in lowercase letters, so you don't need to worry about any uppercase "E".)

Exercise 8-3.

Write a subroutine named `avoids` that takes a word and a string of forbidden letters, and that returns `True` if the word doesn't use any of the forbidden letters.

Next, modify your program to prompt the user to enter a string of forbidden letters and then print the number of words that don't contain any of them. Can you find a combination of five forbidden letters that excludes the smallest number of words?

Exercise 8-4.

Write a subroutine named `uses-only` that takes a word and a string of letters, and that returns `True` if the word contains only letters in the list. Can you make a sentence using only the letters `acefhlo`? Other than "Hoe alfalfa?"

Exercise 8-5.

Write a subroutine named `uses-all` that takes a word and a string of required letters, and returns `True` if the word uses all the required letters at least once. How many words are there that use all the vowels `aeiou`? How about `aeiouy`?

Exercise 8-6.

Write a function called `is_abecedarian` that returns `True` if the letters in a word appear in alphabetical order (double letters are ok). How many abecedarian words are there?

Search

Most of the exercises in the previous section have something in common; they can be solved with the search pattern (and the `index` function we saw in "Searching for a Substring Within the String" on page 111). Most can also be solved using regexes.

Words Longer Than 20 Characters (Solution)

The solution to the simplest exercise—printing all the words of *words.txt* that are longer than 20 characters—is:

```
for 'words.txt'.IO.lines -> $line {
    say $line if $line.chars > 20
}
```

Because the code is so simple, this is a typical example of a possible and useful one-liner (as described in "One-Liner Mode" on page 22). Assuming you want to know the words that are longer than 20 characters, you don't even need to write a script, save it, and run it. You can simply type this at your operating system prompt:

```
$ perl6 -n -e '$_.say if $_.chars > 20;' words.txt
```

The "-e" option tells Perl that the script to be run comes next on the command line between quotation marks. The "-n" asks Perl to read line by line the file after the end of the command line, to store each line in the $_ topical variable, and to apply the content of the script to each line. And the one-line script is just printing the content of $_ if its length is greater than 20.

To simplify a bit, the two options -n and -e may be grouped together as perl6 -ne. In addition, the $_ topical variable can be omitted in method calls (in other words, if a method has no invocant, the invocant will be defaulted to $_). Finally, the trailing semicolon may also be removed. The one-liner above can thus be made somewhat shorter:

```
$ perl6 -ne '.say if .chars > 20' words.txt
```

Remember that, if you're trying this under Windows, you need to replace the single quotes with double quotes (and vice-versa if the scripts itself contains double quotes):

```
C:\Users\Laurent>perl6 -ne ".say if .chars > 20" words.txt
```

Words with No "e" (Solution)

A subroutine that returns True for words that have no "e" (Exercise 8-2) is also quite straightforward:

```
sub has-no-e (Str $word) {
    return True unless defined index $word, "e";
    return False;
}
```

The subroutine simply returns True if the index function did not find any "e" in the word received as a parameter and False otherwise.

Note that this works correctly because the word list used (*words.txt*) is entirely in lowercase letters. The above subroutine would need to be modified if it might be called with words containing uppercase letters.

Since the defined function returns a Boolean value, we could shorten our subroutine to this:

```
sub has-no-e (Str $word) {
    not defined index $word, "e";
}
```

We could also have used a regex for testing the presence of a "e" on the second line of this subroutine:

```
    return True unless $word ~~ /e/;
```

This fairly concise syntax is appealing, but when looking for an exact literal match, the index function is likely to be slightly more efficient (faster) than a regex.

Looking for the words without "e" in our word list and counting them is not very difficult:

```
sub has-no-e (Str $word) {
    not defined index $word, "e";
}

my $total-count = 0;
my $count-no-e = 0;
for 'words.txt'.IO.lines -> $line {
    $total-count++;
    if has-no-e $line {
        $count-no-e++;
        say $line;
    }
}
say "=" x 24;
say "Total word count: $total-count";
say "Words without 'e': $count-no-e";
printf "Percentage of words without 'e': %.2f %%\n",
        100 * $count-no-e / $total-count;
```

The above program will display the following at the end of its output:

```
========================
Total word count: 113809
Words without 'e': 37641
Percentage of words without 'e': 33.07 %
```

So, less than one-third of the words of our list have no "e".

Avoiding Other Letters (Solution)

The avoids subroutine is a more general version of has_no_e, but it has the same structure:

```
sub avoids (Str $word, Str $forbidden) {
    for 0..$forbidden.chars - 1 -> $idx {
        my $letter = substr $forbidden, $idx, 1;
        return False if defined index $word, $letter;
    }
    True;
}
```

We can return False as soon as we find a forbidden letter; if we get to the end of the loop, we return True. Since a subroutine returns the last evaluated expression, we don't need to explicitly use a return True statement in the last code line above. I used this feature here as an example; you might find it clearer to explicitly `return` values, except perhaps for very simple one-line subroutines.

Note that we have here implicitly two nested loops. We could reverse the outer and the inner loops:

```
sub avoids (Str $word, Str $forbidden) {
    for 0..$words.chars - 1 -> $idx {
        my $letter = substr $words, $idx, 1;
        return False if defined index $forbidden, $letter;
    }
    True;
}
```

The main code calling the above subroutine is similar to the code calling `has-no-e` and might look like this:

```
my $total-count = 0;
my $count-no-forbidden = 0;

for 'words.txt'.IO.lines -> $line {
    $total-count++;
    $count-no-forbidden++ if avoids $line, "eiou";
}

say "=" x 24;
say "Total word count: $total-count";
say "Words without forbidden: $count-no-forbidden";
printf "Percentage of words with no forbidden letter: %.2f %%\n",
        100 * $count-no-forbidden / $total-count;
```

Using Only Some Letters (Solution)

`uses-only` is similar to our `avoids` subroutine except that the sense of the condition is reversed:

```
sub uses-only (Str $word, Str $available) {
    for 0..$word.chars - 1 -> $idx {
        my $letter = substr $word, $idx, 1;
        return False unless defined index $available, $letter;
    }
    True;
}
```

Instead of a list of forbidden letters, we have a list of available letters. If we find a letter in word that is not in `available`, we can return `False`. And we return `True` if we reach the loop end.

Using All Letters of a List (Solution)

uses-all is similar to the previous two subroutines, except that we reverse the role of the word and the string of letters:

```
sub uses-all(Str $word, Str $required) {
    for 0..$required.chars - 1 -> $idx {
        my $letter = substr $word, $idx, 1;
        return False unless defined index $word, $letter;
    }
    return True;
}
```

Instead of traversing the letters in $word, the loop traverses the required letters. If any of the required letters do not appear in the word, we can return False.

If you were really thinking like a computer scientist, you would have recognized that uses-all was an instance of a previously solved problem in reverse: if word A uses all letters of word B, then word B uses only letters of word A. So, we can call the uses-only subroutine and write:

```
sub uses-all ($word, $required) {
    return uses-only $required, $word;
}
```

This is an example of a program development plan called *reduction to a previously solved problem*, which means that you recognize the problem you are working on as an instance of a solved problem and apply an existing solution.

Alphabetic Order (Solution)

For is_abecedarian we have to compare adjacent letters. Each time in our for loop, we define one letter as our current letter and compare it with the previous one:

```
sub is_abecedarian ($word) {
    for 1..$word.chars - 1 -> $idx {
        my $curr-letter = substr $word, $idx, 1;
        return False if $curr-letter lt substr $word, $idx - 1, 1;
    }
    return True
}
```

An alternative is to use recursion:

```
sub is-abecedarian (Str $word) {
    return True if $word.chars <= 1;
    return False if substr($word, 0, 1) gt substr($word, 1, 1);
    return is-abecedarian substr $word, 1;
}
```

Another option is to use a while loop:

```
sub is_abecedarian (Str $word):
    my $i = 0;
    while $i < $word.chars -1 {
        if substr($word, $i, 1) gt substr ($word, $i+1, 1) {
            return False;
        }
        $i++;
    }
    return True;
}
```

The loop starts at $i=0 and ends when i=$word.chars -1. Each time through the loop, it compares the *i*th character (which you can think of as the current character) to the *i* + 1th character (which you can think of as the next).

If the next character is less than (alphabetically before) the current one, then we have discovered a break in the abecedarian trend, and we return False.

If we get to the end of the loop without finding a fault, then the word passes the test. To convince yourself that the loop ends correctly, consider an example like 'flossy'. The length of the word is 6, so the last time the loop runs is when $i is 4, which is the index of the second-to-last character. On the last iteration, it compares the second-to-last character (the second "s") to the last (the "y"), which is what we want.

Another Example of Reduction to a Previously Solved Problem

Here is a version of is_palindrome (see Exercise 5-3) that uses two indices; one starts at the beginning and goes up, while the other starts at the end and goes down:

```
sub one-char (Str $string, $idx) {
    return substr $string, $idx, 1;
}
sub is-palindrome (Str $word) {
    my $i = 0;
    my $j = $word.chars - 1;

    while $i < $j {
        return False if one-char($word, $i) ne one-char($word, $j);
        $i++;
        $j--;
    }
    return True;
}
```

Or we could reduce to a previously solved problem and write:

```
sub is-palindrome (Str $word) {
    return is-reverse($word, $word);
}
```

using is-reverse from "Debugging" on page 131 (but you should probably choose the corrected version of the is-reversed subroutine given in the appendix: see "Exercise: is-reverse Subroutine" on page 372).

Debugging

Testing programs is hard. The functions in this chapter are relatively easy to test because you can check the results by hand. Even so, it is somewhere between difficult and impossible to choose a set of words that test for all possible errors.

Taking has_no_e as an example, there are two obvious cases to check: words that have an "e" should return False, and words that don't should return True. You should have no trouble coming up with one of each.

Within each case, there are some less obvious subcases. Among the words that have an "e", you should test words with an "e" at the beginning, the end, and somewhere in the middle. You should test long words, short words, and very short words, like an empty string. The empty string is an example of a *special case*, which is one of the nonobvious cases where errors often lurk.

In addition to the test cases you generate, you can also test your program with a word list like *words.txt*. By scanning the output, you might be able to catch errors, but be careful: you might catch one kind of error (words that should not be included, but are) and not another (words that should be included, but aren't).

In general, testing can help you find bugs, but it is not easy to generate a good set of test cases, and even if you do, you can't be sure your program is correct.

According to a legendary computer scientist:

> Program testing can be used to show the presence of bugs, but never to show their absence!
>
> — Edsger W. Dijkstra

Glossary

file object
    A value that represents an open file.

reduction to a previously solved problem
    A way of solving a problem by expressing it as an instance of a previously solved problem.

special case

A test case that is atypical or nonobvious (and less likely to be handled correctly). The expressions *edge case* and *corner case* convey more or less the same idea.

Exercises

Exercise 8-7.

This question is based on a Puzzler that was broadcast on the radio program *Car Talk* (*http://www.cartalk.com/content/puzzlers*):

> Give me a word with three consecutive double letters. I'll give you a couple of words that almost qualify, but don't. For example, the word committee, c-o-m-m-i-t-t-e-e. It would be great except for the "i" that sneaks in there. Or Mississippi: M-i-s-s-i-s-s-i-p-p-i. If you could take out those i's it would work. But there is a word that has three consecutive pairs of letters and to the best of my knowledge this may be the only word. Of course there are probably 500 more but I can only think of one. What is the word?

Write a program to find it.

Solution: "Exercise 8-7: Consecutive Double Letters" on page 376.

Exercise 8-8.

Here's another *Car Talk* Puzzler (*http://www.cartalk.com/content/puzzlers*)):

> I was driving on the highway the other day and I happened to notice my odometer. Like most odometers, it shows six digits, in whole miles only. So, if my car had 300,000 miles, for example, I'd see 3-0-0-0-0-0.
>
> Now, what I saw that day was very interesting. I noticed that the last 4 digits were palindromic; that is, they read the same forward as backward. For example, 5-4-4-5 is a palindrome, so my odometer could have read 3-1-5-4-4-5.
>
> One mile later, the last 5 numbers were palindromic. For example, it could have read 3-6-5-4-5-6. One mile after that, the middle 4 out of 6 numbers were palindromic. And you ready for this? One mile later, all 6 were palindromic!
>
> The question is, what was on the odometer when I first looked?

Write a program that tests all the six-digit numbers and prints any numbers that satisfy these requirements.

Solution: "Exercise 8-8: Palindromes in Odometers" on page 377.

Exercise 8-9.

Here's another *Car Talk* Puzzler (*http://www.cartalk.com/content/puzzlers*) you can solve with a search:

Recently I had a visit with my mom and we realized that the two digits that make up my age when reversed resulted in her age. For example, if she's 73, I'm 37. We wondered how often this has happened over the years but we got sidetracked with other topics and we never came up with an answer.

When I got home I figured out that the digits of our ages have been reversible six times so far. I also figured out that if we're lucky it would happen again in a few years, and if we're really lucky it would happen one more time after that. In other words, it would have happened 8 times over all. So the question is, how old am I now?

Write a Perl program that searches for solutions to this Puzzler. Hint: you might find the string formatting method `sprintf` useful.

Solution: "Exercise 8-9: Palindromes in Ages" on page 378.

## CHAPTER 9

Arrays and Lists

This chapter presents some of Perl's most useful built-in types, arrays and lists.

Lists and Arrays Are Sequences

Like strings, *lists* and *arrays* are sequences of values. In a string, the values are characters; in a list or in an array, they can be any type. The values in a list or in an array are called *elements* or sometimes *items*.

There are several important differences between lists and arrays. The main ones are that lists are ordered and immutable collections of items: you can't change the number of items in a list and you can't change the individual items either. Arrays, by contrast, are variables and are generally mutable: you can add elements to an array, or remove elements from it. And you can access the individual elements of an array and modify them. For this to be possible, arrays usually have a name (as do other variables), although some arrays are anonymous, which means that they have no name, but have some other ways of accessing them.

A list is also ephemeral (unless it is assigned to a variable or some other thing): it ceases to exist as soon as it has been used, usually as soon as the program control flow goes to the next code line. An array, on the other hand, has some form of persistence: you may be able to use it somewhere else in the program if the variable containing it is still within scope.

There are several ways to create a new list; the simplest is to enumerate its values, separated by commas:

```
> 3, 4, 5
(3 4 5)
> say (3, 4, 5).WHAT;
(List)
```

```
say $_ for 1, 2, 3;
1
2
3
```

You don't need parentheses to create a list, but they are often useful to delimit it, i.e., to stipulate where it starts and where it ends, and, in some cases, to override precedence.

We used lists earlier in this book. If we write:

```
> print "$_ " for 1, 3, 5, 9, "\n";
1 3 5 9
  >
> print "$_ " for 1..10;
1 2 3 4 5 6 7 8 9 10 >
```

we are basically creating and using a list of integers (from the standpoint of the type hierarchy of Perl; this observation is not entirely accurate technically for the second example, since 1..10 has a *Range* type, and it gets transformed into a *Seq* type, but this approximation is good enough for our purposes here).

Arrays are variables whose names start with the sigil @. Named arrays need to be declared before they are used, just as any other variable we've seen so far (except the topical variable, $_). One of the easiest ways to create an array is to assign a list to it:

```
> my @odd_digits = 1, 3, 5, 7, 9;
[1 3 5 7 9]
> say @odd_digits.WHAT;
(Array)
> my @single_digit_numbers = 0..9;
[0 1 2 3 4 5 6 7 8 9]
```

Under the Perl REPL, an array is displayed between square brackets ([and]), while lists are displayed between round parentheses.

If the items don't contain any space characters, it is quite handy to construct a list (and assign it to an array if needed) using the <...> quote-word operator:

```
> my @weekdays = <mon tue wed thu fri>;
[mon tue wed thu fri]
> my @weekend = <sat sun>;
[sat sun]
```

The advantage of this construction is that there is no need to separate the items with commas and no need to insert them between quotes when the items are strings. Basically, the quote-word operator breaks up its content on whitespace and returns a list of words, which can then be used in a loop or assigned to an array as in the example above.

Most of the rest of this chapter will be devoted to arrays rather than lists, but keep in mind that many of the array functions and operators we will study here also work on lists (at least most of those that would not violate the immutability property of lists).

The items of an array (or a list) don't need to be of the same type:

```
> my @heterogeneous-array = 1, 2.3, pi, "str", (1, 2, 4);
[1 2.3 3.14159265358979 str (1 2 4)]
```

Here, the array is composed of an integer, a rational, a float (Num type), a string, and a list of three integers. It may not be advisable for the sake of the developer's mental sanity to use an array with such wildly heterogeneous items, but Perl will not complain about that: it is up to you to make sense of your data.

The previous array even contains a list of items. If you iterate over the elements of this array for example with a for loop statement, this list will arrive as one distinct element; it will not get "flattened" as three elements of the array. Similarly, elems is a method to count the number of items of an array (or of a list). Using it on the above array produces the following result:

```
> say @heterogeneous-array.elems;
5
```

As you can see, the (1, 2, 4) list "counts" as one single array element.

A list within another list is *nested*.

An array that contains no elements is called an empty array; you can create one with empty parentheses, ():

```
> my @empty = ();
[]
```

This code is really assigning an empty list to the array. But this syntax is usually not needed when creating a new empty array, since just declaring an array without defining it has the same effect:

```
> my @empty;
[]
```

So using the empty parentheses (i.e., assigning an empty list) would be needed essentially for resetting an existing array to an empty array.

Arrays Are Mutable

The syntax for accessing the elements of an array or a list uses the square brackets operator. The expression inside the brackets specifies the index or subscript, which can be a literal integer (or some value that can be coerced into an integer), a variable containing a numerical value, a list or a range of numerical values, an expression or a piece of code returning a numerical value, etc. Indices are offsets compared to the beginning of the array or the list (much in the same way as the values returned by the index function on strings), so they start at 0. Thus, the first item of an array has index 0, the second item index 1, and so on:

```
say <sat sun>[1];                  # -> sun  (accessing a list item)
my @weekdays = <mon tue wed thu fri>;      # assigning an array
say "The third day is @weekdays[2]";       # -> The third day is wed
```

You may also use ranges or lists of indices to access *slices* of an array or a list:

```
> my @even-digits = 0, 2, 4, 6, 8;
[0 2 4 6 8]
> my @small-even_digits = @even-digits[0..2];
[0 2 4]
> my @min-max-even-digits = @even-digits[0, 4]
[0 8]
```

If you need a slice in the opposite order, you can use the reverse function to reverse the range:

```
> my @reverse-small-even_digits = @even-digits[reverse 0..2];
[4 2 0]
```

or reverse the data returned by the slice expression:

```
> my @reverse-small-even_digits = reverse @even-digits[0..2];
[4 2 0]
```

Unlike lists, arrays are mutable. When the bracket operator appears after an array on the left side of an assignment, it identifies the element of the array that will be assigned:

```
> my @even-digits = 0, 2, 2, 6, 8;   # Oops, error on the second 2
[0 2 2 6 8]
> @even-digits[2] = 4; # fixing the faulty third digit
4
> say @even-digits
[0 2 4 6 8]
```

The third element of even-digits, which was (presumably by mistake) 2, is now 4. If the index corresponds to an item which does not exist yet in the array, the array will be expanded to include the new element:

```
> my @odds = 1, 3, 5;
[1 3 5]
> @odds[3] = 7;
7
> say @odds;
[1 3 5 7]
```

The elems function or method returns the number of elements of an array. The end function or method returns the index of the last elements of an array:

```
my @nums = 1..5;        # -> [1 2 3 4 5]
say @nums.elems;        # -> 5
say elems @nums;        # -> 5
say @nums.end;          # -> 4
```

The end method returns the result of the elems method minus one because, since indices start at 0, the index of the last element is one less than the number of elements.

The unique function or method returns a sequence of unique elements of the input list or array (i.e., it returns the original list without any duplicate values):

```
> say < a b d c a f d g>.unique;
(a b d c f g)
```

If you know that the input is sorted (and that, therefore, duplicates are adjacent), use the squish function instead of unique, as this is likely to be more efficient. The squish function removes adjacent duplicates.

To know whether two arrays are identical (structurally the same, with the same type and same values), use the eqv equivalence operator. To know whether they just contain the same elements, use the ~~ smart match operator. Between two arrays or lists, the == numeric equality operator will return True if the arrays have the same number of elements and False otherwise, because == coerces its arguments to numeric type, so that it compares the number of elements:

```
> my @even1 = 0, 2, 4, 6, 8;
[0 2 4 6 8]
> my @even2 = reverse 8, 6, 4, 2, 0;
[0 2 4 6 8]
> say @even1 eqv @even2          # same items, structurally the same
True
> say <1 2 3 4 5> eqv 1..5;      # same items, structurally different
False
> say <1 2 3 4 5> ~~ 1..5;       # same items, True
True
> my @array = 1..5;
[1 2 3 4 5]
>  say <1 2 3 4 5> ~~ @array;    # same elements, True
True
>  say <1 2 3 4 6> ~~ @array;    # not the same elements
False
> say <1 2 3 4 5> == <5 6 7 8 9>; # compares the numbers of items
True
```

The <1 2 3 4 5> eqv 1..5 statement returns False because, although they have the same items, the arguments are structurally different entities (one is a list and the other one a range).

Adding New Elements to an Array or Removing Some

We've just seen that assigning an item to an index that does not yet exist will expand the array. There are other ways of expanding an array.

Perl has operators to add elements to, or remove one element from, an array:

shift
> Removes the first item of an array and returns it

pop
> Removes the last item of an array and returns it

unshift
> Adds an item or a list of items to the beginning of an array

push
> Adds an item or a list of items to the end of an array

These are a few examples for each:

```
> my @numbers = <2 4 6 7>;
[2 4 6 7]
> push @numbers, 8, 9;
[2 4 6 7 8 9]
> unshift @numbers, 0, 1;
[0 1 2 4 6 7 8 9]
> my $num = shift @numbers
0
> $num = pop @numbers
9
> say @numbers
[1 2 4 6 7 8]
```

As you might expect by now, these routines also come with a method invocation syntax. For example:

```
> my @numbers = <2 4 6 7>;
[2 4 6 7]
> @numbers.push(8, 9)
[2 4 6 7 8 9]
```

Note, however, that if you push or unshift an array onto another array, you'll get something different than what you might expect:

```
> my @numbers = <2 4 6 7>;
[2 4 6 7]
> my @add-array = 8, 10;
[8 10]
> @numbers.push(@add-array);
[2 4 6 7 [8 10]]
```

As you can see, when @add-array is added as an entity to the @numbers array, @add-array becomes the new last item of the original array. If you want to add the items of @add-array to the original array, you may use the append method instead of push:

```
> my @numbers = <2 4 6 7>;
[2 4 6 7]
> @numbers.append(@add-array);
[2 4 6 7 8 10]
```

Or you can use the "|" prefix operator to flatten the added array into a list of arguments:

```
> my @numbers = <2 4 6 7>;
[2 4 6 7]
> @numbers.push(|@add-array);
[2 4 6 7 8 10]
```

There is also a prepend method that can replace unshift to add individual items of an array at the beginning of an existing array (instead of adding the array as a single entity).

Stacks and Queues

Stacks and queues are very commonly used data structures in computer science.

A stack is a *last in / first out (LIFO)* data structure. Think of piled-up plates. When you put a clean plate on the stack, you usually put it on top; when you take one out, you also take it from the top. So the first plate that you take is the last one that you added. A CS stack implements the same idea: you use it when the first piece of data you need from a data structure is the last one you added.

A queue, by contrast, is a *first in / first out (FIFO)* data structure. This is the idea of people standing in a line waiting to pay at the supermarket. The first person that will be served is the first person who entered the queue.

A stack may be implemented with an array and the push and pop functions, which respectively add an item (or several) at the end of an array and take one from the end of the array. This is a somewhat simplistic implementation of a stack:

```
sub put-in-stack (@stack, $new_item) {
    push @stack, $new_item;
}
sub take-from-stack (@stack) {
    my $item = pop @stack;
    return $item;
}
my @a-stack = 1, 2, 3, 4, 5;
put-in-stack @a-stack, 6;
say @a-stack;
say take-from-stack @a-stack for 1..3;
```

This example will print this:

```
[1 2 3 4 5 6]
6
5
4
```

This stack is simplistic because, at the very least, a more robust implementation should do something sensible when you try to take-from-stack from an empty stack. It would also be wise to add signatures to the subroutines. In addition, you might want to put-in-stack more than one element in one go. Take a look at the solution to the exercise on queues below ("Exercise: Implementing a Queue" on page 379) to figure out on how this stack may be improved.

You could obtain the same stack features using the unshift and shift functions instead of push and pop. The items will be added at the beginning of the array and taken from the beginning, but you will still have the LIFO behavior.

As an exercise, try to implement a FIFO queue on the same model. Hint: you probably want to use an array and the unshift and pop functions (or the push and shift functions). Solution: "Exercise: Implementing a Queue" on page 379.

Other Ways to Modify an Array

The shift and pop functions remove respectively the first and the last item of an array and return that item. It is possible to do almost the same operation on any item of an array, using the delete adverb:

```
my @fruit = <apple banana pear cherry pineapple orange>;
my $removed = @fruit[2]:delete;
say $removed;  # -> pear
say @fruit;    # -> [apple banana (Any) cherry pineapple orange]
```

Notice that the third element ("pear") is removed and returned, but the array is not reorganized; the operation leaves a sort of "empty slot," an undefined item, in the middle of the array. The colon (":") syntax used here is the operator for an adverb (we discussed adverbs in "Regular Expressions (Regexes)" on page 116); for the time being, you may think of it as a kind of special method operating on one element of an item collection.

We have seen how to use array slices to retrieve several items of an array or a list at a time. The same slice syntax can also be used on the left side of an assignment to modify some elements of an array:

```
my @digits = <1 2 3 6 5 4 7 8 9>;
@digits[2..4] = 4, 5, 6;
say @digits;   # -> [1 2 4 5 6 4 7 8 9]
```

Of course, you can't do this with lists, since, as you remember, they are immutable.

The `splice` function may be regarded as the Swiss Army knife of arrays. It can add, remove, and return one or several items to or from an array. The general syntax is as follows:

```
my @out_array = splice @array, $start, $num_elems, @replacement;
```

The arguments for `splice` are the input array, the index of the first element on which to make changes, the number of elements to be affected by the operation, and a list of replacements for the elements to be removed. For example, to perform the slice assignment shown just above, it is possible to do this:

```
my @digits = <1 2 3 6 5 4 7 8 9>
my @removed_digits = splice @digits, 3, 3, 4, 5, 6;
say @removed_digits;      # -> [6 5 4]
say @digits;              # -> [1 2 4 5 6 7 8 9]
```

Here, the `splice` statement removed three elements (6, 5, 4) and replaced them with the replacement arguments (4, 5, 6). It returned the removed items to `@removed_dig its`. The number of replacements does not need to be the same as the number of removed items, in which case the array size will grow or shrink. For example, if no replacement is provided, then `splice` will just remove and return the required number of elements and the array size will be reduced by the same number:

```
my @digits = 1..9;
my @removed_digits = splice @digits, 3, 2;
say @removed_digits;      # -> [4 5]
say @digits;              # -> [1 2 3 6 7 8 9]
```

Conversely, if the number of elements to be removed is zero, no element will be removed, an empty array will be returned, and the elements in the replacement list will be added in the right place:

```
my @digits = <1 2 3 6 4 7 8 9>;
my @removed_digits = splice @digits, 3, 0, 42;
say @removed_digits;      # -> []
say @digits;              # -> [1 2 3 42 6 4 7 8 9]
```

Assuming the `shift` function did not exist in Perl, you could write a `my-shift` subroutine to simulate it:

```
sub my-shift (@array) {
    my @result = splice @array, 0, 1;
    return @result[0];
}
my @letters = 'a'..'j';
my $letter = my-shift @letters;
say $letter;              # -> a
say @letters;             # -> [b c d e f g h i j]
```

We might raise an exception if the array passed to `my-shift` is empty. This could be done by modifying the subroutine as follows:

```
sub my-shift (@array) {
    die "Cannot my-shift from an empty array" unless @array;
    my @result = splice @array, 0, 1;
    return @result[0];
}
```

or by adding a nonempty constraint on the array in the subroutine signature:

```
sub my-shift (@array where @array > 0) {
    my @result = splice @array, 0, 1;
    return @result[0];
}
```

The `@array > 0` expression evaluates to `True` if the number of elements of the array is more than 0, i.e., if the array is not empty. It is equivalent to `@array.elems > 0`.

As an exercise, write subroutines to simulate the `pop`, `unshift`, `push`, and `delete` built-ins. Solution: "Exercise: Other Ways to Modify an Array" on page 383.

Traversing a List

The most common way to traverse the elements of a list or an array is with a `for` loop. The syntax for an array is the same as what we have already seen in earlier chapters for lists:

```
my @colors = <red orange yellow green blue indigo violet>;
for @colors -> $color {
    say $color;
}
```

This works well if you only need to read the elements of the list. But if you want to write or update the elements of an array, you need a doubly pointy block. For example, you might use the `tc` (title case) function to capitalize the first letter of each word of the array:

```
my @colors = <red orange yellow green blue indigo violet>;
for @colors <-> $color {$color = tc $color};
say @colors;   # -> [Red Orange Yellow Green Blue Indigo Violet]
```

Here the `$color` loop variable is a read-and-write alias on the array's items, so that changes made to this alias will be reflected in the array. This works well with arrays, but would not work with lists, which are immutable. You would get an error with a list:

```
> for <red orange yellow> <-> $color { $color = tc $color}
Parameter '$color' expected a writable container, but got Str value...
```

You may also use the syntax of a `for` loop with the `$_` topical variable. For example, this uses the `uc` (uppercase) function to capitalize each word of the previous array:

```
for @colors {
    $_ = $_.uc
}
say @colors; # -> [RED ORANGE YELLOW GREEN BLUE INDIGO VIOLET]
```

Sometimes, you want to traverse an array and need to know the index of the elements you are visiting. A common way to do that is to use the .. range operator to iterate on the indices. For instance, to print the index and the value of each element of an array:

```
for 0..@colors.end -> $idx {
    say "$idx  @colors[$idx]";
}
```

This is useful, for example, for traversing two (or more) arrays in parallel:

```
my @letters = 'a'..'e';
my @numbers = 1..5;
for 0..@letters.end -> $idx {
    say "@letters[$idx] -> @numbers[$idx]";
}
```

which will print:

```
a -> 1
b -> 2
c -> 3
d -> 4
e -> 5
```

You don't really need to specify the index range yourself, as the keys function will return a list of indices for the array or the list:

```
for keys @colors -> $idx {
    say "$idx  @colors[$idx]";
}
```

Another way to iterate over the indices and values of an array is the kv ("keys values") function or method, which returns the index and value of each array item:

```
for @letters.kv -> $idx, $val {
    say "$idx $val";
}
```

In list context, @letters.kv simply returns an interleaved sequence of indexes and values:

```
my @letters = 'a'..'e';
say @letters.kv;    # -> (0 a 1 b 2 c 3 d 4 e)
```

It is the pointy block with two iteration variables that makes it possible to process both an index and a value at each step of the loop. You can of course have more than two iteration variables if needed.

New Looping Constructs

Since the subject of this chapter is arrays and lists, it is probably the right time to briefly study two looping constructs that I left aside so far.

The first one uses the same `for` keyword as above, but with a different syntax for the iteration variable(s):

```
my @letters = 'a'..'e';
for @letters {
    say $^a-letter;
}
```

The `^` in the `$^a-letter` variable is called a *twigil*, i.e., sort of a secondary sigil. When there is a twigil, the first symbol (here, the `$` sign) has the same meaning as usual sigils (here, it denotes a scalar variable), and the second one (here, `^`) extends the variable description and usually modifies its scope. In this specific case, the second character states that the `$^a-letter` variable is a *placeholder parameter* or a *self-declared positional parameter*. This is a positional parameter of the current block that needs not be declared in the signature.

If the block uses more than one placeholder, they are associated to the input according to their lexicographic (alphabetic) order:

```
my @letters = 'a'..'e';
for @letters.kv {
    say "$^a -> $^b";
}
```

which will print:

```
0 -> a
1 -> b
2 -> c
3 -> d
4 -> e
```

As seen just above, the kv function returns an interleaved sequence of indexes and values. Since `$^a` comes before `$^b` in alphabetic order, `$^a` will be bound to the index and `$^b` with the value for each pair of the input.

Placeholders can also be used for subroutines:

```
> sub divide { $^first / $^second }
sub divide ($first, $second) { #`(Sub|230787048) ... }
> divide 6, 4
1.5
```

These placeholders aren't used very often for simply traversing arrays, but we will see later how they are very useful in cases where is would be quite unpractical to have to declare the parameters.

The second new looping construct I want to introduce here uses the `loop` keyword and is similar to the C-style `for` loop (i.e., the loop of the C programming language). In this type of loop, you declare between a pair of parentheses three expressions separated by semicolons: the iteration variable's initial value, the condition on which the loop should terminate, and the change made to the iteration variable on each iteration:

```
loop (my $i = 0; $i < 5; $i++) {
    say $i, " -> " ~ @letters[$i];
}
```

For most common loops, the `for` loops seen earlier are easier to write and usually more efficient than this construct. This special `loop` construct should probably be used only when the exit condition or the change made to the iteration variable is quite unusual and would be difficult to express in a regular `for` loop. As an exception, the `loop` construct with no three-part specification is quite common and even idiomatic for making an infinite loop:

```
loop {
    # do something
    # last if ...
}
```

Map, Filter, and Reduce

When traversing the elements of an array (or a list), so far we have processed one item at a time with a loop. We will now study ways to process all the elements in one go.

Reducing a List to a Value

To add up all the numbers in a list, you can use a `for` loop like this:

```
sub add_all (@numbers) {
    my $total = 0;
    for @numbers -> $x {
        $total += $x;
    }
    return $total;
}
```

`$total` is initialized to 0. Each time through the loop, `$x` gets one element from the list and is added to `$total`. As the loop runs, `total` accumulates the sum of the elements; a variable used this way is sometimes called an *accumulator*.

An operation like this that combines a sequence of elements into a single value is often called a reduction operation because its effect is to *reduce* all the items to one element (this is also sometimes called "folding" in some other programming languages). These ideas are derived from functional programming languages such as LISP (whose name stands for "list processing").

Perl 6 has a reduce function, which generates a single "combined" value from a list of values by iteratively applying to each item of a list a function that knows how to combine two values. Using the reduce function to compute the sum of the first 10 numbers might look like this:

```
> my $sum = reduce { $^a + $^b }, 1..10;
55
```

Remember the *factorial* function of "for Loops" on page 64? It used a for loop to compute the product of the *n* first integers up to a limit. It could be rewritten as follows using the reduce function:

```
sub factorial (Int $num) {
    return reduce { $^a * $^b }, 1..$num;
}
say factorial 10;   # -> 3628800
```

In fact, the code to compute the factorial is so short with the reduce function that it may be argued that it has become unnecessary to write a subroutine for that. You could just "inline" the code:

```
my $fact10 = reduce { $^a * $^b }, 1..10;    # -> 3628800
```

We can do many more powerful things with that, but we'll come back to that later, as it requires a few syntactic features that we haven't seen yet.

The Reduction Metaoperator

Perl 6 also has a reduction operator, or rather a reduction *metaoperator*. An operator usually works on variables or values; a metaoperator acts on other operators. Given a list and an operator, the [...] metaoperator iteratively applies the operator to all the values of the list to produce a single value.

For example, the following also prints the sum of all the elements of a list:

```
say [+] 1, 2, 3, 4;         # ->   10
```

This basically takes the first two values, adds them up, and adds the result to the next value, and so on. Actually, there is a form of this operator, with a backslash before the operator, which also returns the intermediate results:

```
say [\+] 1, 2, 3, 4;        # -> (1 3 6 10)
```

This metaoperator can be used to transform basically any associative infix operator[1] into a list operator returning a single value.

The factorial function can now be rewritten as:

```
sub fact(Int $x){
    [*] 1..$x;
}
my $factorial = fact(10);    # -> 3628800
```

The reduction metaoperator can also be used with relational operators to check whether the elements of an array or a list are in the correct numerical or alphabetical order:

```
say [<] 3, 5, 7;          # -> True
say [<] 3, 5, 7, 6;       # -> False
say [lt] <a c d f r t y>; # -> True
```

Mapping a List to Another List

Sometimes you want to traverse one list while building another. For example, the following function takes a list of strings and returns a new list that contains capitalized strings:

```
sub capitalize_all(@words):
    my @result;
    push @result, $_.uc for @words;
    return @result;
}
my @lc_words = <one two three>;
my @all_caps = capitalize_all(@lc_words); # -> [ONE TWO THREE]
```

@result is declared without any assignment and is thus created as an empty array; each time through the loop, we append the next element. So @result is another kind of accumulator.

An operation like `capitalize_all` is sometimes called a *map* because it "maps" a function (in this case the uc method) to each of the elements in a sequence.

Perl has a map function that makes it possible to do that in just one statement:

```
my @lc_words = <one two three>;
my @all_caps = map { .uc }, @lc_words;     # -> [ONE TWO THREE]
```

Here, the map function applies the uc method to each item of the @lc_words array and returns them to the @all_caps array. More precisely, the map function iteratively assigns each item of the @lc_words array to the $_ topical variable, applies the code

---

1 An infix operator is an operator that is placed between its two operands.

block following the map keyword to $_ in order to create new values, and returns a list of these new values.

To generate a list of even numbers between 1 and 10, we might use the range operator to generate numbers between 1 and 5 and use map to multiply them by two:

```
my @evens = map { $_ * 2 }, 1..5;  # -> [2 4 6 8 10]
```

Instead of using the $_ topical variable, we might also use a pointy block syntax with an explicit iteration variable:

```
my @evens = map -> $num { $num * 2 }, 1..5;  # -> [2 4 6 8 10]
```

or an anonymous block with a placeholder variable:

```
my @evens = map { $^num * 2 }, 1..5;  # -> [2 4 6 8 10]
```

Instead of a code block, the first argument to map can be a code reference (a subroutine reference):

```
sub double-sq-root-plus-one (Numeric $x) {
    1 + 2 * sqrt $x;
}
my @results = map &double-sq-root-plus-one, 4, 16, 42;
say @results;     # -> [5 9 13.9614813968157]
```

The subroutine name needs to be prefixed with the ampersand sigil to make clear that it is a parameter to map and not a direct call of the subroutine.

If the name of the array on the left side and on the right side of the assignment is the same, then the modification seems to be made "in place," i.e., it appears as if the original array is modified in the process.

This is an immensely powerful and expressive function; we will come back to it later.

Filtering the Elements of a List

Another common list operation is to select some elements from a list and return a sublist. For example, the following function takes a list of strings and returns a list that contains only the strings containing a vowel:

```
sub contains-vowel(Str $string) {
    return True if $string ~~ /<[aeiouy]>/;
}
sub filter_words_with_vowels (@strings) {
    my @kept-string;
    for @string -> $st {
        push @kept-string, $st if contains-vowel $st;
    }
    return @kept-string;
}
```

contains-vowel is a subroutine that returns True if the string contains at least one vowel (we consider "y" to be a vowel for our purpose).

The filter_words_with_vowels subroutine will return a list of strings containing at least one vowel.

An operation like filter_words_with_vowels is called a *filter* because it selects some of the elements and filters out the others.

Perl has a function called grep to do that in just one statement:

```
my @filtered = grep { /<[aeiouy]>/ }, @input;
```

The name of the grep built-in function used to filter some input comes from the Unix world, where it is a utility that filters the lines that match a given pattern from an input file.

In the code example above, all of @input strings will be tested against the grep block, and those matching the regex will go into the filtered array. Just like map, the grep function iteratively assigns each item of the @input array to the $_ topical variable, applies the code block following the grep keyword to $_, and returns a list of the values for which the code block evaluates to true. Here, the code block is a simple regex applied to the $_ variable.

Just as for map, we could have used a function reference as the first argument to grep:

```
my @filtered = grep &contains-vowel, @input;
```

To generate a list of even numbers between 1 and 10, we might use the range operator to generate numbers between 1 and 10 and use grep to filter out odd numbers:

```
my @evens = grep { $_ %% 2 }, 1..10;  # -> [2 4 6 8 10]
```

As an exercise, write a program using map to produce an array containing the square of the numbers of the input list and a program using grep to keep only the numbers of an input list that are perfect squares. Solution: "Exercise: Mapping and Filtering the Elements of a List" on page 385.

Most common list operations can be expressed as a combination of map, grep and reduce.

Higher-Order Functions and Functional Programming

Besides their immediate usefulness, the reduce, map, and grep functions we have been using here do something qualitatively new. The arguments to these functions are not just data: their first argument is a code block or a function. We are not only passing to them the data that they will have to use or transform, but we are also passing the code that will process the data.

The reduce, map, and grep functions are what are often called *higher-order functions*, functions that manipulate not only data, but also other functions. These functions can be thought of as generic abstract functions—they perform a purely technical operation: process the elements of a list and apply to each of them a behavior defined in the code block or the function of the first parameter.

These ideas are to a large extent rooted in functional programming, a programming paradigm that is very different from what we have seen so far and that has been implemented historically in languages such as Lisp, Caml, Ocaml, Scheme, Erlang, or Haskell. Perl 6 is not a functional programming language in the same sense as these languages, because it can also use other programming paradigms, but it has incorporated most of their useful features, so that you can use the expressive power and inherent safety of this programming model without being forced to do so if and when you would prefer a different model, and without having to learn a totally new syntax that may sometimes look somewhat abstruse or even clunky.

This is immensely useful and can give you an incredible expressive power for solving certain types of problems. But other types of problems might be better solved with the more "traditional" procedural or imperative programming model, while others may benefit from an object-oriented approach. Perl 6 lets you choose the programming model you want to use, and even makes it possible to seamlessly combine several of them in the same program.

Functional programming is so important in my opinion that a full chapter of this book will be devoted to the functional programming features of Perl (see Chapter 14). Before that, make sure to read "Encapsulating the data" on page 382 in the array and list section of the appendix.

Fixed-Size, Typed, and Shaped Arrays

By default, arrays can contain items of any type, including items of different types, and can auto-extend as you need. Perl will take care of the underlying gory details for you, so that you don't have to worry about them. This is very practical but also comes with a cost: some array operations might be unexpectedly slow, because Perl may have to perform quite a bit of housecleaning behind the scenes, such as memory allocation or reallocation, copying a full array within memory, etc.

In some cases, however, it is possible to know beforehand the size of an array and the data type of its items. If Perl knows about these, it might be able to work faster and use much less memory. It might also help you to prevent subtle bugs.

To declare the type of the elements of an array, just specify it when declaring the array. For example, to declare an array of integers:

```
> my Int @numbers = 1..20;
[1 2 3 4 5 6 7 8 9 10 11 12 13 14 15 16 17 18 19 20]
```

```
> @numbers[7] = 3.5;      # ERROR
Type check failed in assignment to @numbers; expected Int but got Rat
  in block <unit> at <unknown file> line 1
```

Similarly, you can declare the size of an array. Such arrays are sometimes called *shaped arrays*. There are 12 months in a year, so you might tell Perl that your @months array will never contain more than 12 items:

```
> my @months[12] = 1..7;
[1 2 3 4 5 6 7 (Any) (Any) (Any) (Any) (Any)]
> say @months.elems
12
> say @months[3];
4
> say @months[12];
Index 12 for dimension 1 out of range (must be 0..11)
```

Here, Perl has allocated 12 "slots" to the array, even though the last five are currently undefined. Perl may not need to reallocate memory when you define the 10th item of the array. And Perl tells you about your mistake if you accidentally try to access an out-of-range item.

Defining both the type of the elements and the maximal size of the array may lead to a noticeable performance gain in terms of execution speed (at least for some operations) and reduce significantly the memory usage of the program, especially when handling large arrays.

Multidimensional Arrays

The arrays we have seen so far are one-dimensional. In some languages, such arrays are called *vectors*. But arrays can also be multidimensional (you may then call them *matrices*).

For example, you might use a two-dimensional array to store a list of employees with their respective salaries:

```
> my @employees;
[]
> @employees[0;0] = "Liz";
Liz
> @employees[0;1] = 3000;
3000
> @employees[1] = ["Bob"; 2500];
[Bob 2500]
> @employees[2] = ["Jack"; 2000];
[Jack 2000]
> @employees[3] = ["Betty"; 1800];
[Betty 1800]
> say @employees[1;1];
2500
```

```
> say @employees[2];
[Jack 2000]
> say @employees;
[[Liz 3000] [Bob 2500] [Jack 2000] [Betty 1800]]
```

It is possible to have more than two dimensions. For example, we could have a tridimensional matrix to store the temperatures in a chemical reactor, measured in various locations identified by their *x*, *y*, and *z* coordinates:

```
my @temp;
@temp[1;3;4] = 80;
```

For this type of data, however, it is often easier to use the data structure that we will cover in Chapter 10.

Multidimensional arrays can also have a fixed size. For example, this may be a declaration for two-dimensional array where the first dimension is the month in the year and the second the day in the month:

```
my @date[12, 31];
```

Sorting Arrays or Lists

Sorting data is a very common operation in computer science. Perl has a `sort` function that can sort an array or a list and return the sorted result:

```
say sort <4 6 2 9 1 5 11>;  # -> (1 2 4 5 6 9 11)
```

There are several types of sorts. The most common are numeric sort and lexicographic (or alphabetic) sort. They differ in the way they compare individual items to be sorted.

In alphabetic sort, you first compare the first letter of the words to be compared; a word starting with an "a" will always come before a word starting with a "b" (or any other letter) in an ascending sort, irrespective of the value or number of the other characters. You need to compare the second character of two words only if the first character of these words is the same.

Numeric sorting is very different: it is the overall value of the number that is of interest. For example, if we are sorting integers, 11 is larger than 9 because it has more digits. But alphabetic sorting of 9 and 11 would consider 11 to be smaller than 9, because the first digit is smaller.

So an alphabetic or lexicographic sort of the list of integers above would return:

```
(1 11 2 4 5 6 9)
```

The consequence is that, with many programming languages, when you want to sort data, you need to specify which type of sort you want. With consistent data (every item of the same type), Perl 6 is usually clever enough to find out which type of sort is best suited to your needs. So, for example, this code will perform the type of sort that you probably expect:

```
say sort <ac a bc ab abc cb ca>; # ->(a ab abc ac bc ca cb)
```

As you can see, Perl correctly sorts both numeric and string types. Even with mixed data types, sort can do a pretty good job at providing a result that may very well be what you are looking for:

```
say sort <1 b 11 5 cb 4 12 a ab abc 42 ac bc ca >;
        # -> (1 4 5 11 12 42 a ab abc ac b bc ca cb)
```

There are cases, however, where this simple use of the sort function will fail to return what you probably want:

```
say sort <a ab abc A bc BAC AC>; # -> (A AC BAC a ab abc bc)
```

Here, sort puts all strings starting with an uppercase letter before any string starting with a lowercase letter, probably not what you want. It looks even worse if the strings use extended ASCII characters:

```
say sort <a ab àb abc Ñ A bc BAC AC>;
        # -> (A AC BAC a ab abc bc Ñ àb)
```

The reason is that, when sorting strings, sort uses the internal numeric encoding of letters. This was sometimes called "ASCIIbetical" order (by contrast with alphabetical order), but the term is now too limited and somewhat obsolete, because Perl 6 is using Unicode rather than ASCII.

Clearly, these are cases where more advanced sorting techniques are needed.

More Advanced Sorting Techniques

The sort routine typically takes two arguments, a code object and a list of items to be sorted, and returns a new sorted list. If no code object is specified, as in the examples we have seen above, the cmp built-in comparison operator is used to compare the elements. If a code object is provided (and if it accepts two arguments), then it is used to perform the comparison, which tells sort which of the two elements should come first in the final order.

There are three built-in comparison operators that can be used for sorting. They are sometimes called three-way comparators because they compare their operands and return a value meaning that the first operand should be considered less than, equal to, or more than the second operand for the purpose of determining in which order these operands should be sorted. The leg operator coerces its arguments to strings and performs a lexicographic comparison. The <=> operator coerces its arguments to numbers (real) and does a numeric comparison. The aforementioned cmp operator is the "smart" three-way comparator, which compares strings with string semantics and numbers with number semantics.

Most of our simple examples above worked well with strings and numbers because they implicitly used the default `cmp` operator, which "guesses" quite well which type of comparison to perform.

In other words, this:

```
say sort <4 6 2 9 1 5 11>;  # -> (1 2 4 5 6 9 11)
```

is equivalent to this:

```
say sort { $^a cmp $^b }, <4 6 2 9 1 5 11>;
    # -> (1 2 4 5 6 9 11)
```

The code block used here as the first argument to the `sort` routine again uses the placeholder parameters (or self-declared parameters) seen earlier in this chapter. The `cmp` routine receives two arguments that are bound to `$^a` and `$^b` and returns to the `sort` function information about which of the two items should come first in the resulting order.

If you wanted to sort in reverse order, you could just swap the order of the two placeholder parameters:

```
say sort { $^b cmp $^a }, <4 6 2 9 1 5 11>;
    # -> (11 9 6 5 4 2 1)
```

Note that this example is given only for the purpose of explaining some features of the placeholder parameters. To sort the array we've presented here in descending order, it might just be easier to obtain the same result with the following code:

```
say reverse sort <4 6 2 9 1 5 11>;  # -> (11 9 6 5 4 2 1)
```

The reason `sort` does a good job even with mixed strings and integers is because the default comparison function, `cmp`, is pretty clever and guesses by looking at its arguments whether it should perform a lexicographic order or numeric order comparison.

If sorting gets too complicated for `cmp`, or, more generally, when a specific or custom order is required, then you have to write your own ad-hoc comparison subroutine.

For example, if we take again the example of strings with mixed-case letters, we may achieve a case-insensitive alphabetical order this way:

```
say sort { $^a.lc cmp $^b.lc}, <a ab abc A bc BAC AC>;
    # -> (a A ab abc AC BAC bc)
```

or this way:

```
say sort { $^a.lc leg $^b.lc}, <a ab abc A bc BAC AC>;
    # -> (a A ab abc AC BAC bc)
```

Here, when the comparison code block receives its two arguments, the `lc` method casts them to lowercase before performing the comparison. Notice that this has no impact on the case of the output, since the lowercase transformation is local to the comparison code block and has no impact on the data handled by `sort`. We will see shortly that there is a simpler and more efficient way of doing such a transformation before comparing the arguments.

If the comparison specification is more complicated, we may need to write it in a separated subroutine and let `sort` call that subroutine. Suppose we have a list of strings that are all formed of leading digits followed by a group of letters and possibly followed by other irrelevant characters, and that we want to sort the strings according to the group of letters that follows the digits.

Let's start by writing the comparison subroutine:

```
sub my_comp ($str1, $str2) {
    my $cmp1 = $0 if $str1 ~~ /\d+(\w+)/;
    my $cmp2 = $0 if $str2 ~~ /\d+(\w+)/;
    return $cmp1 cmp $cmp2;
}
```

Nothing complicated: it takes two arguments, uses a regex for extracting the group of letters in each of the arguments, and returns the result of the `cmp` function on the extracted strings. In the real world, something might need to be done if either of the extractions fails, but we will assume for our purposes here that this will not happen.

The sorting is now quite straightforward; we just need to pass the above subroutine to the `sort` function:

```
say sort &my_comp, < 22ac 34bd 56aa3 12c; 4abc( 1ca 45bc >;
    # -> (56aa3 4abc( 22ac 45bc 34bd 12c; 1ca)
```

We only need to prefix the comparison subroutine with the "&" ampersand sigil and it works fine: the strings are sorted in accordance to the letter groups that follow the leading digits.

In all the examples above, the comparison subroutine accepted two parameters, the two items to be compared. The `sort` function may also work with a code object taking only one parameter. In that case, the code object is not a comparison code block or subroutine, but is a code object implementing the transformation to be applied to the items before using the default `cmp` comparison routine.

For example, if we take once more the example of strings with mixed-case letters, we may achieve a case-insensitive alphabetical order yet in a new way:

```
say sort { $_.lc }, <a ab abc A bc BAC AC>;
    # -> (a A ab abc AC BAC bc)
```

This could also be written with a placeholder parameter:

```
say sort { $^a.lc }, <a ab abc A bc BAC AC>;
    # -> (a A ab abc AC BAC bc)
```

Here, since the comparison code block takes only one argument, it is meant to transform each of the items to be compared before performing the standard `cmp` routine on the arguments. This not only makes things simpler, but is also probably more efficient, especially if the number of items to be sorted is large and if the transformation subroutine is relatively costly: the transformed values are actually *cached* (i.e., stored in memory for repeated use), so that the transformation is done only once for each item, despite the fact that the comparison routine is called many times for each item in a sort.

Similarly, we could sort numbers according to their absolute values:

```
say sort {$_.abs}, <4 -2 5 3 -12 42 8 -7>; # -> (-2 3 4 5 -7 8 -12 42)
```

If you think about it, the "more complicated" example with digits and letters requiring a separate subroutine is also applying the same transformation to both its arguments. As an exercise, write a (simpler) sorting program using a transformation subroutine and the default `cmp` operator on transformed items. Solution: "Exercise: Advanced Sorting Techniques" on page 386.

Needless to say, the (so-called) advanced uses of the `sort` function presented in this section are yet more examples of the functional programming style. The comparison subroutines and the transformation subroutines are passed around as arguments to the `sort` function, and, more broadly, all of the functions, subroutines, and code blocks used here are higher-order functions or first-class functions.

Debugging

Careless use of arrays (and other mutable objects) can lead to long hours of debugging. Here are some common pitfalls and ways to avoid them:

1. Some array built-in functions and methods modify their argument(s) and others don't.

   It may be tempting to write code like this:

   ```
   @array = splice @array, 1, 2, $new_item;   # WRONG!
   ```

   The `splice` function returns the elements it has deleted from the array, not the array itself, which is modified "in place."

   Before using array methods and operators, you should read the documentation carefully and perhaps test them in interactive mode.

   When traversing an array, for example with `for` or `map`, the `$_` topical variable is an *alias* for the successive items of the array, and not a copy of them. This means that if you change `$_`, the change will be reflected in the array. There may be some cases where this is what you want, and others where you don't care (if you no longer need the original array), but this technique is error-prone and should perhaps be avoided (or at least used only with great care).

```
my @numbers = <1 2 3>;
push @doubles, $_*=2 for @numbers;  # WRONG (probably)
say @numbers; # -> [2 4 6]
```

The error here is that the $_*=2 statement is modifying $_, so that the @numbers array is also modified, whereas the intent was certainly to populate the new numbers into @doubles, not to modify @numbers.

The same code applied to a literal list instead of an array leads to a runtime error because a list is immutable:

```
> push @doubles, $_*=2 for <1 2 3>; # WRONG (definitely)
Cannot assign to an immutable value
```

The fix is quite easy in this case and consists of using an expression that does not modify $_ but returns the new desired value:

```
push @doubles, $_ * 2 for @numbers; # OK
```

The same goes for map:

```
my @numbers = <1 2 3>;
say map { ++$_}, @numbers;          # WRONG (probably)
say @numbers; # -> [2 3 4]
```

Here again, using an expression that does not modify $_ but instead returns the new desired value will fix the problem:

```
my @numbers = <1 2 3>;
say map { $_ + 1}, @numbers;        # -> (2 3 4)
say @numbers; # -> [1 2 3]
```

Glossary

accumulator
    A variable used in a loop to add up or accumulate a result.

alias
    A circumstance where an identifier refers directly to some variable or value, so that a change to it would lead to a change to the variable or value. It essentially means having two names for the same value, container, or object.

array
    A variable containing a mutable sequence of values.

element

One of the values in a list or an array (or some other sequence), also called items.

filter

A processing pattern that traverses a list and selects the elements that satisfy some criterion. `grep` is a Perl implementation of a filter.

list

An immutable sequence of values.

map

A processing pattern that traverses a sequence and performs an operation on each element. Also the name of a Perl built-in function that performs such a processing pattern.

nested array

An array that is an element of another array.

reduce

A processing pattern that traverses a sequence and accumulates the elements into a single result.

Exercises

Exercise 9-1.

Write a subroutine called `nested-sum` that takes an array of arrays of integers and adds up the elements from all of the nested arrays. For example:

```
my @AoA = [[1, 2], [3], [4, 5, 6]];
say nested-sum(@AoA);        # -> 21
```

Solution: "Exercise 9-1: Nested Sum" on page 386.

Exercise 9-2.

Write a subroutine called `cumul-sum` that takes a list of numbers and returns the cumulative sum; that is, a new list where the ith element is the sum of the first $i + 1$ elements from the original list. For example:

```
my @nums = [1, 2, 3, 4];
say cumul-sum(@nums);          # -> [1, 3, 6, 10]
```

Solution: "Exercise 9-2: Cumulative Sum" on page 387.

Exercise 9-3.

Write a subroutine called `middle` that takes a list and returns a new list that contains all but the first and last elements. For example:

```
say middle(1, 2, 3, 4);       # -> (2, 3)
```

Solution: "Exercise 9-3: Middle" on page 388.

Exercise 9-4.

Write a subroutine called `chop-it` that takes an array, modifies it by removing the first and last elements, and returns nothing useful. For example:

```
my @nums = 1, 2, 3, 4;
chop-it(@nums);
say @nums;                    # -> [2, 3]
```

Solution: "Exercise 9-4: Chop" on page 388.

Exercise 9-5.

Write a subroutine called `is-sorted` that takes a list (or array) of numbers as a parameter and returns `True` if the list is sorted in ascending order and `False` otherwise. For example:

```
> is-sorted (1, 2, 2);
True
> is-sorted (1, 2, 1);
False
```

Solution: "Exercise 9-5: Subroutine is-sorted" on page 389.

Exercise 9-6.

Two words are anagrams if you can rearrange the letters from one to spell the other. Write a subroutine called `is-anagram` that takes two strings and returns `True` if they are anagrams.

Solution: "Exercise 9-6: Subroutine is-anagram" on page 390.

Exercise 9-7.

Write a subroutine called `has-duplicates` that takes a list or an array and returns `True` if there is any element that appears more than once. It should not modify the original input.

Solution: "Exercise 9-7: Subroutine has-duplicates" on page 391.

Exercise 9-8.

This exercise pertains to the so-called Birthday Paradox, which you can read about at *http://en.wikipedia.org/wiki/Birthday_paradox.*

If there are 23 students in your class, what are the chances that two of you have the same birthday? You can estimate this probability by generating random samples of 23 birthdays and checking for duplicates. Hint: you can generate random birthdays with the rand and the int functions.

Solution: "Exercise 9-8: Simulating the Birthday Paradox" on page 392.

Exercise 9-9.

Write a subroutine that reads the file *words.txt* and builds a list with one element per word. Write two versions of this function, one using the push method and the other using the idiom unshift. Which one takes longer to run? Why?

Solution: "Exercise 9-9: Comparing push and unshift" on page 393.

Exercise 9-10.

To check whether a word is in our standard word list, you could check each element in turn, but it would be slow because it searches through the words in order.

If the words are in alphabetical order (which is the case of our word list), we can speed things up considerably with a *bisection search* (also known as binary search), which is similar to what you do when you look a word up in the dictionary. You start somewhere in the middle and check to see whether the word you are looking for comes before the word in the middle of the list. If so, you search the first half of the list the same way. Otherwise, you search the second half.

Either way, you cut the remaining search space in half. If the word list has 113,809 words, it will take at most about 17 steps to find the word or conclude that it's not there.

Write a function called bisect that takes a sorted list and a target value and returns information about whether the target value is in the list or not.

Solution: "Exercise 9-10: Bisection Search in a List" on page 394.

Exercise 9-11.

Two words are a "reverse pair" if each is the reverse of the other. For example, "depot" and "toped" form a reverse pair; other examples include "reward" and "drawer," or "desserts" and "stressed." Write a program that finds all the reverse pairs in the *words.txt* file.

Solution: "Exercise 9-11: Reverse Pairs" on page 396.

Exercise 9-12.

Two words "interlock" if taking alternating letters from each forms a new word. For example, "shoe" and "cold" interlock to form "schooled."

Write a program that finds in *words.txt* all pairs of words that interlock. Hint: don't enumerate all pairs, there are many of them!

Solution: "Exercise 9-12: Interlocking Words" on page 399.

Credit: this exercise is inspired by an example at *http://puzzlers.org*.

## CHAPTER 10

Hashes

This chapter presents another built-in type called a hash. Hashes are one of Perl's best and most commonly used features; they are the building blocks of many efficient and elegant algorithms.

A Hash Is a Mapping

A *hash* is like an array, but more general. In an array, the indices or subscripts have to be integers; in a hash, they can be (almost) anything.

A hash contains a collection of indices, which are called *keys*, and a collection of *values*. Each key is associated with a single value. A key and a value together form a pair (an object of the `Pair` type), or a *key-value pair*. A hash can be viewed as a collection of key-value pairs. The values in a hash can also be called *items* or elements, as with arrays.

In other programming languages, hashes are sometimes called dictionaries, *hash tables*, maps, or associative arrays.

In mathematical language, a hash represents a *mapping* from keys to values, so you can also say that each key "maps to" a value. As an example, we'll build a hash that maps from English to Spanish words, so the keys and the values are all strings.

In Perl, hash names start with the "%" sigil. To create a new hash, you just declare it this way:

```
> my %eng2sp;
```

This creates an empty hash. To add items to the hash, you can use curly braces (a.k.a. curly brackets or sometimes simply "curlies"):

```
> %eng2sp{'one'} = 'uno';
uno
```

This line creates an item that maps from the key `'one'` to the value `'uno'`.

If the key is a string containing a single word (i.e., without any space in the middle of it), there is a more idiomatic shortcut to create the same hash entry:

```
> %eng2sp<one> = 'uno';
uno
```

If we print the hash, we see a key-value pair with a `=>` pair constructor operator between the key and value:

```
> say %eng2sp;
one => uno
```

This output format is also an input format. For example, you can create a new hash with three items:

```
> my %eng2sp = ('one' => 'uno', 'two' => 'dos', 'three' => 'tres');
one => uno, three => tres, two => dos
```

Using the `=>` pair constructor operator between keys and values is not required; you may use a comma as well:

```
my %eng2sp = ('one', 'uno', 'two', 'dos', 'three', 'tres');
```

But the pair constructor has the advantage of showing more graphically the key-value relations. The pair constructor operator also makes the use of quotes nonmandatory on its lefthand side (if the key is a string with no space):

```
> my %eng2sp = (one => 'uno', two => 'dos', three => 'tres');
one => uno, three => tres, two => dos
```

You might also use a more concise list syntax for the hash assignment and Perl will happily convert the list into a hash, provided the number of items in the input list is even:

```
> my %eng2sp = <one uno two dos three tres>;
one => uno, three => tres, two => dos
```

You might be surprised by the output. The order of the key-value pairs is usually not the order in which you populated the hash. In general, the order of items in a hash is unpredictable.

But that's not a problem because the elements of a hash are never indexed with integer subscripts. Instead, you use the keys to look up the corresponding values:

```
> say %eng2sp<two>;
dos
```

The key two always maps to the value `'dos'` so the order of the items doesn't matter.

If the key isn't in the hash, you get an undefined value:

```
> say %eng2sp<four>;
(Any)
```

The `elems` method or function works on hashes just as on arrays; it returns the number of key-value pairs:

```
> say %eng2sp.elems;
3
> say elems %eng2sp
3
```

The `:exists` adverb also works on hashes as on arrays; it tells you whether something appears as a *key* in the hash (appearing as a value is not good enough):[1]

```
> %eng2sp<two> :exists;
True
> %eng2sp<four> :exists;
False
```

To see whether something appears as a value in a hash, you can use the `values` method, which returns a collection of values, and then use a loop (or possibly a `grep`) to look for the searched item:

```
my @vals = values %eng2sp;
for @vals -> $value {
    say "Found it!" if $value eq 'uno';        # -> Found it!
}
```

Or more concisely:

```
say "Found it!" if grep {$_ eq 'uno'}, %eng2sp.values;
```

Since `grep` defaults to a smart match, this can be made even more concise:

```
say "Found it!" if grep {'uno'}, %eng2sp.values;  # -> Found it!
```

When looking for values, the program has to search the elements of the list in order (or sequentially), as in "Searching for a Substring Within the String" on page 111. As the list gets longer, the search time gets longer in direct proportion.

By contrast, when looking for keys, Perl uses a *hashing* algorithm that has a remarkable property: it takes about the same amount of time no matter how many items are in the hash. In other words, it performs really fast, compared to the list size, when the searched list is large. This is the reason why the solution to the reverse pair exercise

---

1 Evaluating the value in a Boolean context would also work with our example, but this would return something wrong when the key exists but the value is not defined or otherwise evaluates to a false value (for example, if it is equal to `False`, zero, or an empty string).

(Exercise 9-11) of the previous chapter using a hash was almost three times faster than the bisection search solution (see "Exercise 9-11: Reverse Pairs" on page 396).

As an exercise, use the sample employee data of the multidimensional array of "Multidimensional Arrays" on page 171, load it into a hash, and look up some salaries. Hint: you don't need a multidimensional structure for doing that with a hash. Solution: "Exercise: A Hash Is a Mapping" on page 400.

Common Operations on Hashes

We've seen already that to populate a hash, you can just assign an even list to it. The four syntactical forms below are correct:

```
my %first_quarter = ("jan" => 1, "feb" => 2, "mar" => 3);
my %second_quarter = (apr => 4, may => 5, jun => 6);
my %third_quarter = jul => 7, aug => 8, sep => 9;
my %fourth_quarter = < oct 10 nov 11 dec 12 >;
```

To add an element to a hash, just assign the hash with a key:

```
my %months = ("jan" => 1, "feb" => 2, "mar" => 3);
%months{'apr'} = 4;
say %months;          # -> apr => 4, feb => 2, jan => 1, mar => 3
```

Remember that you can also do the same without having to quote the keys if you use the angle brackets quote-word operator (if the keys are strings):

```
%months<apr> = 4;       # same as: %months{'apr'} = 4;
```

or you can also use the push function with a pair:

```
> push %months, (may => 5);
apr => 4, feb => 2, jan => 1, mar => 3, may => 5
> my $new-pair = jun => 6
jun => 6
> push %months, $new-pair;
apr => 4, feb => 2, jan => 1, jun => 6, mar => 3, may => 5
```

Using push to add a pair to a hash is not exactly the same, though, as making a hash assignment: if the key already exists, the old value is not replaced by the new one—instead, the old and the new ones are placed into an array (or, if the old value is already an array, then the new value is added to the array):

```
> push %months, (jan => '01');
{apr => 4, feb => 2, jan => [1 01], jun => 6, mar => 3, may => 5}
```

To check whether a value is defined for a given key, use `defined`:

```
> say True if defined %months<apr>;
True
```

To obtain the number of items in a hash, use the `elems` method:

```
say %months.elems;                    # -> 6
```

To remove a hash item, use the `:delete` adverb:

```
> push %months, (jud => 7);       # Oops, a typo!
apr => 4, feb => 2, jan => 1, jud => 7, jun => 6, mar => 3, may => 5
> %months{'jud'}:delete;          # typo now removed
7
> say %months
apr => 4, feb => 2, jan => 1, jun => 6, mar => 3, may => 5
```

Note that the `:delete` adverb also returns the value that is being removed.

To iterate over a hash, use:

- kv to retrieve the interleaved keys and values
- keys to retrieve the keys
- values to retrieve the values
- pairs to retrieve the key-value pairs

For example:

```
> for %months.kv -> $key, $val { say "$key => $val" }
jan => 1
apr => 4
mar => 3
jun => 6
may => 5
feb => 2
> say keys %months;
(jan apr mar jun may feb)
> say values %months;
(1 4 3 6 5 2)
> say %months.pairs;
(jan => 1 apr => 4 mar => 3 jun => 6 may => 5 feb => 2)
```

Hash as a Collection of Counters

Suppose you are given a string and you want to count how many times each letter appears. There are several ways you could do it:

- You could create 26 variables, one for each letter of the alphabet. Then you could traverse the string and, for each character, increment the corresponding counter, probably using an ugly and huge 26-part chained conditional.
- You could create an array with 26 elements. Then you could convert each character to a number (using the built-in function ord), use the number as an index into the array, and increment the appropriate counter.

- You could create a hash with characters as keys and counters as the corresponding values. The first time you see a character, you would add an item to the hash. After that, you would increment the value of an existing item.

Each of these options performs the same computation, but each of them implements that computation in a different way.

An *implementation* is a way of performing a computation; some implementations are better than others. For example, an advantage of the hash implementation is that we don't have to know ahead of time which letters appear in the string and we only have to make room for the letters that do appear.

Here is what the code might look like:

```
sub histogram (Str $string) {
    my %histo;
    for $string.comb -> $letter {
        %histo{$letter}++;
    }
    return %histo;
}
```

The name of the function is histogram, which is a statistical term for a collection of counters (or frequencies).

The first line of the function creates an empty hash. The for loop traverses the string. Each time through the loop, if the character $letter is not in the hash, Perl creates a new item with key $letter and defaults the values to 0 when the "++" operator is called on it, so that the first value immediately thereafter is 1. If $letter is already in the hash, the value is incremented.

Here's how it works:

```
> say histogram("We all live in a yellow submarine")
W => 1, a => 3, b => 1, e => 4, i => 3, l => 5, (...) y => 1
```

The histogram indicates that the letters 'W' and 'b' appear only once; 'a' and 'i' appear three times, 'e' appears four times, and so on.

Looping and Hashes

If you use a hash in a for statement, it traverses the pairs of the hash:

```
> for %eng2sp -> $pair { say $pair}
two => dos
three => tres
one => uno
```

We have named the iteration variable `$pair` to point out more clearly that the program is iterating over key-value pairs (actually `Pair` objects). You may use the `key` and `value` (notice the singular) methods to access the key and value of a `Pair`. For example, to reverse the order in which each line is printed:

```
> for %eng2sp -> $pair { say $pair.value ~ " <= " ~ $pair.key; }
dos <= two
tres <= three
uno <= one
```

Again, the keys are in no particular order. To traverse the keys in sorted order, you can use the `keys` (plural) and `sort` functions or methods:

```
my %histo = histogram("We all live in a yellow submarine");
for %histo.keys.sort -> $key {
    say "$key\t%histo{$key}";
}
```

Reverse Lookup

Given a hash `%hash` and a key `$k`, it is easy to find the corresponding value `$val = %hash{$k}`. This operation is called a *lookup* and, as already mentioned, this is fast even when the hash is very large.

But what if you have `$val` and you want to find `$k`? You have three problems: first, there might be more than one key that maps to the value `$val`; depending on the application, you might be able to pick one, or you might have to make an array that contains all of them. Second, there is no simple syntax to do a *reverse lookup*; you have to search. Third, it might be time-consuming if the hash is large.

Here is a function that takes a value and returns the first key that maps to that value:

```
sub reverse-lookup (%hash, $val) {
    for %hash -> $pair {
        return $pair.key if $pair.value eq $val;
    }
    return;
}
```

This subroutine is yet another example of the search pattern. If we get to the end of the loop, that means `$val` doesn't appear in the hash as a value, so we return an undefined value (Nil). Here, the responsibility to react to that situation is left to the caller. An alternative might be to raise an exception, which would still have to be dealt with by the caller. However, since direct lookup with the key is not raising an exception but simply returning an undefined value when the key does not exist, it makes sense for `reverse-lookup` to have the same behavior when the value is not found.

Here is an example of a successful reverse lookup:

```
> my %histo = histogram('parrot');
a => 1, o => 1, p => 1, r => 2, t => 1
> my $key =  reverse-lookup %histo, "2";
r
```

And an unsuccessful one:

```
> say reverse_lookup %histo, "3";
Nil
```

Another more concise way to do reverse lookup would be to use `grep` to retrieve a list of values satisfying our condition:

```
say grep { .value == 2 }, %histo.pairs;    # (r => 2)
```

Another option is to use an expression with the `first` built-in function to retrieve only the first one:

```
my %histo = histogram('parrot');
say %histo.pairs.first: *.value == 1;      # -> p => 1
```

This latter example uses the "*" *whatever* parameter, which we haven't covered yet in this book. Let's just say that, here, the "*" stands successively for every pair of the hash, and the `first` function returns the first pair that matches the condition on the value (see "Currying with the Whatever Star Parameter" on page 324 for details on the "*" parameter).

A reverse lookup is much slower than a forward lookup; if you have to do it often, or if the hash gets big, the performance of your program will suffer.

Testing for Existence

A quite common task is to determine whether something exists or if a given value has already been seen in a program. Using a hash is usually the best solution because finding out whether there is an entry for a given key is very simple and also very efficient: you just need to store the values that you want to watch as a key entry in a hash, and then check for its existence when needed.

In such a case, you often don't really care about the value and you might put basically anything. It is quite common in that case to use "1" as a value, but you might as well store `True` or any other value you like.

Suppose we want to generate 10 random integers between 0 and 49, but want to make sure that the integers are unique. We can use the `rand` method 10 times on the desired range. But the likelihood to twice hit the same number is far from negligible (see Exercise 9-8 on the so-called Birthday Paradox and its solution ("Exercise 9-8: Simulating the Birthday Paradox" on page 392) for a similar situation). For example, trying this:

```
> my @list;
[]
> push @list, 50.rand.Int for 1..10;
> say @list;
[12 25 47 10 19 20 25 42 33 20]
```

produced a duplicate value in the list (25) on the first try. And the second try produced three pairs of duplicates:

```
> say @list;
[45 29 29 27 12 27 20 5 28 45]
```

We can use a hash to reject any generated random integer that has already been seen. The following is a possible way to code this:

```
my @list;
my %seen;
while @list.elems < 10 {
    my $random = 50.rand.Int;
    next if %seen{$random}:exists;
    %seen{$random} = 1;
    push @list, $random;
}
say @list;
```

Every valid integer generated is added to both the %seen hash and the output list. But before doing that, the generated integer is checked against the %seen hash to verify that it has not been seen yet. When this program is finished running, the list has 10 unique (pseudo)random integers.

We have made it step by step and kept two separate data structures, the @list output array and the %seen hash, to make the process as clear as possible. If you think about it, however, @list and %seen have essentially the same content at any step through the loop. We don't really need to keep track of the same data in two places. Since having a hash is important for checking that the output values are unique, we can get rid of @list and write a more concise and probably more idiomatic version of the same program:

```
my %seen;
while %seen.elems < 10 {
        my $random = 50.rand.Int;
        push %seen, ($random => 1) unless %seen{$random}:exists;
}
say keys %seen;       # -> (39 12 46 27 14 21 4 38 25 47)
```

This can be further simplified. It is not really necessary here to check whether the generated integer exists in the hash: if it does exist, the old hash element will be replaced by the new one, and the hash will be essentially unchanged. In addition, when evaluated in a scalar numeric context, a hash returns the number of elements, so the call to .elems is not necessary. This is the new version:

```
my %seen;
%seen{50.rand.Int} = 1 while %seen < 10;
say keys %seen;        # -> (46 19 5 36 33 1 20 45 47 30)
```

This last version is probably more concise and more idiomatic, but that's not meant to say that it is better. It is perfectly fine if you prefer the second or the first version, maybe because you find it clearer. Use whichever version you like better, or your own modified version provided it does the expected work. This is Perl, *there is more than one way to do it* (TIMTOWTDI).

Note however that the pure hash version doesn't keep the order in which the numbers were generated, so (pseudo)randomness might not be as good.

Also note, by the way, that Perl has a `pick` function or method to choose elements at random from a list without repetition.

Hash Keys Are Unique

It is not possible to have the same key in a hash more than once. Trying to map a new value to a key will replace the old value with the new one. Here is an example of hash creation with duplicate keys:

```
> my %friends = (Tom => 5, Bill => 6, Liz => 5, Tom => 7, Jack => 3)
Bill => 6, Jack => 3, Liz => 5, Tom => 7
```

Because two of our friends are named Tom, we lose the data associated with the first of them. This is something you should be careful about: hash keys are unique, so you'll lose some items if the data associated with your keys has duplicates. The next section will show some ways of dealing with this possible problem.

But this key uniqueness property also has very interesting upsides. For example, a typical way of removing duplicates from a list of items is to assign the list items to the keys of a hash (the value does not matter); at the end of the process, the list of keys has no duplicates:

```
> my @array = < a b c d s a z a r e s d z r a >
[a b c d s a z a r e s d z r a]
> my %unique = map { $_ => 1 }, @array;
a => 1, b => 1, c => 1, d => 1, e => 1, r => 1, s => 1, z => 1
> my @unique_array = keys %unique;
[z a e s d c b r]
```

As you can see, duplicates have been removed from the output array. In such a simple case, the `unique` built-in function would have been sufficient to remove duplicates from `@array`, but within a more complex program, it is quite common to use a hash (often called `%seen`) to check whether a value has already been seen.

Hashes and Arrays

Inverting a hash can be very easy if it is known that the values can happen only once (that they are unique). Consider for example a hash mapping months to their number in the year (we limit the example to five months for brevity):

```
> my %months = jan => 1, feb => 2, mar => 3, apr => 4, may => 5;
apr => 4, feb => 2, jan => 1, mar => 3, may => 5
```

We can transform the key-value pairs into a flat list, reverse the list, and assign the reversed list to a new hash:

```
> my %rev_months = %months.kv.reverse;
1 => jan, 2 => feb, 3 => mar, 4 => apr, 5 => may
```

We now have a new hash mapping month numbers to their names. This can be very handy if a hash is known to be bijective, but this approach does not work correctly if a value can happen more than once: in such a case, some pairs will be lost:

```
> my %months = jan => 1, january => 1, feb => 2, february => 2;
feb => 2, february => 2, jan => 1, january => 1
> my %rev_months = %months.kv.reverse;
1 => january, 2 => february
```

Arrays can appear as values in a hash. For example, if you are given a hash that maps from letters to frequencies, you might want to invert it; that is, create a hash that maps from frequencies to letters. Since there might be several letters with the same frequency, each value in the inverted hash should probably be an array of letters.

Here is a function that inverts such a hash:

```
sub invert-hash (%in-hash) {
    my %out-hash;
    for %in-hash.kv -> $key, $val {
        push %out-hash{$val}, $key;
    }
    return %out-hash;
}
```

Each time through the loop, a hash item is assigned to the $key and $val variables, and $key is appended to the value %output-hash for the $val key; if that value does not exist yet, it is created. At the end of the process, the values of %output-hash are all anonymous arrays.

Here is an example:

```
my %rev-hist = invert-hash histogram 'parrot';
say %rev-hist;
dd %rev-hist;
```

This will display:

```
1 => [p a o t], 2 => [r]
Hash %rev-hist = {"1" => $["p", "a", "o", "t"], "2" => $["r"]}
```

Notice that the say function gives a simple representation of the hash data, and that the new dd (short for "data dumper") function used here gives more detailed information. dd is not very commonly used in normal programs, but can be quite useful while debugging a program to display a detailed description of a complex data structure.[2]

%output-hash contains two items (two pairs) whose values are anonymous arrays. You can access the second element of the first array using the hash value %rev-hist{"1"} as if it was any ordinary array name, with this simple syntax:

```
say %rev-hist{"1"}[1];  # -> a
```

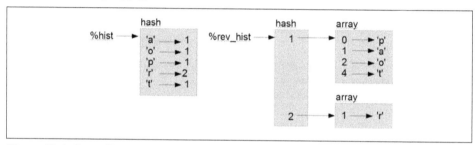

Figure 10-1. State diagram

Figure 10-1 is a state diagram showing %hist and %rev-hist. A hash is represented as a box with the type hash above it and the key-value pairs inside.

Arrays can be values in a hash, as this example shows, but they cannot be keys. If you try, you're likely to end up with a key that contains only one item of the array, but most likely not what you intended:

```
my @a = 'a' .. 'c';
my %h;
%h{@a} = 5;
say %h;  # -> a => 5, b => (Any), c => (Any)
```

Here, Perl interpreted the %h{@a} = 5; assignment as a slice assignment, i.e., it assumed that we were trying to populate three items in one go, one for each element of the array.

---

2 To tell the full truth, dd is not standard Perl 6, it is a Rakudo-specific debugging feature. A future implementation of Perl 6 not based on Rakudo might not have it.

As mentioned earlier, a hash is implemented using a hashing function and that means that the keys have to be *hashable*.[3] A *hashing function* is a function that takes a value (of any kind) and returns an integer. Hashes use these integers, called hash values, to store and look up key-value pairs.

This system works fine if the keys are immutable. But if the keys are mutable, like with arrays, bad things would happen. For example, when you create a key-value pair, Perl would hash the key and store it in the corresponding location. If you modify the key and then hash it again, it would go to a different location. In that case, you might have two entries for the same key, or you might not be able to find a key. Either way, the hash wouldn't work correctly.

That's why keys have to be hashable, and why mutable types like arrays aren't. So Perl will do something else that can be useful (such as creating three distinct hash items in the example above), but will not hash the array itself.

Since hashes are mutable, they can't be used as keys, but they *can* be used as values, so that you can have nested hashes.

Memos

If you played with the `fibonacci` subroutine from "One More Example" on page 87, you might have noticed that the bigger the argument you provide, the longer the subroutine takes to run. Furthermore, the runtime increases extremely quickly.

To understand why, consider Figure 10-2, which shows the *call graph* for `fibonacci` with n=4.

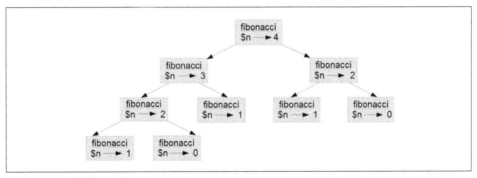

Figure 10-2. Call graph

---

3 This is not entirely true. The keys of a "normal" hash must be hashable and therefore immutable. There is another type of hash, object hashes, for which the need to have immutable keys does not apply.

A call graph shows a set of subroutine frames, with lines connecting each frame to the frames of the functions it calls. At the top of the graph, fibonacci with $n=4 calls fibonacci with $n=3 and $n=2. In turn, fibonacci with $n=3 calls fibonacci with $n=2 and $n=1. And so on.

Count how many times fibonacci(0) and fibonacci(1) are called. This is an inefficient solution to the problem, and it gets much worse as the argument gets bigger.

One solution is to keep track of values that have already been computed by storing them in a hash. A previously computed value that is stored for later use is called a *memo*. Here is a "memoized" version of fibonacci:

```
my %known = 0 => 1, 1 => 1;
say fibonacci(10);
sub fibonacci ($n) {
    return %known{$n} if %known{$n}:exists;
    %known{$n} = fibonacci($n-1) + fibonacci($n-2);
    return %known{$n};
}
```

%known is a hash that keeps track of the Fibonacci numbers we already know. It starts with two items: 0 and 1, which both map to 1.

Whenever fibonacci is called, it checks %known. If the result is already there, it can return immediately. Otherwise, it has to compute the new value, add it to the hash, and return it.

If you run this version of fibonacci and compare it with the original, you will find that it is much faster, especially for a large argument (say more than 30).

Memoizing is a form of *caching*, i.e., storing in memory the result of a (presumably costly) computing operation in order to avoid computing it again. This process is sometimes called "trading memory against CPU cycles." In some cases, such as our Fibonacci recursive example here, the gain can be absolutely huge: calculating the 100th Fibonacci number would take billions of years with the original recursive subroutine and it takes only a split second with the memoized version.

Please note that in the specific case of the Fibonacci function, we are storing values for each successive integer; we could have memoized the Fibonacci numbers in an array rather than in a hash (and it might even be slightly more efficient), but using a hash for such purpose is a more general solution, working even when the memo keys are not consecutive integers.

As an exercise, try to rewrite the fibonacci subroutine using an array instead of a hash to memoize the calculated Fibonacci numbers.

Hashes as Dispatch Tables

You may need a procedure to launch some action depending on the value of a parameter received by the program. To do that, you could use a series of if {...} elsif {...} else {...} statements like this:

```
sub run-stop  { ... };
sub run-start { ... };
my $param = get-param;
if $param eq "stop" {
    run_stop;
} elsif $param eq "start" {
    run-start;
} elsif $param = "h" {
    say $help;
} elsif $param = "help" {
    say $help;
} elsif $param = "v" {
    $verbose = True;
} else {
    die "Unknown option $param";
}
```

This approach is boring and error-prone. Using a dispatch table is often a simpler solution.

A dispatch table is a data structure mapping identifiers to code references or subroutine objects. Applied to the above scenario, it could look like this:

```
sub run-stop  { ... };
sub run-start { ... };
my %dispatch = (
    stop  => &run-stop,
    start => &run-start,
    h     => { say $help; },
    help  => { say $help; },
    v     => { $verbose = True;},
);
my $param = get-param();
die "Unknown option $param" unless %dispatch{$param}:exists;
%dispatch{$param}(); # execute the action specified in %dispatch
```

The %dispatch hash defines the action depending on the parameter used as a key. The %dispatch{$param}() statement calls the required action.

This approach is a bit more concise and slightly cleaner, but there are some other advantages. It is more maintainable: if you need to add one option, you just need to add one entry to the hash and don't have to add code in the middle of a complicated chain of nested if {...} elsif {...} else {...} statements at the risk of breaking up something.

Another upside is that the dispatch table can be dynamically modified at runtime, for example depending on certain external circumstances (for example the day in the month when the program is running) or in accordance with a configuration file. This means that it is possible to dynamically modify the behavior of a program after compile time, while it is already running. This paves the way to some very interesting advanced programming techniques that are beyond the scope of this book.

Note that we have been using hashes for our dispatch tables, and this is the most common way to implement them. If it makes sense to have small integers as keys, you could also implement a dispatch table as an array. This is the case, for example, with numbered menu items where the user is prompted to type a number to indicate which menu option to activate.

Global Variables

In the previous example, %known is created outside the subroutine, so it belongs to the whole main package. Such variables are sometimes called *global* because they can be accessed from any function. Unlike "local" lexical variables, which usually disappear when their scope ends, global variables persist from one subroutine call to the next.

It is common to use global variables for *flags*; that is, Boolean variables that indicate ("flag") whether a condition is true. For example, some programs use a flag named $verbose to control the level of detail in the output:

```
my $verbose = True;
sub example1 {
    say 'Running example1' if $verbose;
    # ...
}
```

Global variables are also sometimes used for environment variables and parameters passed to the program, as well as for storing a large data structure that is the centerpiece of a program, in order to avoid copying it when passing it around as an argument to subroutines.

But, aside from those specific cases, it is usually considered poor practice to use a global variable, because it creates dependencies and unexpected "action-at-a-distance" behaviors between various parts of a program and may lead to difficult-to-track bugs.

In the case of our memoized fibonacci subroutine, the %known hash is useful only within the subroutine. We can improve the implementation by using the state declarator within the subroutine:

```
say fibonacci(10);
sub fibonacci ($n) {
    state %known = 0 => 1, 1 => 1;
```

```
        return %known{$n} if %known{$n}:exists;
        %known{$n} = fibonacci($n-1) + fibonacci($n-2);
        return %known{$n};
    }
```

The `state` declarator makes the variable local to the subroutine and persistent from one call to the subroutine to another: the code line with the `state` statement is executed only once (at the first call of the subroutine) and the content of the variable (the `%known` hash in this case) is kept from one call to the next.

Debugging

As you work with bigger datasets it can become unwieldy to debug by printing and checking the output by hand. Here are some suggestions for debugging large data sets:

Scale down the input
>If possible, reduce the size of the dataset. For example if the program reads a text file, start with just the first 10 lines, or with the smallest example you can find. You can either edit the files themselves, or (better) modify the program so it reads only the first n lines.

>If there is an error, you can reduce n to the smallest value that manifests the error, and then increase it gradually as you find and correct errors.

Check summaries and types
>Instead of printing and checking the entire dataset, consider printing summaries of the data: for example, the number of items in a hash or the total of a list of numbers.

>A common cause of runtime errors is a value that is not the right type. For debugging this kind of error, it is often enough to print the type of a value (think about the `.WHAT` method).

>It is often useful to add typing to your variables. Where you expect a string, make sure you type the variable or subroutine parameter with `Str`. If you expect an integer, type it with `Int`. If you expect an `Int` of a certain range, create a subset for it as in "Checking Types" on page 87 and type the variable with that.

Write self-checks
>Sometimes you can write code to check for errors automatically. For example, if you are computing the average of a list of numbers, you could check that the result is not greater than the largest element in the list or less than the smallest. This is called a "sanity check" because it detects results that are "insane."

>Another kind of check compares the results of two different computations to see if they are consistent. This is called a "consistency check."

Format the output

Formatting debugging output can make it easier to spot an error. We saw an example in "Debugging" on page 90. The dd function displays helpful details on a composite or complex data structure.

Again, time you spend building scaffolding can reduce the time you spend debugging.

Glossary

call graph

A diagram that shows every frame created during the execution of a program, with an arrow from each caller to each callee.

flag

A Boolean variable used to indicate whether a condition is true.

global variable

A variable defined outside any subroutine or other block. Global variables can be accessed from any subroutine.

hash

A mapping from keys to their corresponding values.

hashable

A type that has a hash function. Immutable types like numbers and strings are hashable; mutable types like arrays and hashes are not.

hashing function

A function used by a hash table to compute the location of a key.

hash table

The algorithm used to implement hashes.

implementation

A way of performing a computation.

item

In a hash, another name for a key-value pair.

key

An object that appears in a hash as the first part of a key-value pair.

key-value pair

The representation of the mapping from a single key to its value.

lookup

A hash operation that takes a key and finds the corresponding value.

mapping
> A relationship in which each element of one set corresponds to an element of another set.

memo
> A computed value stored to avoid unnecessary future computation.

reverse lookup
> A hash operation that takes a value and finds one or more keys that map to it.

value
> An object that appears in a hash as the second part of a key–value pair. This is more specific than our previous use of the word "value."

Exercises

Exercise 10-1.

Write a subroutine that reads the words in *words.txt* and stores them as keys in a hash. (It doesn't matter what the values are.) Then you can use the `exists` adverb as a fast way to check whether a string is in the hash.

If you did Exercise 9-10, you can compare the speed of this implementation with a hash and the bisection search.

Solution: "Exercise 10-1: Storing the Word List into a Hash" on page 401.

Exercise 10-2.

Memoize the Ackermann function from Exercise 5-2 and see if memoization makes it possible to evaluate the subroutine with bigger arguments. Hint: no. Solution: "Exercise 10-2: Memoizing the Ackermann Function" on page 401.

Exercise 10-3.

If you did Exercise 9-7, you already have a function named `has-duplicates` that takes a list as a parameter and returns `True` if any object appears more than once in the list.

Use a hash to write a faster, simpler version of `has-duplicates`. Solution: "Exercise 10-3: Finding Duplicates with a Hash" on page 403.

Exercise 10-4.

Two words are "rotate pairs" if you can rotate one of them and get the other (see rotate_word in Exercise 7-3) using the Caesar cipher.

Write a program that reads a word list (e.g., *words.txt*) and finds all the rotate pairs. Solution: "Exercise 10-4: Rotate Pairs" on page 403.

Exercise 10-5.

Here's another Puzzler from *Car Talk* (*http://www.cartalk.com/content/puzzlers*):

> This was sent in by a fellow named Dan O'Leary. He came upon a common one-syllable, five-letter word recently that has the following unique property. When you remove the first letter, the remaining letters form a homophone of the original word, that is a word that sounds exactly the same. Replace the first letter, that is, put it back and remove the second letter and the result is yet another homophone of the original word. And the question is, what's the word?

> Now I'm going to give you an example that doesn't work. Let's look at the five-letter word, "wrack." W-R-A-C-K, you know like to "wrack with pain." If I remove the first letter, I am left with a four-letter word, "R-A-C-K." As in, "Holy cow, did you see the rack on that buck! It must have been a nine-pointer!" It's a perfect homophone. If you put the "w" back, and remove the "r" instead, you're left with the word, "wack," which is a real word, it's just not a homophone of the other two words.

> But there is, however, at least one word that Dan and we know of which will yield two homophones if you remove either of the first two letters to make two, new four-letter words. The question is, what's the word?

You can use the hash from Exercise 10-1 above to check whether a string is in *words.txt*.

To check whether two words are homophones, you can use the CMU Pronouncing Dictionary. You can download it from *http://www.speech.cs.cmu.edu/cgi-bin/cmudict*.

Write a program that lists all the words in *words.txt* (or in the CMU dictionary) that solve the Puzzler. Solution: "Exercise 10-5: Homophones" on page 404.

## CHAPTER 11

Case Study: Data Structure Selection

At this point you have learned about Perl's core data structures, and you have seen some of the algorithms that use them.

This chapter presents a case study with exercises that let you think about choosing data structures and practice using them.

But first, I would like to briefly introduce two conditional structures that have been left aside so far and provide a couple of new possibilities about subroutine signatures.

The Ternary Conditional Operator

Consider the following code that tests the value of a positive integer:

```
my $result;
if $num < 10 {
    $result = "One digit";
} else {
    $result = "More than one digit";
}
say $result;
```

This is quite simple, but a bit long. This can be rewritten in just one line of code:

```
say $num < 10 ?? "One digit" !! "More than one digit";
```

The operator is in two parts: the ?? and the !!, which separate three expressions (hence the name "ternary operator"):

- The condition to be evaluated (is $num less than 10?)
- The expression defining the value if the condition is true
- The expression defining the value if the condition is false

This statement checks if $num is less than 10 and, if true, prints ""One digit"; if the condition is false, it prints "More than one digit."

This operator does not provide any new functionality; it just offers a more concise syntax.

It is possible to nest several ternary operators to examine successively multiple choices:

```
say $value < 10    ?? "One digit"    !!
    $value < 100   ?? "Two digits"   !!
    $value < 1000  ?? "Three digits" !!
                      "More than three digits";
```

This construct is a form of what is sometimes called a *switch statement*, because the C language and many languages derived from it use the switch keyword to describe such a multiple choice conditional.

This is much more concise and often more convenient than nested if ... then ... else conditionals, but the next section provides a more powerful switch type of statement.

The given ... when "Switch" Statement

Perl 6 has a "switch" statement, written with the given and when keywords. The given keyword introduces the variable or expression that will be tested, and each of the when statements specify a condition followed by a block that will execute if the condition is true. By default, the process stops at the first condition that is satisfied.

The example just above can be rewritten as follows:

```
given $value {
    when 0..9       { say "One digit" }
    when $_ < 99    { say "Two digits" }
    when /^\d**3$/  { say "Three digits" }
    default         { say "More than three digits" }
}
```

The given $value statement "topicalizes" the argument, i.e., assigns the content of $value to the $_ topical variable (or, more precisely, aliases it to $_). The argument to given is a simple variable in the example above, but it can be a complex expression whose evaluation is stored (and cached) into $_. Each of the when conditions is checked against $_. I have written these conditions in three different syntactical forms to illustrate some of the various possibilities:

- The first one checks $_ (implicitly) against the 0..9 range.
- The second one compares explicitly $_ to 99.

- The third one uses a regex to check whether $_ has three digits.
- The default statement runs only if the other conditions have failed.

Only one message will be printed, because the matching process stops as soon as one condition has been satisfied, and the default clause will run if no other condition has been met.

If there is no specific operator in the when clause, then it will smart match the expression in the when clause against $_:

```
when $foo { ... }
# equivalent to: when $foo ~~ $_ { ... }
```

Note that the given keyword is not doing much more than topicalizing its argument for the rest of the block. The when clauses are doing the bulk of the real work. In fact, you can even use the when clauses without a given, provided you assign the right value to $_, which, as you hopefully remember, can be done with a for block:

```
my $val = 7;
for $val {
    when 0..6 { say "less than"}
    when 7 {say "Exact";}
    when 8..* {say "greater than";}
}
```

It is possible to add a proceed clause at the end of any of the conditional code blocks to prevent the process from stopping after that code block has succeeded. For example, you might write this:

```
given $value {
    when 0..9      { say "One digit"}
    when 10..99    { say "Two digits"; proceed}
    when 42        { say "The response to the ultimate question"}
    when /^\d**3$/ { say "Three digits" }
    default        { say "More than three digits" }
}
```

Here, if $value is 42, two messages will be displayed, "Two digits" and "The response to the ultimate question," because the proceed clause in the second code block prevents the process from stopping on the first successful match.

Good, it seems, but there is a problem. The proceed clause should be used with some care, as it can easily lead to unexpected results. In fact, *the code above is actually wrong*: if $value has two digits but is not 42 (if it is, say, 43), the default block will also run, because the only other successful match had this proceed clause, and will say that there are "More than three digits" although this is obviously false.

As an exercise, test the above code with various values and try to find a way to fix the bug with the proceed clause. Solution: "Exercise: The given ... when switch statement" on page 405.

Subroutine Named and Optional Parameters

The subroutines that we have seen so far used *positional* parameters, i.e., parameters whose binding with the subroutine call arguments rely on their order within the list of arguments and in the signature. This is usually fine when the number of arguments passed to the subroutine is small (say, three or less).

When the subroutine signature becomes longer, using positional arguments might become cumbersome and error-prone.

Named Parameters

Named arguments may be supplied in any order: the name of the parameter is bound to the argument having the same name. For example:

```
sub divide (:$dividend, :$divisor where $divisor != 0) {
    return $dividend/$divisor;
}
say divide(dividend => 2048, divisor => 128);      # -> 16
# or:
say divide(divisor => 128, dividend => 2048);      # -> 16
```

The arguments are supplied at the subroutine call as a list of pairs using the pair-constructor syntax. In the signature, the parameters are retrieved with the so-called colon-pair syntax: the $dividend parameter is bound to the value of the pair whose key is "dividend" (2048), and $divisor is similarly bound to 128, irrespective of the order of the arguments in the subroutine call.

These named parameters are especially useful when the number of arguments is large. For example, we haven't covered object-oriented programming yet (see Chapter 12), but this is how we could create an object of the (user-defined) Rectangle class:

```
my $rect = Rectangle.new(
    origin_x  => 100,
    origin_y  => 200,
    width     => 23,
    length    => 42,
    color     => 'black'
);
```

Clearly, using five positional parameters would be unpractical.

Optional Parameters

Sometimes, the actual number of arguments is not known in advance: for example, a subroutine may be called with a variable number of arguments. Such a subroutine is said to be *variadic*. You can define a parameter to be optional by postfixing it with a question mark in the subroutine signature:

```
sub my-sub($x, $y?) {  # simple optional parameter
    if $y.defined {
        say "The second parameter has been supplied and defined";
    } else {
        say "The second parameter has not been supplied";
    }
    # ...
}
```

When using positional parameters, the optional parameters always have to be the last ones in the list (after the mandatory ones).

A parameter can also be made optional by supplying a *default value*:

```
sub my-log($number, $base = e) {   # e is a predefined constant
                                   # $base is an optional parameter
    return log($number) / log($base);
}
say my-log(4);       # Natural log (base e)    -> 1.38629436111989
say my-log(32, 2);   # Log base 2              -> 5
say my-log(100, 10); # Common log (base 10)    -> 2
```

Here, if the second argument is not supplied, the default value (*e*) is used instead. Conversely, if there is a second argument, it *overrides* the default value.

Sometimes, having optional or default parameters is not good enough. For example, the subroutine may have to process a list containing any number of values. For situations like this, you can use a *slurpy parameter*, i.e., a kind of array placed at the end of the parameter list that will slurp up all the remaining arguments. This kind of slurpy parameter uses the "*@" twigil. In the following example, the subroutine takes one mandatory parameter (the first number of the list) and a list of additional arguments that will be stored in the @rest array:

```
sub my-sum($first-num, *@rest) {
    say @rest;                     # -> [3 4 5 12 17]
    return $first-num + [+] @rest;
}
say my-sum 1, 3, 4, 5, 12, 17;     # -> 42
```

Some further examples of slurpy parameters have been provided in "Exercise: Implementing a Queue" on page 379.

Word Frequency Analysis

Now, let's get to the case study.

As usual, you should at least attempt the exercises before you read the suggested solutions, which are provided in the following sections of this chapter.

Exercise 11-1.

Write a program that reads a file, breaks each line into words, strips whitespace and punctuation from the words, and converts them to lowercase.

Exercise 11-2.

Go to Project Gutenberg (*http://gutenberg.org*) and download your favorite out-of-copyright book in plain text format.

Modify your program from the previous exercise to read the book you downloaded, skip over the header information at the beginning of the file, and process the rest of the words as before.

Then modify the program to count the total number of words in the book, and the number of times each word is used.

Print the number of different words used in the book. Compare different books by different authors, written in different eras. Which author uses the most extensive vocabulary?

Exercise 11-3.

Modify the program from the previous exercise to print the 20 most frequently used words in a given book.

Exercise 11-4.

Modify the previous program to read a word list (see "Reading Word Lists" on page 141) and then print all the words in the book that are not in the word list. How many of them are typos? How many of them are common words that *should* be in the word list, and how many of them are really obscure?

Random Numbers

Given the same inputs, most computer programs generate the same outputs every time, so they are said to be *deterministic*. Determinism is usually a good thing, since we expect the same calculation to yield the same result. For some applications, though, we want the computer to be unpredictable. Games are an obvious example, but there are more.

Making a program truly nondeterministic turns out to be difficult, but there are ways to make it at least seem nondeterministic. One of them is to use algorithms that generate *pseudorandom* numbers. Pseudorandom numbers are not truly random because they are generated by a deterministic computation, but just by looking at the numbers it is all but impossible to distinguish them from random.

Perl provides functions such as `rand` that generate pseudorandom numbers (which we will simply call "random" numbers from here on).

The function `rand` returns a random number (of `Num` type) between 0.0 and 1.0 (including 0.0 but not 1.0). Each time you call `rand`, you get the next number in a long series. To see a sample, run this loop in the REPL:

```
say rand for 1..5;
```

Used as a method, `rand` returns a random number between 0.0 and the value of the invocant. For example, `10.rand` returns a random number between 0 and 10 (10 not included). You might try it as a one-liner:

```
$ perl6 -e 'say 10.rand for 1..5'
8.23987158729588
9.83276889381497
2.52313276833335
3.44713459548771
1.82329894347025
```

You should hopefully get a different output than I did. If you want to run such a one-liner under Windows, remember that you'll need to replace single quotes with double quotes.

To obtain random integers between 1 and 10, you may use the `Int` and `rand` methods:

```
$ perl6 -e 'say 10.rand.Int + 1 for 1..5'
5
10
1
6
3
```

The `pick` function or method takes a number `$count` and a list as arguments and returns `$count` items chosen at random and without repetition. For example:

```
> say <1 3 4 5 7 9 10 12 14 42>.pick(5);
(5 42 3 4 7)
> say pick 5, <1 3 4 5 7 9 10 12 14 42>;
(42 12 5 1 9)
```

If $count is greater than or equal to the number of items of the list, then all elements from the list are returned in a random sequence.

To obtain random unique integers in a range, you might use `pick` on a range:

```
> say pick 5, 1..20;
(5 3 6 18 7)
> say (1..20).pick(5);
(20 4 18 2 7)
```

If you don't specify the number of random numbers, you'll get one random pick:

```
> say (1..20).pick;
19
```

Exercise 11-5.

Write a function named `choose_from_hist` that takes a histogram as defined in "Hash as a Collection of Counters" on page 187 and returns a random value from the histogram, chosen with probability in proportion to frequency. For example, for the three items (`'a'`, `'a'`, `'b'`), your function should return `'a'` with probability 2/3 and `'b'` with probability 1/3.

Word Histogram

You should attempt the previous exercises before you go on.

For the purpose of presenting the solutions to the above exercises, I've used the plain text of *Emma* (1816), the novel by Jane Austen, downloaded from the Gutenberg project (*http://www.gutenberg.org/files/158/158-0.txt*) and saved in a file called *emma.txt*. Use the same text if you want to compare your solutions and results with mine.

Here is a program that reads the *emma.txt* file and builds a histogram of the words in the file:

```
my %histogram;
my $skip = True; # flag to skip the header

sub process-line(Str $line is copy) {
    if defined index $line, "*END*THE SMALL PRINT!" {
        $skip = False ;
        return;
    }
    return if $skip;
    $line ~~ s:g/<[-']>/ /; # Replacing dashes and apostrophes with spaces
    $line ~~ s:g/<[;:,!?.()"_`]>//; # removing punctuation symbols
    $line = $line.lc;            # setting string to lowercase
    for $line.words -> $word {
        %histogram{$word}++;
```

```
        }
    }
    process-line $_ for "emma.txt".IO.lines;
```

The program reads each line of the *emma.txt* file and, for each line, calls process-line.

The process-line subroutine skips the header lines (i.e., all the lines until a line containing the string "*END*THE SMALL PRINT!" is met). It replaces dashes and apostrophes with spaces, removes various punctuation characters, and sets the line to lowercase. Finally, it splits the line into individual words that are stored and counted with an accumulator in the %histogram hash.

To know whether the program is doing something like what it is supposed to do, we can display a few entries of the %histogram hash:

```
# displaying 20 lines of the histogram
my $count;
for %histogram -> $pair {
    say sprintf "%-24s %d", $pair.key, $pair.value;
    $count++;
    last if $count > 20;
}
```

This prints out the following output:

```
embarrassing            1
hows                    1
appealed                2
bestow                  2
articulate              1
demands                 2
closely                 1
dull                    9
hearts                  1
column                  1
possesses               1
attributed              1
jumped                  2
forwards                2
wittier                 2
expert                  2
attractive              2
asserted                2
oftentimes              1
fancy                   38
finds                   1
```

To count the total number of words in the file, we can add up the values in the histogram:

```
my $word_count = [+] %histogram.values;
say "There are $word_count words in the book.";
```

The number of different words is just the number of items in the hash:

```
my $distinct-words = %histogram.elems;
say "There are $distinct-words distinct words in the book.";
```

Note that you could reduce the above to one code line by interpolating a code block within the output string:

```
say "There are {%histogram.elems} distinct words in the book."
```

And the results:

```
There are 161991 words in the book.
There are 7110 distinct words in the book.
```

Most Common Words

To find the most common words in *emma.txt*, we can sort the %histogram hash according to the values (word frequencies) and retrieve the 10 most frequent words into an array.

```
my @most_commons = (sort { %histogram{$^b} cmp %histogram{$^a} },
                    %histogram.keys)[0..9];
say $_ for map { "$_ \t%histogram{$_} "}, @most_commons;
```

The sort function receives the keys of the histogram and its comparison function compares the values associated with those keys. Since we use the key $^b before the key $^a, the sort will produce a reverse (descending) sort order. The whole sort procedure is placed within parentheses, so that the subscript range [0..9] acts as a slice on the list produced by sort and retains only the first 10 most frequent words. The result is stored in the @most_commons array. The next code line just reprocesses the array to display the words and their respective frequency.

This displays the following output:

```
to      5241
the     5205
and     4897
of      4295
i       3192
a       3130
it      2529
her     2490
was     2400
she     2364
```

If you want to see more interesting words, you might, as a further exercise, filter the histogram and retain only words that have more than, say, four letters.

The @most_commons temporary array is not really needed. We could do the whole thing in a single statement:

```
say $_ for map { "$_ \t%histogram{$_} "},
        (sort { %histogram{$^b} cmp %histogram{$^a} },
        %histogram.keys)[0..9];
```

This is an example of data pipeline (or stream) programming. Such a statement needs to be read from bottom to top and from right to left. The first step is `%histogram.keys`, which produces a list of the histogram keys; this list is fed into the sort statement to produce a list of the keys sorted (in descending order) according to their values; once this whole part between parentheses is completed, the subscript range `[0..9]` retains the 10 most frequent words and feeds them into the map statement, which produces the list of words and frequencies for the final output.

Let me add one word of caution here: sorting the histogram by values and picking up the top 10 to get the most frequent words is probably the easiest way to solve the problem and the shortest code to do it. That's the reason I have used this solution here. But it is not the most efficient solution from the standpoint of runtime, because it involves the cost of sorting a relatively large data set, whereas we are using only a small part of the sorted data. There are some better algorithms to do that from the standpoint of runtime efficiency, but they are more complicated. So, there is a trade-off here between coding efficiency and performance. Assuming this is code that we want to run only once, I have chosen to favor coding efficiency.

Optional Parameters

We saw earlier in this chapter that subroutines can take optional parameters. We can use this functionality to write a subroutine that prints the most common words in the `%histogram` hash extracted from *emma.txt*:

```
display-most-common(%histogram, 5);

sub display-most-common (%hist, Int $num = 10) {
    say $_ for map { "$_ \t%hist{$_} "},
    (sort { %hist{$^b} cmp %hist{$^a} },
    %hist.keys)[0..$num - 1];
}
```

This will display the five top words of the list above ("Most Common Words" on page 212). If we call it without the second parameter:

```
display-most-common(%histogram);
```

we will get the 10 most common words (same list as the one shown in "Most Common Words" on page 212 above), because the default value for the second parameter is 10.

Hash Subtraction

Finding the words from *emma.txt* that are not in the word list *words.txt* is a problem you might recognize as set subtraction; that is, we want to find all the words from one set (the words in *emma.txt*) that are not in the other (the words in *words.txt*).

`subtract` takes hashes `%main` and `%dict` and returns a new hash that contains all the keys from `%main` that are not in `%dict`. Since we don't really care about the values, we set them all to 1:

```
sub subtract (%main, %dict) {
    my %difference;
    for %main.keys -> $word {
        %difference{$word} = 1 unless %dict{$word}:exists;
    }
    return %difference;
}
```

To find the words in *emma.txt* that are not in *words.txt*, we need to load the word list into a hash and call `subtract`, passing the two hashes as arguments. We also add some code to print the first 20 words not found in the word list:

```
my %word-list = map { $_ => 1 }, "words.txt".IO.lines;
my %unknown-words = subtract(%histogram, %word-list);
say %unknown-words.keys.head(20);
```

Notice that rather than using a subscript slice, I have used here the `head` method to print out the first 20 words of the list. This is just another way to get the first "n" items of a list or array. There is also a `tail` method to retrieve the last "n" items of a list or an array.

Here are some of the results from *Emma*:

```
(penetrated unsullied bateses outstepped particularity experienced
italian sunday solicitously blockhead unbleached ult 26th
christian 7th untouched iii greensward houseroom tete)
```

Some of these words are names and ordinal numbers. Others are rare or no longer in common use. But a few are common words that should really be in the list!

Note that I have used a hash (`%unknown-words`) here to store the words of *emma.txt* not found in the word list. Since we are using the data only to print a sample of 20 words, we could have used an array as well.

Constructing New Operators

Learning about hash subtraction is an excellent opportunity to introduce a very interesting functionality of Perl 6: the capacity to construct new operators or to redefine existing ones.

Since we are subtracting two lists of words, it is tempting to use the minus sign to denote this subtraction operation. It is very easy to create such an operator in Perl 6:

```
multi sub infix:<-> (%main, %dict) {
        my %difference;
        for %main.keys -> $word {
                %difference{$word} = 1 unless %dict{$word}:exists;
        }
        return %difference;
}
```

Compared to the definition of the subtract subroutine, the only differences are in the header line. We will cover the details in a later chapter, but let us briefly explain here. Most Perl 6 operators are defined as "multi" subroutines, i.e., subroutines that can be defined several times with different signatures and bodies; Perl will know which one to use depending on the signature. Here we define the minus operator as a multi subroutine whose parameters are two hashes; this will be enough for the Perl compiler to know that we don't want the regular subtraction between numerical values, but something else that applies to two hashes. The minus operator is defined as "infix," which means that the operator will be placed between its two operands.

Calling this new operator is now just as easy as calling the regular subtraction operator between numbers; we just need to use two hashes as operands:

```
my %unknown-words = %histogram - %word-list;
```

The rest of the program works just as before.

This ease of creating new operators is one of the facilities offered by Perl 6 to *extend the language* from within itself. We'll come back to that and other ways to extend the language in later chapters.

As an exercise, write a multi subroutine that creates the new postfix "!" operator for computing the factorial of an integer:

```
say 5!;     # -> 120
```

Also try to think about how you would test this new "!" operator against various input values. Solution: "Exercise: Constructing New Operators" on page 407.

Sets, Bags, and Mixes

Perl 6 has a variety of data structure types called Set, Bag, and Mix that provide many common set operations. They are unordered collections of unique and weighed items. They are immutable (but there also exist mutable versions of these data structures, SetHash, BagHash, and MixHash).

You may create and use a set as follows:

```
> my $s = set <banana apple orange orange banana pear apple>;
set(banana, orange, apple, pear)
> say $s.perl
set("banana","orange","apple","pear")
> say $s.elems;
4
> say $s{'apple'}
True
> say $s{'strawberry'}
False
```

As you can see, duplicates have been removed. Sets only tell us whether or not at least one item of a given name has been seen.

A bag, by contrast, also keeps track of how many of each item have been seen:

```
> my $b = bag <banana apple orange orange banana pear apple orange>;
bag(banana(2), orange(3), pear, apple(2))
> say $b{'banana'}
2
```

Mixes are similar to bags, except that the elements' weights don't have to be integers.

The interesting thing about these collections is that they can use many set operators commonly used in mathematics, such as the $\in$ set membership operator (or use (elem) instead if you don't know how to type $\in$ in your editor[1]), the $\cap$ or (&) set intersection operator, or the $\subseteq$ or (<) subset operator:

```
> say "Found it!" if 'apple' ∈ $s;
Found it!
> say "Is subset!" if <orange banana> ⊂ $s;
Is subset!
> say <orange banana pineapple> ∩ $s;
set(banana, orange)
```

Notice that we haven't used the set keyword to define the <orange banana> list in the second example above. This list has been coerced to a Set to check whether it was a subset of the $s set. This is one of the great things about these collections: most of these set operators can be used with lists, arrays, and hashes.

We can rewrite the hash subtraction program using a set for the word list and the $\in$ (or (elem)) set membership operator:

```
my %histogram;
my $skip = True; # flag to skip the header
sub process-line(Str $line is copy) {
    # (same as above)
}
```

---

1 I can't teach you here how to type these characters, because each editor will require a different method.

```
process-line $_ for "emma.txt".IO.lines;
my $word-list = set "words.txt".IO.lines;
my %unknown-words = subtract(%histogram, $word-list);
say %unknown-words.keys.head(20);

sub subtract (%main, $dict) {
        my %difference;
        for %main.keys -> $word {
                %difference{$word} = 1 unless $word ∈ $dict;
        }
        return %difference;
}
```

The code line in the `for` loop could also be written as follows:

```
            %difference{$word} = 1 unless $word (elem) $dict;
#or:        %difference{$word} = 1 if $word ∉ $dict;
#or:        %difference{$word} = 1 if $word !(elem) $dict;
#or even with the (cont) or ∋ contain operator:
            %difference{$word} = 1 unless $dict (cont) $word;
#or:        %difference{$word} = 1 unless $dict ∋ $word;
#or:        %difference{$word} = 1 if $dict ∌ $word;
# etc.
```

The \ (note that this is unicode character \x2216, not the same as the \ backslash) or (-) operator provides a set difference, so that we needed neither to write a `subtract` subroutine nor to construct our own minus operator:

```
process-line $_ for "emma.txt".IO.lines;
my $word-list = set "words.txt".IO.lines;
my $unknown-words = %histogram.keys (-) $word-list;
say $unknown-words.keys.head(20);
```

There are more than 30 set operators available, covering most of the set operators used in mathematics. I've only shown some that are the most likely to be useful. Check into the official documentation (*https://doc.perl6.org/language/setbagmix*) if you need some others.

As an exercise, you may rewrite the `process-line` subroutine or replace it to use a set or a bag instead of a hash to store the words of *emma.txt* (and possibly adapt the rest of the program where needed), in order to find the words of the *emma.txt* that are not in the *words.txt*. Solution: "Exercise: Sets, Bags, and Mixes" on page 408.

Random Words

To choose random words from the histogram, the simplest algorithm is to build a list with multiple copies of each word, according to the observed frequency, and then choose from the list with the `pick` function:

```
my @array = map {| (.key xx .value)}, %histogram;
say pick 30, @array;
```

The expression map {| (.key xx .value)} reads each pair of the histogram and creates a list with .value copies of the string in .key. The pick function selects 30 random words from the array.

This algorithm works, but it is not very efficient; each time you choose one or some random words, it rebuilds the list, which is as big as the original book. An obvious improvement is to build the list once and then make multiple selections, but the list is still big.

An alternative is:

1. Use keys to get a list of the words in *emma.txt*.

2. Build a list that contains the cumulative sum of the word frequencies (see Exercise 9-2). The last item in this list is the total number of words in the book, *n*.

3. Choose a random number from 1 to *n*. Use a bisection search (see Exercise 9-10) to find the index where the random number would be inserted in the cumulative sum.

4. Use the index to find the corresponding word in the newly created word list.

Exercise 11-6.

Write a program that uses this algorithm to choose a random word from *emma.txt*. Solution: "Exercise: Random Words" on page 410.

Note that Perl offers a shortcut to perform the task at hand: when used on a bag, pick returns a random selection of elements, weighted by the values corresponding to each key. Ideally, we should have used a bag instead of a hash to store our %histo histogram, but we did not know about bags at the time. We can, however, construct a bag from the %histo histogram. Consider the following example:

```
> my %histo = ( banana => 5, pear => 1, orange => 12);
{banana => 5, orange => 12, pear => 1}
> my $fruit-bag = bag map { $_ xx %histo{$_}}, %histo.keys;
bag(banana(5), orange(12), pear)
> for 1..10 { say $fruit-bag.pick: 5}
(banana orange orange orange orange)
(orange orange banana orange banana)
(orange orange banana orange orange)
(pear orange banana banana orange)
(orange banana orange orange orange)
...
```

As you can see, the most common item, "orange," has been picked more often than the others, and the least common, "pear," has not been picked up at all before the fourth draw.

As an exercise, you may want to adapt this code to choose random words from *emma.txt*.

Markov Analysis

If you choose words from *emma.txt* at random, you can get a sense of the vocabulary, but you probably won't get a sentence:

```
this the small regard harriet which knightley's it most things
```

A series of random words seldom makes sense because there is no relationship between successive words. For example, in a real sentence you would expect an article like "the" to be followed by an adjective or a noun, and probably not a verb or adverb.

One way to measure these kinds of relationships is Markov analysis, which characterizes, for a given sequence of words, the probability of the words that might come next. For example, the second chapter of *The Little Prince* (1943), the famous novella written by French writer and pioneer aviator Antoine de Saint-Exupéry, begins:

> The first night, then, I went to sleep on the sand, a thousand miles from any human habitation. I was more isolated than a shipwrecked sailor on a raft in the middle of the ocean. Thus you can imagine my amazement, at sunrise, when I was awakened by an odd little voice. It said:
>
> "If you please–draw me a sheep!"
>
> "What!"
>
> "Draw me a sheep!"
>
> I jumped to my feet, completely thunderstruck. I blinked my eyes hard. I looked carefully all around me. And I saw a most extraordinary small person, who stood there examining me with great seriousness. (...)
>
> Now I stared at this sudden apparition with my eyes fairly starting out of my head in astonishment. Remember, I had crashed in the desert a thousand miles from any inhabited region. And yet my little man seemed neither to be straying uncertainly among the sands, nor to be fainting from fatigue or hunger or thirst or fear. Nothing about him gave any suggestion of a child lost in the middle of the desert, a thousand miles from any human habitation. When at last I was able to speak, I said to him:
>
> "But–what are you doing here?"
>
> And in answer he repeated, very slowly, as if he were speaking of a matter of great consequence:
>
> "If you please–draw me a sheep..."
>
> When a mystery is too overpowering, one dare not disobey. Absurd as it might seem to me, a thousand miles from any human habitation and in danger of death, I took out of my pocket a sheet of paper and my fountain-pen. But then I remembered how my studies had been concentrated on geography, history, arithmetic, and grammar, and I told the little chap (a little crossly, too) that I did not know how to draw. He answered me:

"That doesn't matter. Draw me a sheep..."

But I had never drawn a sheep. So I drew for him one of the two pictures I had drawn so often. It was that of the boa constrictor from the outside. And I was astounded to hear the little fellow greet it with,

"No, no, no! I do not want an elephant inside a boa constrictor. A boa constrictor is a very dangerous creature, and an elephant is very cumbersome. Where I live, every-thing is very small. What I need is a sheep. Draw me a sheep."

In this text, the word "draw" is always followed by the word "me," and the phrase "draw me" is always followed by "a sheep." And the phrase "a thousand" is always fol-lowed by "miles," but the phrase "a thousand miles" may be followed by "from any human habitation" or by "from any inhabited region."

The result of Markov analysis is a mapping from each prefix (like "draw me" and "a thousand miles") to all possible suffixes (like "a sheep" and "from any habitation" or "from any inhabited region").

Given this mapping, you can generate a random text by starting with any prefix and choosing at random from the possible suffixes. Next, you can combine the end of the prefix and the new suffix to form the next prefix, and repeat.

For example, if you start with the prefix "draw me," then the next word has to be "a sheep," because the prefix is always followed by "a sheep" in the text. If a prefix is "a thousand miles," the next suffix might be "from any habitation" or "from any inhabi-ted region."

In this example the lengths of the prefixes are two or three, but you can do Markov analysis with any prefix length.

Exercise 11-7.

Markov analysis:

1. Write a program to read a text from a file and perform Markov analysis. The result should be a hash that maps from prefixes to a collection of possible suf-fixes. The collection might be an array, a hash, a set, a bag, etc.; it is up to you to make an appropriate choice. You can test your program with prefix length two, but it would be nice to write the program in a way that makes it easy to try other lengths.

2. Add a function to the previous program to generate random text based on the Markov analysis. Here is an example from *Emma* with prefix length 2:

   > it was a black morning's work for her. the friends from whom she could not have come to hartfield any more! dear affectionate creature! you banished to abbey mill farm. now i am afraid you are a great deal happier if she had no hesitation in approving. dear harriet, i give myself joy of so sorrowful an event;

For this example, the punctuation has been left attached to the words. The result is almost syntactically correct, but not quite. Semantically, it almost makes sense, but not quite.

What happens if you increase the prefix length? Does the random text make more sense?

3. Once your program is working, you might want to try a mash-up: if you combine text from two or more books, the random text you generate will blend the vocabulary and phrases from the sources in interesting ways.

Credit: this case study is based on an example from Kernighan and Pike, *The Practice of Programming*, Addison-Wesley, 1999.

You should attempt this exercise before you go on. Then you can can study our solution in "Exercise: Markov Analysis" on page 411.

Data Structures

Using Markov analysis to generate random text is fun, but there is also a point to this exercise: data structure selection. In your solution to the previous exercises, you had to choose:

- How to represent the prefixes
- How to represent the collection of possible suffixes
- How to represent the mapping from each prefix to the collection of possible suffixes

The last one is easy: a hash is the obvious choice for a mapping from keys to corresponding values.

For the prefixes, the most obvious options are a string or a list of strings.

For the suffixes, one option is a list; another is a histogram (hash).

How should you choose? The first step is to think about the operations you will need to implement for each data structure. For the prefixes, we need to be able to remove words from the beginning and add words to the end. For example, if the current prefix is "draw me," and the next word is "a," you need to be able to form the next prefix, "me a," in order to find the next suffix, "sheep."

Your first choice might be an array, since it is easy to add and remove elements, but we also need to be able to use the prefixes as keys in a hash, so that sort of rules out arrays.

For the collection of suffixes, the operations we need to perform include adding a new suffix (or increasing the frequency of an existing one), and choosing a random suffix.

Adding a new suffix is equally easy for the list implementation or the hash. Choosing a random element from a list is easy; choosing from a hash is harder to do efficiently (see Exercise 11-6).

So far we have been talking mostly about ease of implementation, but there are other factors to consider in choosing data structures. One is runtime. Sometimes there is a theoretical reason to expect one data structure to be faster than other; for example, we mentioned that a lookup operation is faster for hashes than for arrays, especially when the number of elements is large.

But often you don't know ahead of time which implementation will be faster. One option is to implement both of them and see which is better. This approach is called *benchmarking*. A practical alternative is to choose the data structure that is easiest to implement, and then see if it is fast enough for the intended application. If so, there is no need to go on. If not, there are tools, like `profile` modules, that can identify the places in a program that take the most time.

The other factor to consider is storage space. For example, using a histogram for the collection of suffixes might take less space because you only have to store each word once, no matter how many times it appears in the text. In some cases, saving space can also make your program run faster, and in the extreme, your program might not run at all if you run out of memory. But for many applications, space is a secondary consideration after runtime.

One final thought: in this discussion, we have implied that we should use one data structure for both analysis and generation. But since these are separate phases, it would also be possible to use one structure for analysis and then convert to another structure for generation. This would be a net win if the time saved during generation exceeded the time spent in conversion.

Building Your Own Data Structures

Perl has a number of compound types such as arrays and hashes that you can combine to construct arrays of arrays, arrays of hashes, hashes of arrays, hashes of hashes, arrays of arrays of arrays or hashes, and so on, and this is usually sufficient for most needs. Sometimes, however, you need something very specific that is not built in.

Over the years, computer science has studied and used scores of specific data structures such as linked lists, stacks, queues, circular lists, trees of numerous kinds, etc. We will briefly study a couple of them.

Linked Lists

A linked list is a collection of items in which each item holds a value (or several values) and a link to the next item of the collection. In many programming languages, arrays have a fixed size (contrary to Perl in which arrays can usually grow according to your needs). In those programming languages, a linked list is often used to represent a variable-size collection of items.

We saw in "Stacks and Queues" on page 159 how to use arrays to build stacks and queues. It was fairly easy. In some lower-level programming languages, you would need linked lists for that.

In Perl, a linked list item may be represented by a pair (an object of type Pair). The following code is a very simple example showing how we could implement a stack using a linked list in Perl:

```
sub add-to-stack (Pair $stack-top, $item) {
    my $new-pair = $item => $stack-top;
    return $new-pair;
}

sub take-from-stack (Pair $stack-top) {
    my $new-top = $stack-top.value;
    return $stack-top.key, $new-top;
}

sub create-stack ($item) {
    return $item => Nil;
}

my $stack = create-stack (0);

for 1..5 -> $item {
    $stack = add-to-stack($stack, $item);
}
say "The stack is: ", $stack.perl;

for 1..5 {
    my $value;
    ($value, $stack) = take-from-stack($stack);
    say "$value -- ", $stack;
}
```

Once populated, the resulting stack looks like this:

```
5 => 4 => 3 => 2 => 1 => 0 => Nil
```

This is just given as an example for the construction of a linked list. There is usually no need to use anything like this in Perl, since it is much easier to implement a stack using an array, as seen in "Stacks and Queues" on page 159, although the same principle can be used for building more advanced data structures.

You might still want, as an exercise, to implement a queue (see "Stacks and Queues" on page 159) using a linked list.

Trees

A tree is usually a collection of items in which each item (or *node*) holds a value (or possibly several values) and two or several links to other items of the collection, the children. Think of a family tree or a tree of directories on a hard disk drive to get the general idea. The ultimate nodes that don't have their own children are often called the leaves. There is usually only one ultimate grandparent node, sometimes called the root (if there is more than one ultimate grandparent, then it is not really a tree but several trees or a "forest").

Dozens of different types of trees have been invented and their descriptions have filled entire books about computer science algorithms. Some are designed to keep the data sorted, others to maintain balance between the tree branches, and so on. The data structure is often not very complicated, but the algorithms needed to maintain the required properties sometimes can be a bit hairy.

For example, a typical tree might hold one value and two links, one to the left child and one to the right child. You might implement such a *binary tree* in a similar way as the linked list described above, except that the value would no longer be a link to the next element, but an array of two elements, the links to the two children. Or you could follow more closely the linked list model above and have nested pairs. For example, a binary tree might look like this:

```
my $tree = 1 => (( 2 => 3 ) => (4 => (5 => ((6 => 7) => 8))));
```

The implementation is left as an exercise to the reader.

Quite often, though, a tree may be implemented in Perl as a simpler data structure such as a nested array or hash. The next section examines such an example.

Binary Heaps

A binary heap is a binary tree that keeps a partial order: each node has a value larger that its parent and less than either of its two children; there is no specific order imposed between siblings. (You could also do it the other way around: you could design heaps in which any node has a value less than its parent.)

Because there is no order between siblings, it is not possible to find a particular element without potentially searching the whole heap. Therefore, a heap is not very good if you need random access to specific nodes. But if you're interested in always finding the smallest item, then a heap is a very efficient data structure.

Heaps are used for solving a number of CS problems, and serve as the basis for an efficient and very popular sorting technique called heap sort.

For a human, it is useful to represent a heap in a tree-like form. But a computer can store a heap as a simple array (not even a nested array). For this, the index of an element is used to compute the index of its parent or its two children. The children of an element are the two locations where the indices are about double its index; conversely, the parent of a node is located at about half its index. If the heap starts at index 0, the exact formulas for a node with index $n are commonly as follows:

- parent: `int( ($n-1)/2 )`
- left child: `2*$n + 1`
- right child: `2*$n + 2`

The root node is at index 0. Its children are at positions 1 and 2. The children of 1 are 3 and 4 and the children of 2 are 5 and 6. The children of 3 are 7 and 8, and so on.

Thus, if interpreted as a binary heap, the array:

```
[0, 1, 2, 3, 4, 5, 6, 7, 8]
```

is associated with the tree displayed in Figure 11-1.

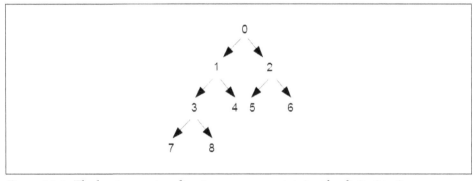

Figure 11-1. The heap corresponding to an array containing the digits 0 to 8

Here is one way to build a heap (in partial alphabetic order) from a list of unordered letters:

```
sub build-heap (@array, $index is copy) {
    my $index-val = @array[$index];
    while ($index) {
        my $parent = Int( ($index - 1) / 2);
        my $parent-val = @array[$parent];
        last if $parent-val lt $index-val;
        @array[$index] = $parent-val;
        $index = $parent;
    }
    @array[$index] = $index-val;
}
```

```
sub heapify (@array) {
    for @array.keys -> $i {
        build-heap @array, $i;
    }
}

my @input = <m t f l s j p o b h v k n q g r i a d u e c>;
heapify @input;
say @input;
```

Note that the heap is built in place (there is no need for a second array). The resulting array is displayed as follows:

```
[a b g d c k j l f h e m n q p t r o i u s v]
```

Is this a correct heap? It's difficult to say at first glance and checking it manually is somewhat tedious. When writing a program for building such a data structure, it is often useful to write some subroutines to display the content in a way that makes it easier to understand the result and check its correctness. The following code shows two examples of such possible subroutines:

```
sub print-heap (@array) {
    my $start = 0;
    my $end = 0;
    my $last = @array.end;
    my $step = 1;
    loop {
        say @array[$start..$end];
        last if $end == $last;
        $start += $step;
        $step *= 2;
        $end += $step;
        $end = $last if $end > $last;
    }
}

sub print-heap2 (@array) {
    my $step = 0;
    for @array.keys -> $current {
        my $left_child = @array[2 * $current + 1];
        say "$current\tNode = @array[$current];\tNo child"
            and next unless defined $left_child;
        my $right_child = @array[2 * $current + 2] // "' '";

        say "$current\tNode = @array[$current];\tChildren: " .
            " $left_child and $right_child";
        $step++;
    }
}
```

The first one displays the related tree level by level:

```
(a)
(b g)
(d c k j)
(l f h e m n q p)
(t r o i u s v)
```

which makes it easy to draw the tree (see Figure 11-2).

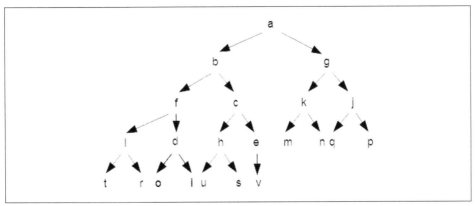

Figure 11-2. The heap corresponding to the array of letters

The second one shows the children for each node and makes it possible to easily check that the partial alphabetic order constraint is satisfied (i.e., each node is smaller than its children):

```
0        Node = a;        Children:  b and g
1        Node = b;        Children:  d and c
2        Node = g;        Children:  k and j
3        Node = d;        Children:  l and f
4        Node = c;        Children:  h and e
5        Node = k;        Children:  m and n
6        Node = j;        Children:  q and p
7        Node = l;        Children:  t and r
8        Node = f;        Children:  o and i
9        Node = h;        Children:  u and s
10       Node = e;        Children:  v and ' '
11       Node = m;        No child
12       Node = n;        No child
(...)
21       Node = v;        No child
```

Debugging

When you are debugging a program, and especially if you are working on a hard bug, here are some things to try:

Reading

Examine your code, read it back to yourself, and check that it says what you meant to say.

Running

Experiment by making changes and running different versions. Often if you display the right thing at the right place in the program, the problem becomes obvious, but sometimes you have to build scaffolding.

Running under a debugger

A *debugger* is a utility program that enables you to run a program step by step, so you can follow the execution path and check the content of important variables at crucial points in the program execution, set break points, etc. Perl 6 provides a debugger, called `perl6-debug`, that makes all these things possible. With the advent of modern high-level languages, many people balk at using a debugger. This is a mistake. A debugger will not help solve every kind of problem, but it can be immensely useful. See "Debugging" on page 266 for more information on the Perl debugger.

Ruminating

Take some time to think! What kind of error is it: syntax, runtime, or semantic? What information can you get from the error messages, or from the output of the program? What kind of error could cause the problem you're seeing? What did you change last, before the problem appeared?

Rubber ducking

If you explain the problem to someone else, you sometimes find the answer before you finish asking the question. Often you don't need the other person; you could just talk to a rubber duck. That's the origin of the well-known strategy called *rubber duck debugging*. I am not making this up; see *https://en.wikipe dia.org/wiki/Rubber_duck_debugging*.

Retreating

At some point, the best thing to do is back off, undoing recent changes, until you get back to a program that works and that you understand. Then you can start rebuilding.

Beginning programmers sometimes get stuck on one of these activities and forget the others. Each activity comes with its own failure mode.

For example, reading your code might help if the problem is a typographical error, but not if the problem is a conceptual misunderstanding. If you don't understand what your program does, you can read it 100 times and never see the error, because the error is in your head.

Running experiments can help, especially if you run small, simple tests. But if you run experiments without thinking or reading your code, you might fall into a pattern we call "random walk programming," which is the process of making random changes until the program does the right thing. Needless to say, random walk programming can take a very long time.

You have to take time to think. Debugging is like an experimental science. You should have at least one hypothesis about what the problem is. If there are two or more possibilities, try to think of a test that would eliminate one of them.

But even the best debugging techniques will fail if there are too many errors, or if the code you are trying to fix is too big and complicated. Sometimes the best option is to retreat, simplifying the program until you get to something that works and that you understand.

Beginning programmers are often reluctant to retreat because they can't stand to delete a line of code (even if it's wrong). If it makes you feel better, copy your program into another file before you start stripping it down. Then you can copy the pieces back one at a time.

Finding a hard bug requires reading, running (with or without a debugger), ruminating, and sometimes retreating. If you get stuck on one of these activities, try the others.

Glossary

benchmarking
The process of choosing between various data structures and algorithms by implementing alternatives and testing them (especially their run durations) on a sample of the possible inputs.

debugger
A program that lets you run your code line by line and check its state at any step during its execution.

default value
The value given to an optional parameter if no argument is provided.

deterministic
Pertaining to a program that does the same thing each time it runs, given the same inputs.

override
To replace a default value with an argument.

pseudorandom
> Pertaining to a sequence of numbers that appears to be random, but is generated by a deterministic program.

rubber duck debugging
> Debugging by explaining your problem to an inanimate object such as a rubber duck. Articulating the problem can help you solve it, even if the rubber duck doesn't know Perl.

Exercises: Huffman Coding

Huffman coding is a technique used for data compression, i.e., to reduce the size of a piece of data (such as, for example, compressing a file).

Variable-Length Codes

If you are familiar with Morse code, you know that it is a system for encoding the letters of the alphabet as a series of dots and dashes. For example, the famous signal . . . - - - . . . represents the letters SOS, which comprise an internationally recognized call for help. The table in Figure 11-3 shows the rest of the codes.

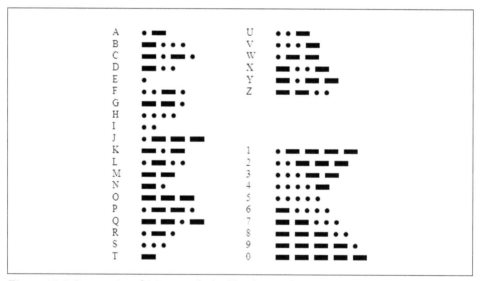

Figure 11-3. International Morse code (public domain)

Morse code (invented between 1836 and 1844) was one of the very first attempts at digital encoding of the alphabet of a plain text. The only known earlier attempt is the braille alphabet (1824-1837).

Notice that some codes are longer than others. By design, the most common letters have the shortest codes. Since there are a limited number of short codes, that means that less common letters and symbols have longer codes. A typical message will have more short codes than long ones, which minimizes the average transmission time per letter.

Codes like this are called variable-length codes. In this exercise, we will look at an algorithm for generating a variable-length code called a Huffman code. It is an interesting algorithm in its own right, but it also makes a useful exercise because its implementation uses a variety of data structures.

Here is an outline of what we will do until the end of this chapter:

1. First, we will use a sample of English text to generate a table of characters and their frequencies.

2. Then we will use this frequency table to generate a code table.

3. Finally, we will encode a message with this code table and then decode it.

The Frequency Table

Since the goal is to give short codes to common letters, we have to know how often each letter occurs. In Edgar Allan Poe's short story "The Gold Bug," one of the characters, William Legrand, uses letter frequencies to crack a cypher. He explains:

> Now, in English, the letter which most frequently occurs is e. Afterwards, the succession runs thus: a o i d h n r s t u y c f g l m w b k p q x z. E however predominates so remarkably that an individual sentence of any length is rarely seen, in which it is not the prevailing character.

So our first mission is to see whether Poe got it right. To check, let's use as a sample the text of "The Gold Bug" itself, which can be downloaded from Project Gutenberg (*http://www.gutenberg.org/files/2147/2147-0.txt*) and a variety of other websites.

Exercise 11-8.

Write a program that counts the number of times each letter appears in a sample text. Download the text of "The Gold Bug" and analyze the frequency of the letters.

Solution: see "Exercise 11-8: The frequency table" on page 413.

Building the Huffman Code

For our purposes, Morse code has one defect: it does not use just two symbols as you might think, but actually three: in addition to the dots and dashes, it it also implicitly using the space between two symbols, as well as a longer space between two letters.

The reason why some space is needed is quite simple. Refer to the Morse code table above and suppose you receive three dots (...). This could be interpreted as the letter "e" three times, or as "ie" or "ei," or as "s," or as the beginning of "h," "v," "3," "4," or "5." Added spaces make it possible to disambiguate between those various possibilities. But they also make code transmission much slower.

In 1951, David A. Huffman invented a code-building technique that avoids this problem: provided that you know where a given letter starts, it is totally unambiguous. For example, we will meet later a Huffman code for a small subset of the alphabet that looks like this:

```
a => ..
e => .-
s => -.-
n => -..
t => --.
d => ---.
r => ----
```

If you start reading a sequence of dots and dashes representing a valid text composed with these seven letters, you can always decode it without any ambiguity. If the first symbol is a dot, then the letter is either an "a" or a "e" depending on the next symbol. If the first symbol is a dash and the next one a dot, then the letter must be either an "s" or an "n" depending on the third symbol. If the two first symbols are dashes, you can similarly determine that the current letter is a "t" (if the third symbol is a dot), or a "d" or a "r," which you can find out by looking at the fourth symbol. In brief, you don't need spaces between the symbols; it is always possible to unambiguously decode a letter.

How can we build such a Huffman code? Let's do it by hand with a very simple alphabet: the four letters of the nucleo-bases of DNA: A, C, T, and G. Suppose we want to encode the following input string:

```
CCTATCCTCGACTCCAGTCCA
```

This gives the following frequency table:

```
C :    10       47.62
T :     5       23.81
A :     4       19.05
G :     2        9.52
```

To build the Huffman code, we start with the two less frequent letters, and merge them into one new temporary symbol, [GA], which we pretend is a new composite letter with a frequency of 6. At this point, we decide that, between two letters, the less frequent one will have an appended dot and the other an appended dash (this is an arbitrary choice; it could be done the other way around). So we say that the symbol for the least common of the two letters ("G") will be [GA]. and the symbol for "A" will be [GA]-.

We are now left with three letters, C, T and [GA]. We merge the two least frequent letters, "T" and "[GA]," and can now tell that the symbol for "T" will be [TGA]. and the symbol for [GA] will be [TGA]-. There are only two letters left, "C" and "TGA," with "C" the least frequent one; so "C" will be a dot and "TGA" a dash.

We can now unroll our dummy letters: "T" is [TGA]., so replacing [TGA] with its symbol, i.e., a dash, the final code for "T" will be -.; similarly, [GA]. now translates into --. By the same substitution process, we can now determine that "A" is --- and "G" --.. So our final Huffman code table is:

```
C => .
T => -.
G => --.
A => ---
```

Notice that, by construction, the most frequent letter (C) has the shortest code and the least common letters (G and A) the longest codes.

Manually encoding the CCTATCCTCGACTCCAGTCCA input string with this code yields the following pseudo-Morse code:

```
..-.----...-..--.---.-...----.-...---
```

Note that our Huffman code is not ambiguous: the first dot can only be a "C," and the second one also. The next symbol is a dash, which can be the beginning of the three other letters, but only "T" can have a dot afterwards. The next sequence of symbols is four dashes. This can only be the three dashes of a "A," with the last dash being the beginning of the next letter; and -. can only be a "T," and so on.

In a real-life Huffman encoding for text file compression, we would not use dots and dashes, but 0 and 1 bits; however, dots and dashes are just another nice way of representing those binary values. So, let's just pretend that dots and dashes are really 0 and 1 binary numbers.

Did we really achieve data compression? Our pseudo-Morse string has 38 binary symbols. The original input string had 21 characters or bytes, that is 168 bits. The data has been compressed by a factor of about 4.4.

Is Huffman coding better than a fixed-length code? A string representation where each letter would be represented by two bits (two bits can represent four letters) would require 42 symbols. So, yes, we did obtain a better data compression than a fixed-length encoding (by about 10%). This may seem to be a small achievement, but this is actually quite good with such a small alphabet. With real text data, Huffman coding can achieve significant data compression.

Exercise 11-9.

1. Write a program that performs Huffman encoding of a simple string of characters. You may start with the DNA example above. Don't worry, though, if you don't get the same Huffman table as the one above: there can be more than one Huffman code for a given input string, but check that you obtain an unambiguous code.

2. Try it with strings having a larger alphabet (you'll probably want to start with a relatively small alphabet, because it can otherwise be tedious to check the result by hand).

3. Write a subroutine to encode an input string into pseudo-Morse using the generated Huffman table.

4. Write a subroutine to decode the pseudo-Morse output you've just generated for the previous question.

Solution: see "Exercise 11-9: Huffman coding of a DNA strand" on page 414.

Moving Forward

Now that you have reached the end of the first part of this book, you should no longer be a pure beginner. By now, you should be able to go through the official Perl 6 documentation (*https://docs.perl6.org*) and find your way.

There are many more things to say about programming. The next three chapters will be devoted to more advanced concepts and new programming paradigms, including:

Object-oriented programming
We will describe how we can construct our own types and methods, which is a way to extend the language.

Using grammars
This is a form of declarative programming in which you define axioms and rules and derive knowledge from these; grammars are a very powerful way to analyze textual content and are used to transform program source code into executable statements.

Functional programming
This is yet another programming paradigm in which computation is expressed as the evaluation of mathematical functions.

Each of these chapters probably deserves a full book in its own right (and might have one some day), but we hope to tell you enough about them to get you going. In my opinion, every programmer should know about these powerful concepts in order to be able to select the best way to solve a given problem.

Perl 6 is a multiparadigm language, so we can really cover these topics in terms of the Perl 6 language. A number of subjects that we have introduced in previous chapters should lead you easily into these new ideas, and this is the reason why I think it is possible to properly cover them with just one chapter for each of these subjects.

There will be far fewer exercises in the second part, because we expect you by now to be able to think up your own exercises and make your own experiments. And there will be only very few suggested solutions, because we are getting at a level where there is really not one right solution, but many possible ways to tackle a problem.

Concerning the Perl language, we have covered a lot of material, but, as we warned from the very beginning, this is far from exhaustive. The following are among the topics that we have not covered (and will not cover); you might want to explore the documentation on them yourself:

Concurrent programming
> Today's computers have multiple processors or multicore processors; Perl 6 offers various ways of taking advantage of these to run computing processes in parallel in order to improve performance and reduce runtime; see the official documentation (*https://docs.perl6.org/language/concurrency*) for more details.

Exception handling
> Managing situations where something goes wrong is an important part of programming. Perl 6 offers various mechanisms to handle such situations. See the official documentation (*https://docs.perl6.org/language/exceptions*) for more details.

Interprocess communication
> Programs often have to run other programs and to communicate with them. See the official documentation (*https://docs.perl6.org/language/ipc*).

Modules
> How to create, use, and distribute Perl 6 modules. See the official documentation (*https://docs.perl6.org/language/modules*).

Native calling interface
> How to call libraries that are written in other programming languages and follow the C calling conventions. See the official documentation (*https://docs.perl6.org/language/nativecall*).

Classes and Objects

At this point you know how to use functions to organize code and built-in types to organize data. The next step is to learn "object-oriented programming," which uses programmer-defined types to organize both code and data.

When software applications start to grow large, the number of details to be handled becomes overwhelming. The only way to manage this complexity is to use abstraction and encapsulation. Object orientation is a very popular and efficient way to implement abstraction and encapsulation.

Perl 6 is an *object-oriented programming language*, which means that it provides features that support object-oriented programming, which has these defining characteristics:

- Programs include class and method definitions.
- Most of the computation is expressed in terms of operations on objects.
- Objects often represent things in the real world, and methods often correspond to the ways things in the real world interact.

Object-oriented programming in Perl 6 is a big topic that may be worth a book by itself (and there will probably be a book or two on the subject at some point). This chapter will hopefully do more than just skim the surface and enable you to create and use objects, but will not cover some of the details and more advanced features.

Objects, Methods, and Object-Oriented Programming

Let us start with a high-level nontechnical overview of object-oriented programming in general and a brief introduction to the jargon associated with it.

In computer science, an object may loosely describe a memory location or an entity having a value, and often be referred to by an identifier. This can be a variable, a data structure, an array, or possibly even a function. This general meaning is not the sense that we will use in this chapter.

In object-oriented programming (OOP), the word *object* has a much more specific meaning: an object is an entity which often has:

- An identity (for example its name).
- Some properties defining its behavior (in the form of special functions that are usually called *methods*); this behavior usually does not change over time and is generally common to all objects of the same type.
- A *state* defined by some special variables (called, depending on the language, attributes, instance data, fields, or members); the state may change over time and is generally specific to each object. In Perl, we speak about *attributes*.

In brief, an object is a set of attributes and methods packed together.

Objects are usually defined in a kind of code package called a *class*. A class defines the methods and the nature of the attributes associated with an object. In Perl 6, a class makes it possible to define new types similar to the built-in types that we have seen before. Very soon, we will start to define some classes and use them to create objects.

You already know informally what a method is, as we have used built-in methods throughout the book. It is a sort of function with a special postfix syntax using the dot notation on the invocant. For example, you may invoke the say method on a simple string:

```
"foo".say;          # -> foo
```

Note that "foo" isn't an object, but a simple string, but you can invoke the say method on it, because Perl can treat it internally as an object when needed. In some OOP languages, this implicit conversion of a native type into an object is sometimes called *autoboxing*.

You probably also remember that methods can be chained in a process where the value returned by a method becomes the invocant for the next method:

```
"foo".uc.say;       # -> FOO

my @alphabet = <charlie foxtrot alpha golf echo bravo delta>;
@alphabet.sort.uc.say;
    # prints: ALPHA BRAVO CHARLIE DELTA ECHO FOXTROT GOLF
```

In OOP, methods applicable to objects are usually defined within classes, often the class that also defined the object or some other class closely related to it. In Perl 6, methods can also be defined in a *role*, which is another type of code package somewhat resembling to a class, as we will see later.

The basic idea of object-oriented programming is that an object is a kind of black box that hides its internals (data and code) from the user; the user can consult or change the state of an object through the methods. Hiding the internals of objects is called *encapsulation*. This often enables a higher-level view and better data abstraction than what we have seen so far; this in turns helps to make programs less buggy (especially large programs).

In addition, OOP usually also offers the following concepts:

- *Polymorphism*, i.e., the possibility for a function or a method to do different things, depending on the type of object which calls it.
- *Inheritance*, i.e., the possibility to derive a class from another class, so that the *child class* inherits some of the properties of the *parent class*, which is a powerful tool for code reuse.

We will now study how all these concepts are implemented in Perl.

Programmer-Defined Types

We have used many of Perl's built-in types; now we are going to define a new type. As an example, we will create a type called `Point2D` that represents a point in two-dimensional space.

In mathematical notation, points are often written in parentheses with a comma separating the coordinates. For example, in Cartesian or rectangular coordinates, $(0, 0)$ represents the origin, and (x, y) represents the point x units to the right and y units up from the origin. x is called the abscissa of the point, and y the ordinate.

There are several ways we might represent points in Perl:

- We could store the coordinates separately in two variables, $x and $y.
- We could store the coordinates as elements in a list, an array, or a pair.
- We could create a new type to represent points as objects.

Creating a new type is a bit more complicated than the other options, but it has advantages that will be apparent soon.

A programmer-defined type is usually created by a *class* (or a role, but we will come back to that later). A barebones class definition for a point type looks like this:

```
class Point2D {
    has $.abscissa;          # "x" value
    has $.ordinate;          # "y" value
}
```

The header indicates that the new class is called `Point2D`. The body is defining two attributes, i.e., named properties associated with the class, here the abscissa and ordinate (or *x* and *y* coordinates) of the point.

Defining a class named `Point2D` creates a *type object*.

The type object is like a factory for creating objects. To create a point, you call the new method on the `Point2D` class:

```
my $point = Point2D.new(
    abscissa => 3,
    ordinate => 4
);
say $point.WHAT;             # -> (Point2D)
say $point.isa(Point2D)      # -> True
say $point.abscissa;         # -> 3
```

You can of course create as many points as you wish.

The new method is called a *constructor* and has not been defined in this example; this is not needed because Perl 6 supplies a default new constructor method for every class (we'll see later how). The method invocation syntax, with the dot notation, is the same as what we have used throughout the book to invoke built-in methods. You are not forced to use this constructor; you can also create your own (and you may name it new or something else), but we will stay with the built-in new method for the time being.

Creating a new object with a class is called *instantiation*, and the object is an *instance* of the class.

Every object is an instance of some class, so the terms "object" and "instance" are interchangeable. But we will often use "instance" to indicate that we are talking about an object belonging to a programmer-defined type.

Attributes

The attributes that we have defined are properties associated with the `Point2D` class, but they are specific to the instance of the class that has been created. They are instance attributes. If we create another `Point2D` object, it will also have these attributes, but the values of these attributes are likely to be different.

Figure 12-1 shows the result of these assignments. A state diagram that shows an object and its attributes is called an *object diagram*.

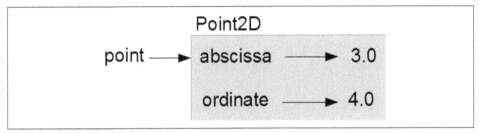

Figure 12-1. Object diagram

The variable $point refers to a Point2D object, which contains two attributes.

Each attribute of the Point2D class should refer to a number, but this is not obvious in the current definition of the class. As it stands right now, we could create a Point2D object with a string for the abscissa, which would not make much sense. We can improve the class definition by specifying a numeric type for the attributes:

```
class Point2D {
    has Numeric $.abscissa;          # "x" value
    has Numeric $.ordinate;          # "y" value
}
```

The instance attributes are private to the class, which means that they normally cannot be accessed from outside the class: you would usually need to invoke a method of the class (i.e., a kind of subroutine defined within the class) to get their value. However, when an attribute is defined with a dot as in $.abscissa:

```
has $.abscissa;
```

Perl automatically creates an implicit *accessor* method, i.e., a method having the same name as the attribute that returns the value of this attribute. Thus, when we wrote:

```
say $point.abscissa;               # -> 3
```

we were not accessing directly the abscissa attribute of the $point object, but we were really calling the abscissa method on the object, which in turn returned the value of that attribute.

You can use such an accessor with dot notation as part of any expression. For example:

```
my $dist-to-center = sqrt($point.abscissa ** 2 + $point.ordinate ** 2);
```

There is another way to declare an attribute in a class, with an exclamation mark twigil instead of a dot:

```
has $!abscissa;
```

In that case, Perl does not create an implicit accessor method and the attribute can only be accessed from methods within the class. Such an attribute is now fully private.

However, if you declare attributes this way, you will not be able to populate them at object creation with the default new constructor and will need to create your own constructor (or indirectly modify new). So don't try that for the time being, as you would not be able to do much with your objects at this point. We'll get back to that later.

By default, object attributes are not mutable; they are read-only. This means you cannot modify them once the object has been created. This is fine for some attributes: if an object represents a person, that person's name and birth date are unlikely to change. Some other attributes may need to be updated, sometimes very frequently. In such cases, attributes can be declared to be mutable with the is rw trait:

```
class Point2D {
    has Numeric $.abscissa is rw;        # "x" value
    has Numeric $.ordinate is rw;        # "y" value
}
```

It is now possible to modify these attributes. For example, we can change the newly created point's abscissa:

```
# First creating a Point2D object:
my $point = Point2D.new(abscissa => 3, ordinate => 4);
say $point;       # -> Point2D.new(abscissa => 3, ordinate => 4)

# Now moving the $point object two units to the right:
$point.abscissa = 5;
say $point;       # -> Point2D.new(abscissa => 5, ordinate => 4)
```

Almost all of the information presented so far about attributes has been related to instance attributes, i.e., to properties related to individual objects. You can also have attributes pertaining to the whole class, which are named *class attributes*. They are less common than instance attributes and are declared with the my declarator (instead of has). A typical example of a class attribute would be a counter at the class level to keep track of the number of objects that have been instantiated.

Creating Methods

The simple Point2D class and its instance $point are not very useful so far. Let's complete the class definition with some methods:

```
class Point2D {
    has Numeric $.abscissa;
    has Numeric $.ordinate;

    method coordinates {        # accessor to both x and y
        return (self.abscissa, self.ordinate)
    }

    method distanceToCenter {
```

```
            (self.abscissa ** 2 + self.ordinate ** 2) ** 0.5
    }
    method polarCoordinates {
        my $radius = self.distanceToCenter;
        my $theta = atan2 self.ordinate, self.abscissa;
        return $radius, $theta;
    }
}
```

We declare three methods in the class:

- coordinates, a simple accessor to the Cartesian coordinates
- distanceToCenter, a method to compute and return the distance between the object and the origin
- polarCoordinates, a method to compute the radius and azimuth ($theta) of the object in the polar coordinates system (notice that polarCoordinates invokes the distanceToCenter method to find the radius component of the polar coordinates)

A method definition is not very different from a subroutine definition, except that it uses the method keyword instead of the sub keyword. This is not a surprise since a method is essentially a subroutine that is defined within a class (or a role) and knows about its *invocant*, i.e., the object that called it and its class. And, of course, it has a different calling syntax.

Another important difference between a subroutine and a method is that, since there may be several methods with the same name defined in different classes (or different roles), a method invocation involves a *dispatch* phase, in which the object system selects which method to call, usually based on the class or type of the invocant. However, in Perl 6, that difference is blurred by the fact that you can have multi subroutines, i.e., subroutines with the same name and a different signature that are also resolved at runtime, depending on the *arity* (number of arguments) and type of the arguments.

Within a method definition, self refers to the *invocant*, the object that invoked the method. There is a shorthand for it, $., so that we could write the coordinates method as follows:

```
method coordinates {        # accessor to both x and y
    return ($.abscissa, $.ordinate)
}
```

The two syntax formats, $. and self, are essentially equivalent.

There is a third syntactic way of doing it, using an exclamation mark instead of a dot:

```
method coordinates {          # accessor to both x and y
    return ($!abscissa, $!ordinate)
}
```

Here, the result would be the same, but this new syntax is not equivalent: $.abscissa is a method invocation, whereas $!abscissa provides direct access to the attribute. The difference is that $!abscissa is available only within the class (and might be slightly faster), while the method invocation syntax can be used somewhere else (for example in another class). We will see in the next section examples of this distinction and its consequences.

We can now create an object and call our methods on it:

```
my $point =  Point2D.new(
    abscissa => 4,
    ordinate => 3
);
say $point.coordinates;        # -> (4 3)
say $point.distanceToCenter;   # -> 5
say $point.polarCoordinates;   # -> (5 0.643501108793284)
```

You might remember from previous chapters that if you use a method without naming an explicit invocant, then the method applies to the $_ topical variable:

```
.say for <one two three>;      # -> one two three (each on one line)
```

Now that we have created an object with some methods, we can also take advantage of the same syntax shortcut. For example if we use for or given to populate the $_ topical variable with the $point object, we can write:

```
given $point {
    say .coordinates;          # -> (4 3)
    say .distanceToCenter;     # -> 5
    .polarCoordinates.say;     # -> (5 0.643501108793284)
}
```

As an exercise, you could write a method called distance_between_points that takes two points as arguments and returns the distance between them using the Pythagorean theorem.

The methods of our class so far are all *accessors*, which means they provide a snapshot of some of the invocant's attributes. If the attributes are mutable (declared with the is rw trait), we can also create some *mutators*, i.e., methods that can be invoked to change those mutable attributes:

```
class Point2D-mutable {
    has Numeric $.abscissa is rw;
    has Numeric $.ordinate is rw;

    # perhaps the same accessors as in the class definition above
```

```
    method new-ordinate (Numeric $ord) {
        self.ordinate = $ord;
    }
}
# Creating the Point2D-mutable object:
my $point = Point2D-mutable.new(abscissa => 3, ordinate => 4);
say $point;  # -> Point2D-mutable.new(abscissa => 3, ordinate => 4)

# Modifying the ordinate:
$point.new-ordinate(6);
say $point;  # -> Point2D-mutable.new(abscissa => 3, ordinate => 6)
```

Rectangles and Object Composition

Sometimes it is obvious what the attributes of an object should be, but other times you have to make decisions. For example, imagine you are designing a class to represent rectangles. What attributes would you use to specify the location and size of a rectangle? You can ignore angle; to keep things simple, assume that the rectangle's edges are either vertical or horizontal.

There are at least two possibilities:

- You could specify one corner of the rectangle (or the center), the width, and the height.
- You could specify two opposing corners.

At this point it is hard to say whether either is better than the other, so we'll implement the first one, just as an example.

Here is the class definition:

```
class Rectangle {
    has Numeric $.width;
    has Numeric $.height;
    has Point2D $.corner;      # lower left vertex

    method area { return $.width * $.height }
    method topLeft { $.corner.abscissa, $.corner.ordinate + $.height; }
    # other methods, e.g. for other corners' coordinates, center, etc.
}
```

The new feature compared to the previous Point2D class definition is that the Rectangle class can now use the Point2D type created previously for defining the corner attribute.

The topLeft method returns the coordinates of the top left angle of the rectangle. This topLeft method gives us an opportunity to explain a bit more the difference between the $. and $! twigils. We have used $.corner.abscissa to obtain the abscissa of the corner, i.e., in effect an accessor invocation. We could have directly accessed the `corner` and `height` attributes of the `Rectangle` class and used the following method definition:

```
method topLeft { $!corner.abscissa, $!corner.ordinate + $!height; }
```

But it would not be possible to use `$!corner!abscissa` or `$.corner!abscissa`, because `abscissa` is not an attribute defined in the `Rectangle` class, and thus cannot be accessed directly there. You can use direct access to the attribute (for example with the `$!abscissa` syntax) only within the class where this attribute is defined, `Point2D`. So, in `Rectangle`, we need to invoke the accessor (i.e., the syntax with `$.`) for obtaining the value of the corner abscissa.

We can now create a `Rectangle` object:

```
my $start-pt =  Point2D.new(abscissa => 4, ordinate => 3);
my $rect = Rectangle.new(corner => $start-pt, height => 10, width => 5);

say "Topleft coord.: ", $rect.topLeft;   # -> Topleft coord.: (4 13)
say "Rectangle area: ", $rect.area;      # -> Rectangle area: 50
```

You might have noticed that the arguments passed to the `Rectangle.new` constructor are not in the same order as in the class definition. I did that on purpose to show that the order is unimportant because we are using named arguments.

Figure 12-2 shows the state of this object.

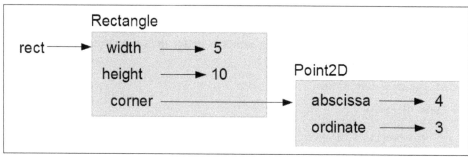

Figure 12-2. Object diagram

Using an object as an attribute of another object, possibly of another class, is called *object composition*. An object that is an attribute of another object is *embedded*. Object composition makes it possible to easily define nested layers of abstraction and is a powerful feature of object-oriented programming. In our "geometry" example, we started to define a low-level object, a `Point2D` instance, and then used that point to build a higher level type, `Rectangle`.

Instances as Return Values

Methods can return instances of another class. For example, the `Rectangle` class can have methods returning instances of `Point2D` for the other corners:

```
method topRightPoint {
    return Point2D.new(
        abscissa => $!corner.abscissa + $!width,
        ordinate => $!corner.ordinate + $!height
    );
}
# other methods for other corners
```

Notice that we don't even bother to give a name to the upper right point (although we could, if we wanted); we create it with the constructor and return it on the fly.

We can use the new method as follows:

```
my $topRightPt = $rect.topRightPoint;
say "Top right corner: ", $topRightPt;
# -> Top right corner: Point2D.new(abscissa => 9, ordinate => 13)
```

Although this is not very useful in such a simple case, we could play it safe and declare a `Point2D` type for `$topRightPt`:

```
my Point2D $topRightPt = $rect.topRightPoint;
```

This way, the code will raise an error if the `topRightPoint` happens to return something other than a `Point2D` instance.

Similarly, the `find-center` method invoked on a `Rectangle` returns a `Point2D` instance representing the center of the `Rectangle`:

```
method find-center { Point2D.new(
        abscissa => $!corner.abscissa + $!width / 2,
        ordinate => $!corner.ordinate + $!height / 2
    );
}
```

This new method can be used as follows:

```
say "Center = ", $rect.find-center;
# -> Center = Point2D.new(abscissa => 6.5, ordinate => 8.0)
```

Inheritance

Inheritance is probably the most emblematic feature of object-oriented programming. It is a mechanism through which it is possible to derive a class from another class. Inheritance is one of the standard ways to implement code reuse in object-oriented programming. It is also another useful way of defining successive layers of abstraction and a hierarchy of types.

The Pixel Class

The `Point2D` class is very general and could be used for a variety of purposes: geometry, vector graphics, animated mangas, and so on. We may want to use it to display graphic data on a screen. For this scenario, let's create a new derived class, `Pixel`, adding new properties to the point, such as color, perhaps transparency, etc.

Do we need to redefine all the attributes and methods for the new class? No, we don't. We can define a new class that *inherits* the properties of the `Point2D` base class and only modify what is no longer suitable or add whatever new features we need. Here, we want a new attribute to represent the pixel color and probably some new methods dealing with this new attribute.

According to the most common standards, a color is defined by three integers (really three octets, i.e., integers between 0 and 255 in decimal notation), representing the red, green, and blue (RGB) components of the pixel:

```
class Pixel is Point2D {
    has %.color is rw;

    method change_color(%hue) {
        self!color = %hue
    }
    method change_color2(Int $red, Int $green, Int $blue) {
        # signature using positional parameters
        self!color = (red => $red, green => $green, blue => $blue)
    }
}
```

The new class *inherits* the properties of `Point2D` thanks to the `is Point2D` trait, except possibly those that are explicitly modified (or overridden) or added in the new class. The new class is sometimes called a child class or subclass, whereas `Point2D` is the parent class. Creating this new class based on `Point2D` is called *subclassing* the `Point2D` parent class.

The new child class inherits the `abscissa` and `ordinate` attributes of the `Point2D` parent class (and their specific type and properties if any), as well as the methods such as `coordinates` defined in the parent class. The child class has a new attribute (the color) and two new methods.

In the preceding code example, we have written two different methods for changing the color only to illustrate two possible syntax formats, for pedagogical purposes. The first one receives a hash as a parameter, and the second one uses positional parameters, which forces the user to remember the order (RGB) in which the arguments must be passed; this can be a source of error and should be avoided when the number of parameters exceeds a certain limit (which will be left up to the reader). On the other hand, anyone working commonly with graphics knows by heart the standard conventional order of colors (i.e., RGB). Also, the second method has the advantage of enabling some type checks (the arguments must be integers). This is a simplified example; in real life, it may be desirable to check that the parameters are octets, i.e., integers between 0 and 255 (which could be done by adding a type constraint or defining a subset of the integer type).

Using the new `Pixel` class is straightforward:

```
say "Original colors: ", $pix.color;

$pix.change_color({:red(195), :green(110), :blue(70),});
say "Modified colors: ", $pix.color;
say "New pixel caracteristics:";
printf \tAbscissa: %.2f\n\tOrdinate: %.2f\n\tColors: R: %d, G: %d, B: %d\n",
      $pix.abscissa, $pix.ordinate,
      $pix.color<red>, $pix.color{"green"}, $pix.color{"blue"};

$pix.change_color2(90, 180, 30);  # positional args
say "New colors:
\tR: {$pix.color<red>}, G: {$pix.color<green>}, B: {$pix.color<blue>} ";
```

This displays the following output:

```
Original colors: {blue => 145, green => 233, red => 34}
Modified colors: {blue => 70, green => 110, red => 195}
New pixel caracteristics:
      Abscissa: 3.30
      Ordinate: 4.20
      Colors: R: 195, G: 110, B: 70
New colors:
      R: 90, G: 180, B: 30
```

To tell the truth, it was not necessary to use two different method names, `change_color` and `change_color2`, as we did in the `Pixel` class definition to simplify matters. It would work the same way if we use these definitions:

```
multi method change_color(%hue) {
    self.color = %hue
}
multi method change_color(Int $red, Int $green, Int $blue) {
    # signature using positional parameters
    self.color = (red => $red, green => $green, blue => $blue)
}
```

Since the `multi method` is defined twice, with the same name but with a different signature, the object system is able to dispatch the invocation to the right method.

The MovablePoint Class

The `$.abscissa` and `$.ordinate` attributes of class `Point2D` are defaulted to read-only. After all, when you define a point in the plan, it usually has a fixed position and there is generally no reason to change its coordinates.

Suppose, however, that our application is about kinematics (the branch of physics dealing with the motion of points or bodies) or is a video game. In such a case, we probably want our points (or sets of points) to move. We need a new class, `Movable Point`, enabling the modification of coordinates.

We don't need to redefine all the attributes and methods for the new class. Again, we can define a new class that *inherits* the properties of the `Point2D` base class and only modifies what is no longer suitable or adds whatever new features we need, for example:

```
class MovablePoint is Point2D {
    has Numeric $.abscissa is rw;
    has Numeric $.ordinate is rw;

    method move (Numeric $x, Numeric $y) {
        $.abscissa += $x;
        $.ordinate += $y;
    }
}
```

Again, the new class inherits the properties of `Point2D` thanks to the `is Point2D` trait, except those that are explicitly modified (or overridden) or added in the new class. Methods that exist in the parent class and are redefined in a child class are said to be *overridden* within that class.

Here, the `$.abscissa` and `$.ordinate` attributes are redefined as read and write (through the `is rw` trait) and a new method, `move`, is defined to modify the position of a point by adding the received parameters to the coordinates of the point.

Note that we have used positional parameters here for the `move` method. We said that it is often better for the sake of clarity to use named parameters, but we have only two parameters here; as it is fairly simple to remember that the `$x` parameter should come before the `$y` parameter, this was a good occasion to illustrate the possibility of using positional parameters.

We can now test our new child class, create a `MovablePoint` instance, display its characteristics, move it to a different location, and display the new position:

```
my $point = MovablePoint.new(
    abscissa => 6,
    ordinate => 7,
    );
```

```
say "Coordinates : ", $point.coordinates;
say "Distance to origin: ", $point.distanceToCenter.round(0.01);
printf "%s: radius = %.4f, theta (rad) = %.4f\n",
    "Polar coordinates", $point.polarCoordinates;

say "--> Moving the point.";
$point.move(4, 5);
say "New coordinates: ", $point.coordinates;
say "Distance to origin: ", $point.distanceToCenter.round(0.01);
printf "%s: radius = %.4f, theta (rad) = %.4f\n",
    "Polar coordinates", $point.polarCoordinates;
```

This produces the following output:

```
Coordinates : (6 7)
Distance to origin: 9.22
Polar coordinates: radius = 9.2195, theta (rad) = 0.8622
--> Moving the point.
New coordinates: (10 12)
Distance to origin: 15.62
Polar coordinates: radius = 15.6205, theta (rad) = 0.8761
```

Here, when the user code invokes the coordinates, distanceToCenter, and polar Coordinates methods, Perl finds that they do not exist in MovablePoint. But, as Mova blePoint subclasses Point2D, the program looks for methods having these names in the parent class and invokes them if it finds them. If it did not find them, it might look into the parent's parent to see if there are any, and so on.

Multiple Inheritance: Attractive, but Is It Wise?

In object-oriented programming, the inheritance mechanism is a traditional way to reuse code; it is even probably the most common way to do it.

A class may have several parent classes and, thus, subclass several other classes. This is what is called *multiple inheritance*. We might want to build a new MovablePixel class inheriting from both MovablePoint and Pixel (and, indirectly, from Point2D). Technically, you can easily do it in Perl:

```
class MovablePixel is MovablePoint is Pixel {
    # ...
}
```

Now, MovablePixel is subclassing both MovablePoint and Pixel and inheriting from both parent classes.

This looks very promising, but it turns out to be more complicated than expected in real situations. If there is a conflict (for example a name collision between two methods), which one shall prevail? Some mechanisms exist to handle such situations (for example in the C++ programming language), and Perl has some metaobject methods to find out about the method resolution order (MRO), but this might quickly leads to severe design problems and to really subtle or complicated bugs. In short, while multiple inheritance originally looked as a attractive idea, it turned out to be complicated to master, because it creates multiple and often implicit dependencies that are quite hard to sort out.

This is the reason why, contrary to C++, relatively more recent OO programming languages such as Java (which came out not so recently, back in 1995) have decided not to implement multiple inheritance.

Perl 6 does not want to forbid such things and allows you to use multiple inheritance if you wish, and it can be useful for simple cases; so don't necessarily rule it out, but remember that, contrary to early expectations, it often leads to a mess and turns out to be quite unmanageable.

Perl offers better concepts for tackling such situations, as we will see shortly.

Roles and Composition

Inheritance is a very powerful concept to describe a hierarchical tree of concepts. For example, you can think of a hierarchy of geometrical figures having more and more specific properties:

1. Polygon
2. Quadrilateral (a polygon with four edges and four corners)
3. Trapezoid (a quadrilateral with one pair of parallel edges)
4. Parallelogram (a trapezoid with two pairs of parallel edges and opposite sides of equal length)
5. Rectangle (a parallelogram with four right angles)
6. Square (a rectangle with all four edges of equal length)

It is relatively easy to imagine a series of classes with a hierarchical inheritance tree reflecting those properties. It gets slightly more complicated, however, if we add the rhombus (a parallelogram with all sides equal), because the square is now *also* a rhombus with four right angles. The square class would subclass both the rectangle and the rhombus, and we might have a possible multiple inheritance issue.

Similarly, we can think of a tree of classes with nested inheritance representing various types of numbers (e.g. integer, rational, real, complex) or animal species (e.g., vertebrate, mammal, carnivoran, canid, dog, Irish setter).

These are great examples for inheritance, but the real world is rarely so hierarchical, and it is often difficult to force everything to fit into such a hierarchical model.

This is one of the reasons why Perl introduces the notion of roles. A role is a set of behaviors or actions that can be shared between various classes. Technically, a role is a collection of methods (with possibly some attributes); it is therefore quite similar to a class, but the first obvious difference is that a role is not designed to be instantiated as an object (although roles can be promoted into classes). The second difference, perhaps more important, is that roles don't inherit: they are used through application to a class and/or composition.

Classes and Roles: An Example

Let's come back to vertebrates, mammals and dogs. A dog is a mammal and inherits some characteristics from the mammals, such as having a neocortex (a region of the brain), hair, and mammary glands, as well as a vertebral column, which all mammals (along with fishes, birds, reptiles, and others) inherit from vertebrates. So far, the class hierarchy seems simple and natural.

But dogs can have very different characteristics and behaviors. To quote the Wikipedia article on dogs: "Dogs perform many *roles* for people, such as hunting, herding, pulling loads, protection, assisting police and military, companionship and, more recently, aiding handicapped individuals" (italic emphasis added). Dogs can also be *feral* animals (i.e., animals living in the wild but descended from domesticated individuals) or stray dogs. All these additional behaviors might be added to the dog class. Similarly, a cat, another mammal, may also be a pet or a feral animal. Mustangs, free-roaming North American horses, are also feral animals, descended from once-domesticated horses; but a mustang may also be captured and brought back to domesticated state. This return to the wild of feral animals is not limited to mammals: pigeons living in our cities are often descended from once-domesticated homing pigeons used in the past. It can even happen with invertebrates, such as swarms of honeybees.

It is apparent that a hierarchical modeling of inheritance trees is not adapted to describe such behaviors.

We can define classes for dogs, cats, and horses as subclasses of mammals (which itself inherits from vertebrates). Besides that, we define roles for pet or feral animals. In addition, we can create new classes subclassing the dog, horse, and cat classes and doing some specific roles; or we can assign roles to individual instances of a class. This could look like this (this is a dummy example that cannot be tested):

```
class Vertebrate { method speak {say "vertebrate"};}
class Mammal  is Vertebrate  { method speak { say "mammal" } }
class Bird    is Vertebrate  { method fly    {} }
class Dog     is Mammal      { method bark   {} }
class Horse   is Mammal      { method neigh  {} }
class Cat     is Mammal      { method meow   {} }
class Mouse   is Mammal      { method squeek {} }
```

```
class Duck     is Bird        { method quack  {} }
# ...

role Pet-animal {
    method is-companion() {...}
    # other methods
}
role Shepherd    { ... }    # sheep keeper
role Feral       { ... }    # animal back to wild life
role Guide       { ... }    # blind guide
role Human-like  { ... }    # animal behaving like a human
# ...

class Guide-dog        is Dog    does Guide      { ... }
class Shepherd-dog     is Dog    does Shepherd   { ... }
class Stray-dog        is Dog    does Feral      { ... }
class Pet-cat          is Cat    does Pet-animal { ... }
class Feral-cat        is Cat    does Feral      { ... }
class Mustang          is Horse  does Feral      { ... }
class Domestic-canary  is Bird   does Pet-animal { ... }
# ...
# Role can also be applied to instances:
my $garfield = Pet-cat.new(...);
my $mickey   = Mouse.new(...);
$mickey does Human-like;
my $donald   = Duck.new(...);
$donald does Human-like;
my $pluto    = Dog.new(...);
$pluto does Pet-animal;
my $snoopy   = Dog.new(...);
$snoopy does Pet-animal does Human-like;
```

A role is applied to a class or an object with the does trait (as opposed to is for inheritance). These different keywords reflect the semantic difference associated to them: composing a role into a class or an object provides this class or object with the *supplementary behavior* associated with the role, but it does not follow that the object receiving the role is *the same thing* as or of the same nature as the role.

If the Pet-animal and feral roles had been defined as classes, then the Pet-cat and Feral-cat classes would have undergone double inheritance, with the potential problems associated with that. By applying a role to a class, you avoid constructing a multiple-inheritance tree that is probably not really justified and can be complicated to conceptualize and difficult to maintain. Judicious use of classes and roles can lead to a model that is simpler, more natural, and closer to the real relations between the entities and behaviors under scrutiny.

In addition, if you inadvertently compose several roles with two methods having the same name, this immediately raises an error (unless a method of the same name exists within the class, in which case it prevails), rather than dispatching silently to one of the two methods as in the case of multiple inheritance. In that case, naming conflicts are identified immediately (at compile time), which has the benefit of immediately finding a bug that might otherwise go unseen for a while.

Role Composition and Code Reuse

Classes are meant for managing instances and roles are meant for managing behaviors and code reuse. The following example shows how classes and roles can play together:

```
role Drawable {
    has $.color is rw;
    method draw { ... }
}
class Figure {
    method area { ... }
}
class Rectangle is Figure does Drawable {
    has $.width;
    has $.height;
    method area {
        $!width * $!height;
    }
    method draw() {
        for 1..$.height {
            say 'x' x $.width;
        }
    }
}
Rectangle.new(width => 10, height => 4).draw;
```

Please note that the ellipsis ... used in the code above is meant here to represent some code that is left to your implementation. However, this is actually valid code and it will compile and even run without any problem. The ellipsis is used to represent functionality that is not yet there but is supposed to be implemented at a later point. This will work as long as you don't invoke these methods (you would get a runtime error) or set up a situation where they would need to be defined (which would cause a compile-time error). In the case of the draw method in the Drawable role, role composition into the Rectangle class works only because draw is redefined in the Rectangle class; without this redefinition, it would have raised a compile-time error. Similarly, the method area { ... } code of the Figure class would raise a runtime error if it were called without having been redefined in the Rectangle class. The ellipsis has been used here only as a convenient way to represent code whose implementation is not important for our example because it is being redefined anyway. In real coding, it is probably best advised not to use the ellipsis, except as a temporary expedient for code that is not yet developed but will be implemented.

The code example above draws an ASCII rectangle:

```
~ perl6 test_drawable.pl6
xxxxxxxxxx
xxxxxxxxxx
xxxxxxxxxx
xxxxxxxxxx
```

Roles, Classes, Objects, and Types

A role can be applied to an entire class or only to some instances of the class:

```
role Guide { ...}
class Guide-dog is Dog does Guide {
    ...
}   # Composing the Guide role into the Guide-dog class
    # inheriting from the Dog class

my $doggy = new Dog;    # creating a Dog object
$doggy does Guide;      # applying the role to the object
```

Roles and classes are different, but both are or define types. This means that a role can be used as a type for a variable declaration where you might expect a class name. For example, the Guide role sketched in the code snippet above does effectively create a Guide type. So a Blind role for a human might have an attribute of Guide type, which might represent a guide-dog, a guide-horse, a human guide, or even a guiding robot.

```
class Human {
    has Dog $dog;       # May contain any dog, with or without
                        # a guide role
}
role Blind {
    has Guide $guide;   # May contain any Guide type, whether
                        # a dog, a horse, a human or a robot
}
```

A number of Perl 6 built-in types are defined by roles and not by classes, such as IO, Iterable, Iterator, Numeric, Rational, Real, etc.

Method Delegation

Delegation is another way to link an object to another piece of code. The delegation technique has been relatively well studied at the theoretical level and implemented in a few specialized research languages, but mainstream generalist languages implementing delegation are rather rare.

Rather than defining methods in a class or in a role, the idea is to invoke methods belonging to another object, as if they were methods of the current class. In Perl 6, delegation may be performed at the level of a class or a role. A delegated object is simply an attribute defined in the class or in the role with the handles keyword, which makes it possible to specify which methods of the delegated object may be used in the current class:

```
class BaseClass {
    method Don-Quijote()    { "Cervantes"   }
    method Hamlet()         { "Shakespeare" }
    method Three-Sisters () { "Chekhov"     }
    method Don-Carlos()     { "Schiller"    }
}
class Uses {
    has $.base is rw handles < Don-Quijote Hamlet Three-Sisters >;
}

my $user = Uses.new;
$user.base = BaseClass.new(); # implementing an object-handler
say $user.Don-Quijote;
say $user.Hamlet;
say $user.Three-Sisters;
say $user.Don-Carlos;
```

This displays the following output:

```
Cervantes
Shakespeare
Chekhov
Method 'Don-Carlos' not found for invocant of class 'Uses'
  in block <unit> at delegate.pl6 line 16
```

The program properly displays the names of writers returned by the first three methods, because they have been sort of "imported" into the Uses class, but it fails on the last one, because "Don-Carlos" is not part of the handler's list. The error on the last method is a runtime exception and the program would stop running even if there were some more correct code afterward.

Note that the Uses class does not know from where the methods will be imported; it only knows about the names of the methods that will be imported. It is only when the $user object is created and the $user.base attribute is added to it that the object is dynamically associated with the methods defined in BaseClass. By the way, this process could be done in just one step:

```
my $user = Uses.new( base => BaseClass.new() );
```

There is no need to enumerate the methods to be handled. The Uses class can import all the methods of BaseClass:

```
class Uses {
    has $.base is rw handles BaseClass;
}
```

This will work as before, except of course that it will not fail on the Don-Carlos method this time, since this method is also imported now:

```
Cervantes
Shakespeare
Chekhov
Schiller
```

Polymorphism

Polymorphism is a way to supply a common or close interface to different types. In a certain way, the inheritance examples studied previously offer a form of polymorphism: the `coordinates`, `distanceToCenter`, and `PolarCoordinates` methods are polymorphic, since they can apply to `Point2D`, `movablePoint`, and `pixel` types. But these are trivial forms of polymorphism. We will speak of polymorphism when the relevant methods or functions are doing something different from each other, at least at the implementation level, even if they share the same name and interface.

Outside of object-oriented programming, Perl's *multi* subroutines implement a form of polymorphism, since they can behave differently depending on the type and number of their arguments. Within the OOP context, it is often the type of the invocant (its class or possibly one of its roles) that will determine, usually at runtime, which of the possible methods will be invoked.

For example, we might want to create a new class for points in a three-dimensional space. The methods will have to be different, but it seems interesting to offer the user an interface that is the same (or almost) as for two-dimensional points:

```
class Point3D {
    has Numeric $.x;
    has Numeric $.y;
    has Numeric $.z;

    method coordinates () {        # accessor to the 3 coordinates
        return $.x, $.y, $.z
    }
    method distanceToCenter () {
        return ($.x ** 2 + $.y ** 2 + $.z ** 2) ** 0.5
    }
    method polarCoordinates () {
      return self.sphericalCoordinates;
    }
    method sphericalCoordinates {
      my $rho = $.distanceToCenter;
      my $longitude = atan2 $.y, $.x;          # theta
      my $latitude = acos $.z / $rho;          # phi
      return $rho, $longitude, $latitude;
    }
    method cylindricalCoordinates {
      # ...
      }
}
```

The methods in this new class are not the same as those in Point2D, but methods with similar semantics have the same name; it is thus possible to use either class without being lost with different names.

The distanceToCenter method has exactly the same interface. The coordinates method returns a list of three values instead of two, but the calling convention is the same. Note that it might also have been possible to design Point2D so that this method would also return a third zero value, in order to have exactly the same interface (after all, a point in the plane might be considered as a point in the 3D space with a zero height); complying to exactly the same interface is not mandatory, but only a possible implementation decision that might make for a more intuitive interface.

The notion of polar coordinates does not have a well-defined meaning in a 3D space, but I have chosen here to keep the name in our interface because it is intuitively quite similar to the idea of spherical coordinates; it does nothing more than invoke the sphericalCoordinates method on its invocant and return the return values.

Please note that mathematicians, physicists, astronomers, engineers, geographers, and navigators all use the same basic system for spherical coordinates, but their conventions are different concerning the origin, angle range, angle measurement units, and rotation direction, and the names of the various values or symbols associated with them. So you might find some different formulas in a textbook. The conventions and formulas we have used here are commonly used in geography and some branches of mathematics. A real general-purpose class might have to take these varying conventions into account and implement the necessary conversions.

Encapsulation

Encapsulation is the idea of hiding the data and the code of a library or a module from the user. It is not specific to object-oriented programming, but it is a fundamental concept of OOP.

In object-oriented programming, encapsulation consists of protecting the data in an object from being tampered with directly (and possibly made inconsistent) by the user, who can access such data only through methods. This is achieved by providing to the user methods that are commonly called *accessors* (or *getters*) and *mutators* (or *setters*). This makes it possible to ensure that the object properties will be validated by its methods.

Encapsulation is a strong form of data abstraction and procedural abstraction. Seen from the outside, an object is a black box having some specified properties and behaviors. This way, these properties and behaviors are *hidden* from the user. They're not hidden in the sense that the user cannot know about them (at least in the open source world, it is easy to know that), but hidden in the sense that it is usually not possible to use that knowledge to bypass the supplied interface. This means that the internal implementation of the object may change without having to modify the external behavior. If you are going to use insider knowledge, your code will probably break when the internal implementation is modified, so don't do that.

Various programming languages don't have the same rules for guaranteeing encapsulation. Some are stricter than others, some are less restrictive for read access than for write access, and others don't make such a distinction but rather rely on the visibility level specified for an attribute, for example "public" or "private" (with sometimes an intermediate "protected" level).

Perl 6 lets you choose the encapsulation model you want to apply to your objects and attributes. All attributes are private. If you declare a class as follows:

```
class Point2D {
    has $!abscissa;
    has $!ordinate;
    # …
    method value_x { return $!abscissa }
    method value_y { return $!ordinate }
}
```

the $!x and $!y coordinates will be accessible only from within the class. This is why we have added accessor methods. In addition, the attributes are immutable by default.

But as we have seen earlier, if you declare this class as follows:

```
class Point2D {
    has $.abscissa;
    has $.ordinate;
    # ...
}
```

the coordinates will still be private attributes, but Perl 6 will automatically generate accessor methods having the same names as the attributes, so that it will be possible to access them from outside the class almost as if they were public:

```
class Point2D {
    # ...
}
my $point = Point2D.new(abscissa => 2, ordinate => 3);
say $point.abscissa;        # -> 2
```

Whether the attribute is mutable or not is managed separately by the is rw trait. In brief, Perl 6 offers a default access mode, but you can fine-tune it and get what you need.

Private Methods

Methods are the normal way to use objects, whether with read-only or read and write access. They usually form the *interface* of a class, that is the part of the class that is made public and available to programmers wishing to use them. It is thus natural and legitimate for methods to be public, i.e., accessible from outside the class.

But a class may also contain numerous methods that are part of the internal cooking recipes of the class, i.e., the way it does things internally, and that are not meant to be used from outside the class. It is possible to prevent their use from outside the class by making these methods private. A Perl 6 private method is prefixed with an exclamation mark:

```
method !private-behavior($x, $y) {
    ...
}
```

You will also need to use an exclamation mark to call them:

```
$my-object!private-behavior($val1, $val2)
```

Private methods are really internal to a given class. In particular, they are not inherited by child classes.

Constructing Objects with Private Attributes

Constructing objects with private attributes raises a little difficulty. Let's consider the following program:

```
class Point3D {
    has $.x;
    has $.y;
    has $!z;

    method get {
        return ($!x, $!y, $!z);
    }
};

my $a = Point3D.new(x => 23, y => 42, z => 2);
say $_ for $a.get;
```

In this example, we have declared $.x and $.y as "public" (so to speak) attributes, and $.z as a truly private attribute. Running this code displays this:

```
23
42
(Any)
```

Oops, what is going on? It seems that the get method is not able to read $!z, since it returns an undefined value. This method is defined within the class, so it should be able to access this attribute. In fact, get is not the problem, it is $!z that is not defined within the object, because it hasn't been properly initialized during object construction.

The guilt lies with the new implicit constructor which, by default, initializes only "public" attributes.

Here, the simplest solution is probably to add a BUILD submethod in the class definition.

A *submethod* is a public method of a class that is not inherited in its child classes. Semantically, it is really equivalent to a subroutine, but it is called with a method syntax (hence the name). Submethods are especially useful to perform object construction and destruction tasks that should not be inherited by subclasses, as well as for tasks that are so specific to a given type that classes derived from it will almost surely have to redefine them.

Initializing private attributes at object instantiation might look like this:

```
class Point3D {
    has $.x;
    has $.y;
    has $!z;

    submethod BUILD (:$!x, :$!y, :$!z) {
        say "Initialization";
        $!x := $!x;
        $!y := $!y;
        $!z := $!z;
    }
    method get {
        return ($!x, $!y, $!z);
    }
};

my $a = Point3D.new(x => 23, y => 42, z => 2);
say $_ for $a.get;
```

The program now works as desired and displays all three attributes:

```
Initialization!
23
42
2
```

This works because the default new constructor, a method defined in the Mu ultimate superclass and inherited by default by any Perl 6 class, calls the default BUILD submethod. If we redefine BUILD in our class, it will supersede the default one called by new. By redefining BUILD, we force the constructor to take into account the private attribute that was not used previously.

Quite a bit of simplification is possible. Since passing arguments to a routine binds the arguments to the parameters, a separate binding step is unnecessary if the attributes are used as parameters. Hence, the BUILD submethod in the example above could also have been written simply as:

```
submethod BUILD(:$!x, :$!y, :$!z) {
    say "Initialization!";
}
```

While we are speaking about the intricacies of object construction, note that since new is a method inherited from the Mu superclass, you can override it if you wish. The default new constructor can only be used with named arguments. Assuming you absolutely want to use positional parameters, you could override new with your own method, like so:

```
class Point2D {
    has Numeric $.abscissa;
    has Numeric $.ordinate;

    method new ($x, $y) {
        self.bless(abscissa => $x, ordinate => $y);
    }
    method coordinates {        # accessor to both coordinates
        return (self.abscissa, self.ordinate)
    }
    # other methods
};

my $point = Point2D.new(3, 5);
say $_ for $point.coordinates;
```

This will duly display the two coordinates. bless is a low-level method for object construction, inherited from Mu and called automatically when you invoke new to construct an object. You usually don't need to know about it, except when you want to write your own custom constructor.

You can give the constructor a different name than new, for example:

```
class Point2D {
    has Numeric $.abscissa;
    has Numeric $.ordinate;

    method construct ($x, $y) {
     self.bless(abscissa => $x, ordinate => $y);
    }
    method coordinates {        # accessor to both coordinates
        return (self.abscissa, self.ordinate)
    }
    # other methods
};

my $point = Point2D.construct(3, 5);
say $_ for $point.coordinates;
```

Think twice, though, before you override new or create your own custom constructor with a different name, as it may make it more complicated to subclass your Point2D class.

Interface and Implementation

One of the goals of object-oriented design is to make software more maintainable, which means that you can keep the program working when other parts of the system change, and modify the program to meet new requirements.

A design principle that helps achieve that goal is to keep interfaces separate from implementations. For objects, that means that the public interface of the methods provided by a class should not depend on how the attributes are represented.

For example, we designed a Point2D class in which the main attributes were the point's Cartesian coordinates. We may find out that, for the purpose of our application, it would be easier or faster to store the point's polar coordinates in the object attributes. It is entirely possible to change the internal implementation of the class, and yet keep the same interface. In order to do that, we would need the constructor to convert input parameters from Cartesian into polar coordinates, and store the latter in the object attribute. The polarCoordinates method would return the stored attributes, whereas methods returning the Cartesian coordinates may have to do the backward conversion (or may perhaps be stored separately in private attributes). Overall, the change can be made with relatively heavy refactoring of the Point2D class, but users of the class would still use the same interface and not see the difference.

After you deploy a new class, you might discover a better implementation. If other parts of the program are using your class, it might be time-consuming and error-prone to change the interface.

But if you designed the interface carefully, you can change the implementation without changing the interface, which means that other parts of the program don't have to change.

Object-Oriented Programming: A Tale

Most tutorials and books teaching object-oriented programming tend to focus on the technical aspects of OOP (as we have done in this chapter so far), and that's a very important part of it, but they sometimes neglect to explain the reasons for it. They say "how," but not "why." We've tried, and hopefully succeeded, in explaining the "why," but this section attempts to explain OOP from the standpoint of the reasons for it and its benefits, independently of any technical consideration, in the form of a parable (the code examples are only pseudocode and are not supposed to compile, let alone run).

The Fable of the Shepherd

Once upon a time, there was a sheep farmer who had a flock of sheep. His typical workday looked like this:

```
$shepherd.move_flock($pasture);
$shepherd.monitor_flock();
$shepherd.move_flock($home);
```

Eventually, due to successful wool sales, he expanded his farming activities and his day became like this:

```
$shepherd.move_flock($pasture);
$shepherd.monitor_flock();
$shepherd.move_flock($home);
$shepherd.other_important_work();
```

But now the shepherd wanted to devote more time to other_important_work(), so he decided to hire a minion to handle the sheep-related work, so the work was now split like this:

```
$shepherd-boy.move_flock($pasture);
$shepherd-boy.monitor_flock();
$shepherd-boy.move_flock($home);
$shepherd.other_important_work();
```

This did give the shepherd more time for other_important_work(), but unfortunately the $shepherd-boy had a tendency to cry wolf, so the farmer had to replace him with a new assistant:

```
$sheep-dog.move_flock($pasture);
$sheep-dog.monitor_flock();
$sheep-dog.move_flock($home);
$shepherd.other_important_work();
```

$sheep-dog was more reliable and demanded less pay than $shepherd-boy, so this was a win for the farmer.

The Moral

We can learn a few things from this parable.

Delegation

To handle complexity, delegate to a suitable entity, e.g., the farmer delegates some of his work to $shepherd-boy.

Encapsulation

Tell objects what to do, rather than micromanage, e.g.:

```
$sheep-dog.monitor_flock();
```

rather than something like:

```
$sheep-dog.brain.task.monitor_flock;
```

At a high level, we do not particularly care what the internals of the object are. We only care what the object can do.

An object becomes harder to change the more its internals are exposed.

Polymorphism

$sheep-dog and $shepherd-boy both understood the same commands, so replacing the latter with the former was easier than it would have been otherwise.

The fable of this section is adapted from a post by "Arunbear" on the PerlMonks website (http://www.perlmonks.org/?node_id=1146129). Thanks to "Arunbear" for allowing me to reuse it.

Debugging

This section is about using a debugger, a program that is designed to help you to debug your programs. "What? There is a tool to debug my programs, and you're telling me only now?" you might complain. Well, it's not quite that. A debugger is not going to do the debugging for you; you'll still have to do the hard investigation work, but a debugger can help you a lot in figuring out why your program isn't doing what you think it should be doing. Or, rather, why what your program is doing isn't quite what you want it to do.

Debuggers are a bit like people with a strong personality: some people love them and others hate them. Often, people who don't like debuggers simply never took the time to learn how to use them, but there are also many expert programmers who don't like them and whom we can't suspect of not having seriously tried. Whether you like debuggers or not is probably a matter of personal taste, but they can provide invaluable help, if you know how to use them.

The Perl 6 Debugger

Rakudo-Perl 6 ships with an interactive debugger that you call with the perl6-debug command (or, on some installs at least, perl6-debug-m). You can just fire this command, followed by the name of the program to be debugged, just as you would normally use perl6 with the name of a program to run the program. One word of warning: you can run the debugger on a program only if the program compiles with no errors; a debugger is not aimed as finding compile-time errors, but only execution or semantic errors.

Once you've launched the debugger, you will see something like this:

```
>>> LOADING while_done.pl6
+ while_done.pl6 (1 - 3)
| while True {
|     my $line = prompt "Enter something ('done' for exiting)\n";
|     last if $line eq "done";
>
```

This says that it is loading the *while_done.pl6* program, and displays the first lines of the program; the last line at the bottom (">") is a prompt where you can enter some commands. The program is stopped at the first statement that actually does something and waits for your input. The code line that is waiting to be executed is highlighted in a different color.

Getting Some Help

The first command you probably want to issue is "h," which will display the debugger help and return to the prompt. Below, we have omitted most of the output for brevity:

```
> h
<enter>             single step, stepping into any calls
s                   step to next statement, stepping over any calls
so                  step out of the current routine
[...]
q[uit]              exit the debugger
>
```

Take the time to issue that command and read the various possible instructions you can enter. We will describe the most common ones. As you can see above, just use "q" or "quit" to exit the debugger.

Stepping Through the Code

The main characteristic of a debugger is that it lets you run the program step by step. Each time you hit the Enter key, the program will move forward one step (e.g., one code line). It will enter into any subroutine if the code line is a subroutine call, but you can step over the subroutine call by issuing the "s" command at the debugger prompt: this will run the subroutine and bring you to the first code line after the subroutine call (and any nested call of other subroutines) is over. If you entered into a subroutine but are no longer interested in stepping through it, just issue the "so" command to step out of it.

At any point through that process, you can look at the content of variables or even call methods on them. To view a variable, just type its name and then press Enter:

```
> $line
"foo"
```

You can also view an array or a hash, or use the index or the key, for example @array[10] or %hash{"bar"}, to visualize one specific item of the array or the hash.

You may also use "s" (or "say") or "p" (or "print") to evaluate and display an expression in the current scope.

Stopping at the Right Place with Breakpoints

You might find it tedious to run through the program step by step until you get to the interesting part. As it happens, you can get there immediately using a *breakpoint*. For adding a breakpoint, you type bp add line, where line is the line number where you want the program to stop running and resume stepping line by line. Then you enter the "r" command and the program will run until it reaches one of the breakpoints that you have set. The execution will also stop if the program runs into an exception; in that case, you can still access variables to try to figure out what went wrong. If it does not hit a breakpoint or an exception, it will run to the end.

You can view all breakpoints (bp list), remove one breakpoint (bp rm line), or remove all breakpoints (bp rm all). You can also set a breakpoint in another file (for example if you are using a module) by using the following syntax: bp add file:line, where "file" is the filename.

You're all set to start using the debugger

You probably know enough by now to make good use of the Perl 6 debugger, step through your program, and find out where it does something that isn't what you intended. It wasn't so much to learn, was it? Try it!

We'll cover a couple of additional goodies, though.

Logging Information with Trace Points

It is possible to set trace points on specific lines of code and variables (or expressions), with the command tp add line $var. This will record the value of $var each time the programs hits the chosen line. Then you simply run the program for a while and, at some point, you can visualize how the variable changed over time, using the command tp show.

For example, we used it to log the variable $rotated-word in the solution to the Caesar's cipher exercise (see "Exercise 7-3: Caesar's Cipher" on page 375) for the "ABC-Dabcd" input string with a rotation of 25 letters; the tp show command displayed how the coded output string was progressively populated letter by letter:

```
> tp show
>>> rotate.pl6:23
*
* Z
* ZA
* ZAC
* ZACB
* ZACBz
* ZACBza
* ZACBzab
```

Stepping Through a Regex Match

The debugger can also provide useful information when the code is trying to match a regex. For example, suppose we're running a program under the debugger in which we have the following code:

```
"foobar" ~~ /f.+b/;
```

If you run the regex step by step, color highlighting will show atom by atom where it is in the regex and which part of the string has been matched. (We can't show the color highlighting here, but you should try it to see it.)

With the above regex, you'll see that the regex engine tries to match the "f" of the pattern and that it finds an "f" at the beginning of the string; next, you'll see that the regex engines tries to match the ".+" subpattern and that it matches the whole string; then, when the regex engine tries to match the final "b" of the pattern, you'll see that the regex engine backtracks and gives away the "r" and then the "a"; finally, the regex engine succeeds with "foob".

If you have difficulty understanding how regexes work or are mystified by backtracking, just run the debugger on a few regexes and observe what's going on step by step. You don't even have to write a program; you can use it as a one-liner. For example, to test the above regex as a one-liner under Windows, just type the following command at the prompt:

```
C:\Users\Laurent>perl6-debug-m -e "'foobar' ~~ /f.+b/;"
```

As usual, change double quotes to single quotes and the other way around if you are using a Unix-like platform.

Our final word on the debugger: remember you can always hit "h" to get help on the command you need.

Glossary

attribute

A state property akin to a variable within an OOP framework. An instance attribute is one of the named values associated with an object. Class attributes are variables associated with the whole class.

child class

A new class created by inheriting from an existing class; also called a *subclass*.

class

A programmer-defined type. A class definition creates a new type object (a form of abstract definition) and makes it possible to instantiate concrete objects representing real data.

delegation

Defining a class or a role in which it is possible to invoke methods belonging to another object.

embedded object

An object that is stored as an attribute of another object.

encapsulation

The principle that the interface provided by an object should not depend on its implementation, in particular the representation of its attributes. This is also called *information hiding*.

inheritance

The ability to define a new class that is a modified version of a previously defined class.

instance

An object that belongs to a class and contains real data.

instantiate

To create a new object.

method

A special kind of subroutine defined within a class or a role that can be called using the dot notation syntax.

multiple inheritance

A situation in which a child class is derived and inherits from more than one parent class.

object

An entity that encloses its state (attributes) and its behavior (methods).

object composition

Using an object as part of the definition of another object, especially using an object as an attribute of another object.

object diagram

A diagram that shows objects, their attributes, and the values of the attributes.

override

when the method of a parent class is redefined in a child class, it is said to be overridden within that child class.

parent class

The class from which a child class inherits.

polymorphic

Pertaining to a function that can work with more than one type.

role

A collection of methods quite similar to a class but that is not designed to build objects. A role contains methods that can be applied to a class or an object to add new behaviors to them.

subclassing

Creating a child class derived from an existing parent class.

type object

An object that contains information about a programmer-defined type. The type object can be used to create instances of the type.

CHAPTER 13

Regexes and Grammars

Regular expressions or regexes were introduced in "Regular Expressions (Regexes)" on page 116 and "Substitutions" on page 130. You might want to review those sections before reading this chapter if you don't remember much about regexes. You don't need to remember the details of everything we covered earlier and we will explain again briefly specific parts of the functionality that we will be using, but you are expected to understand generally how regexes work.

A Brief Refresher

Regexes, as we have studied them so far, are about string exploration using patterns. A pattern is a sequence of (often special) characters that is supposed to describe a string or part of a string. A pattern matches a string if a correspondence can be found between the pattern and the string.

For example, the following code snippet searches the string for the letter "a", followed by any number (but at least one) of letters "b" or "c", followed by zero or more digits followed by a "B" or a "C":

```
my $str = "foo13abbccbcbcbcbb42Cbar";
say ~$/ if $str ~~ /a <[bc]>+ (\d*) [B|C]/;   # -> abbccbcbcbcbb42C
say ~$0;                                       # -> 42
```

This code uses the ~~ smart match operator to check whether the $str string matches the /a <[bc]>+ (\d*) [B|C]/ pattern. Remember that spaces are usually not significant in a regex pattern (unless specified otherwise).

The pattern is made of the following components:

a

    A literal match of letter "a".

`<[bc]>+`

The `<[bc]>` is a character class meaning letter "b" or "c"; the + quantifier says characters matching the character class "b" or "c" can be repeated one or more times.

`(\d*)`

The \d atom is a digit character class, the * quantifier means 0 or more occurrences of the previous atom, and the enclosing parentheses request a capture of these digits (if any) into the $0 variable (a special variable that is really a shortcut for $/[0]).

`[B|C]`

B|C is an alternation (either a "B" or a "C"), and the square brackets regroup this alternation into one subpattern (and also enable proper precedence).

If the match is successful (as is the case in this example), the result is stored into the *match object*, $/. Printing ~$/ displays a stringified version of the match object. And printing $0 (or $/[0]) displays the capture (part of the match that is between parentheses, in this case the number "42").

This is what might be called low-level matching: pattern recognition is done mostly at the individual character level. Perl 6 offers ways to group and name regex patterns so that these individual patterns can then be used as building blocks for higher level matching: recognizing words and sequences of words (rather than just characters), for the purpose of performing what is called lexical analysis (or *lexing*) and grammatical analysis (or *parsing*) on a piece of text.

This chapter is mostly devoted to this higher type of matching, leading to the creation of full-fledged *grammars* that can analyze structured text such as XML or HTML texts, JSON or YAML documents, or even computer programs: Perl 6 programs are actually parsed using a Perl 6 grammar written in Perl 6.

Grammars are a very important topic in computer science, but, obviously, most programmers don't commonly write full-fledged grammars for parsing programming languages. However, writing a simple grammar and a simple parser might be, or perhaps should be, a much more common task.

Quite often, people spend a lot of effort at deciphering a simple configuration file with low-level techniques, whereas writing a simple parser might be a lot easier and much more efficient. Perl 6 offers all the tools to do that very easily.

Sometimes, you also need to develop a domain-specific language (DSL), i.e., a usually relatively small sublanguage (a.k.a. *slang*) adapted to a specific field of knowledge (scientific, engineering, business, art, or other) with its own conventions, symbols, operators, and so on. With a grammar and Perl's ability to create its own operators, you can often express specialized knowledge within the terminology framework of subject-matter experts.

Declarative Programming

Both regexes and grammars are examples of yet another programming paradigm that we haven't really explored so far: *declarative programming*. This is a programming model in which, contrary to ordinary imperative or procedural programming, you don't state how to do something and don't choose your control flow. Rather, you specify a set of definitions, rules, properties, and possibly some constraints and actions, and let the program apply those to derive some new information about the input data.

This form of programming is widely used in logic programming (e.g., Prolog), artificial intelligence, expert systems, data analysis, database query languages (e.g., SQL), text and source code recognition (e.g., Lex and Flex), program compilation (e.g., Yacc or Bison), configuration management, makefiles, and also in some ways functional programming.

Captures

As we noted in the regex examples at the beginning of this chapter, round parentheses not only group things together, but also *capture* data: they make the string matched by the subpattern within the parentheses available as a special variable:

```
my $str = 'number 42';
say "Number is $0" if $str ~~ /number \s+ (\d+) /;  # -> Number is 42
```

Here, the pattern matched the $str string, and the part of the pattern within parentheses was captured in the $0 special variable. Where there are several parenthesized groups, they are captured in variables named $0, $1, $2, etc. (from left to right):

```
say "$0 $1 $2" if "abcde" ~~ /(a) b (c) d (e)/;       # -> a c e
```

This is fine for simple captures, but the numbering of captures can become tedious if there are many captures and somewhat complicated when there are nested parentheses in the pattern:

```
if 'abc' ~~ / ( a (.) (.) ) / {
    say "Outside: $0";                 # Outside: abc
    say "Inside: $0[0] and $0[1]";     # Inside: b and c
}
```

When it gets complicated, it is often better to use another feature called *named captures*. The standard way to name a capture is as follows:

```
if 'abc;%' ~~ / $<capture_name> = \w+ / {
    say ~$<capture_name>;                # abc
}
```

The use of the named capture, $<capture_name>, is a shorthand for accessing the $/ match object as a hash, in other words: $/{ 'capture_name' } or $/<capture_name>.

Named captures can be nested using regular capture group syntax:

```
if 'abc' ~~ / $<overall>=( a $<part1>=(.) $<part2>=(.) ) / {
    say "Overall: $<overall>";           # Overall: abc
    say "Part 1: $<overall><part1>";     # Part 1: b
    say "Part 2: $<overall><part2>";     # Part 2: c
}
```

Assigning the match object to a hash gives you easy programmatic access to all named captures:

```
if 'abc' ~~ / $<overall>=( a $<part1>=(.) $<part2>=(.) ) / {
    my %capture = $/.hash;
    say ~%capture<overall>;              # -> abc
    for kv %capture<overall> -> $key, $val {
        say $key, " ", ~$val;            # -> part2 c \n part1 b
    }
}
```

But you might as well do the same thing directly on the match object without having to perform an extra hash assignment:

```
if 'abc' ~~ / $<overall>=( a $<part1>=(.) $<part2>=(.) ) / {
    say "Overall: $<overall>";           # -> Overall: abc
    for kv %<overall> -> $key, $val {
        say $key, " ", ~$val;            # -> part2 c \n part1 b
    }
}
```

Remember that, in the above code, $<overall> is really a shortcut for $/<overall>, i.e., for a hash type of access to the $/ match object.

There is, however, a more convenient way to get named captures, which is discussed in the next section.

Named Rules (a.k.a. Subrules)

It is possible to store pieces of regexes into *named rules*. The following example uses a named regex, which is one of the kinds of named rules, to match a text line:

```
my regex line { \N* \n }  # any number of characters other
                          # than new line, followed by 1 new line
if "abc\ndef" ~~ /<line> def/ {
```

```
        say "First line: ", $<line>.chomp;      # First line: abc
    }
```

Notice that the syntax with a block of code is akin to a subroutine or method definition. This is not a coincidence; we will see that named rules are very similar to methods. Notably, rules can call each other (or even sometimes call themselves recursively) just like methods and subroutines, and we will see that this is a very powerful and expressive feature.

A named regex can be declared with `my regex name { regex body }`, and called with `<name>`.

As you can see in the example above, a successful named regex creates a named capture with the same name. If you need a different name for the capture, you can do this with the syntax `<capturename=regexname>`. In this example, we call the same named regex twice and, for convenience, use a different name to distinguish the two captures:

```
my regex line { \N* \n }
if "abc\ndef\n" ~~ / <first=line> <second=line> / {
    say "First line: ", $<first>.chomp;   # -> First line: abc
    say "Second line: ", $<second>.chomp; # -> Second line: def
    print $_.chomp for $<line>.list;      # -> abc  def
}
```

Here, we have used `chomp` method calls to remove the newline characters from the captures. There is in fact a way to match on the newline character but exclude it from the capture:

```
my regex line { \N* )> \n }
if "abc\ndef\n" ~~ / <first=line> <second=line> / {
    say "First line: ", ~$<first>;        # -> First line: abc
    say "Second line: ", ~$<second>;      # -> Second line: def
    print $<line>.list;                   # -> abc  def
}
```

This relatively little-known token, ")>", marks the endpoint of the match's overall capture. Anything after it will participate in the match but will not be captured by the named regex. Similarly, the "<)" token indicates the start of the capture.

Named regexes are only one form (and probably not the most common) of the named rules, which come in three main flavors:

- Named regex, in which the regex behaves like ordinary regexes
- Named tokens, in which the regex has an implicit `:ratchet` adverb, which means that there is no backtracking

- Named rules, in which the regex has an implicit :ratchet adverb, just as named tokens, and also an implicit :sigspace adverb, which means that whitespace within the pattern (or, more specifically, between word characters) is not ignored

In the two examples above, we did not need the regexes to backtrack. We could (and probably should) have used a named token instead of a named regex:

```
my token line { \N* \n }
if "abc\ndef" ~~ /<line> def/ {
    say "First line: ", $<line>.chomp;    # First line: abc
}
```

But, for a rule to match, we would have to remove the space from *within the pattern*:

```
my rule line { \N*\n }
if "abc\ndef" ~~ /<line> def/ {
    say "First line: ", $<line>.chomp;    # First line: abc
}
```

Collectively, these three types of named rules are usually referred to as *rules*, independently of the specific keyword used for their definition.

Remember the various regexes we experimented for extracting dates from a string in "Extracting Dates" on page 127? The last example used subpatterns as building blocks for constructing the full pattern. We could now rewrite it, with the added feature of recognizing multiple date formats, as follows:

```
my $string = "Christmas : 2016-12-25.";
my token year { \d ** 4 }
my token month {
    1 <[0..2]>                          # 10 to 12
    || 0 <[1..9]>                       # 01 to 09
};
my token day { (\d ** 2) <?{1 <= $0 <= 31 }> }
my token sep { '/' || '-' }
my rule date {   <year> (<sep>) <month> $0 <day>
             || <day> (<sep>) <month> $0 <year>
             || <month>\s<day>',' <year>
}

if $string ~~ /<date>/ {
    say ~$/;                            # -> 2016-12-25
    say "Day\t= "    , ~$/<date><day>;  # -> 25
    say "Month\t= "  , ~$/<date><month>;  # -> 12
    say "Year\t= "   , ~$/<date><year>;   # -> 2016
}
```

The first four named tokens define the basic building blocks for matching the year, the month, the day, and possible separators. Then, the date named rule uses these building blocks to define an alternation between three possible date formats.

This code checks that the day in the month is between 0 and 31 and that the month is between 01 and 12, and this is probably sufficient to recognize dates in a text in most cases, but this would recognize "2016-11-31" as a date, although November only has 30 days. We may want to be a little bit stricter about valid dates and prevent that by adding a negative code assertion to the date named rule:

```
my rule date { [    <year> (<sep>) <month> $0 <day>
                 || <day> (<sep>) <month> $0 <year>
                 || <month>\s<day>',' <year>
               ] <!{ $<day> > 30 and $<month> ==  2|4|6|9|11}>
}
```

This is better, but we can still match an invalid date such as "2016-02-30."

Exercise 13-1.

As an exercise, change the code assertion to reject a "Feb. 30" date. If you feel courageous, you might even want to check the number of days in February depending on whether the date occurs in a leap year. You may also want to try to define and test other date formats. Solution: "Exercise 13-1: Getting the February Dates Right" on page 420.

Rules can (and usually should) be grouped in grammars; that's in fact what they have been designed for.

Grammars

Grammars are a powerful tool used to analyze textual data and often to return data structures that have been created by interpreting that text.

For example, any Perl 6 program is parsed and executed using a Perl 6 grammar written in Perl 6, and you could write a grammar for parsing (almost) any other programming language. To tell the truth, programmers rarely write grammars for parsing programming languages. But grammars are very useful for performing many tasks that are much more common than parsing programs.

If you ever tried to use regexes for analyzing a piece of HTML (or XML) text,[1] you probably found out that this is quickly becoming next to impossible, except perhaps for the most simple HTML data. For analyzing any piece of such data, you need an actual parser which, in turn, will usually be based on an underlying grammar.

---

1 Don't try to do it. Now, I warned you: just don't do it.

If you didn't like grammar in school, don't let that scare you off grammars. Grammars are nothing complicated; they just allow you to group named rules, just as classes allow you to group methods of regular code.

A grammar creates a namespace and is introduced with the keyword grammar. It usually groups a number of named rules, in the same way a class groups a number of methods. A grammar is actually a class that inherits from the Grammar superclass, which provides methods such as parse to analyze a string and .parsefile to analyze a file. Moreover, you can actually write some methods in a grammar, and even import some roles. And, as we shall see, grammars are often associated with some *actions classes* or objects.

Unless told otherwise, the parsing methods will look for a default rule named "TOP" (which may be a named regex, token, or rule) to start the parsing. The date parsing rules used above might be assembled into a grammar as follows:

```
grammar My-date {
    rule TOP { \s*?
                [    <year> (<sep>) <month> $0 <day>
                  || <day> (<sep>) <month> $0 <year>
                  || <month>\s<day>',' <year>
                ] \s*
                <!{ ($<day> > 30 and $<month> ==  2|4|6|9|11)}>
             }
    token year  { \d ** 4 }
    token month { 1 <[0..2]> || 0 <[1..9]> }
    token day   { (\d ** 2) <?{1 <= $0 <= 31 }> }
    token sep   { '/' || '-' }
}

for " 2016/12/25 ", " 2016-02-25 ", " 31/04/2016 " -> $string {
        my $matched = My-date.parse($string);
        say ~$matched if defined $matched;
}
```

This will print out:

```
2016/12/25
2016-02-25
```

The code assertion within the "TOP" rule prevents invalid dates such as "31/04/2016" from being matched; you would need to add some code for handling the end of February dates, as we did in the solution to the previous exercise (see "Exercise 13-1: Getting the February Dates Right" on page 420) if this is important. You may want to do it as an exercise.

Besides that, this code is not very different from our earlier code, but there are a few changes that are significant.

We renamed the date rule as TOP because this is the default name searched by parse for the top-level rule. A grammar creates its own namespace and lexical scope, and we no longer need to declare our rules with the my declarator (which is required for rules declared outside of a grammar).

Within a grammar, the order in which the rules are defined is generally not relevant, so that we could define the TOP rule first, even though it uses tokens that are defined afterwards (which again would have not been possible with rules used outside a grammar). This is important because, within a grammar, you can have many rules that call each other (or rules that call themselves recursively), which would be unpractical if the order of the rule definitions mattered.

If you're parsing the input string with the .parse method, the TOP rule is automatically anchored to the start and end of the string, which means that the grammar has to match the whole string to be successful. This is why we had to add patterns for spaces at the beginning and at the end of our TOP rule to match our strings that have some spaces before and after the date itself. There is another method, .subparse, which does not have to reach the end of the string to be successful, but we would still need to have the space pattern at the beginning of the rule.

Grammar Inheritance

A grammar can inherit from another grammar, just as a class can inherit from another class.

Consider this very simple (almost simplistic) grammar for parsing a mail message:

```
grammar Message {
    rule  TOP    { <greet> $<body>=<line>+? <end> }
    rule greet   { [Hi||Hello||Hey] $<to>=\S+? ',' }
    rule end     { Later dude ',' $<from>=.+ }
    token line   { \N* \n}
}
```

We can test it with the following code:

```
my $msg = "Hello Tom,
I hope you're well and that your car is now repaired.
Later dude, Liz";

my $matched = Message.parse($msg);
if defined $matched {
    say "Greeting \t= ", ~$matched<greet>.chomp;
    say "Addressee\t= $matched<greet><to>";
    say "Author   \t= $matched<end><from>";
    say "Content  \t= $matched<body>";
}
```

This will print out the following:

```
Greeting          = Hello Tom,
Addressee         = Tom
Author            = Liz
Content           = I hope you're well and that your car is now repaired.
```

Suppose now that we want a similar grammar for parsing a more formal message and we figure out that we could reuse part of the Message grammar. We can have our new child grammar inherit from the existing parent:

```
grammar FormalMessage is Message {
    rule greet { [Dear] $<to>=\S+? ',' }
    rule end { [Yours sincerely|Best regards] ',' $<from>=.+ }
}
```

The is Message trait in the header tells Perl that FormalMessage should inherit from the Message grammar. Only two rules, greet and end, need to be redefined; the others (the TOP rule and the line token) will be inherited from the Message grammar.

Let's try some code to run it:

```
my $formal_msg = "Dear Thomas,
enclosed is our invoice for June 2016.
Best regards, Elizabeth.";
my $matched2 = FormalMessage.parse($formal_msg);
if defined $matched2 {
    say "Greeting \t= ", ~$matched2<greet>.chomp;
    say "Addressee\t= $matched2<greet><to>";
    say "Author   \t= $matched2<end><from>";
    say "Content  \t= $matched2<body>";
}
```

This will print:

```
Greeting          = Dear Thomas,
Addressee         = Thomas
Author            = Elizabeth.
Content           = enclosed is our invoice for June 2016.
```

Actions Objects

A successful grammar match gives you a parse tree of match objects (objects of the Match type). This tree recapitulates all the individual "submatches" that contributed to the overall match, so it can quickly become very large and complicated. The deeper that match tree gets, and the more branches in the grammar there are, the harder it becomes to navigate the match tree to get the information you are actually interested in.

To avoid the need for diving deep into a match tree, you can supply an actions object. After each successful match of a named rule in your grammar, it tries to call a method with the same name as the grammar rule, giving it the newly created match object as a positional argument. If no such method exists, it is skipped. (Action methods are sometimes also called *reduction methods*.) If it exists, the action method is often used to construct an *abstract syntax tree (AST)*, i.e., a data structure presumably simpler to explore and to use than the match object tree, or it can do any other thing deemed to be useful.

In this somewhat simplistic example of a basic arithmetic calculator, the actions don't try to build an AST, but simply do the bulk of the calculation work between the various tokens matched by the grammar:

```
grammar ArithmGrammar {
    token TOP { \s* <num> \s* <operation> \s* <num> \s*}
    token operation { <[^*+/-]> }
    token num { \d+ | \d+\.\d+ | \.\d+ }
}
class ArithmActions {
    method TOP($/) {
        given $<operation> {
            when '*' { $/.make([*] $/<num>)}
            when '+' { $/.make([+] $<num>)}
            when '/' { $/.make($<num>[0] / $<num>[1]) }
            when '-' { $/.make([-] $<num>) }
            when '^' { $/.make($<num>[0] ** $<num>[1]) }
        }
    }
}
for '  6*7  ', '46.2 -4.2', '28+ 14.0 ',
    '70 * .6 ', '126    /3', '6.4807407 ^ 2' -> $op {
        my $match = ArithmGrammar.parse($op, :actions(ArithmActions));
        say "$match\t= ", $match.made;
}
```

This prints the following output:

```
    6*7          = 42
46.2 -4.2        = 42
28+ 14.0         = 42
70 * .6          = 42
126    /3        = 42
6.4807407 ^ 2    = 42.00000002063649
```

The aim of this example is not to describe how to implement a basic calculator (there are better ways to do that, we'll come back to that), but only to show how actions may be used in conjunction with a grammar.

The grammar is quite simple and is looking for two decimal numbers separated by an infix arithmetic operator. If there is a match, $/<num> (or $<num> for short) will refer to an array containing the two numbers (and $/<operation> will contain the arithmetic operator).

The `parse` method is called with an `actions:` named argument, the `ArithmActions` class, which tells Perl which actions object to use with the grammar. In this example, we don't really pass an action object, but simply the name of the actions class (actually a type object), because there is no need to instantiate an object. In other cases, for example if there was a need to initialize or somehow use some object attributes, we would need to pass an actual object that would have to be constructed beforehand.

Whenever the `TOP` rule succeeds, the `TOP` method of class `ArithmActions` is invoked with the match object for the current rule as the argument. This method calls the `make` method on the match object and returns the result of the actual arithmetic operation between the two numbers. Then, the `made` method in the caller code (within the for loop) returns that result.

A Grammar for Parsing JSON

JSON (*JavaScript Object Notation*) is an open-standard format for text data derived from the object notation in the JavaScript programming language. It has become one of the commonly used standards for serializing data structures, which makes it possible, for example, to exchange them between different platforms and different programming languages, to send them over a network, and to store them permanently in files on disks.

The JSON Format

The JSON format is quite simple and is composed of two types of structural entities:

- Objects or unordered lists of name–value pairs (basically corresponding to hashes in Perl)
- Arrays, or ordered lists of values

Values can be either (recursively) objects or arrays as defined just above, or basic data types, which are strings, numbers, Boolean (true or false), and *null* (empty value or undefined value). A string is a sequence of Unicode characters between quotation marks, and numbers are signed decimal numbers that may contain a fractional part and may use exponential "E" notation.

Our JSON Sample

To illustrate the format description above and for the purpose of our tests, we will use an example borrowed from the Wikipedia article on JSON (*https://en.wikipedia.org/wiki/JSON*), which is a possible JSON description of a person:

```
{
  "firstName": "John",
  "lastName": "Smith",
```

```
  "isAlive": true,
  "age": 25,
  "address": {
    "streetAddress": "21 2nd Street",
    "city": "New York",
    "state": "NY",
    "postalCode": "10021-3100"
  },
  "phoneNumbers": [
    {
      "type": "home",
      "number": "212 555-1234"
    },
    {
      "type": "office",
      "number": "646 555-4567"
    },
    {
      "type": "mobile",
      "number": "123 456-7890"
    }
  ],
  "children": [],
  "spouse": null,
  "Bank-account": {
    "credit": 2342.25
  }
}
```

Compared to the Wikipedia example, we've added a `Bank-account` object to provide the possibility of testing JSON noninteger numbers.

Writing the JSON Grammar Step by Step

Let's take each of the JSON entities in turn and handle them with rules.

Numbers

The example JSON document above only has integers and decimal numbers, but we need to be able to recognize numbers such as "17," "−138.27," "1.2e-3," ".35," etc. We can use the following token to do so:

```
token number {
    [\+|\-]?              # optional sign
    [ \d+ [ \. \d+ ]? ]   # integer part and optional fractional part
      | [ \. \d+ ]        # or only a fractional part
    [ <[eE]> [\+|\-]? \d+ ]?    # optional exponent
}
```

JSON strings

There are many possible patterns to define a string. For our sample JSON document, the following rule will be sufficient:

```
token string {
    \" <[ \w \s \- ' ]>+ \"
}
```

This will match a double-quoted sequence of alphanumeric characters, spaces, dashes, and apostrophes.

For a real JSON parser, a rule using a negative character class excluding anything that cannot belong to a string might be better, for example:

```
token string {
    \" <-[\n " \t]>* \"
}
```

i.e., a double-quoted sequence of any characters other than double quotes, newlines, and tabulations.

You might want to study the JSON standards[2] to figure out exactly what is accepted or forbidden in a JSON string. For our purposes, the first rule above will be sufficient.

JSON objects

JSON objects are lists of key–value pairs. Lists are delimited by curly braces and pairs separated by commas. A key–value pair is a string followed by a colon, followed by a value (to be defined later). This can be defined as follows:

```
rule object     { '{' <pairlist> '}' }
rule pairlist   { [<pair> [',' <pair>]*] }
rule pair       { <string> ':' <value>  }
```

We can use a regex feature that we haven't seen yet, the quantifier modifier, to simplify the `pairlist` rule. To more easily match things like comma-separated values, you can tack on a % modifier to any of the regular quantifiers to specify a separator that must occur between each of the matches. So, for example /a+ % ','/ will match "a" or "a,a" or "a,a,a", etc.

Thus, the `pairlist` rule can be rewritten as follows:

```
rule pairlist   {<pair> + % \,}
```

or:

```
rule pairlist   {<pair> * % \,}
```

---

2 Since JSON is actually not completely standardized, I will not provide a specific link; look it up and make up your mind.

if we accept that a `pairlist` may also be empty.

JSON arrays

Arrays are comma-separated lists of values between square brackets:

```
rule array      { '[' <valueList> ']'}
rule valueList {   <value> * % \, }
```

Here, we again used the modified quantifier just shown.

JSON values

Values are objects, arrays, string, numbers, Booleans (true or false), or *null*:

```
token value { | <object> | <array> | <string> | <number>
              | true     | false   | null
}
```

The JSON Grammar

We have defined all the elements of the JSON grammar; we only need to declare a grammar and add a TOP rule to complete it:

```
grammar JSON-Grammar {
    token TOP      { \s* [ <object> | <array> ] \s* }
    rule object    { '{' \s* <pairlist> '}' \s* }
    rule pairlist { <pair> * % \, }
    rule pair      { <string>':' <value> }
    rule array     { '[' <valueList> ']'}
    rule valueList { <value> * % \, }
    token string   { \" <[ \w \s \- ' ]>+ \"  }
    token number   {
      [\+|\-]?
      [ \d+ [ \. \d+ ]? ] | [ \. \d+ ]
      [ <[eE]> [\+|\-]? \d+ ]?
    }
    token value    { <object> | <array> | <string> | <number>
                     | true   | false   | null
    }
}
```

We can now test the grammar with our sample JSON string and try to print the match object:

```
my $match = JSON-Grammar.parse($JSON-string);
say ~$match if $match;
```

This produces the following output:

```
{
  "firstName": "John",
  "lastName": "Smith",
```

```
    "isAlive": true,
    "age": 25,
    "address": {
      "streetAddress": "21 2nd Street
      "city": "New York",
      "state": "NY",
      "postalCode": "10021-3100"
    },
    "phoneNumbers": [
      {
        "type": "home",
        "number": "212 555-1234"
      },
      {
        "type": "office",
        "number": "646 555-4567"
      },
      {
        "type": "mobile",
        "number": "123 456-7890"
      }
    ],
    "children": [],
    "spouse": null,
    "Bank-account": {
        "credit": 2342.25
    }
  }
```

The sample JSON document has been fully matched. This JSON grammar works perfectly on it, and takes less than 20 lines of code. If you think about it, this is really powerful. Test it for yourself. Try to change the grammar in various places to see if it still works. You could also try to introduce errors into the JSON document (for example to remove a comma between two values of a list) and the match should no longer occur (or, at least, should not be the same).

You may object that this grammar covers only a subset of JSON. This is sort of true, but not really: it is almost complete. True, I would not recommend using this grammar in a production environment for parsing JSON documents, because it has been built only for pedagogical purposes and may not comply with every single fine detail of the JSON standards.

Take a look at the grammar of the Perl 6 `JSON::Tiny` module (*https://github.com/moritz/json*), which can parse any valid JSON document. It is not much more complicated than what we have shown here (except for the use of proto regexes, a topic that we haven't covered here), and it is not much longer, as it contains about 35 code lines.

Adding Actions

The JSON grammar works fine, but printing out the tree of parse objects just for our relatively small JSON document will display about 300 lines of text, as it provides all the details of everything that has been matched, rule by rule and subpattern by subpattern. This can be very useful in helping you to understand what the grammar does (especially when it does not work as expected), but exploring that tree to extract the data can be quite tedious. You can use *actions* to populate a simpler tree structure (often called an abstract syntax tree) containing only the information you really need.

Let us add an actions class to build an abstract syntax tree (AST):

```
class JSON-actions {
    method TOP($/) {
        make $/.values.[0].made;
    };
    method object($/) {
        make $<pairlist>.made.hash.item;
    }
    method pairlist($/) {
        make $<pair>>>.made.flat;
    }
    method pair($/) {
        make $<string>.made => $<value>.made;
    }
    method array($/) {
        make $<valueList>.made.item;
    }
    method valueList($/) {
        make [$<value>.map(*.made)];
    }
    method string($/) { make ~$0 }
    method number($/) { make +$/.Str; }
    method value($/) {
        given ~$/ {
            when "true"  {make Bool::True;}
            when "false" {make Bool::False;}
            when "null"  {make Any;}
            default { make $<val>.made;}
        }
    }
}
```

For this actions class to work, we need to make a small change to the grammar. The value method uses a `val` named capture to access its content; we need to add the relevant named captures to the `value` token:

```
token value { <val=object> | <val=array> | <val=string>
              | <val=number> | true | false | null
}
```

We can now call our grammar with the following syntax:

```
my $j-actions = JSON-actions.new();
my $match = JSON-Grammar.parse($JSON-string, :actions($j-actions));
say $match.made;
```

Notice that here, we've used an actions object rather than simply the actions class, but this is just for the purpose of showing how to do it; we could have used the class directly as before.

The last statement in the above code prints out the AST. We have reformatted the output to better show the structure of the AST:

```
{
    Bank-account => {
        credit => 2342.25
    },
    address => {
        city => New York,
        postalCode => 10021-3100,
        state => NY,
        streetAddress => 21 2nd Street
    },
    age => 25,
    children => [],
    firstName => John,
    isAlive => True,
    lastName => Smith,
    phoneNumbers => [
        {number => 212 555-1234, type => home}
        {number => 646 555-4567, type => office}
        {number => 123 456-7890, type => mobile}
    ],
    spouse => (Any)
}
```

In this case, the top structure is a hash (it could also have been an array with a different JSON input string). We can now explore this hash to find the data of interest to us. For example:

```
say "Keys are: \n", $match.made.keys;
say "\nSome values:";
say $match.made{$_} for <firstName lastName isAlive>;
say $match.made<address><city>;
say "\nPhone numbers:";
say $match.made<phoneNumbers>[$_]<type number>
    for 0..$match.made<phoneNumbers>.end;
```

This will display the following output:

```
Keys are:
(lastName Bank-account phoneNumbers children address age firstName spouse
isAlive)
```

```
Some values:
John
Smith
True
New York

Phone numbers:
(home 212 555-1234)
(office 646 555-4567)
(mobile 123 456-7890)
```

Inheritance and Mutable Grammars

The capacity for a grammar to inherit from another one opens the door to very rich possibilities in terms of extending the Perl 6 language itself. It is possible, for example in the context of a module or a framework, to "subclass" the standard Perl grammar, i.e., to write a new child grammar that inherits from the standard Perl grammar, but adds a new feature, overloads an operator, or modifies some other syntax element, and to run this program with the same Perl 6 compiler, but with this locally modified grammar.

This means that it is actually possible to dynamically extend the language for new needs, often without even changing the compiler or the virtual machine. These are, however, advanced topics that are more geared toward language gurus than to beginners. So we only mention these exciting possibilities with the hope of whetting your appetite and pushing you to study these further, but will not dwell further on them in this book.

Debugging

Writing grammars is a lot of fun, but it can also be difficult or even tedious when you start.

When you started to practice programming with this book, you probably made a lot of small mistakes that initially prevented your programs from compiling and running, or from doing what you expected. With practice, however, you hopefully gradually made fewer errors and spent less time chasing bugs.

When you begin to learn grammars (and to a lesser extent regexes), you may feel like you are starting again at square one. Even very good programmers often make silly mistakes when they start writing grammars. It is a different programming paradigm, and it requires a new learning phase.

In this case, small is beautiful. Start with small regexes and small rules, and with small test input. Test individual regexes or rules under the REPL, and add them to your code only when you're confident that they do what you want.

Write test cases at the same time as your code (or actually even before you write the code), and make sure that you pass all the relevant tests before moving on. And add new tests when you add new rules.

One standard debugging technique is to add print statements to the code in order to figure out various information about the state of the program (such as the value of variables, the flow of execution of the program, etc.). You can also do that with regexes and grammars.

Let's take the example of the very simple grammar for matching dates of "Grammars" on page 279 and let's suppose that you have written this grammar:

```
grammar My-Date {
    token TOP { \s* <year> '-' <month> '-' <day> }
    token year  { \d ** 4 }
    token month { 1 <[0..2]> || 0 <[1..9]> }
    token day   { (\d ** 2) <?{1 <= $0 <= 31 }> }
}
my $string = " 2016-07-31 ";
say so My-Date.parse($string);                    # -> False
```

This test fails.

At this point, it has already become a bit difficult to figure out why the grammar fails (unless we have thoroughly tested each of the three tokens before building the grammar, but let's assume for the sake of this discussion that we haven't). Let's try not to randomly change things here or there and see if it works better; we would likely spend hours doing that and probably not get anywhere. Let's be more methodical.

Let's first test the building-block tokens, year, month, and day. We've seen before that the parse method looks *by default* for the TOP rule in the grammar, but you can specify another rule, and that's what we need here. We can test these tokens individually:

```
say so My-Date.parse("2016", :rule<year>);   # -> True
say so My-Date.parse("07",   :rule<month>);  # -> True
say so My-Date.parse("31",   :rule<day>);    # -> True
```

These three tokens seem to work fine. At this point, you might be guessing where the problem is, but let's assume you don't.

We need to debug the "TOP" token. We can just use the common debugging method of printing where we are at various stages of the program. You can insert a print statement block in a named rule. Let's try to change the TOP token to this:

```
token TOP { \s* <year>  { say "matched year"; }
            '-' <month> { say "matched month";}
            '-' <day>   { say "matched day";  }
          }
```

This displays the following output:

```
matched year
matched month
matched day
```

So, even the "TOP" token seems to work almost to the end. At this point, we should be able to figure out that we lack final spacing in the "TOP" token.

So either we should add an optional spacing at the end of the token:

```
token TOP { \s* <year> '-' <month> '-' <day> \s*}
```

or change it to a rule:

```
rule TOP { \s* <year> '-' <month> '-' <day> }
```

or it was possibly the test string that was wrong (because it wasn't supposed to have spaces) and needed to be fixed.

If you have an actions class, you can also add print statements to the actions methods.

Remember also that the Perl debugger (see "Debugging" on page 266) can be very helpful. We briefly showed in "Stepping Through a Regex Match" on page 269 how to go step by step through a regex match. Most of what has been described there also applies to debugging grammars.

Finally, there is a very good module, `Grammar::Tracer` (*https://github.com/jnthn/grammar-debugger/*), for debugging regexes and grammars that works with Rakudo. If you add:

```
use Grammar::Tracer;
```

to your program, then any grammar within the lexical scope will print out debugging information about the rules that tried to match, those that succeeded, and those that failed.

You can also use the following:

```
use Grammar::Debugger;
```

to do the same thing step by step. Just type "h" at the prompt for a list of available commands.

Glossary

Abstract syntax tree (AST)
A data structure often summarizing the match object and used for further exploitation of the useful data. The match object is populated automatically by Perl, whereas the AST contains information explicitly inserted by the programmer.

actions class

A class used in conjunction with a grammar to perform certain actions when a grammar rule matches something in the input data. If a method with the same name as a rule in the grammar exists in the actions class, it will be called whenever the rule matches.

capture

The fact that parts of the target string that are matched by a regex (or a grammar) can be retrieved through the use of a number of dedicated special variables.

declarative programming

A programming model where you specify definitions, rules, properties, and constraints, rather than statements and instructions, and let the program derive new knowledge from these definitions and rules. Regexes and grammars are examples of declarative programming.

grammar

A high-level tool for performing lexical and grammatical analysis of structured text. In Perl 6, a grammar is more specifically a namespace containing a collection of named rules aimed at this type of analysis.

lexing

Performing a lexical analysis of a source text, and especially dividing it into "words" or tokens.

Match object

In Perl 6, an object (of type `Match`), usually noted `$/`, which contains (sometimes very) detailed information about what was successfully matched by a regex or a grammar. The `$/` match object will be set to `Nil` if the match failed.

parsing

Performing a grammatical analysis of a source text, and especially assembling words or tokens into sentences or expressions and statements that make some semantic sense.

rule

In broad terms, named rules are regexes that use a method syntax and are usually stored in a grammar. More specifically, one category of these named rules (along with named regexes and tokens).

Exercise: A Grammar for an Arithmetic Calculator

The arithmetic calculator presented in "Actions Objects" on page 282 is very simplistic. In particular, it can parse simple arithmetic expressions composed of two operands separated by one infix operator, but not much more than that.

We would like to be able to parse more complicated arithmetic expressions. The calculator should also be able to handle:

- Expressions with several different operators (among the four basic arithmetic operators) and multiple operands
- Standard precedence rules between operators (for example, multiplications should be performed prior to additions)
- Parentheses to override usual precedence rules

These are a few examples of expressions the calculator should parse and compute correctly:

```
3 + 4 + 5;
3 + 4 * 5;    # result should be 23
(3 + 4) * 5; # result should be 35
```

Exercise 13-2.

Your mission, [Dan|Jim], should you choose to accept it, is to write such a grammar. As usual, should you fail, the Government shall deny any knowledge of your actions class.

There are many possible ways to accomplish this; the solution presented in "Exercise: A Grammar for an Arithmetic Calculator" on page 422 is only one of them.

## CHAPTER 14

Functional Programming in Perl

Functional programming is a programming paradigm that treats computation as the evaluation of mathematical functions and avoids changing-state and mutable data. It is a declarative programming paradigm, which means programming is done with expressions or declarations instead of statements. In functional code, the output value of a function depends only on the arguments that are input to the function, so calling a function twice with the same argument will produce the same result each time. Eliminating side effects, i.e., changes in state that do not depend on the function inputs, can make it much easier to understand and predict the behavior of a program, which is one of the key motivations for the development of functional programming.

Perl is not a functional language in the sense that it also uses several other programming paradigms that we have seen abundantly throughout this book. It does however offer extensive functional programming features and capabilities, some of which have been introduced in various sections of this book and will be briefly reviewed here before we get further.

Higher-Order Functions

As early as Chapter 3 on functions and subroutines, in "Functions and Subroutines as First-Class Citizens" on page 47, we have seen that functions, subroutines, and other code objects are *first-class objects* or *first-class citizens* in Perl, which means that they can be passed around as values. A Perl 6 function is a value you can assign to a variable or pass around as an argument to a function or a return value from another function.

A Refresher on Functions as First-Class Objects

Our initial very simple example of a higher-order function was something like this:

```
sub do-twice(&code) {
    &code();
    &code();
}
sub greet {
    say "Hello World!";
}
do-twice &greet;
```

in which the greet subroutine was passed as an argument to the do-twice subroutine, with the effect of printing the greeting message twice. A function that is passed as an argument to another function is often called a *callback function*.

The & sigil placed before the greet subroutine name in the argument list (as well as before the code parameter in the signature and in the body of the do-twice subroutine) tells Perl that you are passing around a subroutine or some other callable code object.

In computer science, a subroutine that can take another subroutine as an argument is sometimes called a *higher-order function*.

More interesting examples of higher-order function are found with the reduce, map, and grep functions studied in "Map, Filter, and Reduce" on page 165, as well as the sort function ("Sorting Arrays or Lists" on page 172 and "More Advanced Sorting Techniques" on page 173).

Let's consider for example the task of sorting by date records consisting of an identifier followed by a date in the DD-MM-YYYY format, such as "id1;13-05-2015" or "id2;17-04-2015". The records need quite a bit of transformation before we can compare them for the sake of finding the chronological order in which they should be sorted, so we might write a separate comparison function:

```
sub compare ($rec1, $rec2) {
    my $cmp1 = join ",", reverse split /<[;-]>/, $rec1;
    my $cmp2 = join ",", reverse split /<[;-]>/, $rec2;
    return $cmp1 cmp $cmp2;
}
```

Each modified record is constructed by chaining three functions. These lines should be read from right to left: first, the input value is split into four items; these items are then reversed and then joined, so that the result for "id1;13-05-2015" is "2015,05,13,id1", which is adapted for a comparison with the cmp operator. We will come back soon to this form of pipeline programming and others ways of performing these operations.

We can now pass the compare subroutine to the sort function:

```
.say for sort &compare, <id1;13-05-2015 id2;17-04-2015
                         id3;21-02-2016 id4;12-01-2015>;
```

This displays:

```
id4;12-01-2015
id2;17-04-2015
id1;13-05-2015
id3;21-02-2016
```

Please note that this is provided as an example of callback functions used with the sort built-in function. We will see at the end of the next subsection a simpler way to accomplish the same type of sort using an anonymous subroutine.

Anonymous Subroutines and Lambdas

We have also seen that a subroutine does not need to have a name and can be *anonymous*. For example, it may be stored directly in a scalar variable:

```
my $greet = sub {
    say "Hello World!";
};
do-twice $greet;              # prints "Hello World" twice
```

We don't even need to store the code of the anonymous function in the $greet variable; we can pass it directly as an argument to the do-twice subroutine:

```
do-twice(sub {say "Hello World!"} );
```

Since this anonymous subroutine does not take an argument and does not return a useful value, we can simplify the syntax further and pass a simple anonymous code block to do-twice:

```
do-twice {say "Hello World!"};   # prints "Hello World" twice
```

You've already seen several useful examples of anonymous subroutines in this book (see "Map, Filter, and Reduce" on page 165 for details):

- With the reduce function to compute the sum of the first 20 integers:

```
my $sum = reduce { $^a + $^b }, 1..20; # -> 210
```

- With the map function to capitalize the first letter of a list of cities (using the tc built-in):

```
> .say for map {.tc}, <london paris rome washington madrid>;
London
Paris
Rome
Washington
Madrid
```

- With the `grep` function to generate a list of even numbers by filtering out odd numbers:

```
my @evens = grep { $_ %% 2 }, 1..17; # -> [2 4 6 8 10 12 14 16]
```

The example with `reduce` is of special interest. In principle, contrary to a subroutine, you cannot easily pass arguments to a code block (because it has no signature). But the use of the self-declared positional parameters (or placeholders) with the $^ twigil makes it possible to use parameters within the block.

Because of this possibility, the anonymous code block becomes what is commonly called a *lambda* in computer science (and in mathematics), i.e., a kind of nameless function. Lambda calculus, a mathematical theory invented in the 1930s by Alonzo Church, is the root of most of today's functional programming languages.

Actually, the two other examples above using the $_ topical variable are also lambdas. Although we haven't mentioned it, some other constructs we saw earlier are also lambdas. In particular, consider the "pointy block" syntax used twice in the following for loops displaying the multiplication tables:

```
for 1..9 -> $mult {
    say "Multiplication table for $mult";
    for 1..9 -> $val {
        say "$mult * $val = ", $mult * $val;
    }
}
```

This is another form of lambda where the "function" parameter is defined by the pointy block loop variable.

The sorting example presented in "A Refresher on Functions as First-Class Objects" on page 297 just above may also be rewritten with an anonymous code block (taking advantage of the `sort` syntax using a code block with a single argument described in "More Advanced Sorting Techniques" on page 173):

```
my @in = <id1;13-05-2015 id2;17-04-2015 id3;21-02-2016>;
.say for sort { join ",", reverse split /<[;-]>/, $_ }, @in;
```

Here again, the somewhat long code block passed as an argument to the `sort` function is a lambda.

Closures

In computer programming, a *closure* (or *lexical closure*) is a function that can access variables that are lexically available where the function is defined, even if those variables are no longer in scope in the code section where the function is called.

Consider the following example:

```
sub create-counter(Int $count) {
    my $counter = $count;
    sub increment-count {
        return $counter++
    }
    return &increment-count;
}
my &count-from-five = create-counter(5);
say &count-from-five() for 1..6; # prints numbers 5 to 10
```

The create-counter subroutine initializes the $counter variable to the value of the received parameter, defines the increment-count subroutine, and returns this subroutine. The main code calls create-counter to dynamically create the &count-from-five code reference (and could call it many times to create other counters counting from 6, 7, and so on). Then, &count-from-five is called six times and prints out numbers between 5 and 10, each on its own line.

The magical thing here is that the $counter variable is out of scope when &count-from-five is called, but &count-from-five can access it, return its value, and increment it because $counter was within the lexical scope at the time the increment-count was defined. It is commonly said that increment-count "closes over" the $counter variable. The increment-count subroutine is a closure.

The above example is a bit contrived and its syntax somewhat awkward because I wanted to show an example of a named closure (increment-count is a named subroutine). It is usually simpler and more idiomatic to use anonymous closures and to rewrite the example as follows:

```
sub create-counter(Int $count) {
    my $counter = $count;
    return sub {
        return $counter++
    }
}
my &count-from-five = create-counter(5);
say &count-from-five() for 1..6; # prints numbers 5 to 10
```

You could even simplify create-counter further with implicit return statements:

```
sub create-counter(Int $count) {
    my $counter = $count;
    sub { $counter++ }
}
```

but this is arguably less clear because the code's intent is less explicit.

The last create-fifo example in the solution to the FIFO queue exercise ("Encapsulating the data" on page 382) is another example of the same mechanism:

```
sub create-fifo {
    my @queue;
    return (
        sub {return shift @queue;},
        sub ($item) {push @queue, $item;}
        ) ;
}
my ($fifo-get, $fifo-put) = create-fifo();
$fifo-put($_) for 1..10;
print " ", $fifo-get() for 1..5; # ->  1 2 3 4 5
```

In Perl 6, all subroutines are closures, which means that all subroutines can access to lexical variable that existed in the environment at the time of their definition, but they don't necessarily act as closures.

In fact, all code objects, even simple anonymous code blocks, can act as closures, which means that they can reference lexical variables from the outer scope, and this is in effect what is going on with the loop variable of a pointy block or in the following map block:

```
my $multiplier = 7;
say  map {$multiplier * $_}, 3..6; # -> (21 28 35 42)
```

Here the block passed to map references the variable $multiplier from the outer scope, making the block a closure.

Languages without closures cannot easily provide higher-order functions that are as easy to use and powerful as map.

Here is yet another example of a block acting as a closure for a counter implementation:

```
my &count;
{
    my $counter = 10;
    &count = { say $counter++ };
}
&count() for 1..5;
```

This closure saves a reference to the $counter variable when the closure is created. The call to the &count code block successfully displays and updates $counter, even though that variable is no longer in lexical scope when the block is executed.

List Processing and Pipeline Programming

Quite often, a computation can be expressed as a series of successive transformations on a list of values. Perl provides functions able to work on the items of a list and apply simple actions, callback functions, or code blocks to these items. We have already seen and used abundantly several such functions:

- `map` applies a transformation to each item of a list.
- `grep` is a filter that keeps only the items for which the function or code block associated with `grep` evaluates to true.
- `reduce` uses each item of a list to compute a single scalar value.
- `sort` sorts the elements of a list in accordance to the rules defined in the passed code block or subroutine.

We have discussed several examples where these functions can be used together in a sort of data pipeline in which the data produced by each step of the pipeline is fed to the next step. For example, in an earlier section ("A Refresher on Functions as First-Class Objects" on page 297), we used this:

```
my $cmp1 = join ",", reverse split /<[;-]>/, $rec1;
```

As we said, this type of code should be read from right to left (and from bottom to top if written over several code lines): `$rec1` is fed to `split`, which splits the data item into four pieces; the pieces are then reversed and fed to `join` to reconstruct a single data item where the pieces are now in reverse order.

Similarly, we could produce a list of pet animals belonging to single women living in Kansas with the following code chaining several methods:

```
my @single-kansas-women-pets =
    map { .pets },
    grep { !.is-married },
    grep { .gender eq "Female" },
    grep { .state eq "Kansas" },
        @citizens;
```

This one should be read bottom to top. It takes a list of all citizens, filters those from Kansas who are female, filters those who are not married, and finally generates the list of pets of such persons. Note that `.pets` may return one animal, a list of several animals, or an empty list. `map` "flattens" the lists thus produced, so the final result going into the array is a flat list of animals (and not a nested list of lists).

These pipelines are very powerful and expressive, and can get a lot done in a few code lines.

Feed and Backward Feed Operators

In the previous examples, the steps were laid out in reverse order; you may consider this inconvenient, although it is easy to get used to.

Perl 6 provides the ==> *feed* operator (sometimes called *pipe* in other languages) that makes it possible to write the various pipeline steps in a "more natural," left to right, order.

For example, reusing the example of sorting records by dates from earlier in this chapter, you could rewrite it like so:

```
"id1;13-05-2015"
    ==> split(/<[;-]>/)
    ==> reverse()
    ==> join(",")
    ==> my @out;   # @out is now: [2015,05,13,id1]
```

By the way, if you're using such pipeline operations on a large input, and depending on your platform architecture, Perl 6 may be able to run these various operations in parallel on different CPUs or cores, thereby improving significantly the performance of the overall process.

There is also a backward feed operator, <==, enabling us to write the pipeline in reverse order:

```
my $out <== join(",")
        <== reverse()
        <== split(/<[;-]>/)
        <== "id1;13-05-2015";
```

The Reduction Metaoperator

We already met this metaoperator in "Map, Filter, and Reduce" on page 165. A meta-operator acts on other operators. Given a list and an operator, the [...] *reduction meta-operator* applies the operator iteratively to all the values of the list to produce a single value.

For example, the following prints the sum of all the elements of a list or a range:

```
say [+] 1..10;     # -> 55
```

Similarly, we can write a factorial function as:

```
sub fact (Int $n where $n >= 0) {
    return [*] 1..$n;
}
say fact 20;       # -> 2432902008176640000
say fact 0;        # -> 1
```

(Note that this yields the correct result even for the edge case of factorial 0, which is defined mathematically to be 1.)

The Hyperoperator

A hyperoperator applies the specified operator to each item of a list (or two lists in parallel) and returns a modified list (somewhat similarly to the map function). It uses the so-called French or German quote marks, « » (Unicode codepoints U+00AB and

U+00BB), but you can use their ASCII-equivalent double angle brackets, << >>, if you prefer (or don't know how to enter those Unicode characters with your editor).

Our first example will multiply each element of a list by a given number (5):

```
my @b = 6..10;
my @c = 5 «*» @b;
say @c;              # prints 30 35 ... 50 (5*6, 5*7, ...)
```

We can also combine two lists and, for example, add respective values:

```
my @a = 1..5;
my @b = 6..10;
my @d = @a >>+<< @b;
say @d;              # -> [7 9 11 13 15]
```

You can also use hyperoperators with a unary operator:

```
my @a = 2, 4, 6;
say -« @a;           # prints:  -2 -4 -6
```

Hyperoperators with unary operators always return a list the same size as the input list. Infixed hyperoperators have a different behavior depending on the size of their operands:

```
@a >>+<< @b;   # @a and @b must have the same size
@a <<+<< @b;   # @a can be smaller
@a >>+>> @b;   # @b can be smaller
@a <<+>> @b;   # Either can be smaller, Perl will do
               # probably what you mean (DWIM principle)
```

Hyperoperators also work with modified assignment operators:

```
@x >>+=<< @y   # Same as: @x = @x >>+<< @y
```

The Cross (X) and Zip (Z) Operators

The cross operator uses the capital letter X. It takes two or more lists as arguments and returns a list of all lists that can be constructed combining the elements of each list (a form of "Cartesian product"):

```
my @a = 1, 2;
my @b = 3, 4;
my @c = @a X @b;     # -> [(1,3), (1,4), (2,3), (2,4)]
```

The cross operator may also be used as a metaoperator and apply the operator that it modifies to each item combination derived from its operands:

```
my @a = 3, 4;
my @b = 6, 8;
say @a X* @b;    # -> 18 24 24 32
```

If no additional operator is supplied (as in the first example above), X acts as if a comma is provided as default additional operator.

The Z zip operator interleaves the lists like a zipper:

```
say 1, 2 Z <a b c > Z 9, 8;    # -> ((1 a 9) (2 b 8))
```

The Z operator also exists as a metaoperator, in which case, instead of producing nested inner lists as in the example above, the zip operator will apply the supplied additional operator and replace these nested lists with the values thus generated. For instance, in the following example, the ~ concatenate operator is used to merge the inner lists produced by the zip operator into strings:

```
say 1, 2, 3 Z~ <a b c > Z~ 9, 8, 7; # -> (1a9 2b8 3c7)
```

List Operators: A Summary

The list operators above are powerful and can be combined together to produce incredibly expressive constructs.

As an exercise, try to solve the following small quizzes (please don't read on until you have tried them and try to do them with the operators we've just seen):

- Given that the lcm built-in function returns the least common multiple of two numbers, write a program which displays the smallest positive number divisible by all numbers between 1 and 20.
- Write a program that computes the sum of all digits of factorial 100.
- Find the difference between the square of the sum of the 100 first integers and the sum of the squares of the 100 first integers.

Please, again, don't read further until you have tried to solve these quizzes (and hopefully succeeded).

The reduction operator makes it possible to apply an operator to all elements of a list. Thus, using it with the lcm function gives the LCM of numbers between 1 and 20:

```
say [lcm] 1..20;                         # -> 232792560
```

For the sum of the digits of factorial 100, we use the [ ] reduction metaoperator twice, once with the multiplication operator to compute factorial 100, and another time with the addition operator to sum the digits of the result:

```
say [+] split '', [*] 2..100;            # -> 648
```

For the square of the sum minus the sum of the squares, it is easy to compute the sum of the 100 first integers with the reduction operator. The <<...>> hyperoperator easily supplies a list of the squares of these integers, and another application of the reduction operator reduces this list to a sum:

```
say ([+] 1..100)**2 - [+] (1..100) «**» 2; # -> 25164150
```

Creating New Operators

We have briefly seen ("Constructing New Operators" on page 214) that you can build new operators or redefine existing ones for new types.

The example we gave was to define the minus sign (–) as an infix operator between two hashes in order to perform a kind of mathematical set subtraction, i.e., to find all keys of the first hash that are not in the second hash.

In the previous paragraph, the word *infix* means that this is a binary operator (two operands) that will be placed between the two operands.

There are other flavors of operators:

Prefix
    A unary operator placed before the operand, for example the minus sign in the expression – 1

Postfix
    A unary operator placed after the operand, for example the exclamation mark used as a mathematical symbol for the factorial: 5!

Circumfix
    An operator made of two symbols placed around the operand(s), for example the parentheses (. . .) or the angle brackets < . . . >

Postcircumfix
    An operator made of two symbols placed after an operand and around another one, for example the square brackets in @a[1]

To declare a new operator, you usually need to specify its type (prefix, postfix, etc.), followed by a colon, followed by the operator symbol or name between angle brackets, followed by the function signature and body defining the operator. For example, we could define a prefix % operator as follows:

```
multi sub prefix:<%> (Int $x) {   # double operator
    2 * $x;
}
say % 21;   # -> 42
```

This is just an example to show how operator construction works; % would probably not be a good name for a double operator. The interesting point, though, is that we have reused an existing operator (the modulo operator), but the compiler does not get confused because modulo is an infix operator and our new operator is defined as a prefix operator.

A better naming example might be to use an exclamation mark (!) as a postfix factorial operator, just as in mathematical notation:

```
multi sub postfix:<!> (Int $n where $n >= 0) {
    [*] 2..$n;
}
say 5!;                         # -> 120
```

Note that the exclamation mark used as a prefix operator (i.e., placed before its operand) is a negation operator, but there is usually no possible confusion between the two operators because one is a prefix operator and our new operator is a postfix operator (although you might have to be a bit careful on where to put whitespace if your expression is somewhat complicated). The multi keyword isn't strictly required here, but it is probably good practice to put it anyway, just to cover the cases where it is needed.

As another example, you could define the Σ (sum) operator as follows:

```
multi sub prefix:<Σ> (@*num-list) {
    [+] @num-list;
}
say Σ (10, 20, 12);             # -> 42
```

The benefit of using the Σ operator over using [+] directly may not be very obvious, but it is sometimes very useful to create a "domain-specific language" (DSL), i.e., a sublanguage specifically adapted for a specific context or subject matter (e.g., math or chemistry), which allows a particular type of problem or solution to be expressed more clearly than the existing core language would allow. In Perl 6, the grammars and the ease of creating new operators make this creation of DSL quite an easy task.

The new operator does not have to be declared between angle brackets. The following declarations could all be used to define an addition operator:

```
infix:<+>
infix:<<+>>
infix:«+»
infix:('+')
infix:("+")
```

You can also specify the precedence of your new operators (relative to existing ones). For example:

```
multi sub infix:<mult> is equiv(&infix:<*>) { ... }
multi sub infix:<plus> is equiv(&infix:<+>) { ... }
mutli sub infix:<zz> is tighter(&infix:<+>) { ... }
mutli sub infix:<yy> is  looser(&infix:<+>) { ... }
```

In one of his articles ("Structured Programming with go to Statements," December 1974), Donald Knuth, a very famous computer scientist, uses the :=: symbol as a pseudocode operator to express the variable interchange (or swap) of two values, i.e., the following operation:

```
# Caution: this is pseudocode, not working code, at this point
my $a = 1; my $b = 2;
$a :=: $b;
say "$a $b";  # -> 2 1
```

In Knuth's paper, this is just a pseudocode shortcut to discuss more easily Tony Hoare's quicksort algorithm (see "Exercise: Quick Sort" on page 334), but we can easily implement that symbol:

```
multi sub infix:<:=:> ($a is rw, $b is rw) {
    ($a, $b) = $b, $a;
}
```

Note that this can also be written this way:

```
multi sub infix:<:=:> ($a is rw, $b is rw) {
    ($a, $b) .= reverse;   # equivalent to: ($a, $b) = ($a, $b).reverse
}
```

We can now test it for real on the following examples:

```
my ($c, $d) = 2, 5;
say $c :=: $d;            # -> (5 2)
# using it to swap two array elements:
my @e = 1, 2, 4, 3, 5;
@e[2] :=: @e[3];
say @e;                  # -> [1 2 3 4 5]
```

Now, the pseudocode above now just works fine as real code. A sort algorithm such as the one following ("Our Own Version of a Sort Function" on page 311) may typically have code lines like these to swap two elements of an array:

```
if $some-condition {
    my ($x, $y) = @array[$i], @array[$i + gap];
    @array[$i], @array[$i + gap] = $y, $x;
}
```

If the above :=: operator is defined, we could just rewrite these lines as follows:

```
@array[$i] :=: @array[$i + gap] if $some-condition;
```

A final interesting point. Suppose we want to use the ⊕ operator for the mathematical set union between two hashes. This could easily be written as follows:

```
multi sub infix:<⊕> (%a, %b) {
    my %c = %a;
    %c{$_} = %b{$_} for keys %b;
    return %c
}
```

This works fine:

```
my %q1 = jan => 1, feb => 2, mar => 3;
my %q2 = apr => 4, may => 5, jun => 6;
```

```
my %first_half = %q1 ⊕ %q2;
say %first_half;
# {apr => 4, feb => 2, jan => 1, jun => 6, mar => 3, may => 5}
```

So far, so good, nothing really new. But the new infix ⊕ operator has now become almost the same as a Perl built-in operator, so that we can use it together with the reduction metaoperator:

```
my %q1 = jan => 1, feb => 2, mar => 3;
my %q2 = apr => 4, may => 5, jun => 6;
my %q3 = jul => 7, aug => 8, sep => 9;
my %q4 = oct => 10, nov => 11, dec => 12;
my %year = [⊕] %q1, %q2, %q3, %q4;
say %year;
# {apr => 4, aug => 8, dec => 12, feb => 2, jan => 1,
# jul => 7, jun => 6, mar => 3, may => 5, nov => 11,
# oct => 10, sep => 9}
```

Everything works as if this new operator was part of the Perl 6 grammar. And that's in effect what has happened here: we have extended the language with a new operator. This possibility of extending the language is key to the ability of Perl 6 to cope with future needs that we can't even think of at present time.

Creating Your Own Map-Like Functions

We have seen in this chapter and in "Map, Filter, and Reduce" on page 165 how higher-order functions such as the reduce, map, grep, and sort functions can be powerful and expressive. There are some other such built-in functions in Perl, but we would like to be able to create our own.

Custom versions of map, grep, etc.

Let's see how we could write our own custom versions of such functions.

my-map, a pure Perl version of map

Let's start by trying to rewrite in pure Perl the map function. It needs to take a subroutine or a code block as its first argument, to apply it to an array or a list, and to return the modified list:

```
sub my-map (&code, @values) {
    my @temp;
    push @temp, &code($_) for @values;
    return @temp;
}
my @result = my-map { $_ * 2 }, 1..5;
say @result;                    # -> [2 4 6 8 10]
```

This works exactly as expected on the first trial. (I have attempted the same experiment with some other languages in the past, including Perl 5; it took quite a few tries before getting it right, especially regarding the calling syntax. Here, everything falls into place naturally.) To tell the truth, the test in this code example is very limited and there may very well be some edge cases when my-map does not work the same way as map, but our aim was not to clone map exactly; the point is that it is quite simple to build a higher-order subroutine that behaves essentially the same way as map.

my-grep

Writing our pure-Perl version of grep is just about as easy:

```
sub my-grep (&code, @values) {
    my @temp;
    for @values -> $val {
        push @temp, $val if &code($val);
    }
    return @temp;
}
my @even = my-grep { $_ %% 2 }, 1..10;
say @even;                    # -> [2 4 6 8 10]
```

Our Own Version of a Sort Function

We can similarly write our own version of a sort function.

The Perl sort function implements a sort algorithm known as *merge sort*.[1] Some previous versions of the Perl language (prior to version 5.8) implemented another algorithm known as *quick sort*.[2] The main reason for this change was that, although quick sort is on average a bit faster than merge sort, there are specific cases where quick sort is much less efficient than merge sort (notably when the data is almost sorted). These cases are very rare with random data, but not in real situations: it is quite common that you have to sort a previously sorted list in which only a few elements have been added or modified.

In computing theory, it is frequently said that, for sorting n items, both merge sort and quick sort have an *average complexity* of $O(n \log n)$, which essentially means that the number of operations to be performed is proportional to $n \log n$ if the number of items to be sorted is n, with quick sort being usually slightly faster; but quick sort has a *worst-case complexity* of $O(n^2)$, whereas merge sort has a *worst-case complexity* of $O(n \log n)$. When the number of items n to be sorted grows large, n^2 becomes very

---

1 Merge sort is presented in some detail in "The Merge Sort Algorithm" on page 325.

2 Quick sort is presented in "Exercise: Quick Sort" on page 334.

significantly larger than *n* log *n*. In other words, merge sort is deemed to be better because it remains efficient in all cases.

Suppose now that we want to implement another sorting algorithm whose performance is alleged to be better. For this example, we will use a somewhat exotic sorting algorithm known as *comb sort* (a.k.a. Dobosiewicz's sort), the details of which can be found on Wikipedia (*https://en.wikipedia.org/wiki/Comb_sort*). This algorithm is said to be *in place*, which means that it does not need to copy the items into auxiliary data structures, and has generally good performance (often better than merge sort), but is not very commonly used in practice because its theoretical analysis is very difficult (in particular, it seems that it has a good worst-case performance, but no one has been able to prove this formally so far). In fact, we don't really care about the real performance of this sort algorithm; it is very unlikely that a pure Perl implementation of the comb sort will outperform the built in sort function implemented in C and probably very carefully optimized by its authors. We only want to show how a sort subroutine could be implemented.

To work the same way as the internal sort, a sort function must receive as parameters a comparison function or code block and the array to be sorted, and the comparison routine should use placeholder parameters ($^a and $^b in the code below). This is a possible basic implementation:

```
sub comb_sort (&code, @array) {
    my $max = @array.elems;
    my $gap = $max;
    loop {
        my $swapped = False;
        $gap = Int($gap / 1.3);      # 1.3: optimal shrink factor
        $gap = 1 if $gap < 1;
        my $lmax = $max - $gap - 1;
        for (0..$lmax) -> $i {
            my ($x, $y) = (@array[$i], @array[$i+$gap]);
            (@array[$i], @array[$i+$gap], $swapped) = ($y, $x, True)
                if &code($x, $y) ~~ More;  # or: if &code($x, $y) > 0
        }
        last if $gap == 1 and ! $swapped;
    }
}
```

This can be tested with the following code:

```
my @v;
my $max = 500;
@v[$_] = Int(20000.rand) for (0..$max);

comb_sort {$^a <=> $^b}, @v;
.say for @v[0..10], @v[493..499]; # prints array start and end
# prints (for example):
# (14 22 77 114 119 206 264 293 298 375 391)
# (19672 19733 19736 19873 19916 19947 19967)
```

The inner loop compares items that are distant from each other by `$gap` values, and swaps them if they are not in the proper order. At the beginning, `$gap` is large, and it is divided by a shrink factor at each iteration of the outer loop. Performance heavily depends on the value of the shrink factor. At the end, the gap is 1 and the comb sort becomes equivalent to a bubble sort. The optimal shrink factor lies somewhere between 1.25 and 1.33; I have used a shrink factor of 1.3, the value suggested by the authors of the original publications presenting the algorithm.

An Iterator Version of map

These `my-map`, `my-grep`, and `comb_sort` functions are pedagogically interesting, but they aren't very useful if they do the same thing as their built-in counterparts (and are probably slower). However, now that we have seen how to build them, we can create our own versions that do things differently.

Say we want to create a function that acts like `map` in the sense that it applies a transformation on the items of the input list, but does that on the items one by one, on demand from a consumer process, and pauses when and as long as the consumer process does not need anything. This could be described as an *iterator* returning modified elements on demand from the source list. You might think that this does not have much to do with `map`, but it might also be considered as a form of `map` with delayed evaluation, which processes only the elements of the input lists that are necessary for the program, not more than that.

The idea of processing only what is strictly required is often called *laziness*, and this is a very useful idea. Lazy list processing can be very useful not only because it avoids processing data that is not needed, and therefore can contribute to better resource usage and better performance, but also because it makes it possible to consider *infinite* lists: so long as you can guarantee that you are only going to use a limited number of elements, you don't have any problem considering lists that are potentially unlimited. Perl 6 provides the concepts and tools to do this.

To reflect these considerations, we will call our subroutine `iter-map`. Since we might want to also write a `iter-grep` subroutine and possibly others, we will write separately an iterator and a data transformer.

We can use a closure to manufacture an iterator:

```
sub create-iter(@array) {
    my $index = 0;
    return sub { @array[$index++];}
}
my $iterator = create-iter(1..200);
say $iterator() for 1..5; # -> 1, 2, 3, 4, 5
```

Now that the iterator returns one value at a time, we can write the `iter-map` subroutine:

```
sub iter-map (&code-ref, $iter) {
    return &code-ref($iter);
}
my $iterator = create-iter(1..200);
say iter-map { $_ * 2 }, $iterator() for 1..5; # -> 2, 4, 6, 8, 10
```

Since we have called the iter-map function only 5 times, it has done the work of multiplying values by 2 only 5 times, instead of doing it 200 times, 195 of which are for nothing. Of course, multiplying a number by 2 isn't an expensive operation and the array isn't very large, but this shows how laziness can prevent useless computations. We will come back to this idea, since Perl 6 offers native support to lazy lists and lazy processing.

As already noted, an additional advantage of using a function such as iter-map is that it is possible to use virtually infinite lists. This implementation using an infinite list works just as before:

```
my $iterator = create-iter(1..*);
say iter-map { $_ * 2 }, $iterator() for 1..5;
    # prints 2, 4, 6, 8, 10
```

An Iterator Version of grep

If we try to write a iter-grep subroutine on the same model:

```
my $iterator = create-iter(reverse 1..10);
sub iter-grep (&code_ref, $iter) {
    my $val = $iter();
    return $val if &code_ref($val);
}
# simulating ten calls
say iter-grep { $_ % 2 }, $iterator for 1..10;
```

it doesn't quite work as desired, because this will print alternatively odd values (9, 7, 5, etc.) and undefined values (for the even values of the array). Although we haven't specified it yet, we would prefer iter-grep to supply the next value for which the $code-ref returns True. This implies that iter-grep has to loop over the values returned by the iterator until it receives a proper value.

That might look like this:

```
my $iterator = create-iter(reverse 1..10);
sub iter-grep (&code_ref, $iter) {
    loop {
        my $val = $iter();
        return unless defined $val;  # avoid infinite loop
        return $val if &code_ref($val);
    }
}
# simulating ten calls
for 1..10 {
```

```
    my $val = iter-grep { $_ % 2 }, $iterator;
    say "Input array exhausted!" and last unless defined $val;
    say $val;
}
```

This now works as expected:

```
9
7
5
3
1
Input array exhausted!
```

However, we still have a problem if the array contains some undefined values (or "empty slots"). This would be interpreted as the end of the input array, whereas there might be some additional useful values in the array. This is sometimes known in computer science as the "semi-predicate" problem. Here, iter-grep has no way to tell the difference between an empty slot in the array and the end of the array. A more robust implementation therefore needs a better version of create-iter returning something different for an undefined array item and array exhaustion. For example, the iterator might return a false value when done with the array, and a pair with the array item as a value otherwise. A pair will be considered to be true, even if its value isn't defined:

```
sub create-iter(@array) {
    my $index = 0;
    my $max-index = @array.end;
    return sub {
    return False if $index >= $max-index;
    return ("a_pair" => @array[$index++]);
    }
}
my @array = 1..5;
@array[7] = 15;
@array[9] = 17;
push @array, $_ for 20..22;
.say for '@array is now: ', @array;
my $iterator = create-iter(@array);
sub iter-grep (&code_ref, $iter) {
    loop {
        my $returned-pair = $iter();
        return unless $returned-pair;  # avoid infinite loop
        my $val = $returned-pair.value;
        return $val if defined $val and &code_ref($val);
    }
}
for 1..10 {
    my $val = iter-grep { $_ % 2 }, $iterator;
    say "Input array exhausted!" and last unless defined $val;
```

```
    say $val;
    }
```

Running this script displays the following:

```
@array is now:
[1 2 3 4 5 (Any) (Any) 15 (Any) 17 20 21 22]
1
3
5
15
17
21
Input array exhausted!
```

This now works fully as desired.

Although `iter-map` did not suffer from the same problem, you might want as an exercise to modify `iter-map` to use our new version of `create-iter`.

The advantage of the iterator functions seen above is that they process only the items that are requested by the user code, so that they perform only the computations strictly required and don't waste CPU cycles and time doing unnecessary work. We have gone through these iterating versions of the `map` and `grep` functions as a form of case study for pedagogical purposes, in order to explain in practical terms the idea of laziness.

This is what would have been necessary to implement lazy iterators in earlier versions of Perl (e.g., Perl 5), but much of this is not required with Perl 6, which has built-in support for lazy lists and lazy operators, as we will see soon.

The gather and take Construct

A useful construct for creating (possibly lazy) lists is `gather { take }`. A `gather` block acts more or less like a loop and runs until `take` supplies a value. This construct is also a form of iterator.

For example, the following code returns a list of numbers equal to three times each of the even numbers between 1 and 10:

```
my @list = gather {
    for 1..10 {
        take 3 * $_ if $_ %% 2
    }
};
say @list;                 # -> [6 12 18 24 30]
```

Here, `gather` loops on the values of the range and `take` "returns" the wanted values.

If you think about it, the code above seems to be doing a form of combination of a map and a grep.

We can indeed simulate a map. For example:

```
my @evens = map { $_ * 2 }, 1..5;
```

could be rewritten with a gather { take } block:

```
my @evens = gather {take $_ * 2 for 1.. 5}; # [2 4 6 8 10]
```

And we could simulate a grep similarly:

```
my @evens = gather {take $_ if $_ %% 2 for 1..10};
```

Since take also admits a method syntax, this could be rewritten as:

```
my @evens = gather {.take if $_ %% 2 for 1..10};
```

These code examples don't bring any obvious advantage over their map or grep counterparts and are not very useful in themselves, but they illustrate how a gather { take } block can be thought of as a generalization of the map and grep functions. And, as already mentioned, the first example in this section actually does combine the actions of a map and a grep.

In fact, we can write a new version of my-map:

```
sub my-map (&coderef, @values) {
    return gather {
        take &coderef($_) for @values;
    };
}
say join " ", my-map {$_ * 2}, 1..10;
# prints: 2 4 6 8 10 12 14 16 18 20
```

Writing a new version of my-grep is just about as easy and left as an exercise to the reader.

Calling the take function only makes sense within the context of a gather block, but it does not have to be within the block itself (or within the lexical scope of the gather block); it can be within the *dynamic scope* of the gather block

Although we haven't covered this concept before, Perl has the notion of *dynamic scope*: contrary to lexical scope, dynamic scope encloses not only the current block, but also the subroutines called from within the current block. Dynamic scope variables use the "*" twigil. Here is an example:

```
sub write-result () { say $*value; }
sub caller (Int $val) {
    my $*value = $val * 2;
    write-result();
}
caller 5;              # -> 10
```

In the code above, the `$*value` dynamic variable is declared and defined in the `caller` subroutine and used in the `write-result` subroutine. This would not work with a lexical variable, but it works with a dynamic variable such as `$*value`, because the scope of `$*value` extends to the `write-result` subroutine called by `caller`.

Similarly, the `take` function can work within the dynamic scope of the `gather` block, which essentially means that the `take` function can be called within a subroutine called from the `gather` block. For example:

```
my @list = gather {
    compute-val($_) for 1..10;
}
sub compute-val(Numeric $x) {
    take $x * $x + 2 * $x - 6;
}
say @list[0..5];        # -> (-3 2 9 18 29 42)
```

As you can see, the `take` function is not called within the `gather` block, but it works fine because it is within the dynamic scope of the gather block, i.e., within the `compute-val` subroutine, which is itself called in the `gather` block.

One last example will show how powerful the `gather { take }` construct can be.

Let's consider this problem posted on the Rosetta Code site (*http://rosettacode.org/ wiki/Same_Fringe*): write a routine that will compare the leaves ("fringe") of two binary trees to determine whether they are the same list of leaves when visited left-to-right. The structure or balance of the trees does not matter; only the number, order, and value of the leaves is important.

The solution in Perl 6 uses a `gather { take }` block and consists of just six code lines:

```
sub fringe ($tree) {
    multi sub fringey (Pair $node) {fringey $_ for $node.kv;}
    multi sub fringey ( Any $leaf) {take $leaf;}
    gather fringey $tree;
}
sub samefringe ($a, $b) { fringe($a) eqv fringe($b) }
```

Perl 6 is the clear winner in terms of the shortest code to solve the problem.

As a comparison, the Ada example is almost 300 lines long, and the C and Java programs slightly over 100 lines. By the way, the shortest solutions besides Perl 6 (Clojure, Picolisp, Racket) run in about 20 lines and are all functional programming languages, or (for Perl 5 for example) are written using functional programming concepts. Although the number of code lines is only one of many criteria to compare programs and languages, this is in my humble opinion a testimony in favor of the functional programming paradigm and its inherent expressiveness.

Lazy Lists and the Sequence Operator

Let's come back now to the idea of lazy lists and study how Perl 6 can handle and use them.

The Sequence Operator

Perl provides the ... sequence operator to build lazy lists. For example, this:

```
my $lazylist := (0, 1 ... 200);
say $lazylist[42];              # -> 42
```

produces a lazy list of successive integers between 0 and 200. The Perl 6 compiler may or may not allocate some of the numbers (depending on the implementation), but it is not required to produce the full list immediately. The numbers that have not been generated yet may be created and supplied later, if and when the program tries to use these values.

As explained below, if you want to generate consecutive integers, you can actually simplify the lazy list definition:

```
my $lazylist := (0 ... 200);
```

If you assign a sequence to an array, it will generate all the values of the sequence immediately, since assignment to an array is eager (nonlazy). However, you can force laziness with the lazy built-in when assigning to an array:

```
my @lazyarray = lazy 1 ... 200;    # -> [...]
say @lazyarray.elems;              # -> Cannot .elems a lazy list
say @lazyarray[199];               # -> 200
say @lazyarray[200];               # -> (Any)
say @lazyarray.elems;              # -> 200
```

Here, the @lazylist array is originally lazy. Evaluating one item past the last element of the array forces Perl to actually generate the full array (and the array is no longer lazy). After that, no further elements can be generated, and .elems stays at 200 (unless you actually assign values to elements past the 200th element).

When given two integers, one for the first and the last items of a list, the sequence operator will generate a list of consecutive integers between the two supplied integers. If you supply two initial items defining implicitly a step, this will generate an arithmetic sequence:

```
my $odds = (1, 3 ... 15);    # (1 3 5 7 9 11 13 15)
my $evens = (0, 2 ... 42);   # (0 2 4 6 8 ... 40 42)
```

You may remember that in "Lists and Arrays Are Sequences" on page 153, we said that parentheses are usually not necessary for constructing a list, unless needed for precedence reasons. The above code is one such example: try to run that code without parentheses and observe the content of the $odds and $evens variables.

When three initial numbers in geometric progression are supplied, the sequence operator will produce a geometric sequence, as in this example producing the powers of two:

```
say (1, 2, 4 ... 32);              # -> (1 2 4 8 16 32)
```

The sequence operator may also be used to produce noninteger numbers, as shown in this example under the REPL:

```
> say (1, 1.1 ... 2);
(1 1.1 1.2 1.3 1.4 1.5 1.6 1.7 1.8 1.9 2)
```

Contrary to the .. range operator, the sequence operator can also count down:

```
say (10 ... 1);                    # (10 9 8 7 6 5 4 3 2 1)
```

Infinite Lists

One of the great things about lazy lists is that, since item evaluation is postponed, they can be infinite without consuming infinite resources from the computer:

```
my $evens = (0, 2 ... Inf);        # (...)
say $evens[18..21];                # -> (36 38 40 42)
```

The Inf operand is just the so-called "Texas" or ASCII equivalent of the ∞ infinity symbol. The above could have been written:

```
my $evens = (0, 2 ... ∞);
say $evens[21];                    # -> 42
```

The most common way to indicate an infinite lazy list, though, is to use the * whatever argument:

```
my $evens = (0, 2 ... *);
say $evens[21];                    # -> 42
```

Using an Explicit Generator

The sequence operator ... is a very powerful tool for generating lazy lists. Given one number, it just starts counting up from that number (unless the end of the sequence is a lower number, in which case it counts down). Given two numbers to start a sequence, it will treat it as an arithmetic sequence, adding the difference between those first two numbers to the last number generated to generate the next one. Given three numbers, it checks to see if they represent the start of an arithmetic or a geometric sequence, and will continue it.

However, many interesting sequences are neither arithmetic nor geometric. They can still be generated with the sequence operator provided one term can be deduced from the previous one (or ones). For this, you need to explicitly provide the code block to generate the next number in the sequence. For example, the list of odd integers could also be generated with a generator as follows:

```
say (1, { $_ + 2 } ... 11);        # -> (1 3 5 7 9 11)
```

We now have yet another way of defining the factorial function:

```
my $a;
my @fact = $a = 1, {$_ * $a++} ... *;
say @fact[0..8];          # -> (1 1 2 6 24 120 720 5040 40320)
```

or, possibly more readable:

```
my @fact = 1, { state $a = 1; $_ * $a++} ... *;
say @fact[0..8];          # -> (1 1 2 6 24 120 720 5040 40320)
```

This approach is much more efficient than those we have seen before for repeated use, since it automatically caches the previously computed values in the lazy array. As you might remember from "Memos" on page 195, *caching* is the idea of storing a value in memory in order to avoid having to recompute it, with the aim of saving time and CPU cycles.

And we can similarly construct a lazy infinite list of Fibonacci numbers:

```
my @fibo = 0, 1, -> $a, $b { $a + $b } ... *;
say @fibo[0..10];   # -> (0 1 1 2 3 5 8 13 21 34 55)
```

This can be rewritten in a more concise (albeit possibly less explicit and less clear) way using the * whatever placeholder parameter:

```
my @fibo = 0, 1, * + * ... *;
say @fibo[^10];     # -> (0 1 1 2 3 5 8 13 21 34)
```

Just as for factorial, this is more efficient than the implementations we've seen previously, because the computed values are cached in the lazy array.

Similarly the sequence of odd integers seen at the beginning of this section could be generated in a slightly more concise form with the whatever "*" parameter:

```
say (1, * + 2  ... 11);        # -> (1 3 5 7 9 11)
```

This syntax with an asterisk is called a *whatever closure*; we will come back to it below.

There is, however, a small caveat in using the sequence operator with an explicit generator: the end value (the upper bound) has to be one of the generated numbers for the list to stop at it. Otherwise, it will build an infinite list:

```
my $nums = (0, { $_ + 4 } ... 10);
say $nums[0..5];     # -> (0 4 8 12 16 20)
```

As you can see in this example, the generator "jumps over the end point" (it goes beyond 10), and the list is in fact infinite. This is usually not a problem in terms of the computer resources, since it is a lazy infinite list, but it is probably a bug if you expected the list not to run above 10. In this specific case, it is very easy to compute an end point that will be matched (e.g., 8 or 12), but it may be more complicated to find a valid end point. For example, it is not obvious to figure out what the largest

Fibonacci number less than 10,000 might be without computing first the series of such numbers until the first one beyond 10,000.

In such cases where it is difficult to predict what the end point should be, we can define another code block to test whether the sequence should stop or continue. The sequence will stop if the block returns a true value. For example, to compute Fibonacci numbers until 100, we could use this under the REPL:

```
> my @fibo = 0, 1, -> $a, $b { $a + $b } ... -> $c { $c > 100}
[0 1 1 2 3 5 8 13 21 34 55 89 144]
```

This is better, as it does stop the series of numbers, but not quite where we wanted: we really wanted it to stop at the last Fibonacci under 100, and we're getting one more. It would be quite easy to remove or filter out the last generated Fibonacci number, but it's even better not to generate it at all. A slight change in the syntax will do that for us:

```
> my @fibo = 0, 1, -> $a, $b { $a + $b } ...^ -> $c { $c > 100}
[0 1 1 2 3 5 8 13 21 34 55 89]
```

Switching from ... to ...^ means the resulting list does not include the first element for which the termination test returned true.

Similarly, we can limit the *whatever closure* syntax seen above as follows:

```
> say 0, 1, * + * ...^ * > 100;
(0 1 1 2 3 5 8 13 21 34 55 89)
```

Currying and the Whatever Operator

Currying (or partial application) is a basic technique of functional programming, especially in pure functional programming languages such as Haskell. The "curry" name comes from the American mathematician Haskell Curry, one of the founders (with Alonzo Church) of logical mathematical theories, including lambda-calculus and others. (And, as you might have guessed, the Haskell programming language derived its name from Curry's first name.)

To curry a function having several arguments means replacing it with a function having only one argument and returning another function (often a closure) whose role is to process the other arguments.

In some pure functional programming languages, a function can only take one argument and return one result. Currying is a technique aimed at coping with this apparent limitation. Perl does not have such a limitation, but currying can still be very useful to reduce and simplify the arguments lists in subroutine calls, notably in cases of repeated recursive calls.

Creating a Curried Subroutine

The standard example is an *add* function. Suppose we have an add mathematical function, add(x, y), taking two arguments and returning their sum.

In Perl, the add subroutine is very simple:

```
sub add (Numeric $x, Numeric $y) {return $x + $y}
```

A curried version of it would be another function add_y(x) returning a function adding *y* to its argument.

This could be done with a closure looking like this:

```
sub make-add (Numeric $added-val) {
    return sub ($param) {$param + $added-val;}
    # or: return sub {$^a + $added-val;}
}
my &add_2 = make-add 2;
say add_2(3);          # -> 5
say add_2(4.5);        # -> 6.5
```

The &add_2 code reference is a curried version of our mathematical add function. It takes only one argument and returns a value equal to the argument plus two.

We can of course create other curried subroutines using make-add with other arguments:

```
my &add_3 = make-add 3;
say &add_3(6);          # -> 9
```

There is not much new here: the &add_2 and &add_3 are just closures that memorize the increment value passed to the make-add subroutine. This can be useful when some functions are called many times (or recursively) with many arguments, some of which are always the same: currying them makes it possible to simplify the subroutine calls.

Currying an Existing Subroutine with the assuming Method

If a subroutine already exists, there is often no need to create a new closure with the help of a "function factory" (such as make-add) as we've done just above. It is possible to curry the existing function, using the assuming method on it:

```
sub add (Numeric $x, Numeric $y) {return $x + $y}
my &add_2 = &add.assuming(2);
add_2(5);               # -> 7
```

The assuming method returns a callable object that implements the same behavior as the original subroutine, but has the values passed to assuming already bound to the corresponding parameters.

It is also possible to curry built-in functions. For example, the `substr` built-in normally takes three arguments: the string on which to operate, the start position, and the length of the substring to be extracted. You might need to make a number of extractions on the same very long string. You can create a curried version of `substr` always working on the same string:

```
my $str = "Cogito, ergo sum";
my &string-start-chars = &substr.assuming($str, 0);
say &string-start-chars($_) for 6, 13, 16;
```

This will print:

```
Cogito
Cogito, ergo
Cogito, ergo sum
```

Note that we have "assumed" two parameters here, so that the curried subroutine "remembers" the first two arguments and only the third argument needs be passed to `&string-start-chars`.

You can even curry Perl 6 operators (or your own) if you wish:

```
my &add_2 = &infix:<+>.assuming(2);
```

Currying with the Whatever Star Parameter

A more flexible way to curry a subroutine or an expression is to use the *whatever star* (*) argument:

```
my &third = * / 3;
say third(126);          # -> 42
```

The *whatever star* (*) is a placeholder for an argument, so that the expression returns a closure.

It can be used in a way somewhat similar to the $_ topical variable (except that it does not have to exist when the declaration is made):

```
> say map 'foo' x * , (1, 3, 2);
(foo foofoofoo foofoo)
```

It is also possible to use multiple whatever terms in the same expression. For example, the `add` subroutine could be rewritten as a whatever expression with two parameters:

```
my $add = * + *;
say $add(4, 5);          # -> 9
```

or:

```
my &add = * + *;
say add(4, 5);           # -> 9
```

You might even do the same with the multiplication operator:

```
my $mult = * * *;
say $mult(6, 7);          # -> 42
```

and the compiler won't get confused and will figure out correctly that the first and third asterisks are whatever terms and that the second asterisk is the multiplication operator; in other words that this is more or less equivalent to:

```
my $mult = { $^a * $^b };
say $mult(6, 7);          # -> 42
```

or to:

```
my $mult = -> $a, $b { $a * $b }
say $mult(6, 7);          # -> 42
```

To tell the truth, the compiler doesn't get confused, but the user might, unless she or he has been previously exposed to some functional programming languages that commonly use this type of syntactic construct.

These ideas are powerful, but you are advised to pay attention so you don't fall into the trap of code obfuscation.

That being said, the functional programming paradigm is extremely expressive and can make your code much shorter. And, overall, shorter code, provided it remains clear and easy to understand, is very likely to have fewer bugs than longer code.

Using a Functional Programming Style

In this chapter, we have seen how to use techniques derived from functional programming to make our code simpler and more expressive. In a certain way, though, we haven't fully applied functional programming. All of the techniques we have seen stem from functional programming and are a crucial part of it, but the true essence of functional programming isn't really about using higher-order functions, list processing and pipeline programming, anonymous subroutines and closures, lazy lists and currying, and so on. The true essence of functional programming is a specific mindset that treats computation as the evaluation of mathematical functions and avoids changing-state and mutable data.

Instead of simply using techniques derived from functional programming, we can go one step further and actually write code in functional programming style. If we are going to avoid changing-state and mutable data, this means that we will no longer use variables (or at least not change them, and thus treat them as immutable data) and do things differently.

The Merge Sort Algorithm

Consider the example of a classical and efficient sorting technique called the merge sort, invented by John von Neumann in 1945. It is based on the fact that if you have two sorted arrays, it is significantly faster to merge the two arrays into a single sorted array by reading each array in parallel and picking up the appropriate item from either of the arrays than it would be to blindly sort the data of the two arrays.

Merge sort is a "divide and conquer" algorithm which consists of recursively splitting the input unsorted array into smaller and smaller sublists, until each sublist contains only one item (at which point the sublist is sorted, by definition), and then merging the sublists back into a sorted array.

To avoid adding unnecessary complexity, we will discuss here implementations that simply sort numbers in ascending order.

A Nonfunctional Implementation of Merge Sort

Here's how we could try to implement a merge sort algorithm using purely imperative/procedural programming:

```
# ATTENTION: buggy code
sub merge-sort (@out, @to-be-sorted, $start = 0, $end = @to-be-sorted.end) {
    return if $end - $start  < 2;
    my $middle = ($end + $start) div 2;
    my @first = merge-sort(@to-be-sorted, @out, $start, $middle);
    my $second = merge-sort(@to-be-sorted, @out, $middle, $end);
    merge-lists(@out, @to-be-sorted, $start, $middle, $end);
}
sub merge-lists (@in, @out, $start, $middle, $end) {
    my $i = $start;
    my $j = $middle;
    for $start..$end   -> $k {
        if $i < $middle and ($j >= $end or @in[$i] <= @in[$j]) {
            @out[$k] = @in[$i];
            $i++;
        } else {
            @out[$k] = @in[$j];
            $j++;
        }
    }
}
my @array = reverse 1..10;
my @output = @array;
merge-sort2 @output, @array;
say @output;
```

This program always works on the full array (and its copy) and the sublists are not really extracted: the extraction is simulated by the use of subscript ranges.

This code is not very long, but nonetheless fairly complicated. If you try to run it, you'll find that there is a bug: the last item of the original array is improperly sorted. For example, if you try to run it on the list of 10 consecutive integers in reverse order

---

(i.e., ordered from 10 to 1) used in the test at the end of the above code, you'll get the following output array:

```
[2 3 4 5 6 7 8 9 10 1]
```

As an exercise, try fixing the bug before reading any further. (The fix is explained next.)

It is likely that you'll find that identifying and correcting the bug is quite difficult, although this bug is actually relatively simple (when I initially wrote this code, I encountered some more complicated bugs before arriving at this one). It is quite hard to properly use the array subscripts and insert the data items in the right place, avoiding off-by-one and other errors.

Here's a corrected version:

```
sub merge-sort (@out, @to-be-sorted, $start = 0, $end = @to-be-sorted.elems) {
    return if $end - $start < 2;
    my $middle = ($end + $start) div 2;
    merge-sort(@to-be-sorted, @out, $start, $middle);
    merge-sort(@to-be-sorted, @out, $middle, $end);
    merge-lists(@out, @to-be-sorted, $start, $middle, $end);
}
sub merge-lists (@in, @out, $start, $middle, $end) {
    my $i = $start;
    my $j = $middle;
    for $start..$end - 1  -> $k {
        if $i < $middle and ($j >= $end or @in[$i] <= @in[$j]) {
            @out[$k] = @in[$i];
            $i++;
        } else {
            @out[$k] = @in[$j];
            $j++;
        }
    }
}
my @array = pick 20, 1..100;
my @output = @array;
merge-sort2 @output, @array;
say @output;
```

The main change is in the signature of the merge-sort subroutine: the default value for the $end parameter is the size (number of items) of the array, and no longer the subscript of the last elements of the array (so the bug was an off-by-one error). Making this correction also makes it necessary to change the pointy block (for $start.. $end - 1 -> ...) in the merge-lists subroutine.

For 20 random integers between 1 and 100, this prints out something like the following:

```
[11 13 14 15 19 24 25 29 39 46 52 57 62 68 81 83 89 92 94 99]
```

The point is that it is difficult to understand the detailed implementation of the algorithm, and fairly hard to debug, even using the Perl debugger presented in "Debugging" on page 266.

A Functional Implementation of Merge Sort

Rather than modifying the entire array at each step through the process (and being confused with the management of subscripts), we can recursively split the data into actual sublists and work on these sublists.

This can lead to the following implementation:

```
sub merge-sort (@to-be-sorted) {
    return @to-be-sorted if @to-be-sorted < 2;
    my $middle = @to-be-sorted.elems div 2;
    my @first = merge-sort(@to-be-sorted[0 .. $middle - 1]);
    my @second = merge-sort(@to-be-sorted[$middle .. @to-be-sorted.end]);
    return merge-lists(@first, @second);
}
sub merge-lists (@one, @two) {
    my @result;
    loop {
        return @result.append(@two) unless @one;
        return @result.append(@one) unless @two;
        push @result, @one[0] < @two[0] ?? shift @one !! shift @two;
    }
}
```

The code is shorter than the previous implementation, but that's not the main point.

The merge-sort subroutine is somewhat similar to the previous implementation, except that it recursively creates the sublists and then merges the sublists.

It is the merge-lists subroutine (which does the bulk of the work in both implementations) that is now much simpler: it receives two sublists and merges them. Most of this work is done in the last code line; the two lines before it are only taking care of returning the merged list when one of the input sublists ends up being empty.

This functional version of the program captures the essence of the merge sort algorithm:

- If the array has less than two items, it is already sorted, so return it immediately (this is the base case stopping the recursion).
- Else, pick the middle position of the array to divide it into two sublists, and call merge-sort recursively on them.
- Merge the sorted sublist thus generated.
- Return the merged list to the caller.

I hope that you can see how much clearer and simpler the functional style implementation is. To give you an idea, writing and debugging this latter program took me about 15 minutes, i.e., about 10 times less than the nonfunctional version. If you don't believe me, try to implement these two versions for yourself. (It's a good exercise even if you *do* believe me.)

The exercise section of this chapter ("Exercise: Quick Sort" on page 334) will provide another (and probably even more telling) example of the simplicity of functional programming compared to more imperative or procedural approaches.

Debugging

This time, we will not really talk about debugging proper, but about a quite closely related activity, testing.

Testing code is an integral part of software development. In Perl 6, the standard Test module (shipped and installed together with Rakudo) provides a testing framework which enables automated, repeatable verification of code behavior.

The testing functions emit output conforming to the *Test Anything Protocol* or TAP (*http://testanything.org/*), a standardized testing format which has implementations in Perl, C, C++, C#, Ada, Lisp, Erlang, Python, Ruby, Lua, PHP, Java, Go, JavaScript, and other languages.

A typical test file looks something like this:

```
use v6;
use Test;      # a Standard module included with Rakudo
use lib 'lib';

# ...

plan $num-tests;

# .... tests

done-testing;  # optional with 'plan'
```

We ensure that we're using Perl 6, via the use of the v6 pragma, then we load the Test module and specify where our libraries are. We then specify how many tests we plan to run (such that the testing framework can tell us if more or fewer tests were run than we expected) and when finished with the tests, we use done-testing to tell the framework we are done.

We have already seen a short example of the use of the Test module in "Exercise: Constructing New Operators" on page 407 (solution to the exercise of "Constructing New Operators" on page 214).

The Test module exports various functions that check the return value of a given expression, and produce standardized test output accordingly.

In practice, the expression will often be a call to a function or method that you want to unit-test. You may want to check:

- Truthfulness:

  ```
  ok($value, $description?);
  nok($condition, $description?);
  ```

  The ok function marks a test as passed if the given $value evaluates to true in a Boolean context. The nok function marks a test as passed if the given value evaluates to false. Both functions accept an optional $description of the test. For example:

  ```
  ok  $response.success, 'HTTP response was successful';
  nok $query.error,      'Query completed without error';
  ```

- String comparison:

  ```
  is($value, $expected, $description?)
  ```

  The is function marks a test as passed if $value and $expected compare positively with the eq operator. The function accepts an optional description of the test.

- Approximate numeric comparison:

  ```
  is-approx($value, $expected, $description?)
  ```

  is-approx marks a test as passed if the $value and $expected numerical values are approximately equal to each other. The subroutine can be called in numerous ways that let you test using relative or absolute tolerance of different values. (If no tolerance is set, it will default to an absolute tolerance of 10^{-5}.)

- Regex:

  ```
  like($value, $expected-regex, $description?)
  unlike($value, $expected-regex, $description?)
  ```

  The like function marks a test as passed if the $value matches the $expected-regex. Since we are speaking about regexes, "matches" in the previous sentence really means "smart matches." The unlike function marks a test as passed if the $value does not match the $expected-regex.

  For example:

  ```
  like 'foo', /fo/, 'foo looks like fo';
  unlike 'foo', /bar/, 'foo does not look like bar';
  ```

- And many other functions that you can study in the following documentation: *https://docs.perl6.org/language/testing.html.*

In principle you could use ok for every kind of comparison test, by including the comparison in the expression passed as a value:

```
ok factorial(4) == 24, 'Factorial - small integer';
```

However, it is better (where possible) to use one of the specialized comparison test functions, because they can print more helpful diagnostics output in case the comparison fails.

If a test fails although it appears to be successful, and you don't understand why it fails, you may want to use the diag function to get additional feedback. For example, assume that the test:

```
ok $foo, 'simple test';
```

is failing and that you don't have enough feedback to understand why; you may try:

```
diag "extensive feedback" unless
    ok $foo, 'simple test';
```

This might give you the additional information you need.

Suppose we want to test a subroutine to determine whether a given string is a palindrome (as discussed in several chapters in this book, see for example Exercise 5-3 and "Another Example of Reduction to a Previously Solved Problem" on page 148). You could perform that test by writing something like this:

```
# file is-palindrome.p6
use v6;

sub is-palindrome($s) { $s eq $s.flip }

multi sub MAIN( $input ) {
    if is-palindrome( $input ) {
        say "'$input' is palindrome.";
    }
    else {
        say "'$input' is not palindrome.";
    }
}

multi sub MAIN(:$test!) {
    use Test;
    plan 4;
    ok is-palindrome(''), 'empty string';
    ok is-palindrome('aba'), 'odd-sized example';
    ok is-palindrome('abba'), 'even-sized example';
    nok is-palindrome('blabba'), 'counter example';
}
```

Usually, tests are stored in different files placed in a "t" subdirectory. Here, for this short test, everything is in the same file, but two multi MAIN subroutines are supplied to either test whether a passed parameter is a palindrome, or to run the test plan. See "Program Arguments and the MAIN Subroutine" on page 69 and "The MAIN subroutine" on page 411 if you need a refresher on the MAIN subroutine.

You can run these tests as follows:

```
$ perl6 is-palindrome.p6 abba
'abba' is palindrome.
$ perl6 is-palindrome.p6 abbaa
'abbaa' is not palindrome.
$
$ perl6 is-palindrome.p6 --test
1..4
ok 1 - empty string
ok 2 - odd-sized example
ok 3 - even-sized example
ok 4 - counter example
```

Try this example, play with it, change some lines, add new tests, and see what happens.

Writing such unit tests may appear to be tedious work. The truth, though, is that it is manual testing that is somewhat tedious and, if you try, you'll find that writing and using such test scenarios makes the testing work much less cumbersome. You usually write the tests once, and run them very often. And you will be surprised how many bugs you will find even if you are sure your code is correct! Also, once you've written a test suite for something, you might still be using it years later, for example for non-regression testing after a software change. This can be not only a time saver, but also a guarantee that you're supplying good quality software.

Many organizations actually write their tests even before writing the programs. This process is called *test-driven development* and there are many areas where it is quite successful. In fact, the Rakudo/Perl 6 compiler had a very large test suite (more than 40,000 tests) long before the compiler was ready. In a way, the test suite even became the true specification of the project, so that you could use the same test suite for verifying another implementation of Perl 6.

An additional advantage of such an approach is that measuring the ratio of tests that pass may often be a better metric of software completion than the usual "wet finger in the wind" estimates, such as, say, a ratio of the number of code lines written versus the estimate of the final number of code lines.

Glossary

algorithmic complexity

A rough measure of the number of computing operations (and time) needed to perform some computing on relatively large data sets, and, more precisely, a measure of how an algorithm scales when the data set grows.

anonymous subroutine

A subroutine that has no name. Also commonly called a *lambda*. Although they are not exactly the same thing, pointy blocks can also be assimilated to anonymous subroutines.

cache

To cache a value is to store it in memory (in a variable, an array, a hash, etc.) in order to avoid the need to compute it again, thereby hopefully saving some computation time.

callback function

A function or subroutine that is passed as an argument to another function.

closure

A function that can access variables that are lexically available where the function is defined, even if those variables are no longer in scope where the function is called.

currying

Currying a function that takes several arguments means to create another function that takes fewer arguments (where the missing arguments are stored within the new curried function).

first-class object

An object that can be passed around as an argument to or as a return value from a subroutine. In Perl, subroutines are first-class objects (also called first-class citizens).

higher-order function

A function or subroutine that takes another subroutine (or a simple code block) as an argument. The `map`, `grep`, `reduce`, and `sort` built-in functions are examples of higher-order functions.

iterator

A piece of code that returns values on demand and keeps track of where it has arrived, so as to be able to know what the next value to be provided should be.

laziness

A process of delayed evaluation whereby, for example, one populates a list or processes the items of a list only on demand, when required, to avoid unnecessary processing.

metaoperator

An operator that acts on another operator to provide new functionality.

pipeline programming

A programming model in which pieces of data (usually lists) undergo successive transformations as in a pipeline or an assembly line.

reduction

A process through which a list of values is reduced to a single value. For example, a list of numbers can be reduced to an average, a maximum value, or a median. Some languages call this process *folding*.

test-driven development

A development methodology where the tests are written from the specifications before the actual program, so that it becomes easier to check that the program complies with the specifications.

Exercise: Quick Sort

Exercise 14-1.

Quick sort is a "divide and conquer" sorting algorithm invented by Tony Hoare in 1959. It relies on partitioning the array to be sorted. To partition an array, an element called a *pivot* is selected. All elements smaller than the pivot are moved before it and all greater elements are moved after it. The lesser and greater sublists are then recursively sorted through the same process and finally reassembled together.

One of the difficulties is to select the right pivot. Ideally it should be the median value of the array items, since this would give partitions of approximately equal sizes, thereby making the algorithm optimally efficient, but finding the median for each partition would take some time and ultimately penalize the performance. Various variants of the quick sort have been tried, with different strategies to (usually arbitrarily) select a pivot.

The following is a typical nonfunctional implementation of the quick sort algorithm.

```
sub quicksort(@input) {
    sub swap ($x, $y) {
        (@input[$x], @input[$y]) = @input[$y], @input[$x];
    }
    sub qsort ($left, $right) {
```

```
        my $pivot = @input[($left + $right) div 2];
        my $i = $left;
        my $j = $right;
        while $i < $j {
            $i++ while @input[$i] < $pivot;
            $j-- while @input[$j] > $pivot;
            if $i <= $j {
                swap $i, $j;
                $i++;
                $j--;
            }
        }
        qsort($left, $j) if $left < $j;
        qsort($i, $right) if $j < $right;
    }
    qsort(0, @input.end)
}
my @array = pick 20, 1..100;
quicksort @array;
say @array;
```

The array is modified in place (which has the advantage of requiring limited memory), which means that the original array is modified.

For functional programming, internal data is immutable, so that you're copying data fragments into new lists, rather than modifying them "in place."

In the same spirit as what we've done in "A Functional Implementation of Merge Sort" on page 328 for the merge sort algorithm, try to write a functional style implementation of the quick sort algorithm. Hint: this can be done in about half a dozen lines of code.

Solution: "Exercise: Making a Functional Implementation of Quick Sort" on page 425.

## CHAPTER 15

Some Final Advice

> Everyone knows that debugging is twice as hard as writing a program in the first place. So if you're as clever as you can be when you write it, how will you ever debug it?
>
> —Brian Kernighan, *The Elements of Programming Style*

Make It Clear, Keep It Simple

Writing a real-life program is not the same thing as learning the art of programming or learning a new language.

Because the goal of this book is to lead you to learn more advanced concepts or new syntax, I have often been pushing new ways of doing things. But this does not mean that you should try to pack your most advanced knowledge into each of your programs. Quite the contrary.

The rule of thumb is "KISS": keep it simple, stupid. The KISS engineering principle (originated in the US Navy around 1960) states that most systems work best if they are kept simple rather than made complicated; therefore simplicity should be a key goal in design and unnecessary complexity should be avoided. This does not mean, however, that you should write simplistic code.

As an example, if you're looking for a literal substring within a string, use the simple `index` built-in function, rather than firing the regex engine for that. Similarly, if you know the position and length of the substring, then use the `substr` function. But if you need a more "fuzzy" match with perhaps some alternatives or a character class, then a regex is very likely the right tool.

Another related tenet is "YAGNI": you aren't gonna need it. This acronym comes from a school of programming known as "extreme programming" (XP). Even if you don't adhere to all the XP principles, this idea is quite sound and well-founded: don't add any functionality until it is really needed.

Try to make your programs as clear as possible, and as simple as you can. Use more advanced concepts if you have to, but don't do it for the sake of showing how masterful you are. Don't try to be clever or, at least, don't be *too* clever.

Remember that code is not only used by the compiler, but read by humans. Think about them.

Think about the person who will have maintain your code. As some people like to put it: "Always code as if the person who ends up maintaining your code is a violent psychopath who knows where you live." And, if nothing else will convince you, remember that the person maintaining your code might be you a year from now. You may not remember then how that neat trick you used really works.

A final quote from Edsger Dijkstra on this subject: "Simplicity is prerequisite for reliability."

Dos and Don'ts

Don't repeat yourself (DRY)
Avoid code duplication. If you have the same code in different places of your program, then something is most likely wrong. Maybe the repeated code should go into a loop or a separate subroutine, or perhaps even in a module or a library. Remember that copy and paste is a source of evil.

Don't reinvent the wheel
Use existing libraries and modules when you can; it is likely that they have been thoroughly tested and will work better than the quick fix you're about to write. The Perl 6 ecosystem has a large and growing collection of software modules (*http://modules.perl6.org*) that you can use in your programs.

Use meaningful identifiers
If your variables, subroutines, methods, classes, grammars, modules, and programs have sensible names that convey clearly what they are or what they do, then your code will be clearer and might need fewer comments. Very short names like $i or $n are usually fine for loop variables, but pretty much anything else needs a name that clearly explains what the content or the purpose is. Names like $array or %hash may have sometimes been used in the examples of this book to indicate more clearly the nature of the data structure, but they are not recommended in real-life programs. If your hash contains a collection of words, call it %words or %word-list, not %hash. The % sigil indicates that it is a hash anyway.

Make useful comments and avoid useless ones

A comment like this:

```
my $count = 1;      # assigns 1 to $count
```

is completely useless. In general, your comments should explain neither what your code is doing nor even how it is doing it (this should be obvious if your code is clear), but rather *why* you are doing it: perhaps you should refer to a math theorem, a law of physics, or a business rule.

Remove dead code and code scaffolding

Even when writing new code, you may at some point create variables that you don't use in the final version of your code. If so, remove them; don't let them distract the attention of your reader. If you modify an existing program, clean up the place after you've changed it. Remember the Boy Scout rule: leave the place better and cleaner than you found it.

Test aggressively

Nobody can write any piece of significant software without having a number of initial bugs. Edsger Dijkstra is quoted as saying: "If debugging is the process of removing software bugs, then programming must be the process of putting them in." It is unfortunately very true. Even though Dijkstra also said that "Testing shows the presence, not the absence of bugs," testing is an essential part of software development. Write extensive test plans, use them often, and update them as the functionality evolves. See "Debugging" on page 329 for some automated testing tools.

Avoid premature optimization

In the words of Donald Knuth: "Premature optimization is the source of all evil (or at least most of it) in programming."

Don't use magical numbers

Consider this:

```
my $time-left = 31536000;
```

What is this 31,536,000 number coming out of nowhere? There's no way to know just by looking at this line of code. Compare with this:

```
my $secondsInAYear = 365 * 24 * 60 * 60;
# ...
my $time-left = $secondsInAYear;
```

Isn't the second version clearer? Well, to tell the truth, it would be even better to use a constant in such a case:

```
constant SECONDS-PER-YEAR = 365 * 24 * 60 * 60;
```

Avoid hardcoded values

Hardcoded values are bad. If you have to use some, define them as variables or constants at the beginning of your program, and use those variables or constants instead. Hardcoded file paths are especially bad. If you have to use some, use some variables with relative paths:

```
my $base-dir = '/path/to/application/data';
my $input-dir = "$base-dir/INPUT";
my $result-dir = "$base-dir/RESULT";
my $temp-dir = "$base-dir/TEMP";
my $log-dir = "$base-dir/LOG";
```

At least, if the path must change, you only have to change the top code line.

Don't ignore errors returned by subroutines or built-in functions

Not all return values are useful; for example, we usually don't check the return value of a print statement, but that's usually fine because we are interested in the side effect, the fact of printing something out to the screen or to a file, rather than the return value. In most other cases, you need to know if something went wrong in order to take steps to either recover from the error condition, if possible, or to abort the program gracefully (e.g., with an informative error message) if the error is too serious for the program to continue.

Format your code clearly and consistently

The compiler might not care about code indentation, but human readers do. Your code formatting should help clarify the structure and control flow of your programs.

Be nice and have fun.

Use Idioms

Any language has its own "best practice" methods of use. These are the idioms that experienced programmers use, ways of doing things that have become preferred over time. These idioms are important. They protect you from reinventing the wheel. They are also what experienced users expect to read; they are familiar and enable you to focus on the overall code design rather than get bogged down in detailed code concerns. They often formalize patterns that avoid common mistakes or bugs.

Even though Perl 6 is a relatively new language, a number of such idioms have become honed over time. Here are a few of these idiomatic constructs.[1]

---

1 When two solutions are suggested, the second one is usually the more idiomatic one.

Creating a hash from a list of keys and a list of values
 Using slices:

```
my %hash; %hash{@keys} = @values;
```

 Using the *zip* operator and a metaoperator with the pair constructor:

```
my %hash = @keys Z=> @values;
```

For existence tests, the hash values only need to be true. Here is a good way to create a hash from a list of keys:

```
my %exists = @keys X=> True;
```

 Or, better yet, use a set:

```
my $exists = @keys.Set;
say "exists" if $exists{$object};
```

Making mandatory attributes (or subroutine parameters)
 This is a nice way of making a mandatory attribute in a class:

```
has $.attr = die "The 'attr' attribute is mandatory";
```

This code uses the default value mechanism: if a value is supplied, then the code for the default value does not run. If no value is supplied, then the code dies with the appropriate error message. The same mechanism can be used for subroutine parameters.

 Or you could use the `is required` trait:

```
> class A { has $.a is required };
> A.new;
The attribute '$!a' is required,
but you did not provide a value for it.
```

 You can even pass a explanatory message:

```
> class A { has $.a is required("We need it") };
> A.new;
The attribute '$!a' is required because We need it,
but you did not provide a value for it.
```

Iterating over the subscripts of an array
 The first solution that comes to mind might be:

```
for 0 .. @array.end -> $i {...}
```

 That's alright, but this is probably even better:

```
for @array.keys -> $i {...}
```

Iterating over the subscripts and values of an array

The .kv method, in combination with a pointy block taking two parameters, allows you to easily iterate over an array:

```
for @array.kv -> $i, $value {...}
```

Printing the number of items in an array

Two possible solutions:

```
say +@array;
# or:
say @array.elems;
```

Do something every third time

Use the %% divisibility operator on the loop variable:

```
if $i %% 3 {...}
```

Do something n times

Use the right-open range operator:

```
for 0 ..^ $n {...}
# or, simpler:
for ^$n {...}
```

Split a string into words (splitting on space)

A method call without an explicit invocant always uses the $_ topical variable as an implicit invocant. Thus, assuming the string has been topicalized into $_:

```
@words = .split(/\s+/);
# or, simpler:
@words = .words;
```

An infinite loop

A loop statement with no parentheses and no argument loops forever:

```
while True {...}
# or, more idiomatic:
loop {...}
```

Of course, the body of the loop statement must have some kind of flow control statement to exit the loop at some point.

Returning the unique elements of a list

The unique method removes duplicates from the input list:

```
return @array.unique;
```

Or, if you know that your list is sorted, you can use the squish function (which removes adjacent duplicates).

Adding up the items of a list

Use the reduce function or the reduction metaoperator:

```
my $sum = @a.reduce(* + *);
# or, simpler:
my $sum = [+] @a;
# or yet simpler, using the sum built-in:
my $sum = @a.sum;
```

Swapping two variables

Use the .= mutating method call with the reverse function:

```
( $x, $y ) =   $y, $x;
# or:
( $x, $y ) .= reverse; # equivalent to: ($x, $y) = ($x, $y).reverse
```

Generating random integers between 2 and 6

Use the .. range operator and the pick method:

```
$z = 2 + Int(5.rand);
# or, better:
$z = (2..6).pick;
```

Count by steps of 3 in an infinite loop

Use the ... sequence operator with the "*" whatever star operator and a pointy block:

```
for 3, * + 3 ... * -> $n {...}
# or:
for 3, 6, 9 ... * -> $n {...}
```

Loop on a range of values, discounting the range limits

Use the open range operator:

```
for ($start+1) .. ($end-1) -> $i {...}
# or, better:
for $start ^..^ $end -> $i {...}
```

What's Next?

A book like this one can't tell you everything about programming, nor about Perl 6. At this point, you should know how to write a program to solve an average-difficulty problem, but a lot of work has been done in the last decades to solve harder problems. So where should you go from here?

Read books about algorithmics, the science of algorithms. Many good books exist on the subject, but I especially recommend the following two (you should be aware, though, that they are not easy):

- Thomas H. Cormen, Charles E. Leiserson, Ronald L. Rivest, and Clifford Stein, *Introduction to Algorithms*, The MIT Press

- Donald Knuth, *The Art of Computer Programming*, Addison-Wesley (many volumes, many editions)

Read other books about programming, even if they target other programming languages or no specific programming language. They're likely to have a different approach on various points; this will offer you a different perspective and perhaps better comprehension, and will complement what you have read here. Read tutorials, articles, blogs, and forums about programming. Participate when you can. Read *Introduction to Perl 6* (*http://perl6intro.com/*), which exists in eight different languages as of this writing. Read the official Perl 6 documentation (*https://docs.perl6.org*).

This book has more than a thousand code examples, which is quite a lot, but may not be sufficient if you really want to learn more. You should also read code samples written by others. Look for open source libraries or modules, and try to understand what they do and how they do it. Try to use them.

Having said that, I should stress that you can read as many books as you want about the theory of swimming, but you'll never know swimming until you really get around to doing it. The same is true about learning to program and learning a programming language. Write new code. Modify existing examples, and see what happens. Try new things. Go ahead, be bold, dive into the pool and swim. The bottom line is: you will really learn by doing.

Learning the art of programming is great fun. Enjoy it!

Solutions to the Exercises

This (long) chapter provides solutions to the exercises suggested in the main matter of this book. However, it contains much more than that.

First, in many cases, it provides several different solutions, illustrating different approaches to a problem, discussing their respective merits or drawbacks and often showing solutions that may be more efficient than others.

Second, it often provides a lot of additional information or complementary examples.

Just the sheer volume of code examples of this chapter is likely to teach you a lot about programming in general and about the Perl 6 language in particular.

Finally, this chapter sometimes introduces (with examples) new concepts that are covered only in later chapters of the book. Having seen such examples may help you to get a smoother grasp to these new ideas when you get to these chapters. In a few cases, this chapter covers or introduces notions that will not be covered anywhere else in the book.

When you solve an exercise, even if you're confident that you did it successfully, please make sure to consult the solutions in this chapter and to try them: you're likely to learn quite a bit from them.

Exercises of Chapter 3: Functions and Subroutines

Exercise 3-1: Subroutine right-justify

The aim is to write a subroutine that prints a string with enough leading spaces so that the last letter of the string is in column 70 of the display.

This is the first real exercise of this book, so let's do it step by step:

```
use v6;
sub right-justify ($input-string) {
    my $str_length = chars $input-string;
    my $missing_length = 70 - $str_length;
    my $leading-spaces = " " x $missing_length;
    say $leading-spaces, $input-string;
}
right-justify("Larry Wall");
right-justify("The quick brown fox jumps over the lazy dog");
```

This subroutine:

- Assigns the input string length to the `$str_length` variable
- Computes into the `$missing_length` variable the number of spaces that will need to be added at the beginning of the displayed line to have it end in column 70
- Creates the `$leading-spaces` string with the needed number of spaces
- Prints out the `$leading-spaces` and `$input-string` one after the other to obtain the desired result

This displays the following:

```
                                                              Larry Wall
                            The quick brown fox jumps over the lazy dog
```

We can, however, make this code shorter by composing some of the statements and expressions:

```
sub right-justify ($input-string) {
    my $leading-spaces = " " x (70 - $input-string.chars);
    say $leading-spaces, $input-string;
}
```

It could even be boiled down to a shorter single-line subroutine:

```
sub right-justify ($input-string) {
    say " " x 70 - $input-string.chars, $input-string;
}
```

This works fine, but it may be argued that this last version is less clear. In fact, the `$leading-spaces` temporary variable used in the previous version had a name that self-documented what the subroutine is doing. You can make very concise code as in the last example above, but sometimes it may become a little bit too terse, so there is a tradeoff between concision and clarity.

Note that there are two built-in functions, `printf` and `sprintf`, that can perform a similar task, but we will cover them later. There is also a `.fmt` method for producing formatted output.

Exercise 3-2: Subroutine do-twice

To add an addressee to the greeting, we need to:

- Pass a second argument in the call to do-twice (the string "World")
- Add a new parameter in the do-twice subroutine signature ($addressee)
- Add this new parameter as an argument in the calls to $code
- Add a signature with one parameter ($addr) in the definition of the greet subroutine
- Use this new parameter in the print statement

This leads to the following code:

```
sub do-twice($code, $addressee) {
    $code($addressee);
    $code($addressee);
}
sub greet (Str $addr) {
    say "Hello $addr!";
}
do-twice &greet, "World";
```

This displays:

```
Hello World!
Hello World!
```

For the next question, we replace the greet subroutine by the print-twice subroutine:

```
sub do-twice($code, $message) {
    $code($message);
    $code($message);
}
sub print-twice($value) {
    say $value;
    say $value;
}
do-twice &print-twice, "What's up doc";
```

This prints "What's up doc" four times.

Finally, we add the new do-four subroutine and let it call the do-twice subroutine twice, printing the message eight times:

```
sub do-twice($code, $message) {
    $code($message);
    $code($message);
}
sub print-twice($value) {
```

```
        say $value;
        say $value;
    }
    sub do-four ($code, $message) {
        do-twice $code, $message;
        do-twice $code, $message;
    }
    do-four &print-twice, "What's up doc";
```

Exercise 3-3: Subroutine print-grid

To print a grid such as the one requested in the exercise, we need to print each line one by one, and we basically have two types of lines: the three "dotted lines" and the eight lines without dashes, which we'll call "empty lines" for lack of a better name, because they are are partly empty (no dashes).

To avoid code repetition, one way to do it is to create a string for each of the two line types and to print these strings in accordance with the needs.

This is one possible solution:

```
    use v6;

    my $four-dashes = "- " x 4;
    my $dotted_line = ("+ " ~ $four-dashes ) x 2 ~ "+" ;
    my $spaces = " " x 9;
    my $empty-line = ("|" ~ $spaces ) x 2 ~ "|" ;

    sub say-four-times($value) {
        say $value;
        say $value;
        say $value;
        say $value;
    }
    sub print-grid {
        say $dotted_line;
        say-four-times $empty-line;
        say $dotted_line;
        say-four-times $empty-line;
        say $dotted_line;
    }
    print-grid;
```

There are obviously better ways to do something four times than just repeating say $value; four times as in say-four-times above, but this will be covered in Chapter 4 (see "for Loops" on page 64).

To draw a similar grid with four rows and four columns, we first need to modify the strings used for printing the lines:

```
my $dotted_line = ("+ " ~ $four-dashes ) x 4 ~ "+" ;
# ...
my $empty-line = ("|" ~ $spaces ) x 4 ~ "|" ;
```

In addition to that, we could modify print-grid to just print each line the required number of times. But that would involve quite a bit of code repetition, and the aim of this exercise is to use subroutines to permit code reuse.

There are now two things that we repeatedly need to do four times. It makes sense to write a do-four-times subroutine that will be used both for creating say-four-times (in charge of printing the four empty lines) and for calling entire rows four times. This subroutine will be passed the code reference for doing the specific actions required:

```
my $four-dashes = "- " x 4;
my $dotted_line = ("+ " ~ $four-dashes ) x 4 ~ "+" ;
my $spaces = " " x 9;
my $empty-line = ("|" ~ $spaces ) x 4 ~ "|" ;

sub do-four-times ($code) {
    $code();
    $code();
    $code();
    $code();
}
sub say-four-times($value) {
    do-four-times(sub {say $value});
}
sub print-bottom-less-grid {
    say $dotted_line;
    say-four-times $empty-line;
}
sub print-grid {
    do-four-times(&print-bottom-less-grid);
    say $dotted_line;
}
print-grid;
```

In addition, rather than declaring global variables for the line strings, it is better practice to declare and define them within the subroutines where they are used. We also no longer need the say-four-times subroutine; we can just pass the relevant arguments to the do-four-times subroutine to the same effect. This could lead to the following program:

```
sub do-four-times ($code, $val) {
    $code($val);
    $code($val);
    $code($val);
    $code($val);
}
sub print-bottom-less-grid($dot-line) {
```

```
    say $dot-line;
    my $spaces = " " x 9;
    my $empty-line = ("|" ~ $spaces ) x 4 ~ "|" ;
    do-four-times(&say, $empty-line);
}
sub print-grid {
    my $four-dashes = "- " x 4;
    my $dotted_line = ("+ " ~ $four-dashes ) x 4 ~ "+" ;
    do-four-times(&print-bottom-less-grid, $dotted_line);
    say $dotted_line;
}
print-grid;
```

Exercises of Chapter 4: Conditionals and Recursion

Exercise Suggested in "Stack Diagrams for Recursive Subroutines": Subroutine do-n-times

We need a subroutine that takes a function and a number, $num, as arguments, and that calls the given function $num times.

The do-n-times subroutine is recursive and is calling itself each time with a decremented argument. It stops "recursing" when this argument is 0. $subref is an anonymous subroutine called within the body of do-n-times:

```
sub do-n-times ($coderef, Int $num) {
    return if $num <= 0;
    $coderef();
    do-n-times $coderef, $num - 1;
}

my $subref = sub { say "Carpe diem";}

do-n-times $subref, 4;
```

This prints:

```
Carpe diem
Carpe diem
Carpe diem
Carpe diem
```

Exercise 4-1: Days, Hours, Minutes, and Seconds

The following is one possible way of converting a number of seconds into a number of days, hours, minutes, and seconds:

```
days-HMS(240_000);
```

```
sub days-HMS (Int $seconds) {
    my $minutes = $seconds div 60;
    my $sec_left = $seconds mod 60;
    my ($hours, $min_left) = $minutes div 60, $minutes mod 60;
    my ($days, $hours_left) = $hours div 24, $hours mod 24;
    say "$days $hours_left $min_left $sec_left";
            #  prints: 2 18 40 0
}
```

The first two lines do the integer division and modulo operation separately. For the next two cases, we do both operations in one single line, using a list syntax.

The $minutes, $hours, and $days variables are all computed in essentially the same way. The code could be made more modular by using a subroutine to compute $minutes, $hours, and $days. Although fruitful subroutines will really be studied in the course of the next chapter, we have seen a couple of examples of them and can provide the gist of how they could be used:

```
sub div_mod (Int $input, Int $num-base) {
    return $input div $num-base, $input mod $num-base;
}
sub days-HMS (Int $seconds) {
    my ($minutes, $sec_left) = div_mod $seconds, 60;
    my ($hours, $min_left)   = div_mod $minutes, 60;
    my ($days, $hours_left)  = div_mod $hours, 24;
    say "$days $hours_left $min_left $sec_left";
}
```

To ask a user to enter a number of seconds, you might do this:

```
my $sec = prompt "Please enter the number of seconds: ";
days-HMS $sec.Int;
```

In real life, it would usually be good to verify that the user-provided input is a positive integer and ask again if it is not. As a further exercise, you might try to insert the above code into a recursive subroutine that prints an error message and calls itself again if the user input is not valid. The solution to the next exercise ("Exercise 4-2: Fermat's Theorem" on page 352) gives an example of a recursive subroutine designed to prompt the user to supply input again; this might help you figure out how to do it if you encounter difficulty.

Try replacing the following code line:

```
say "$days $hours_left $min_left $sec_left";
```

with this one:

```
printf "%d days %d hours %d minutes %d seconds \n", days-HMS 240_000;
```

to see a better-formatted output.

Exercise 4-2: Fermat's Theorem

The check-fermat subroutine checks whether:

$$a^n + b^n = c^n$$

is true for the supplied values of a, b, c, and n:

```
sub check-fermat (Int $a, Int $b, Int $c, Int $n) {
    if $a**$n + $b**$n == $c**$n {
        if $n > 2 {
            say "Holy smokes, Fermat was wrong!" if $n > 2;
        } elsif $n == 2 or $n ==1 {
            say "Correct";
        }
        return True;
    }
    return False
}

say "Correct for 3, 4, 5, 2" if check-fermat 3, 4, 5, 2;
get-input();

sub get-input {
    say "Your mission, Jim, should you decide to accept it, is to ";
    say "provide values of A, B, C and n satisfying Fermat's equation:";
    say "   A ** n + B ** n = C * *n";
    my $a = prompt "Please provide a value for A: ";
    my $b = prompt "Please provide a value for B: ";
    my $c = prompt "Please provide a value for C: ";
    my $n = prompt "Please provide a value for the exponent: ";
    if check-fermat($a.Int, $b.Int, $c.Int, $n.Int) {
        say "The equation holds true for your values";
    } else {
        say "Nope. The equation is not right."
    }
    my $try-again = prompt "Want to try again (Y/N)?";
    get-input if $try-again eq 'Y';
}
```

Fermat's last theorem has been proven and, needless to say, the mission is truly impossible if $n > 2$; perhaps this time Jim Phelps should decline to accept the mission.

Exercise 4-3: Is It a Triangle?

This is a possible routine to find out whether you can make a triangle with three given stick lengths:

```
sub is-triangle ( Numeric $x, Numeric $y, Numeric $z) {
    my $valid = True;
    $valid = False if $x > $y + $z;
```

```
    $valid = False if $y > $x + $z;
    $valid = False if $z > $x + $y;
    if $valid {
        say "Yes";
    } else {
        say "No";
    }
}
is-triangle 1, 3, 4;   # -> Yes
is-triangle 1, 3, 6;   # -> No
```

Another way to do this would be to start by finding the greatest length and test only that one, but that does not make the algorithm significantly simpler.

Prompting the user to input three lengths has been shown in the previous two exercises; there is nothing really new here. However, this is one new way of doing it:

```
my ($a, $b, $c) = split " ",
    prompt "Please enter three lengths (separated by spaces): ";
is-triangle $a.Int , $b.Int , $c.Int;
```

Exercise 4-4: The Fibonacci Numbers

The Fibonacci numbers are a sequence of numbers in which the first two numbers are equal to 1 and any subsequent number is the sum of the two preceding ones, for example:

```
1, 1, 2, 3, 5, 8, 13, 21, 34, ...
```

Printing the first 20 Fibonacci numbers:

```
sub n_fibonacci (Int $n) {
    my $fib1 = 1;
    my $fib2 = 1;
    say $_ for $fib1, $fib2;
    for 3..$n {
        my $new_fib = $fib1 + $fib2;
        say $new_fib;
        ($fib1, $fib2) = $fib2, $new_fib;
    }
}
n_fibonacci 20;
```

Printing the *n*th Fibonacci number:

```
my $n = prompt "Enter the searched Fibonacci number: ";
$n = $n.Int;
say fibo($n);

sub fibo (Int $n) {
    my ($fib1, $fib2) = 1, 1;
    for 3..$n {
        my $new_fib = $fib1 + $fib2;
```

```
        ($fib1, $fib2) = $fib2, $new_fib;
    }
    return $fib2;
}
```

Exercise 4-5: The recurse Subroutine

Examining the code of the recurse subroutine, the first thing you should notice is that each time it is called recursively, the first argument ($n) is decremented by one compared to the previous call. If the initial value of $n is a *positive integer*, the succession of calls will eventually lead to the base case where $n == 0, and the cascade of recursive calls will eventually stop.

If $n is not an integer or if it is negative, we will get into infinite recursion.

One way to visualize how the program runs is to display the subroutine parameters at each call:

```
sub recurse($n,$s) {
    say "Args : n = $n, s = $s";
    if ($n == 0) {
        say $s;
    } else {
        recurse $n - 1, $n + $s;
    }
}
recurse 3, 0;
```

This would print:

```
Args : n = 3, s = 0
Args : n = 2, s = 3
Args : n = 1, s = 5
Args : n = 0, s = 6
6
```

To guard against arguments leading to infinite recursion, we can add integer type constraints to the subroutine signature and some code to stop recursion if the first argument is negative, for example:

```
sub recurse(Int $n, Int $s) {
    say "Args : n = $n, s = $s";
    if $n == 0 {
        say $s;
    } elsif $n < 0 {
        die 'STOP! negative $n, we need to give up';
    } else {
        recurse $n - 1, $n + $s;
    }
}
```

Now, if we call `recurse` with a negative value for $n, we get an error message:

```
Args : n = -1, s = 0
STOP! negative $n, we need to give up
  in sub recurse at recurse2.pl6 line 6
  in block <unit> at recurse2.pl6 line 12
```

And if we call it with a noninteger value for $n:

```
===SORRY!=== Error while compiling recurse2.pl6
Calling recurse(Rat, Int) will never work with declared
signature (Int $n, Int $s)
at recurse2.pl6:12
------> <BOL><HERE>recurse 1.5, 0;
```

Another possibility might be to use a feature of Perl 6 which we haven't covered yet, *multi* subroutines, described in "Multi Subroutines" on page 89. The idea is to declare two versions of the `recurse` subroutine, which have the same name but different signatures. The compiler will figure out which version of `recurse` to call depending on which signature applies to the arguments passed to the subroutine:

```
multi recurse(Int $n where $n >= 0, $s) {
    say "Args : n = $n, s = $s";
    if ($n == 0) {
        say $s;
    } else {
        recurse $n - 1, $n + $s;
    }
}

multi recurse($n , $s) {
    say "Args : n = $n, s = $s";
    # do something else for such a case, for example:
    # recurse (abs $n.Int), $s; # calling the 1st version of recurse
    # or simply:
    say 'STOP! invalid $n, we need to give up';
}
```

If the first parameter is a positive integer, the first version of `recurse` will be called. Otherwise, the second version will run:

```
$ perl6 recurse.pl6
Args : n = 6.1, s = 0
STOP! negative $n, we need to give up

$ perl6 recurse.pl6
Args : n = -1, s = 0
STOP! invalid $n, we need to give up
```

Try running the following code for the second definition of `recurse`:

```
multi recurse($n , $s) {
    say "Args : n = $n, s = $s";
```

```
        recurse (abs $n.Int), $s;
    }
```

to see what is happening in that case.

Exercises of Chapter 5: Fruitful Functions

Exercise: Compare

This is the solution to the exercise at the end of "Return Values" on page 77. Here's a subroutine that takes two numbers and compares them, and returns 1 if the first one is larger than the second, 0 if they are equal, and –1 otherwise (i.e., if the second is larger than the first):

```
sub compare (Numeric $x, Numeric $y) {
    return 1 if $x > $y;
    return 0 if $x == $y;
    return -1;
}

say compare 4, 7;   # -1
say compare 7, 4;   # 1
say compare 5, 5;   # 0
```

Note: this exemplifies a three-way compare function commonly used for sorting in a number of programming languages, including older versions of Perl (such as Perl 5). In Perl 6, the operators implementing this functionality (the three-way comparators cmp, leg, and <=>) return special types of values: Order::More, Order::Less, and Order::Same. (See "Sorting Arrays or Lists" on page 172 for more details.)

Exercise: Hypotenuse

This is the solution to the exercise at the end of "Incremental Development" on page 79. The aim is to use an incremental development plan for calculating the hypotenuse of a right triangle (using the Pythagorean theorem).

We could start with an outline of the subroutine:

```
sub hypotenuse(Numeric $x, Numeric $y) {
    return 0;
}
say hypotenuse 3, 4;
```

This will obviously print 0.

Next, we calculate the hypotenuse and print it within the subroutine:

```
sub hypotenuse(Numeric $x, Numeric $y) {
    my $hypotenuse = sqrt ($x ** 2 + $y ** 2);
    say "hypotenuse = $hypotenuse";
```

```
        return 0.0;
    }
    say hypotenuse 3, 4;
```

This prints:

```
hypotenuse = 5
0
```

The subroutine is calculating correctly the hypotenuse (5), but is still returning the 0 dummy value. We can now return safely the result (and remove the scaffolding):

```
sub hypotenuse(Numeric $x, Numeric $y) {
    my $hypotenuse = sqrt ($x ** 2 + $y ** 2);
    return $hypotenuse;
}
say hypotenuse 3, 4;
```

This prints correctly the value of the hypotenuse.

Finally, we can, if we wish, remove the temporary variable to further simplify the sub-routine:

```
sub hypotenuse(Numeric $x, Numeric $y) {
    return sqrt ($x ** 2 + $y ** 2);
}
say hypotenuse 3, 4;
```

Exercise: Chained Relational Operators

This is the solution to the exercise in "Boolean Functions" on page 82. We need a sub-routine to figure out whether $x \le y \le z$ is true or false. We simply need to test it with a chained relational operator and return that:

```
sub is-between(Numeric $x, Numeric $y, Numeric $z) {
    return $x <= $y <= $z;
}
say is-between 3, 5, 6; # True
say is-between 3, 8, 7; # False
say is-between 6, 5, 6; # False
say is-between 6, 6, 7; # True
```

Note that the tests provided here are just a limited number of examples, given for illustration purposes. A more complete test suite might be needed (testing for example negative and noninteger numbers). We will see later better ways of building more robust test suites (see for example "Debugging" on page 329 and the exercise solution in "Exercise: Constructing New Operators" on page 407).

Exercise 5-2: The Ackermann Function

Write a subroutine to compute the Ackermann function. The Ackermann function, $A(m, n)$, is defined as follows:

$$A(m, n) = \begin{cases} n + 1 & \text{if } m = 0 \\ A(m - 1, 1) & \text{if } m > 0 \text{ and } n = 0 \\ A(m - 1, A(m, n - 1)) & \text{if } m > 0 \text{ and } n > 0 \end{cases}$$

Here's one way to compute the Ackermann function in Perl:

```
sub ack (Int $m, Int $n) {
    return $n + 1 if $m == 0;
    return ack($m - 1, 1) if $n == 0;
    return ack($m - 1, ack($m, $n-1));
}
say ack 3, 4;     # -> 125
```

We have used parentheses to better show the structure, but it works well without them. Even in the last code line with two calls to the subroutine, the subroutine signature with two integer numbers is sufficient for the Perl compiler to understand which arguments are associated with which call:

```
sub ack (Int $m, Int $n) {
    # say "m n = $m, $n";
    return $n + 1 if $m == 0;
    return ack $m - 1, 1 if $n == 0;
    return ack $m - 1, ack $m, $n-1;
}
```

The Ackermann function is defined for nonnegative integers. As a further exercise, modify the ack subroutine to prevent negative arguments. We discussed two different ways of doing that in "Checking Types" on page 87.

Exercise 5-3: Palindromes

Write a recursive subroutine that checks if a word is a palindrome:

```
sub first_l(Str $word where $word.chars >= 2){
    return substr $word, 0, 1;
}

sub last_l(Str $word){
    return substr $word, *-1, 1;
}

sub middle_l(Str $word){
    return substr $word, 1, *-1;
}
```

```
sub is_palindrome(Str $word) {
    return True if $word.chars <= 1;
    return False if first_l($word) ne last_l($word);
    return is_palindrome(middle_l($word))
}
for ("bob", "otto", "laurent", "redivider", "detartrated") -> $x {
    say "Is $x a palindrome? Answer: ", is_palindrome($x);
}
```

Result:

```
Is bob a palindrome? Answer: True
Is otto a palindrome? Answer: True
Is laurent a palindrome? Answer: False
Is redivider a palindrome? Answer: True
Is detartrated a palindrome? Answer: True
```

The third parameter (length) of the `substr` built-in function is optional. In that case, `substr` will return all characters from a given position. So the `first_l` subroutine could be simplified as follows:

```
sub first_l(Str $word where $word.chars >= 2){
    return substr $word, 0;
}
```

And the `last_l` subroutine could benefit from the same simplification.

Note: the built-in `flip` function or `.flip` method of Perl returns a reversed version of a string and would provide a much easier solution:

```
sub is_palindrome(Str $word) {
    return $word eq $word.flip;
}
```

Exercise 5-4: Powers

Write a recursive subroutine checking whether a number is a power of another number:

```
sub is-power-of (Int $a, Int $b) {
    return False unless $a %% $b;
    return True if $a == $b;
    return is-power-of Int($a/$b), $b;
}

say is-power-of 16, 4;
say is-power-of 25, 5;
say is-power-of 125, 5;
say is-power-of 600, 20;
say is-power-of 8000, 20;
```

Example run:

```
True
True
True
False
True
```

Adding an execution trace to visualize the recursive calls:

```
sub is-power-of (Int $a, Int $b) {
    return False unless $a %% $b;
    return True if $a == $b;
    say "$a\t$b";
    return is-power-of Int($a/$b), $b;
}
```

Running is-power-of with arguments 1024 and 2, with a printed trace of $a and $b:

```
1024    2
512     2
256     2
128     2
64      2
32      2
16      2
8       2
4       2
True
```

Exercise 5-5: Finding the GCD of Two Numbers

Write a subroutine that returns the greatest common divisor of two numbers:

```
sub gcd(Int $a, Int $b) {
    return $a if $b == 0;
    return $b if $a == 0;
    return gcd($b, $a mod $b);
}

say gcd 125, 25;
say gcd 2048, 256;
say gcd 256, 4096;
say gcd 2048, 1;
say gcd 0, 256;
say gcd 33, 45;
```

Note that there is a simpler method to find the GCD of two numbers without using the modulo function. It is known as *Euclid's algorithm* and is considered the oldest known algorithm (*https://en.wikipedia.org/wiki/Euclidean_algorithm*). The Euclidean algorithm is based on the observation that the GCD of two numbers does not change if the larger number is replaced by its difference with the smaller number.

This might be implemented in Perl with the following recursive subroutine:

```
sub gcd(Int $a, Int $b) {
    return gcd($b, $a - $b) if $a > $b;
    return gcd($a, $b - $a) if $b > $a;
    return $a;
}
```

This code works perfectly well in *almost* all cases, at least for all strictly positive input values, but try to follow the flow of execution if one of the two arguments passed to the subroutine, say $b, is zero. In this case, gcd enters an infinite recursion. This is often called an *edge case* or a *corner case*, i.e., a special input value for which an apparently well-working program ceases to function properly.

We have a similar problem for negative input values.

One solution might be to add a signature constraint (or use a type subset):

```
sub gcd(Int $a where $a > 0, Int $b where $b > 0) {
    ...
}
```

but this is not really satisfactory because the GCD of any nonzero integer and 0 is well defined mathematically and is equal to the first number.

Leaving aside for the moment the case of negative numbers, we could rewrite our subroutine as follows:

```
sub gcd(Int $a, Int $b) {
    return $a if $b == 0;
    return $b if $a == 0;
    return gcd($b, $a - $b) if $a > $b;
    return gcd($a, $b - $a) if $b > $a;
    return $a;
}
```

Concerning negative numbers, there is a theorem stating that the GCD of a and b is the same as the GCD of a and $-b$:

```
gcd(a,b) = gcd(-a,b) = gcd(a,-b) = gcd(-a,-b)
```

We can modify further the gcd subroutine:

```
sub gcd(Int $a is copy, Int $b is copy) {
    $a = -$a if $a < 0;
    $b = -$b if $b < 0;
    return $a if $b == 0;
    return $b if $a == 0;
    return gcd($b, $a - $b) if $a > $b;
    return gcd($a, $b - $a) if $b > $a;
    return $a;
}
```

This is now working fine, but remember that a recursive subroutine may be called many times and, for each call, the first four code lines in the program above are executed, although they are really useful only at the first call: once these conditions have been checked during the first call to the subroutine, we know that the arguments must be and remain valid in the chain of recursive calls, so these checks are useless after the first call. This is somewhat wasteful and may lead to unnecessary performance problems.

Ideally, it might be better to separate these four lines that check the preconditions from the cascade of recursive calls. For example, we might write two subroutines:

```
sub gcd1(Int $c, Int $d) {
    return gcd1($d, $c - $d) if $c > $d;
    return gcd1($c, $d - $c) if $d > $c;
    return $c;
}

sub gcd(Int $a is copy, Int $b is copy) {
    $a = -$a if $a < 0;
    $b = -$b if $b < 0;
    return $a if $b == 0;
    return $b if $a == 0;
    return gcd1 $a, $b;
}
```

Now, gcd is making all the necessary checks on the initial arguments and calls the recursive gcd1 subroutine with arguments that have been sanitized and will not lead to infinite recursion. Note that we have renamed the parameters within gcd1 for better clarity, but this was not necessary; it would just work the same if we had kept $a and $b.

The preceding code works perfectly well.

There may be a last problem, though. Someone being not careful enough (or wanting to be too clever) might decide to call directly gcd1, thus annihilating the benefits of the checks made by gcd. To prevent that, we can make good use of the fact that subroutines have lexical scope in Perl 6 and can be made local to another subroutine: we can declare and define gcd1 within the body of the gcd subroutine, so that gcd1 can be called only from within the gcd subroutine:

```
sub gcd(Int $a is copy, Int $b is copy) {
    sub gcd1($c, $d) {
        return gcd1($d, $c - $d) if $c > $d;
        return gcd1($c, $d - $c) if $d > $c;
        return $c;
    }
    $a = -$a if $a < 0;
    $b = -$b if $b < 0;
    return $a if $b == 0;
```

```
        return $b if $a == 0;
        return gcd1 $a, $b;
    }

    say gcd 125, 25;        # 25
    say gcd 2048, 256;      # 256
    say gcd 256, 4096;      # 256
    say gcd 2048, 1;        # 1
    say gcd 0, 256;         # 256
    say gcd 33, 45;         # 3
    say gcd -4, 6;          # 2
```

Chapter 6 will come back to lexical scoping.

You may be interested to know that there is a built-in gcd function in Perl 6.

Exercises of Chapter 6: Iteration

Exercise 6-1: Square Root

We need a subroutine to find the square root of a number by computing successively better approximations of the root, using Newton's method.

For this exercise, I've made the following somewhat arbitrary decisions:

- I have chosen an *epsilon* value of 10^{-11} (or 1e-11).
- I have used $a/2 as the initial estimate of $\sqrt{\$a}$.

Note that it might make more sense to make this initial estimate within the my-sqrt subroutine, rather than having the caller pass it as an argument. The rationale for doing it in the caller is that, in some cases, the caller might have information on the range of the input value and might therefore be able to provide a better initial estimate, leading the algorithm to converge toward the solution slightly faster.

Here's an implementation of Newton's method for computing the square root of a number:

```
sub my-sqrt ($a, $estimate is copy) {
    my $epsilon = 1e-11;
    while True {
        # say "-- Intermediate value: $estimate";
        my $y = ($estimate + $a/$estimate) / 2;
        last if abs($y - $estimate) < $epsilon;
        $estimate = $y;
    }
    return $estimate;
}

sub print-result ($a, $r, $s, $d) {
```

```
        printf "%d  %.13f  %.13f  %.6e \n", $a, $r, $s, $d;
}

sub test-square-root {
    say "a  mysqrt(a)\t     sqrt(a)\t      diff";
    for 1..9 -> $a {
        my $init-estimate = $a/2;
        my $result = my-sqrt $a, $init-estimate;
        my $sqrt = sqrt $a;
        my $diff = abs($result - $sqrt);
        print-result($a, $result, $sqrt, $diff);
    }
}

test-square-root;
```

The printf ("formatted print") function used in the print-result subroutine is derived from the C programming language. Its first argument is a *format string*, which describes how each of the following arguments should be formatted. Here, the format string requests the compiler to output the first subsequent argument as a signed integer (the %d part of the format string), the next two arguments as floating-point numbers with 13 digits after the decimal point (the %.13f part), and the last argument as a floating-point number in scientific notation with 6 digits after the decimal point (%.6e).

Exercise 6-2: Pi Estimate

Pi estimate according to Srinivasa Ramanujan's algorithm:

```
sub factorial(Int $n) {
    return 1 if $n == 0;
    return $n * factorial $n-1;
}

sub estimate-pi {
    #`{ ======================================
        Algorithm by Srinivasa Ramanujan
        (see http://en.wikipedia.org/wiki/Pi)
        ======================================
    }
    my $factor = 2 * 2.sqrt / 9801;
    my $k = 0;
    my $sum = 0;
    while True {
        my $num = factorial(4*$k) * (1103 + 26390*$k);
        my $den = factorial($k)**4 * 396**(4*$k);
        my $term += $factor * $num / $den;
        # say "Intermediate term = $term";
        last if abs($term) < 1e-15;
        $sum += $term;
        $k++;
```

```
    }
    return 1 / $sum;
}

say estimate-pi;
# say pi - estimate-pi;
```

This prints 3.14159265358979.

Notice how we have used a multiline comment to give some additional information about the subroutine.

Uncommenting the intermediate print statement shows the steps toward the solution:

```
Intermediate term = 0.31830987844047
Intermediate term = 7.74332048352151e-009
Intermediate term = 6.47985705171744e-017
-4.44089209850063e-016
```

Exercises of Chapter 7: Strings

Exercise: String Traversal

This is the solution to the exercise in "String Traversal with a while or for Loop" on page 115. The backward traversal of a word with a `while` loop may be written as follows:

```
my $fruit = "banana";
my $index = $fruit.chars;
while $index > 0 {
    $index--;
    my $letter = substr $fruit, $index, 1;
    say $letter;
}
```

The `chars` method returns the length of the string. The `substr` function will find letters under `$index` between 0 and `$length – 1`. It is therefore practical to decrement the `$index` variable before using the `substr` function.

The `while` loop of the preceding code example can be written more concisely:

```
my $fruit = "banana";
my $index = $fruit.chars;
while $index > 0 {
    say substr $fruit, --$index, 1;
}
```

Here, we print directly the value returned by `substr`, without using a temporary variable, and we decrement the `$index` variable within the expression using `substr`. We need to use the prefix form of the decrement operator because we need `$index` to be decremented before it is used by `substr`.

The loop would be even more concise if we used a `while` with a statement modifier (or the postfix syntax of `while`):

```
my $fruit = "banana";
my $index = $fruit.chars;
say substr $fruit, --$index, 1 while $index;
```

This is the same idea, using the `flip` function to reverse the string:

```
my $fruit = flip "banana";
my $index = 0;
say substr $rev_fruit, $index++, 1 while $index < $rev_fruit.chars;
```

The aim of this exercise was to train you to use loops to traverse the string. Combining the `flip` and `comb` functions or methods would of course make our solution much simpler (and probably faster):

```
.say for "banana".flip.comb;
```

Exercise: The Ducklings

This is the solution for the exercise in "String Traversal with a while or for Loop" on page 115. The first idea that may come to mind for this exercise is to build a modified list of prefixes this way:

```
for 'J' .. 'N', 'Ou', 'P', 'Qu' -> $letter { #...}
```

But this does not work properly because it creates a list of four elements in which the first element is itself a sublist "J" to "N":

```
> say ('J'..'N', 'Ou', 'P', 'Qu').perl;
("J".."N", "Ou", "P", "Qu")
```

We will come back to this later in the book, but let us just say that we need to *flatten* this combination of lists into one single iterable list, which can be done with the `flat` method or function or the "|" operator:

```
for ('J' .. 'N', 'Ou', 'P', 'Qu').flat      -> $letter {#...}
# or: for flat 'J' .. 'N', 'Ou', 'P', 'Qu' -> $letter {...}
# or: for |('J' .. 'N'), 'Ou', 'P', 'Qu'    -> $letter {...}
# Note: parentheses needed in the last example above with |
# to overcome precedence problem
```

With this small difficulty removed, the solution is now easy:

```
my $suffix = 'ack';
for ('J' .. 'N', 'Ou', 'P', 'Qu').flat -> $letter {
    say $letter ~ $suffix;
}
```

Here again, we could make the code slightly more concise with the postfix syntax of `for` and the `$_` topical variable:

```
my $suffix = 'ack';
say "$_$suffix" for flat 'J' .. 'N', 'Ou', 'P', 'Qu';
```

Here, we introduced another simple and common way of concatenating two strings: simply inserting the two variables one after the other within double quotes and letting variable interpolation do the work.

Exercise: Counting the Letters of a String

This is the solution to the exercise in "String Traversal with a while or for Loop" on page 115. This subroutine counts the number of occurrences of a specific letter within a word (or any string):

```
sub count (Str $word, Str $letter) {
    my $count = 0;
    for $word.comb -> $letter {
        $count++ if $letter eq 'a';
    }
    return $count;
}
say count "banana", "a";    # -> 3
```

The solution to Exercise 7-1 ("Exercise 7-1: Counting Letters" on page 372) uses the index and substr functions to perform the same count.

Exercise: Simulating a Regex with a Loop

This is the solution to the exercise in "Regular Expressions (Regexes)" on page 116. The aim is to find in a string any letter that is immediately preceded by the letter "l" and followed by the letter "w".

If you try to do the specified search with the techniques we've seen so far, you'll find out that there are a number of edge cases, making it quite complicated.

This is a possible solution:

```
sub traverse (Str $word, Str $start_letter, Str $end_letter) {
    my $found_start = False;
    my $capture_next = False;
    my $target_letter;
    for 0..$word.chars - 1 -> $idx {
        my $letter = substr $word, $idx, 1;
        next unless $letter eq $start_letter or $found_start;
        if ($capture_next) {
            $target_letter = $letter;
            $capture_next = False;
            next;
        }
        if $letter eq $start_letter and not $found_start {
            $found_start = True;
            $capture_next = True;
```

```
                next;
            }
            # if we get there, we have found a candidate target letter
            if $letter eq $end_letter {
                return $target_letter
            } else {
                # wrong match, let's start again, we need to backup
                if $target_letter eq $start_letter {
                    $target_letter = $letter;
                    $capture_next = False;
                } elsif $letter eq $start_letter {
                    $capture_next = True;
                } else {
                    $capture_next = False;
                    $found_start = False;
                }
            }
        }
    }
    return;  # not found!
}

for <s b   l w   l o   s m   y l   a z> -> $st, $end {
    say "$st $end: ", traverse "yellow submarine", $st, $end;
}
```

As you can see, this is quite complicated because of the various edge cases that need to be handled. Compare this with the one-line regex that does the same:

```
say ~$0 if "yellow submarine" ~~ /l(.)w/;
```

To tell the truth, we haven't chosen the simplest way of doing it.

It is much easier to loop on every letter of the string except the first one and the last one and, for each such letter, to check what the previous letter and the next are. Then you simply need to return the current letter if the previous and the next match the conditions:

```
sub traverse (Str $word, Str $start_letter, Str $end_letter) {
    my $found_start = False;
    my $capture_next = False;
    my $target_letter;
    for 1..$word.chars - 2 -> $idx {
        if $start_letter eq substr $word, $idx - 1, 1
          and $end_letter eq substr $word, $idx + 1, 1 {
            return substr $word, $idx, 1;
        }
    }
    return;  # not found!
}

for <s b   l w   l o   s m   y l   a z> -> $st, $end {
    say "$st $end: ", traverse "yellow submarine", $st, $end;
}
```

In the test cases at the end, we use a `for` loop in a pointy block construct in which we use *two* of the items in the list each time through the loop. The spacing between the items of the list is technically useless and irrelevant to the way the syntactic construct works; the spaces are just formatting help for the reader to better see how the letters will be grouped in the process.

This displays:

```
s b: u
l w: o
l o: l
s m: Nil
y l: e
a z: Nil
```

This is much simpler than the previous attempt, but it would still be quite difficult to change something, for example to add a new condition: the structure of the code would probably need to be reworked quite a bit.

Even compared with this simpler solution, the regex solution really shines orders of magnitude brighter.

Exercise: Regex Exercises

This is the solution to the exercises in "Exercises on Regexes" on page 126. As is often the case in Perl, and even more so with regexes, there is more than one way to do it (TIMTOWTDI). Most of the exercises suggested here have more than one solution (and sometimes many).

With regexes, you also have to think carefully about the input data to figure out what should be matched and what should be rejected.

Ten digits in a row

Here's a way to find 10 consecutive digits in a string:

```
my $string = "567867 8778689 6765432 0123456789 897898";
say ~$0 if $string ~~ /(\d ** 10)/; # -> 0123456789
```

We are simply using the \d (digit) character class together with a quantifier specifying this class 10 times.

Note that we have used capturing parentheses here in order to populate the matched number into $0. We could also omit parentheses and retrieve the number from the match object:

```
my $string = "567867 8778689 6765432 0123456789 897898";
say ~$/ if $string ~~ /\d ** 10/; # -> 0123456789
```

Also, the above solutions would match any 10-digit sequence within a longer sequence of digits, which may or may not be what you need. For example:

```
my $string = "567867 87786896765432 0123456789 897898";
say ~$0 if $string ~~ /(\d ** 10)/; # -> 8778689676
```

If you want to match more precisely a sequence of 10 digits (not more than 10), you need to specify what you want to have "around" the match. For example, to match the sole 10-digit sequence above, you might use the nondigit character class:

```
my $string = "567867 87786896765432 0123456789 897898";
say ~$0 if $string ~~ /\D (\d ** 10) \D/; # -> 0123456789
```

But that would not match a 10-digit sequence at the start or the end of the string:

```
my $string = "5678670001 87786896765432 0123456789 897898";
say ~$0 if $string ~~ /\D (\d ** 10) \D/; # -> 0123456789
```

A better solution might be to use word boundary anchors:

```
my $string = "5678670001 87786896765432 0123456789 897898";
say ~$0 if $string ~~ /<< (\d ** 10) >>/; # -> 5678670001
```

Quite a bit of reflection may sometimes be needed to ensure that we match exactly what we want.

An octal number

Here's a possible solution for finding an octal number (i.e., a number composed only of digits between 0 and 7) in a string:

```
my $string = "567867 8778689 6765432 0123456789 897898";
say ~$0 if $string ~~ /\D (<[0..7]>+) \D/; # -> 6765432
```

The character class is <[0..7]> for digits between 0 and 7. The + quantifier means as many as possible of this character class. And the \D (nondigit) are there to prevent the regex from matching part of a larger number with nonoctal digits (for example from matching 567 in the first number). Depending on the exact requirement, using word boundary anchors as in the previous exercise's solution might be better.

First word at the start of the string

To find the first word in a string, we can just search the first sequence of word characters (characters belonging to the \w character class) in the string:

```
my $string = "The greatest thing you'll ever learn " ~
             "is just to love and be loved in return. " ~
             "(Nature Boy, Nat King Cole)";
say ~$0 if $string ~~ /(\w +)/;  # -> The
```

First word starting with an "a"

Here's a way to find the first word starting with the letter "a" in a sentence:

```
my $string = "Four scores and seven years ago our fathers ...";
say ~$0 if $string ~~ /\W (a \w+)/;   # -> and
```

First word starting with a lowercase vowel

To make sure that the match does not start with a vowel in the middle of a word, we might start the pattern with a \W (nonword character) or, better, with a << left word boundary:

```
my $string = "Democracy is the worst form of government, " ~
             "except for all the others. (Churchill)";
say ~$0 if $string ~~ /<< (<[aeiouy]> \w*)/;   # -> is
```

Here we use a * (rather than +) quantifier because a word containing only one vowel is eligible as a word starting with a vowel.

A mobile number

For a 10-digit number starting with "06" or "07", the easiest solution is probably to use a <[67]> character class:

```
my $string = "567867 8778689 0123456789 0723456789 3644";
say ~$0 if $string ~~ /(0<[67]>\d ** 8)/;   # -> 0723456789
```

First word starting with a vowel (lower- or uppercase)

We can simply ignore case for the whole word:

```
my $string = " Ask not what your country can do for you — " ~
             " ask what you can do for your country. (JFK)";
say ~$0 if $string ~~ /:i << (<[aeiouy]> \w*)/;   # -> Ask
```

Repeated letters

We can capture any letter and check whether the next one is the same as the capture:

```
say ~$0 if 'appeal' ~~ /((\w)$0);   # -> pp
```

For capturing the second group of repeated letters:

```
say ~$1 if 'coffee' ~~ /(\w)$0.*((\w)$0)/;   # -> ee
```

And for the third group:

```
say ~$2 if 'Mississippi' ~~ /(\w)$0.*(\w)$0.*((\w)$0)/; # -> pp
```

Exercise: is-reverse Subroutine

This is the solution to the exercise in "Debugging" on page 131. The second bug in the is-reverse subroutine is located on this line:

```
while $j > 0 {
```

The $j index should be allowed to loop down until 0 (included) if we want to compare the first letter of $word2 with the last letter of $word1.

The corrected version of the is-reverse subroutine might be:

```
sub is-reverse(Str $word1, Str $word2) {
    return False if $word1.chars != $word2.chars;

    my $i = 0;
    my $j = $word2.chars - 1;

    while $j >= 0 {
        return False if substr($word1, $i, 1) ne substr($word1, $j, 1);
        $i++; $j--;
    }
    return True;
}
```

Exercise 7-1: Counting Letters

Counting the number of "a" letters in a word with the index function implies looking for the first "a" from the beginning of the string, then looking for the next one from the position immediately after, and so on until no more "a" letters are found.

Here, we make an infinite loop from which we break out with the last statement when index no longer finds an "a". The $count counter is incremented each time an "a" is found, and the $idx keeps track of the current position within the string:

```
sub count_a {
    my $word = "banana";
    my $count = 0;
    my $idx = 0;
    while True {
        $idx = index $word, 'a', $idx;
        last unless $idx.defined;
        $idx++;
        $count++;
    }
    return $count;
}
say count_a();  # -> 3
```

Adapting it for any string and any letter is just a matter of passing the right arguments to the subroutine and using within the subroutine its parameters instead of hard-coded values:

```
sub count_index (Str $word, Str $letter) {
    my $count = 0;
    my $idx = 0;
    while True {
        $idx = index $word, $letter, $idx;
        last unless $idx.defined;
        $idx++;
        $count++;
    }
    return $count;
}
say count_index "When in the Course of human events...", "n"; # 5
```

Counting a given letter in a given word with the substr function is straightforward: we just need to loop over each letter of the word and increment a counter when needed:

```
sub count_substr (Str $word, Str $letter) {
    my $count = 0;
    for 0..$word.chars - 1 {
        $count++ if $letter eq substr $word, $_, 1;
    }
    return $count;
}
say count_substr "I have a dream that one day...", "a"; # -> 4
```

Exercise 7-2: Lowercase Letters

Only any_lowercase5 and any_lowercase7 are correctly checking whether the input string contains at least one lowercase letter.

If you did not determine that yourself, really try to find by yourself the mistakes in the others before reading on; you should be able to find the errors in the other sub-routines (except perhaps any_lowercase4, which is admittedly a bit tricky).

The any_lowercase5 and any_lowercase7 subroutines perform the search as follows:

- any_lowercase5 sets $flag to False before the loop, changes it to True if any character in the string is True, and returns $flag after the completion of the loop.

- any_lowercase7 is also correct (and probably slightly better than any_lower case5). It returns True if any character is lowercase and returns False only if it gets a chance to go to the end of the loop.

The other subroutines have the following mistakes (some have arguably several mistakes; we're going to list at least one of them):

- `any_lowercase1` is only checking the first character of its argument and exiting the loop thereafter.

- `any_lowercase2` is calling the `is-lower` subroutine on the string `"char"`, not on the `$char` variable (it also has the same defect as `any_lowercase1`).

- `any_lowercase3` is returning `True` or `False` depending on only the last character of the input string.

- `any_lowercase4` suffers from a somewhat nasty operator precedence problem: the assignment `$flag = $flag ...` is executed before the or relational operator is executed, so that the latter part has no effect. Changing the faulty line to:

```
$flag = $flag || is-lower $char;    # higher priority operator
# or
$flag = ($flag or is-lower $char); # parens to override precedence
```

    would solve the problem.

- `any_lowercase6` is almost correct in terms of its algorithm, but returns the strings `"True"` or `"False"` instead of the Boolean values `True` or `False`.

- `any_lowercase8` returns `False` if any character is not lowercase.

- `any_lowercase9` also returns `False` if any character is not lowercase.

The following is an example of the loop you could write to test each subroutine, each with three input strings:

```
for <FOO bar Baz> -> $str {
    say "1. $str: ", any_lowercase1 $str;
    say "2. $str: ", any_lowercase2 $str;
    say "3. $str: ", any_lowercase3 $str;
    say "4. $str: ", any_lowercase4 $str;
    say "5. $str: ", any_lowercase5 $str;
    say "6. $str: ", any_lowercase6 $str;
    say "7. $str: ", any_lowercase7 $str;
    say "8. $str: ", any_lowercase8 $str;
    say "9. $str: ", any_lowercase9 $str;
}
```

It would be possible to replace the nine print statements with a simple loop, but this requires using features that we haven't studied yet.

You'll see in other chapters ways to better organize test cases, for example in "Debugging" on page 329.

Exercise 7-3: Caesar's Cipher

Implementing a letter rotation cipher:

```
sub rotate-one-letter (Str $letter, Int $shift) {
    my $upper-end = 'Z'.ord;         # last uppercase letter
    my $lower-end = 'z'.ord;         # last lowercase letter

    my $rotated-ord = $letter.ord + $shift;
    if $letter ~~ /<[a..z]>/ {                 # lowercase
        $rotated-ord -= 26 if $rotated-ord > $lower-end;
    } elsif $letter ~~ /<[A..Z]>/ {            # uppercase
        $rotated-ord -= 26 if $rotated-ord > $upper-end;
    } else {
        return $letter;
    }
    return $rotated-ord.chr;
}

sub rotate-one-word (Str $word, Int $shift is copy) {
    $shift = $shift % 26;
    $shift = 26 + $shift if $shift < 0;
    my $rotated-word = "";
    for 0..$word.chars - 1 {
        $rotated-word ~= rotate-one-letter substr($word, $_, 1), $shift;
    }
    return $rotated-word;
}

sub rot13 (Str $word) {
    return rotate-one-word $word, 13;
}

say rotate-one-word "ABDCabcd", 25;
say rotate-one-word "cheer", 7;
say rotate-one-word "melon", -10;

say rot13("Fbzr cebsnavgl");
```

If you are interested in decoding only ROT13, the `tr` transliteration operator can give you much shorter code. For example `tr/a..m/n..z/` will transliterate all letters in the a..m range into their respective equivalents in the n..z range.

We can code ROT13 in a simple Perl one-liner (see "One-Liner Mode" on page 22):

```
$ perl6 -e 'my $w = "foobar"; $w ~~ tr/a..mn..z/n..za..m/; say $w;'
sbbone

$ perl6 -e 'my $w = "sbbone"; $w ~~ tr/a..mn..z/n..za..m/; say $w;"
foobar
```

It is quite easy to add the ranges for capital letters. You might want to do it as a further exercise.

Exercises of Chapter 8: Word Play

Exercise 8-7: Consecutive Double Letters

With the looping techniques used in Chapter 8, we could write this:

```
sub is_triple_double (Str $word) {
    # Tests if a word contains three consecutive double letters.
    my $i = 0;
    my $count = 0;
    while $i < $word.chars - 1 {
        if substr($word, $i, 1) eq substr($word, $i + 1, 1) {
            $count++;
            return True if $count == 3;
            $i += 2;
        } else {
            $count = 0;
            $i++;
        }
    }
    return False;
}

for 'words.txt'.IO.lines -> $word {
    say $word if is_triple_double $word;
}
```

This is, however, a typical case where regexes might prove more efficient than looping (in terms of coding efficiency, i.e., as an approximation, how many code lines are needed for performing a given task).

We discussed in Chapter 7 that regex captures are populating the $0, $1, $2, etc. special variables. A regex pattern matching any repeated letter might therefore be /(.) $0/, where the character found by $0 is the same as the character found by the dot.

Similarly, a regex pattern matching three pairs of repeated letters in a row might be:

```
say ~$/ if "abbccdde" ~~ /(.)$0 (.)$1 (.)$2/; # -> bbccdd
```

With this, the program to find the words with three double letters in the *words.txt* file takes just three code lines:

```
for 'words.txt'.IO.lines -> $word {
    say $word if $word ~~ /(.) $0 (.) $1 (.) $2/;
}
```

Both programs find four words, which are variations on "bookkeeper" and "book-keeping."

The regex version is so simple that you can code it directly at the operating system command line prompt as a one-liner (see "One-Liner Mode" on page 22):

```
$ perl6 -ne '.say if /(.) $0 (.) $1 (.) $2/' words.txt
bookkeeper
bookkeepers
bookkeeping
bookkeepings
```

Exercise 8-8: Palindromes in Odometers

The following is a possible program for solving the palindromic odometer puzzle:

```
sub is-palindrome ($number, $start, $len) {
    # Checks if the relevant substring is a palindrome
    my $substring = substr $number, $start, $len;
    return $substring eq flip $substring;
}

sub check ($num) {
    # Checks whether the integer num has the properties described
    return (is-palindrome($num, 2, 4) and
        is-palindrome($num + 1, 1, 5) and
        is-palindrome($num + 2, 1, 4) and
        is-palindrome($num + 3, 0, 6));
}

say 'The following are the possible odometer readings:';
for 1e5..1e6 - 4 -> $number {
    say $number if check $number;
}
```

Another way to do it would be to use regexes to find out whether we have palin-dromes:

```
sub check ($num) {
    # Checks whether the integer num has the properties described
        $num ~~ /^..(.)(.)$1$0/ and
        $num + 1 ~~ /^.(.)(.).$1$0/ and
        $num + 2 ~~ /^.(.)(.)$1$0/ and
        $num + 3 ~~ /^(.)(.)(.)$2$1$0/;
}

say 'The following are the possible odometer readings:';
for 1e5..1e6 - 4 -> $number {
    say $number if check $number;
}
```

This code is shorter, but is also slower: it takes almost twice as long to execute on my computer. So there is a tradeoff here: The first, faster, way is probably better if you need to run your program many times or often, but you might prefer the second version if this is just a one-off computation. It's up to you to decide.

Exercise 8-9: Palindromes in Ages

The following program iterates over possible age differences between 15 and 75 and, for each age, calculates all palindromic possibilities.

```
say 'diff #instances';
check_diffs();
say 'daughter  mother';
num_instances(18, True);

sub are_reversed(Int $i, Int $j) {
    # $j (mother's age) will always be 2 digits
    return $j eq flip sprintf '%02d', $i; # format $i on 2 digits
}

sub num_instances (Int $diff, Bool $flag) {
    # computes and counts all possibilities for one age difference
    my $daughter = 0;
    my $count = 0;
    while True {
        my $mother = $daughter + $diff;
        if are_reversed($daughter, $mother)
            or are_reversed($daughter, $mother+1) {
            $count++;
            printf "%02d\t%d\n", $daughter, $mother if $flag;
        }
        last if $mother > 99;
        $daughter++;
    }
    return $count;
}

sub check_diffs () {
    # enumerates all possible age differences
    for 15..75 -> $diff {
        my $nb_cases = num_instances $diff, False;
        say "$diff    $nb_cases" if $nb_cases > 0;
    }
}
```

The `while True` statement creates an infinite loop. The loop is stopped, however, by the `last` control flow statement when the mother's age exceeds 99. We will see in "New Looping Constructs" on page 164 a more idiomatic way to build an infinite loop, but this is sufficient for now.

The `sprintf` function used here transforms any number below 10 into a two-digit number string with a leading 0. Its syntax is similar to that of the `printf` function seen earlier. The difference is that it only creates a new string, but does not print it.

Using the `.fmt` method instead of the `sprintf` function, as well as the method syntax for `flip`, may render the `are_reversed` subroutine somewhat nicer:

```
sub are_reversed(Int $i, Int $j) {
    return $j eq $i.fmt('%02d').flip; # format $i on 2 digits
}
```

Exercises of Chapter 9: Arrays and Lists

Exercise: Implementing a Queue

This is the solution to the exercise in "Stacks and Queues" on page 159. Here is a somewhat simplistic implementation of a queue using an array and the unshift and pop functions:

```
sub enqueue (@queue, $new_item) {
    unshift @queue, $new_item;
}
sub dequeue (@queue) {
    my $item = pop @queue;
    return $item;
}
my @line = 1, 2, 3, 4, 5;
enqueue @line, 6;
say @line;
say dequeue @line for 1..3;
```

Improving the queue subroutine signatures

Let us try to make our queue a bit more robust.

First, we want to add some signatures to our subroutines. We might be tempted to write something like:

```
sub enqueue (Array @queue, $new_item) {
    unshift @queue, $new_item;
}
```

But that does not work, because that would essentially tell Perl that the @queue parameter is an array of arrays. What we need here is the following signature syntax:

```
sub enqueue (@queue where Array, $new_item) {
    unshift @queue, $new_item;
}
sub dequeue (@queue where Array) {
    my $item = pop @queue;
    return $item;
}
```

We probably don't want any type signature here for the $new_item parameter of enqueue, because we want our queue to be able to operate on any data type in order to make it as generic as possible. But, just as we said it about stacks ("Stacks and

Queues" on page 159), we might want to be able to add several items to the data structure in one go.

Slurpy (or variadic) parameters

There are several ways to insert several elements to the queue, but the simplest is probably to use a signature with a *slurpy* parameter (or *variadic* parameter): an array or hash parameter is marked as slurpy by a leading asterisk, which means it can bind to an arbitrary amount of arguments (zero or more). These are called "slurpy" because they slurp up any remaining arguments to a function, like someone slurping up noodles. This also means that a positional slurpy parameter can only be the last one in the signature:

```
sub enqueue (@queue where Array, *@new_items) {
    unshift @queue, $_ for @new_items;
    # or: unshift @queue, |@new_items;
}
sub dequeue (@queue where Array) {
    my $item = pop @queue;
    return $item;
}
my @line = 4, 5, 6, 7, 8;
enqueue @line, 3, 2, 1;
say @line;
say dequeue @line for 1..3;
```

This will display:

```
[1 2 3 4 5 6 7 8]
8
7
6
```

See also "Optional Parameters" on page 207 for more details on slurpy parameters.

Note that, for an enqueue subroutine, we can't simply write:

```
sub enqueue (@queue where Array, *@new_items) {
    unshift @queue, @new_items;
}
```

because, when given an array as a second argument, unshift inserts the new items as a sublist. Using the for loop or the "|" flattening operator solves this slight difficulty.

Another possibility is to use the prepend built-in function instead of unshift, since it does add the flattened elements of the array at the beginning of the queue:

```
sub enqueue (@queue where Array, *@new_items) {
    prepend @queue, @new_items;
}
```

A queue using shift and append

The order in which the arguments are passed is a bit counterintuitive. Also, we might prefer not having to use a loop to add the new elements. It is slightly easier to use the push and shift combination, and to replace push by append, which does more or less the same thing as push but flattens the list just as prepend did earlier:

```
sub enqueue (@queue where Array, *@new_items) {
    append @queue, @new_items;
}
sub dequeue (@queue where Array) {
    my $item = shift @queue;
    return $item;
}
my @line = 1, 2, 3, 4;
enqueue @line, 6, 7, 8;
say @line;
say dequeue @line for 1..3;
```

This will display:

```
[1 2 3 4 6 7 8]
1
2
3
```

Exceptions

Finally, one additional weakness needs to be fixed: what happens if the queue is empty when we try to dequeue an item? Raising an exception or aborting the program might be what's needed. We might also decide to return an undefined value and let the caller deal with it:

```
sub enqueue (@queue where Array, *@new_items) {
    append @queue, @new_items;
}
sub dequeue (@queue where Array) {
    return unless @queue;
    my $item = shift @queue;
    return $item;
}
my @line;
enqueue @line, 1, 2, 3;
say @line;
for 1..4 -> $count {
    my $item = dequeue @line;
    if defined $item {
        say $item;
    } else {
        say "ERROR: The queue is empty !";
    }
}
```

This produces the following output:

```
[1 2 3]
1
2
3
ERROR: The queue is empty !
```

The dequeue subroutine could be made simpler by using the ternary conditional operator (see "The Ternary Conditional Operator" on page 203) and returning the Nil value if the queue is empty:

```
sub dequeue (@queue where Array) {
    @queue ?? @queue.shift !! Nil
}
```

As a further exercise, you might want to apply to the example code for stacks (seen in "Stacks and Queues" on page 159) the changes we have made above to the management of queues.

Encapsulating the data

Another problem with our implementation of queues is that the @file queue is fully accessible to the developer, who might be tempted to peek directly into the array or, worse, to modify it, without using the enqueue and dequeue subroutines designed to keep the queue consistent.

We might want to prevent that and make it impossible for the user to tamper with the queue or otherwise access it by any other means than the adequate subroutines. Hiding the information about the implementation or otherwise making it inaccessible by other means than those that have been designed for that purpose is often called data *encapsulation*. One common way to achieve data encapsulation is through object-oriented programming, which we cover in Chapter 12.

We can, however, obtain a similar result by combining variable scoping and some material briefly covered in "Functions and Subroutines as First-Class Citizens" on page 47.

Consider the following implementation of a queue:

```
sub create-fifo {
    my @queue;
    return (
        sub {return shift @queue;},
        sub ($item) {push @queue, $item;}
        ) ;
}
my ($fifo-get, $fifo-put) = create-fifo();
$fifo-put($_) for 1..10;
print " ", $fifo-get() for 1..5; # ->  1 2 3 4 5
```

The centerpiece here is the `create-fifo` subroutine. The `@queue` array holding the data is lexically scoped to this subroutine and cannot be accessed directly from anywhere else in the program. `create-fifo` returns two anonymous subroutines, one to dequeue items and one to enqueue them. These subroutines are lexical *closures*, which means in simple terms that they can access `@queue`, because they have been defined within its scope, even if they are called from somewhere else. Even when `create-fifo` has completed, those subroutines can still access it because they sort of give an extra life to the array as long as the subroutines are accessible.

The rest of the code should be clear: when `create-fifo` is called, it manufactures the two anonymous subroutines that are stored in the `$fifo-get` and `$fifo-put` variables. A subroutine such as `create-fifo` is sometimes called a *function factory* because it generates other subroutines at runtime. Finally, `$fifo-put` is called ten times to populate the queue with integers from 1 to 10, and `$fifo-get` is called five times to get the first five items of the queue. The queue is encapsulated: there is no way to access its data other than using the two anonymous subroutines.

Making it possible to enqueue a list of items (rather than a single one) and managing exceptions (such as trying to get an item from an empty queue) are left as an exercise for the reader.

The techniques used here borrow heavily on a programming paradigm called *functional programming*, a model of programming used by languages such as Lisp, Caml, Clojure, and Haskell. This paradigm is quite different from almost everything we have seen so far, just as object-oriented programming is yet another different paradigm. As you gain more experience as a programmer, you should make a point to understand these different paradigms, because they offer different ways of doing things, and they all have specific advantages for specific types of problems. Knowing all of them gives you more expressive power. One of the good things with Perl 6 is that it gives you a modern and powerful tool to use each of these programming paradigms. Chapter 14 is all about functional programming. Meanwhile, make sure to read "Higher-Order Functions and Functional Programming" on page 169.

Exercise: Other Ways to Modify an Array

Simulating the pop function

This is the solution to the exercise in "Other Ways to Modify an Array" on page 160. The `my-pop` subroutine uses `splice` to simulate the `pop` function:

```
sub my-pop (@array where @array > 0) {
    my @result = splice @array, @array.end, 1;
    return @result[0];
}
my @letters = 'a'..'j';
my $letter = my-pop @letters;
```

```
say $letter;           # -> j
say @letters;          # -> [a b c d e f g h i]
```

Here, the expression @array.end returns the index of the last item of the array. It is also possible to count the array items from the end and access the last and penulti-mate items of a list or an array using the following syntax:

```
> say (1..9)[*-1];
9
> say (1..9)[*-2];
8
```

The my-pop subroutine could be rewritten as follows:

```
sub my-pop (@array where @array > 0) {
    my @result = splice @array, *-1, 1;
    return @result[0];
}
```

You don't have to specify the number of elements with splice if you just want the rest. We can also avoid using the @result intermediate array. So we could simplify my-pop as:

```
sub my-pop (@array where @array > 0) {
    @array.splice(*-1)[0]
}
```

Simulating the push function

The only slight difficulty in this exercise is to manage a signature with a "variadic" list of parameters (or slurpy parameters). This was explained in "Slurpy (or variadic) parameters" on page 380:

```
sub my-push (@array, *@list) {
    my @result = splice @array, @array.end + 1, 0, @list;
    return @array; # push returns the modified list
                   # (seldom used for arrays)
}
my @letters = 'a'..'j';
my-push @letters, 'k', 'l', 'm';
say @letters;      # -> [a b c d e f g h i j k l m]
```

Simulating the unshift function

To simulate the unshift function, we can again use slurpy parameters:

```
sub my-unshift (@array, *@list) {
    my @result = splice @array, 0, 0, @list;
    return @array; # unshift returns the modified list
                   # (seldom used for arrays)
}
my @letters = 'd'..'j';
```

```
my-unshift @letters, 'a'..'c';
say @letters;       # -> [a b c d e f g h i j]
```

Simulating the delete subscript adverb

Remember the `delete` adverb removes the value, but leaves the slot undefined within the array. The `splice` function would also remove the slot, so this might not be what is really needed here if we want to simulate the behavior of `delete` (although, in a sense, it might also be considered to be an improvement to remove the slot altogether). To really simulate `delete`, it is probably better to just "undefine" the value:

```
sub my-delete (@array, $idx) {
    my $item = @array[$idx];
    @array[$idx] = Nil;
    return $item;
}
my @letters = 'a'..'j';
my $letter = my-delete @letters, 4;
say $letter;        # -> e
say @letters;       # -> [a b c d (Any) f g h i j]
```

Exercise: Mapping and Filtering the Elements of a List

This is the solution to the exercise in "Map, Filter, and Reduce" on page 165. Producing an array containing the square of the numbers in the input list is very straightforward:

```
my @squares = map { $_ ** 2 }, 3, 5, 7;     # -> [9 25 49]
```

To keep the elements of a list that are perfect squares, one way is to check for each number whether its square root is an integer. For example:

```
my @filt = grep { my $sq = sqrt $_; $sq == $sq.Int}, 3, 9, 8, 16;
say @filt;                                    # -> [9 16]
```

This is working fine with the sample data of the example test, but the program will abort if we try it with a negative input value. We want to avoid that exception and just consider that a negative number can never be a perfect square.

Since the code block here would be getting a bit more complicated, we might prefer to use a function reference instead:

```
sub is-square (Numeric $num} {
    return False if $num < 0;
    my $sq = sqtr $num;
    return $sq == $sq.Int;
}
my @filt = grep &is-square, 3, 9, -6, 16;    # -> [9 16]
```

Exercise: Advanced Sorting Techniques

This is the solution to the exercise in "More Advanced Sorting Techniques" on page 173. The transformation subroutine that can extract the letter groups from the strings is quite straightforward:

```
sub my_comp (Str $str) {
    return $0 if $str ~~ /^\d+ (\w+)/;
    Nil;    # returning Nil if the regex did not match
}
```

The sort is just the same as in the original chapter:

```
say sort &my_comp, <22ac 34bd 56aa3 12c; 4abc( 1ca 45bc>;
    # -> (56aa3 4abc( 22ac 45bc 34bd 12c; 1ca)
```

The transformation subroutine is simple enough to be easily replaced by a code block:

```
my @unsorted = <22ac 34bd 56aa3 12c; 42acd 12cd; 4abc( 1ca 45bc 3dab!>;
my @sorted = sort {/\d+ (\w+)/; $0 // Nil}, @unsorted;
say @sorted;
    # -> [56aa3 4abc( 22ac 42acd 45bc 34bd 12c; 1ca 12cd; 3dab!]
```

This can also be written with a method invocation syntax:

```
my @sorted = @unsorted.sort: {/\d+ (\w+)/; $0 // Nil};
```

Exercise 9-1: Nested Sum

The most obvious way to compute the sum of all values contained in nested lists or arrays is to use nested loops. For example:

```
my @AoA = [[1, 2], [3], [4, 5, 6]];
sub nested-sum (@array) {
    my $sum;
    for @array -> $item {
        for $item.flat -> $nested_item {
            $sum += $nested_item;
        }
    }
    return $sum
}
say nested-sum @AoA;  # -> 21
```

The only slight syntactical difficulty here is that we need to flatten the $item sublists in order to traverse them. This could also be done with the "|" operator:

```
for |$item -> $nested_item {
```

Here is another way to do it, using a for loop for traversing the outer array and a reduction operator for adding the elements of the nested lists:

```
my @AoA = [[1, 2], [3], [4, 5, 6]];
sub nested-sum (@array) {
    my $sum;
    for @array -> $item {
        $sum += [+] $item;
    }
    return $sum
}
say nested-sum @AoA;  # -> 21
```

Using map for flattening the nested lists and the reduction operator can make this code considerably shorter:

```
my @AoA = [[1, 2], [3], [4, 5, 6]];
sub nested-sum (@array) {
    return [+]  map {|$_}, @array;
}
say nested-sum @AoA;  # -> 21
```

Comparing this solution needing one line of actual code with the first one shows how expressive the functional programming style can be for handling arrays and lists and hopefully tells you one of the reasons why we have been insisting on this programming style in this chapter.

These solutions work well because it is known that there are at most lists and nested lists (lists of lists). What if the level of "nestedness" is not known in advance and can be higher than two? A solution would be to use a recursive subroutine to explore the tree of lists:

```
my @AoA = [[1,2], [3], [4,5,6], [3, [7,6, [3,2]]]];
sub nested-sum ($input) {
    my $sum = 0;
    for |$input -> $item {
        if $item.WHAT ~~  Int {
            $sum += $item;
        } else {
            $sum += nested-sum $item;
        }
    }
    return $sum;
}
say nested-sum @AoA;  # -> 42
```

Remember that a recursive approach is often an efficient tool when dealing with nested or chained data.

Exercise 9-2: Cumulative Sum

To compute the cumulative sum of a list of numeric values, we just need an accumulator and we push the value of the accumulator each time through the iteration on the array:

```
my @numbers = <2 5 7 6 5 3 6 8>;
say cumul-sum(@numbers); # -> [2 7 14 20 25 28 34 42]

sub cumul-sum (@array) {
    my @cumulative;
    my $partial_sum = 0;
    for @array -> $element {
        $partial_sum += $element;
        push @cumulative, $partial_sum;
    }
    return @cumulative;
}
```

But guess what? The code can be much shorter with functional programming. Remember that the reduction metaoperator can give you a list of partial results:

```
my @numbers = <2 5 7 6 5 3 6 8>;
say [\+] @numbers;    # -> (2 7 14 20 25 28 34 42)
```

You might think at this point that I designed these exercises to make my point about the expressive power of functional programming. Not at all! Both this exercise and the previous one are straight from the list chapter of Allen Downey's *Think Python* book, on which this book is loosely based. I didn't write these two exercises, but only the solutions presented here.

Exercise 9-3: Middle

The easiest way to produce a new list that contains all but the first and last elements of a given list is probably to simply use a slice:

```
say middle(5..10);    # -> (6 7 8 9)
sub middle (@array) {
    return @array[1..*-2]
}
```

Note that *-1 refers to the index of the last element of an array. To discard the last element, we limit the range to *-2.

Exercise 9-4: Chop

The basic difference with the previous exercise is that the array should be modified in place, rather than returned from the function.

Here's one possible solution, which uses the shift and pop functions to remove respectively the first and the last element of the array:

```
my @nums = 5..10;
chop-it(@nums);
say @nums;   # -> [6 7 8 9]

sub chop-it (@array) {
```

```
    shift @array;
    pop @array;
    return;
}
```

Using a slice is somewhat simpler; just make sure to assign the slice to the array in order to modify the array in place:

```
sub chop-it (@array) {
    @array = @array[1..*-2];
    return;
}
```

Exercise 9-5: Subroutine is-sorted

To check whether a list is sorted, we just need to iterate over its items, keep track of the previous value, and compare the current value with the previous one. Return False if any pair of values does not satisfy the comparison, and return True upon getting to the end of the iteration:

```
sub is-sorted (@array) {
    my $previous = @array[0];
    for @array -> $current {
        return False if $current < $previous;
        $previous = $current;
    }
    return True;
}
say is-sorted < 2 4 5 7 7 8 9>;    # -> True
say is-sorted < 2 4 5 7 6 8 9>;    # -> False
```

Another approach might be to simply compare the input list with a sorted version of the same:

```
sub is-sorted (@array) {
    return @array eqv @array.sort;
}
say is-sorted < 2 4 5 7 7 8 9>;    # -> True
say is-sorted < 2 4 5 7 6 8 9>;    # -> False
```

While this leads to short and simple code, this is not an optimal solution, because it forces the program to sort the input array, which is significantly more costly than just traversing the array, at least when the array to be checked is large.

Once again, functional programming and especially the reduction hyperoperator can lead to much shorter code than the first solution, without incurring the cost of an additional sort:

```
sub is-sorted (@array) {
    return [<=] @array }
}
```

```
say is-sorted < 2 4 5 7 7 8 9>;    # -> True
say is-sorted < 2 4 5 7 6 8 9>;    # -> False
```

By the way, this last version of is-sorted will "short-circuit" and return False as soon as it has found values not in the proper order, without iterating over the rest of the list.

Exercise 9-6: Subroutine is-anagram

When comparing two words to see if they are anagrams, we can start by returning False if they are not the same length, since anagrams obviously have the same letter count. This might make the process faster if the detailed process to compare two strings is time consuming, by avoiding the time-consuming part for cases that will obviously not match.

We don't want to try every permutation of letters. The easiest way to check for anagrams is probably to start by *normalizing* the input strings, i.e., reorganizing them in such a way that they can easily be compared. The most obvious way is just to sort the letters of the two words and compare the results:

```
sub is-anagram (Str $word1, Str $word2) {
    return False if $word1.chars != $word2.chars;
    return False if $word1.comb.sort ne $word2.comb.sort;
    True;
}
for <ban bane post stop pots stop post pots pots taps> -> $w1, $w2 {
    say "$w1 $w2:\t", is-anagram $w1, $w2;
}
```

This produces the following output:

```
$ perl6 anagrams.pl6
ban bane:      False
post stop:     True
pots stop:     True
post pots:     True
pots taps:     False
```

Note that this works correctly because the ne operator coerces its argument into a string before performing the comparison.

This code can be made shorter (but possibly slightly less efficient) by returning directly the comparison of the sorted versions:

```
sub is-anagram (Str $word1, Str $word2) {
    return $word1.comb.sort eq $word2.comb.sort;
}
```

Exercise 9-7: Subroutine has-duplicates

Within the context of what we have seen so far, the easiest way to find out if a list of strings has duplicates is probably to sort the list, so that possible duplicates will be adjacent, and to compare each item of the sorted array with the previous (or next) one:

```
say has-duplicates( < a b c df g xy z r e >); # -> False
say has-duplicates( < a b c df g xy z c e >); # -> True

sub has-duplicates (@array) {
    my @sorted = sort @array;
    for 1..@sorted.end -> $i {
        return True if @sorted[$i] eq @sorted[$i - 1];
    }
    False;
}
```

Here, the loop starts on index 1 (and not 0) because each item is compared with the previous one.

Another way is to iterate on the elements of the sorted array and to keep track of the previous item to enable the comparison:

```
say has-duplicates( < a b c d f y z r e >); # -> False
say has-duplicates( < a b c d f y z c e >); # -> True

sub has-duplicates (@array) {
    my @sorted = sort @array;
    my $previous = shift @sorted;
    for @sorted -> $item {
        return True if $item eq $previous;
        $previous = $item;
    }
    False;
}
```

Another possibility is to use the unique function of Perl 6, which returns a sequence of unique values from the input list or array. Comparing the item count of the output of unique with the element count of the original list will tell us whether some duplicates were removed by unique:

```
sub has-duplicates (@array) {
    my @unique-items = unique @array;
    return False if @unique-items.elems == @array.elems;
    True;
}
```

This could be rewritten more concisely by chaining the method invocations:

```
sub has-duplicates (@array) {
    @array.unique.elems != @array.elems;
}
```

Note that Perl also has a `repeated` built-in function, which is the counterpart of `unique` and returns the duplicates of a list:

```
say <a b c d b f d>.repeated;  # -> (b d)
```

The `has-duplicates` subroutine can just coerce the output of `repeated` into a Boolean:

```
sub has-duplicates (@array) {
    ?@array.repeated
}
```

Another efficient way of finding or removing duplicates from a list or an array is to use *hashes*, a built-in data structure which we cover in Chapter 10 (see Exercise 10-3).

Exercise 9-8: Simulating the Birthday Paradox

For simulating the birthday paradox, we need to generate random integers between 1 and 365 (each integer representing a date in the year). For the sake of simplicity, we will generate random integers between 0 and 364, which is equivalent for our purposes.

We will run the simulation 1,000 times:

```
sub has-duplicates (@array) {
    return ?@array.repeated
}

sub check-birthdays (Int $num-students) {
    my @blist;
    for 1..$num-students {
        push @blist, 365.rand.Int; # random numbers between 0 and 364
    }
    return has-duplicates(@blist);
}

my $dupl-count = 0;
my $nb-tests = 1000;
for 1..$nb-tests {
    $dupl-count++ if check-birthdays 23; # 23 students
}
say "On $nb-tests tests, $dupl-count had at least one duplicate birthday";
```

Note that we have reused the `has-duplicates` subroutine of the previous exercise here. It is so short that its code could have been inlined in the `check-birthdays` subroutine, but it is generally considered good practice to reuse software components that have been developed and tested.

Running the program four times gave the following results:

```
$ perl6 birthdays.pl6
On 1000 tests, 498 had at least one duplicate birthday

$ perl6 birthdays.pl6
On 1000 tests, 505 had at least one duplicate birthday

$ perl6 birthdays.pl6
On 1000 tests, 527 had at least one duplicate birthday

$ perl6 birthdays.pl6
On 1000 tests, 491 had at least one duplicate birthday
```

This simulation confirms that with a sample of 23 persons, there is an approximate 50% probability that at least two will have the same birthday.

Note that Perl has a roll built-in that returns randomly selected elements from a list. This can make the check-birthdays subroutine significantly more concise:

```
sub check-birthdays (Int $num-students) {
    has-duplicates( (^365).roll($num-students) )
}
```

Exercise 9-9: Comparing push and unshift

Populating an array with either push or unshift is something you've seen before. The only new thing here is to compare runtimes of various solutions. The now function returns the number of seconds elapsed since a theoretical start point called "the Epoch," usually January 1, 1970. Calling now once before running a script and once after will tell us how long it ran through a simple subtraction.

```
my $start_push = now;
my @push_array;
for 'words.txt'.IO.lines -> $line {
    push @push_array, $line;
}
say "push took " ~ now - $start_push ~ " seconds.";
@push_array = ();

my $start_unsh = now;
my @unsh_array;
for 'words.txt'.IO.lines -> $line {
    unshift @unsh_array, $line;
}
say "unshift took " ~ now - $start_unsh ~ " seconds.";
@unsh_array = ();
```

This is a sample run of this program:

```
push took 1.870107 seconds.
unshift took 2.2291266 seconds.
```

Try it for yourself. Run it several times, and you should probably notice that push is consistently faster than unshift, even though the difference is not that large.

The reason is presumably that since unshift is inserting items at the start of the array, Perl has to move data around in order to reorganize the whole array many times over, whereas, using push for inserting items at the end of the array implies less internal housekeeping.

As a further exercise, you may try to explore other ways to populate an array, such as append or splice.

If you are just going to insert each line from the input file into an array without changing anything to those lines, then slurping the data into the array without a loop will be simpler and much faster:

```
my $start_slurp = now;
my @slurp_array = 'words.txt'.IO.lines;
say "slurp took " ~ now - $start_slurp ~ " seconds.";
```

This is four to five times faster:

```
slurp took 0.42602506 seconds.
```

Note that you don't really need to call the now function at the beginning of the program: you can use INIT now to retrieve the time when the program began to run:

```
my @slurp_array = 'words.txt'.IO.lines;
say "slurp took " ~ (now - INIT now) ~ " seconds.";
```

Exercise 9-10: Bisection Search in a List

We can start with a recursive bisection algorithm:

```
sub bisect (@word_list, Str $word) {
    my $index = (@word_list.elems / 2).Int;
    return False if $index == 0 and @word_list[$index] ne $word;
    my $found = @word_list[$index];
    if $word lt $found {
        # search the first half
        return bisect @word_list[0..$index-1], $word;
    } elsif $word gt $found {
        # search the second half
        return bisect @word_list[$index+1..*-1], $word;
    }
    True;      # if we get there, we've found the word
}

for <a f w e q ab ce> -> $search {
    if bisect [<a b d c e f g>], $search {
        say "found $search";
```

```
    } else {
        say "did not find $search";
    }
}
```

This will display the following output:

```
found a
found f
did not find w
found e
did not find q
did not find ab
did not find ce
```

There are a couple of weaknesses, though, in this implementation. First, on each recursive call, bisect passes as an argument an array that may be quite large, and this may not be very efficient both in terms of memory usage (to store the successive subsets of the original array) and in terms of CPU cycles (the time to copy these arrays).

In addition, we can figure out whether the target word can be found in the list (and there are many cases where we don't need more information than that), but we don't know where it was found (i.e., on which subscript of the original array), which is often what is really needed.

A better option might be to have only one copy of the original array, say as a global variable, and to pass around subscript ranges. But global variables are usually very much frowned upon because they tend to go against the tenets of structured programming and can be dangerous (even though this would arguably be a case where a global variable does make some sense). We can actually do better than global variables and still have the benefit of not passing the whole array around again and again thanks to the fact that, in Perl 6, subroutines are *closures*, which means that they can use variables that exist in the environment where they are created.

In the following code, bisect is no longer a recursive subroutine; it is a very simple subroutine that just sets up the environment for bisect2, which is the recursive routine and is defined within the body of bisect. Because the array and the searched word exist within bisect, bisect2 will be able to access to them. The parameters to bisect2 are now just two subscripts representing the range in which it will have to look up the word:

```
sub bisect (Str $word, @word_list) {
    sub bisect2 ($low_idx, $high_idx) {
        my $mid_idx = (($low_idx + $high_idx) /2).Int;
        my $found = @word_list[$mid_idx];
        return $mid_idx if $word eq $found;
        return -1 if $low_idx >= $high_idx;
        if $word lt $found {
            # search the first half
```

```
            return bisect2 $low_idx, $mid_idx - 1;
        } else {
            # search the second half
            return bisect2 $mid_idx+1, $high_idx;
        }
    }
    my $max_index = @word_list.end;
    return bisect2 0, $max_index;
}

for <a f w e q ab ce g> -> $search {
    my $result = bisect $search, [<a b d c e f g>];
    if $result == -1 {
        say "did not find $search";
    } else {
        say "found $search on position $result";
    }
}
```

As a further exercise, adapt the above program to search for various English words in *words.txt*. Notice how fast this is. Please be aware that it works correctly because the words in this file are listed in alphabetical order.

Try to change the code to count and display the number of steps necessary to find a given word. Compare this with the number of steps it would take on average for a linear search (i.e., traversing the array linearly until the word is found or can be declared to be absent). Can you guess why this search algorithm is sometimes called a *logarithmic search*?

You may also want to try to write a nonrecursive solution using a loop.

Exercise 9-11: Reverse Pairs

Finding reverse pairs requires reading each word of the list and checking the list to see whether the reversed words exist in the list. This means that you are going to look up about 113,000 words in a list having 113,000 words. Your lookup method needs to be efficient. The obvious solution is to use the bisection search implemented in the previous exercise:

```
sub bisect (Str $word, @word_list) {
    # see the code in the previous exercise
}

my @array = 'words.txt'.IO.lines;

for @array -> $word {
    my $reverse = $word.flip;
    my $res = bisect $reverse, @array;
    say "$word and $reverse form a reverse pair" if $res >= 0;
```

```
}
say now - INIT now;
```

On my laptop (a decent box, but not a racehorse), the whole process ran in about 42 seconds, i.e., less than 0.4 millisecond per lookup.

If you think about it, the `for` loop in the code above is really filtering from the word list those words belonging to a reverse pair. This could be implemented with a `grep` using the `bisect` subroutine to select the matches:

```
say "$_ and $_.flip() form a reverse pair"
    for @array.grep( { bisect( .flip, @array ) >= 0 } );
```

With the algorithm used here, each reverse pair is found twice (once for each word of the pair). When examining any given word from the list, we actually don't need to search backward in the part of the list before that word because if that word forms a pair with another word that comes before in alphabetic order, we've already found the pair when processing that other word. So it would be more efficient and faster to search only forward, i.e., to look for the reverse word in the part of the list coming after the word being examined. As a further exercise, modify the `for` loop to search words forward.

Comparing bisection search with hash lookup

Bisection search is fairly fast, but hash lookup is even faster. Although we haven't studied hashes yet, try the following code:

```
my %hash = map { $_ => 1}, 'words.txt'.IO.lines;
for %hash.keys -> $word {
    my $reverse = $word.flip;
    say "$word and $reverse form a reverse pair"
        if %hash{$reverse}:exists;
}
say now - INIT now;
```

Don't worry about understanding the code for the time being, but notice how much shorter it is. And how much faster it runs: on the same laptop, the execution time is about 16 seconds (less than 0.15 millisecond per lookup). I hope this will whet your appetite for Chapter 10.

Note that the output of this example is not sorted because a hash does not keep the order of the input data, as we will see in Chapter 10. It would be fairly easy to keep the sort order, for example by using an array in addition to the hash, but that is not really the subject here.

Creating and using a module

Coming back to the `bisect` subroutine, copying and pasting this subroutine from the program of the previous exercise into the code of this exercise is not the best way to reuse code. Suppose a bug is found in that subroutine. It now needs to be fixed in two different programs; the chance that the bug gets corrected in one program and forgotten for the other is quite significant. Even if it is not forgotten, this is twice the work, and increases the chance of making another mistake in the process. The bug fix also needs testing twice. Even if there is no bug, we might need an enhancement and this again has to be done twice.

A good way to reuse software while maintaining only one copy of the reused subroutine is to insert it into a Perl module, i.e., in a separate file that will be loaded into our programs needing to use it.

The module file might be named *BisectSearch.pm* and contain the following code:

```
unit module BisectSearch;

sub bisect (Str $word, @word_list) is export {
    sub bisect2 ($low_idx, $high_idx) {
        my $mid_idx = (($low_idx + $high_idx) /2).Int;
        my $found = @word_list[$mid_idx];
        return $mid_idx if $word eq $found;
        return -1 if $low_idx >= $high_idx;
        if $word lt $found {
            # search the first half
            return bisect2 $low_idx, $mid_idx - 1;
        } else {
            # search the second half
            return bisect2 $mid_idx+1, $high_idx;
        }
    }
    my $max_index = @word_list.end;
    return bisect2 0, $max_index;
}

sub some-other-sub is export {
    # does something useful
}
```

Note that the module name given at the top of the code and the root file name have to correspond. The only other change to the code of the subroutine is adding the is export trait to the signature of the subroutine.

Now a Perl program will be able to load this module and use the bisect and some-other-sub subroutines. For example:

```
use lib ".";  # tells Perl to look for modules in the current dir
use BisectSearch;

my @array = 'a'..'m';
for < a f w e q ab ce g > -> $search {
    my $result = bisect $search, @array;
    if $result == -1 {
```

```
            say "did not find $search";
        } else {
            say "found $search : item # $result";
        }
    }
```

Perl has a list of places to look for modules, which may vary from one Perl installation to another. The first line use lib "."; tells Perl to also look for modules in the current directory. This is just an example; you might prefer using a dedicated directory for your modules. The second line use BisectSearch; tells Perl to load the module and import the exported subroutines. Now the program can use the bisect subroutine just as if it had been defined within the program.

That's it, folks! Simple, isn't it? Just try it! Well, there are a few more things to know about modules, but you already know enough to create and use modules.

You might want to review some of the other subroutines we have written so far and stick those that might be useful again into a module. Hint: some of the array and string subroutines we've seen are likely candidates.

Exercise 9-12: Interlocking Words

First, it seems that it was a good idea to create the BisectSearch module; it's going to be reused immediately.

Second, we need some thinking. The first idea that might come to mind to solve the problem might be to have a nested loop on the word list in order to find all pairs of two words, interlock them, and see if the resulting combined string exists in the list. But this is quite bad, because it means creating 113,000 squared pairs, i.e., more than 12.5 billion pairs. Even if a relatively large part of these pairs can be eliminated before having to look up the word list, since a pair can be interlocked only if the letter count difference between the two words is 0 or 1, checking all these pairs will take ages.

Let us see what happens if we work the other way around: for each word on the word list, we "intersplit" the word into one string with the even-rank letters and one with the odd-rank letters, and then check if these substrings belong to the list. At most, we will need 226,000 searches—in fact much less because we don't need to look up the second string if the first string did not match anything:

This is our suggested solution:

```
use lib ".";
use BisectSearch;

my @array = 'words.txt'.IO.lines;
for @array -> $word {
    my ($word1, $word2) = intersplit($word);
    say "$word: $word1, $word2" if bisect($word1, @array) >= 0
        and bisect($word2, @array) >= 0;
```

```
    }
    sub intersplit (Str $word) {
        my @letters = $word.comb;
        my $evens = join '', map {@letters[$_] if $_ %% 2}, @letters.keys;
        my $odds = join '', map {@letters[$_] if $_ % 2}, @letters.keys;
        return ($evens, $odds);
    }
```

The intersplit subroutine is not optimal in the sense that it traverses the @letters array twice each time it is called. We can improve it using a pointy block taking two parameters (one odd- and one even-rank letters):

```
    sub intersplit (Str $word) {
        my (@evens, @odds);
        for $word.comb -> $even, $odd {
            push @evens, $even;
            push @odds, $odd;
        }
        @evens.join, @odds.join;
    }
```

As a further exercise, can you find any words that are three-way interlocked; that is, every third letter forms a word, starting from the first, second, or third? Hint: it will probably be easier if you start from the revised version of intersplit just above.

Exercises of Chapter 10: Hashes

Exercise: A Hash Is a Mapping

This is the solution to the exercise at the end of "A Hash Is a Mapping" on page 183. Here's how to populate one pair at a time:

```
my %wages;
%wages{"Liz"} = 3000;
%wages{"Bob"} = 2500;
%wages{"Jack"} = 2000;
%wages{"Betty"} = 1800;
say "Bob's salary is %wages{'Bob'}";
for <Liz Jack> -> $employee {
    say "The salary of $employee is %wages{$employee};
}
```

You can avoid quotation marks around the keys by using the <...> angle brackets operator:

```
my %wages;
%wages<Liz> = 3000;
%wages<Bob> = 2500;
# ...
say "Bob's salary is %wages<Bob>";
```

And here's how to assign the full hash in one go:

```
my %wages = Liz => 3000, Bob => 2500, Jack => 2000, Betty => 1800;
say %wages; # -> Betty => 1800, Bob => 2500, Jack => 2000, Liz => 3000
```

Exercise 10-1: Storing the Word List into a Hash

The standard way to store the word list in a hash might be to read each line of the file in a for loop and store each word as the key of the hash. The content of the value is not important; we will store 1 (it may also make sense to store the True Boolean value):

```
my %words;
for 'words.txt'.IO.lines -> $line {
    %words{$line} = 1
}
```

An alternative approach is to assign to the hash the output of a map expression returning a pair for each line of the file:

```
my %hash = map { $_ => 1}, 'words.txt'.IO.lines;
```

Exercise 10-2: Memoizing the Ackermann Function

The original implementation of the Ackermann function looked like this:

```
sub ack ($m, $n) {
    return $n + 1 if $m == 0;
    return ack($m - 1, 1) if $n == 0;
    return ack($m - 1, ack($m, $n-1));
}
```

It is not possible to memoize the cases where either $m or $n is zero, because the other value is unknown. Only the code corresponding to the last code line can be memoized, but that's okay because it does the bulk of the work anyway.

The next problem is that the hashes seen so far had only one key, but the Ackermann function takes two parameters. The simple workaround is to create a composite key, i.e., to concatenate the two parameters with a separator to create the keys of the hash. This leads to this possible solution:

```
my %ack-memo;
sub mem-ack (Int $m, Int $n) {
    return $n + 1 if $m == 0;
    return mem-ack($m - 1, 1) if $n == 0;
    %ack-memo{"$m;$n"} = mem-ack($m - 1, mem-ack($m, $n-1))
        unless %ack-memo{"$m;$n"}:exists;
    return %ack-memo{"$m;$n"};
}
say mem-ack 3, 4;
```

To benchmark the two solutions, you may use the following code:

```
my %ack-memo;
sub mem-ack (Int $m, Int $n) {
    return $n + 1 if $m == 0;
    return mem-ack($m - 1, 1) if $n == 0;
    %ack-memo{"$m;$n"} = mem-ack($m - 1, mem-ack($m, $n-1))
        unless %ack-memo{"$m;$n"}:exists;
    return %ack-memo{"$m;$n"};
}
my $start = now;
say mem-ack 3, 4;
say "mem-ack runtime: ", now - $start;
dd %ack-memo;

sub ack ($m, $n) {
    return $n + 1 if $m == 0;
    return ack($m - 1, 1) if $n == 0;
    return ack($m - 1, ack($m, $n-1));
}
$start = now;
say ack 3, 4;
say "ack runtime: ", now - $start;
```

But don't try to run it with values of $m greater than 3; it is useless. If we were to find an Ackermann value for a pair of numbers already seen, that would mean that we have entered an infinite loop. So there is in fact no point trying to memoize the Ackermann function.

We have used composite keys for %ack-memo, but we can use multidimensional hashes just as there are multidimensional arrays (see "Multidimensional Arrays" on page 171). We only need to have two keys, each between its pair of curly brackets:

```
my %h;
%h{'a'}{'b'}= 'ab';
%h{'a'}{'c'}= 'ac';
%h{'a'}{'d'}= 'ad';
%h{'b'}{'c'}= 'bc';
dd %h;
# -> Hash %h = {:a(${:b("ab"), :c("ac"), :d("ad")}), :b(${:c("bc")})}
```

or we can use a semicolon to separate the keys:

```
my %i;
%i{'a';'b'} = 'ab';
%i{'a';'c'} = 'ac';
%i{'b';'c'} = 'bc';
dd %i; # -> Hash %i = {:a(${:b("ab"), :c("ac")}), :b(${:c("bc")})}
```

Exercise 10-3: Finding Duplicates with a Hash

We need to loop on the array, store the array elements in a hash, and detect whether an element is found in the hash. Here's one way to do that:

```
sub has-duplicates (@array) {
    my %seen;
    for @array -> $elmt {
        return True if %seen{$elmt}:exists;
        %seen{$elmt} = 1;
    }
    return False;
}
```

As a further exercise, generate a list of 50,000 random integers between 0 and 1,000,000,000, and then, using the various methods we have demonstrated, check to see whether this list contains any duplicates and measure the runtime of these various methods. If you encounter difficulties doing this, take a look at the solutions to the "has duplicates" (see "Exercise 9-7: Subroutine has-duplicates" on page 391) and "birthday paradox" (see "Exercise 9-8: Simulating the Birthday Paradox" on page 392) exercises to get some coding clues. An example of simple benchmarking is presented in the exercise just above.

Once your subroutines are working properly, launch the whole process at least 10 times to see if the differences are significant.

Exercise 10-4: Rotate Pairs

Consider the word "iron" and rotate it by three letters. This gives the word "folk." This also means that if "folk" is rotated by 23 letters, we will get "iron." Since we are going to scan all the words of our word list, we will find this "rotate pair" when we try a shift of three letters on "iron," so that there no need to try a 23-letter rotation on "folk." More generally, we need to try only rotations between 1 and 13 letters.

The following code iterates through the words of the list, rotates each of them by every shift between 1 and 13, and looks up the result in the hash:

```
sub rotate-one-letter (Str $letter, Int $shift) {
    my $last  = 'z'.ord;        # last lower-case letter
    my $rotated-ord = $letter.ord + $shift;
    if $letter ~~ /<[a..z]>/ {
        $rotated-ord -= 26 if $rotated-ord > $last;
    } else {
        return $letter;
    }
    return $rotated-ord.chr;
}

sub rotate-one-word (Str $word, Int $shift) {
    my $rotated-word = "";
```

```
        for 0..$word.chars - 1 {
            $rotated-word ~= rotate-one-letter substr($word, $_, 1), $shift;
        }
        return $rotated-word;
    }

    my %words = map { $_ => 1}, 'words.txt'.IO.lines;

    for %words.keys -> $string {
        for 1..13 -> $shift {
            my $rotated = rotate-one-word $string, $shift;
            say " $string and $rotated are shifted by $shift"
                if %words{$rotated}:exists;
        }
    }
```

Rotating each word of a 113,000 list by each shift between 1 and 13 is quite long. Running the program on the word list will take some time, probably on the order of 10 to 15 minutes. Using the .trans built-in (see the documentation (*https:// docs.perl6.org/routine/trans*)) might speed up the process. Try it and judge for yourself.

Exercise 10-5: Homophones

We are looking for words that *sound* the same when we remove either the first or the second letter.

This is a solution using both the *words.txt* word list and the CMU phonetic dictionary:

```
    my %phonetic;

    sub load-phonetic ($file-name) {
        for $file-name.IO.lines -> $line {
            next if $line !~~ /^\w/;
            my ($key, $val) = $line.split("   ", 2);
            $key = lc $key;
            %phonetic{$key} = $val;
        }
    }

    load-phonetic('cmu_dict.txt');
    my %words = map { $_ => 1}, 'words.txt'.IO.lines;

    say "Starting the search";

    for %words.keys -> $word {
        next unless %phonetic{$word}:exists;
        my $shorter = $word.substr(1);
        next unless %words{$shorter}:exists;
        next unless %phonetic{$shorter}:exists;
```

```
    next unless %phonetic{$word} eq %phonetic{$shorter};
    my $other-shorter = $word.substr(0, 1) ~ $word.substr(2);
    next unless %words{$other-shorter}:exists;
    next unless %phonetic{$other-shorter}:exists;
    next unless %phonetic{$other-shorter} eq %phonetic{$shorter};
    say "$word $shorter $other-shorter %phonetic{$shorter}"
}
```

But this is somewhat inefficient because we don't actually need the word list, since the CMU dictionary is another word list that we can use (and we can't use words that would be in the word list and not in the CMU dictionary, because the program wouldn't be able to figure out how they sound). The following program uses only the CMU dictionary and saves the time to load the word list and do checks on it:

```
my %phonetic;

sub load-phonetic ($file-name) {
    for $file-name.IO.lines -> $line {
        next if $line !~~ /^\w/;
        my ($key, $val) = $line.split(" ", 2);
        $key = lc $key;
        %phonetic{$key} = $val;
    }
}

load-phonetic('cmu_dict.txt');

for %phonetic.keys -> $word {
    my $shorter = $word.substr(1);
    next unless %phonetic{$shorter}:exists;
    next unless %phonetic{$word} eq %phonetic{$shorter};
    my $other-shorter = $word.substr(0, 1) ~ $word.substr(2);
    next unless %phonetic{$other-shorter}:exists;
    next unless %phonetic{$other-shorter} eq %phonetic{$shorter};
    say "$word $shorter $other-shorter %phonetic{$shorter}"
}
```

Exercises of Chapter 11

Exercise: The given ... when switch statement

This is the solution to the exercise in "The given ... when "Switch" Statement" on page 204. To test the switch statement with various values, you might write something like this:

```
for <5 42 43 101 666 1024 2048> -> $value {
    given $value {
        when 0..9      { say "$_: One digit"}
        when 10..99    { say "$_: Two digits" ; proceed; }
        when 42        { say "$_: Response to the question" }
```

```
        when /^\d**3$/ { say "$_: Three digits" }
        default        { say "$_: More than three digits" }
    }
    say '';
}
```

This will display the following result:

```
5: One digit

42: Two digits
42: Response to the question

43: Two digits
43: More than three digits

101: Three digits
(...)
```

You can see the error when the input value is 43.

As a solution, it is possible to change the order of the when clauses:

```
for <5 42 43 101 666 1024 2048> -> $value {
    given $value {
        when 0..9      { say "$_: One digit"}
        when 42        { say "$_: Response to the question"; proceed; }
        when 10..99    { say "$_: Two digits"}
        when /^\d**3$/ { say "$_: Three digits" }
        default        { say "$_: More than three digits" }
    }
    say '';
}
```

This now works correctly, but the output for 42 is no longer in the same order. If we want to keep the original order, we may need to add a when statement with an empty block:

```
for <5 42 43 101 666 1024 2048> -> $value {
    given $value {
        when 0..9      { say "$_: One digit"}
        when 10..99    { say "$_: Two digits"; proceed}
        when 42        { say "$_: Response to the question"; }
        when 10..99    { }
        when /^\d**3$/ { say "$_: Three digits" }
        default        { say "$_: More than three digits" }
    }
    say '';
}
```

Or we could remove the need for proceed by inserting the code for the 42 case into the two-digit block:

```
for <5 42 43 101 666 1024 2048> -> $value {
    given $value {
        when 0..9      { say "$_: One digit"}
        when 10..99    { say "$_: Two digits";
                         say "$_: Response to the question" if $_ == 42
                       }
        when /^\d**3$/ { say "$_: Three digits" }
        default        { say "$_: More than three digits" }
    }
    say '';
}
```

It would also be possible to nest a when subexpression within the when 10..99 expression:

```
for <5 42 43 101 666 1024 2048> -> $value {
    given $value {
        when 0..9      { say "$_: One digit"}
        when 10..99    { say "$_: Two digits";
                         when 42 {say "$_: Response to the question";}
                       }
        when /^\d**3$/ { say "$_: Three digits" }
        default        { say "$_: More than three digits" }
    }
    say '';
}
```

Exercise: Constructing New Operators

This is the solution to the exercise in "Constructing New Operators" on page 214. The "!" negation operator is a prefix operator (i.e., placed before the term that it negates). For the factorial operator, we need a postfix operator (placed after the term upon which it acts), so this difference will be sufficient to enable the Perl compiler to distinguish between the two operators.

We use the reduction metaoperator to compute the result:

```
sub postfix:<!> (Int $n) {
    [*] 2..$n;
}
say 5!; # -> 120
```

The signature ensures the operand is an integer (failing which we get an error). We may want to guard against a negative integer, which we can do by raising an error if $n is negative. In addition, we can use the Test standard module to automatize our tests:

```
sub postfix:<!> (Int $n) {
    fail "The operand is not a positive integer" if $n < 0;
    [*] 2..$n
}
use Test;
```

```
plan 5;
dies-ok {(-1)!}, "Factorial fails for -1";
eval-dies-ok "(2.5)!", "Factorial fails for 2.5";
ok 0! == 1, "Factorial 0";
ok 1! == 1, "Factorial 1";
ok 5! == 120, "Factorial of a larger integer";
done-testing;
```

The plan 5; line says that the test plan contains five individual tests. Then the two first tests check that the factorial operator fails for invalid input values. And it checks the output for some valid input.

The done-testing specifies that the test has finished. This function is really useful when you don't have a plan, for example when you don't know yet how many tests you'll run. Here, we have a plan, so using done-testing isn't necessary.

The following is the output of the tests:

```
1..5
ok 1 - Factorial fails for -1
ok 2 - Factorial fails for 2.5
ok 3 - Factorial 0
ok 4 - Factorial 1
ok 5 - Factorial of a larger integer
```

If we had a test error on test 3, we would have obtained something like this:

```
ok 1 - Factorial fails for -1
ok 2 - Factorial fails for 2.5
not ok 3 - Factorial 0

# Failed test 'Factorial 0'
# at test_fact.pl6 line 8
ok 4 - Factorial 1
ok 5 - Factorial of a larger integer
1..5
# Looks like you failed 1 test of 5
```

Here, we have put the tests in the same file as the subroutine definition for the sake of simplicity of the example. Normally, the tests would be in a separate file, usually in a "t" directory and with a .t extension.

Testing and the Test module are further discussed in "Debugging" on page 329. More information about testing can be found in the Perl 6 documentation (*https://doc.perl6.org/language/testing*).

Exercise: Sets, Bags, and Mixes

This is the solution to the exercise in "Sets, Bags, and Mixes" on page 215. We can't just replace the %histogram with a bag, because bags are immutable (i.e., cannot be changed after creation) and the %histogram hash is populated progressively as the lines of the book are being read from the file. You may use a baghash (the mutable version of a bag) and are encouraged to try it.

However, the aim here is to extract the words of the book that are not in the word list. In other words, we no longer care about word frequencies, but just need a unique list of words that appear at least once in the book, so a set would be sufficient to satisfy our needs. The question is how to populate the set at creation time.

We can change the process-line subroutine so that it processes the line as previously but, instead of populating a hash, just returns the list of words. And we can create the set with a map function calling that subroutine:

```
my $skip = True;                        # flag to skip the header
sub process-line(Str $line is copy) {
    $skip = False if defined index $line, "*END*THE SMALL PRINT!";
    next if $skip;
    $line ~~ s:g/<[-']>/ /;             # Replacing dashes and
                                        # apostrophes with spaces
    $line ~~ s:g/<[;:,!?.()"_`]>//;     # removing punctuation symbols
    $line = $line.lc;                   # setting string to lowercase
    return $line.words;
}

my $book-set = set map { process-line $_}, "emma.txt".IO.lines;
my $word-list = set "words.txt".IO.lines;
my $unknown-words = $book-set (-) $word-list;
say $unknown-words.keys.head(20);
```

This works well, but once we've done that, we can also get rid of the $book-set data structure and just filter directly the words extracted from the book:

```
my $skip = True; # flag to skip the header

sub process-line($line is copy) {
    # (same as above)
}

my $word-list = set "words.txt".IO.lines;
my @unknown-words = unique grep {$_ ∉ $word-list},
                    grep { $_ },
                    map { | process-line $_},
                    "emma.txt".IO.lines;
say @unknown-words.head(20);
```

Testing such a program may take some time, because it has to process the full book each time. For the purposes of initial testing, one tip is to reduce the amount of input data to speed up the tests. You may achieve that by preparing a smaller file with just a limited number of lines from the original *emma.txt* file. Another simple way is to read only some lines from the book, which you can do with a slice on the code line that reads the file. For example, to read only the first 2,000 lines of the book file:

```
my @unknown-words = unique grep {$_ ∉ $word-list},
                    grep { $_ },
                    map { | process-line $_},
                    ("emma.txt".IO.lines)[0..1999];
```

This can also be used to get rid of the header. Since the actual text of the book starts on line 254, we can have:

```
my @unknown-words = unique grep {$_ ∉ $word-list},
                    grep { $_ },
                    map { | process-line $_},
                    ("emma.txt".IO.lines)[253..1999];
```

and remove from `process-line` the code to skip the header.

Exercise: Random Words

This is the solution to the exercise in "Random Words" on page 217. We have made a `BisectSearch` module containing a `bisect` subroutine. It would be great to reuse it, but we can't because it is currently doing string comparisons and we need numerical comparisons.

The best solution at this point is probably to make a copy of the subroutine and modify it to make numeric comparisons. The subroutines can have the same name provided they are declared as multi subroutines and have a different signature: the first parameter of the new multi subroutine should be an `Int` instead of a `Str`. Since the changes to be made are quite small and easy, this is left as an exercise for the reader.

The program using that module might look like this:

```
use lib ".";
use BisectSearch;
my %histogram;

sub process-line(Str $line is copy) {
    $line ~~ s:g/<[-']>/ /;
    $line ~~ s:g/<[;:,!?.()"_`]>//;
    $line = $line.lc;
    return $line.words;
}
%histogram{$_}++ for grep {$_},
                    map { | process-line $_},
                    ("emma.txt".IO.lines)[253..*];
my (@words, @freqs);
my $total_freq = 0;
for %histogram.kv -> $word, $freq {
    $total_freq += $freq;
    push @words, $word;
    push @freqs, $total_freq;
}
my $rand_int = $total_freq.rand.Int;
```

```
my $idx = bisect $rand_int, @freqs;
say @words[$idx];
```

Exercise: Markov Analysis

This is the solution to the exercise in "Markov Analysis" on page 219. But before we present our solution, we want to briefly introduce a functionality that is useful for retrieving and validating the command-line arguments passed to a program: the MAIN subroutine.

The MAIN subroutine

The arguments passed to a program are usually stored in the @*ARGS special array. You can just browse the items of this array to retrieve the arguments. The following one-liner is an example of this:

```
$ perl6 -e 'say $_ for reverse @*ARGS' one two three
three
two
one
```

There is however another way to do it, the MAIN subroutine that we briefly discussed in "Program Arguments and the MAIN Subroutine" on page 69. If there is a subroutine called MAIN in the program, then the program will start by executing this subroutine, whose parameters will be the arguments passed to the program. This means that the signature of the MAIN subroutine will make it possible to retrieve the parameters and check their validity.

In our example solution below, the MAIN subroutine is declared as follows:

```
sub MAIN (Str $book, Int $word-count, Int $order = 2,
          Int $start-line = 0) {
    # body of subroutine here
}
```

The program will thus check that the arguments passed to it match the MAIN subroutine signature. In the example, the first parameter has to be a string and the second one an integer; the third and fourth parameters are optional and will be defaulted respectively to 2 and 0 if the corresponding arguments are not provided.

If the arguments passed to the program don't match the MAIN signature, the program will die after having printed an automatically generated usage message:

```
$ perl6  markov.pl6 emma.txt 100 2 foo
Usage:
  markov.pl6 <book> <word-count> [<order>] [<start-line>]
```

The $start-line parameter has to be an integer. Since the corresponding argument ("foo") is not an integer, the program displays a message showing the program usage.

Validating the command-line arguments passed to a program can sometimes be a relatively tedious task. But, with this MAIN subroutine signature mechanism, it can often be reduced to a single line of code, the MAIN signature.

Solution to the Markov analysis exercise

This is a possible way to perform a Markov analysis of a text file:

```
my %prefixes;

sub MAIN (Str $book, Int $word-count, Int $order = 2,
             Int $start-line = 0) {
    process-line($order, $_) for ($book.IO.lines)[$start-line..*];
    say make-text($order, $word-count);
}

sub process-line($order, Str $line is copy) {
    $line ~~ s:g/<[-']>/ /;
    $line ~~ s:g/<[;:,!?.()"_`]>//; # removing punctuation symbols
    $line = $line.lc;               # setting string to lowercase
    return unless $line ~~ /\w/;
    process-words($order, $line.words);
}

sub process-words ($order, @new-words) {
    state @word-buffer = ();
    push @word-buffer, |@new-words;
    while (@word-buffer.elems >= $order * 2) {
        my $key = @word-buffer.shift ~ " " ~
            (join ' ', @word-buffer[0..$order - 2]);
        my $value = @word-buffer[$order -1];
        push %prefixes{$key}, $value;
    }
}

sub make-text (Int $order, Int $w-count) {
    my @prefix = %prefixes.keys.pick.words;
    my $count = 0;
    my $text = join " ", @prefix;
    while $count <= $w-count {
        my @possible-suffixes = |%prefixes{join " ", @prefix};
        last unless @possible-suffixes;
        my $new-word = |@possible-suffixes.pick;
        $text ~= " $new-word";
        shift @prefix;
        push @prefix, |$new-word;
        $count++
    }
    return $text;
}
```

This program may be called on the *emma.txt* file with the following syntax:

```
$ perl6  markov.pl6 emma.txt 100 2 253
```

Exercise: The Huffman Code

Exercise 11-8: The frequency table

This is the solution to the exercises in "Exercises: Huffman Coding" on page 230. We have already seen problems similar to this one. This is a possible solution using the pipeline programming model described in "Most Common Words" on page 212:

```
my %frequencies;
%frequencies{$_}++ for grep {/<[a..z]>/}, map {.lc},
    "goldbug.txt".IO.lines.comb;
my $total_count = [+] values %frequencies;
say "$_ :\t%frequencies{$_} \t",
    sprintf "%5.2f", %frequencies{$_}*100/$total_count
    for reverse sort {%frequencies{$_}}, %frequencies.keys;
```

This displays:

```
e :     7625    13.10
t :     5485     9.42
a :     4477     7.69
o :     4208     7.23
i :     4183     7.18
n :     3912     6.72
s :     3516     6.04
h :     3372     5.79
r :     3278     5.63
d :     2533     4.35
l :     2324     3.99
u :     1893     3.25
c :     1523     2.62
m :     1499     2.57
f :     1392     2.39
w :     1303     2.24
p :     1169     2.01
y :     1146     1.97
g :     1143     1.96
b :     1031     1.77
v :      525     0.90
k :      351     0.60
x :      120     0.21
j :      111     0.19
q :       60     0.10
z :       44     0.08
```

Remember that Edgar Allan Poe's character claimed the succession of the most commonly used letters in English ran as follows:

```
e a o i d h n r s t u y c f g l m w b k p q x z
```

So it appears that Poe's character was approximately right, but certainly not very accurate, in his estimates of the letter frequencies in an English text. It appears that he especially grossly underestimated the frequency of the "t" letter. Running the same program against the text of Jane Austen's novel *Emma* that we have used previously produces very close results:

```
e :     87029    12.57
t :     60035     8.67
a :     54884     7.93
o :     53877     7.78
n :     47773     6.90
i :     47172     6.82
s :     42920     6.20
h :     42819     6.19
r :     41453     5.99
d :     28870     4.17
l :     27971     4.04
(...)
```

Exercise 11-9: Huffman coding of a DNA strand

At each step in the algorithm, we need to look for the two letters with the lowest frequencies. Rather than having to repeatedly go through all the items in the frequency hash (or to sort the values each time), we will use a data structure maintaining the values sorted according to our needs.

We start with the %frequencies hash built in the previous exercise and transform it into a sorted collection of pairs mapping each letter to its frequency. We create an insert-pair subroutine that adds the newly created pairs (the dummy letters) at the right place in the pair array to keep the array sorted according to our needs:

```
my %code;
my @pairs;
push @pairs, $_ => %frequencies{$_} for
    sort {%frequencies{$_}}, %frequencies.keys;

sub insert-pair (@list, $new-elem) {
    my $val = $new-elem.value;
    for @list.keys -> $i {
        if @list[$i].value >= $val {
            splice @list, $i, 0, $new-elem;
            return;
        }
    }
    push @list, $new-elem; # putting the new element at the end of
                           # the list if right place not found earlier
}
```

We loop over the pairs, pick up the two with the smallest frequencies, merge them into a new pair, and add it at the right place with the insert-pair subroutine. The loop ends when there are only two pairs left. At the same time, we populate at each step of the loop the new %code hash with the partial codes found:

```
loop {
    my $least1 = shift @pairs;
    my $least2 = shift @pairs;
    my $new-pair = $least1.key ~ $least2.key => $least1.value + $least2.value;
    insert-pair @pairs, $new-pair;
    %code{$least1.key} =  $least1.key ~ $least2.key ~ "|.";
    %code{$least2.key} =  $least1.key ~ $least2.key ~ "|-";
    last if @pairs <= 2;
}
%code{@pairs[0].key} = ".";
%code{@pairs[1].key} = "-";
```

At the end of the loop, the pair array contains two pairs:

```
[c => 10 tga => 11]
```

and the %code hash contains the partial codes for each letter or dummy letter:

```
{a => ga|-, c => ., g => ga|., ga => tga|-, t => tga|., tga => -}
```

We then use another loop to substitute the pseudoletters and get rid of them, until we are left with only the actual letters of the original input string:

```
loop {
    my $done = True;
    for %code.keys -> $letter {
        next if $letter.chars > 1;
        my ($val, $code) = split '|', %code{$letter};
        next unless defined $val and defined $code;
        $done = False;
        my $result = %code{$val} ~ $code;
        %code{$letter} = $result;
    }
    last if $done;
}
my %encode;
%encode{$_} = %code{$_} for grep {$_.chars < 2 }, %code.keys;
```

The %encode hash contains the Huffman table:

```
c => .
t => -.
g => --.
a => ---
```

Exercise 11-9: Huffman coding of a more complex string

For this question, we will use a small paragraph specially written to contain only a few letters of the alphabet:

Eastern Tennessee anteaters ensnare and eat red ants, detest ant antennae (a tart taste) and dread Antarean anteater-eaters. Rare Andean deer eat tender sea reeds, aster seeds and rats' ears. Dessert? Rats' asses.

As a first step, we will fold all letters to lowercase and use only the letters, eliminating spaces and punctuation from the computation of the frequency table:

```
my $string = "Eastern Tennessee anteaters ensnare and eat red ants, detest ant
antennae (a tart taste) and dread Antarean anteater-eaters. Rare
Andean deer eat tender sea reeds, aster seeds and rats' ears. Dessert?
Rats' asses.";

my %frequencies;
%frequencies{$_}++ for grep { /\w/ }, $string.lc.comb;
```

This eloquent treatise on the eating habits of various fauna yields the following frequency table:

```
e :    40      23.53
a :    32      18.82
t :    24      14.12
s :    22      12.94
n :    20      11.76
r :    19      11.18
d :    13      7.65
```

Using the same code as in the previous question generates the following Huffman table:

```
a => ..
e => .-
s => -.-
n => -..
t => --.
d => ---.
r => ----
```

Exercise 11-9: Encoding the input string

We want not only to encode an input string with the Huffman code, but we also want to then be able to decode it and to recognize the original input. Because of that, we no longer want to filter out punctuation from the translation table, which will therefore grow much larger than before. Spaces (both horizontal spaces and line returns) will be handled differently: we'll keep them unchanged in the encoded pseudo-Morse string, as this will make it easier to check and to display the result.

The frequency table now includes punctuation characters that exist in the input string:

```
%frequencies{$_}++ for grep {/<[\w] + [.,()'?-]>/}, $string.lc.comb;
```

The frequency table now has 14 entries:

```
e :     40      22.10
a :     32      17.68
t :     24      13.26
s :     22      12.15
n :     20      11.05
r :     19      10.50
d :     13       7.18
. :      3       1.66
, :      2       1.10
' :      2       1.10
) :      1       0.55
- :      1       0.55
? :      1       0.55
( :      1       0.55
```

And the Huffman table (%encode hash) now looks like this:

```
e => .-
a => ---
s => -..
n => ..-
t => --.
r => ...
d => -.--
. => -.-.-.
( => -.-..-.
' => -.-.--.
? => -.-..--
) => -.-...-
- => -.-....
, => -.-.---
```

The encoding subroutine is very simple:

```
sub encoding (Str $input, %encode) {
    my $output;
    for $input.lc.comb -> $letter {
        $output ~= %encode{$letter} // $letter;
    }
    return $output;
}
```

Each letter of the input is converted to lowercase (since we have limited our table to lowercase), translated into its pseudo-Morse code equivalent and concatenated to the output string. If a letter is not found in the %encode hash, then it is stored into the output as it is: this makes it possible to insert the spaces and end-of-line characters into the output string.

The result is as follows (slightly reformatted to fit in this book):

```
.------..--..-.....- --.,-.-.-.-.--.,...-.- ---.,----.------.,-..,-..
.-..-.........---.,...- ---.,--.-- .------. ......--.-- ---.,---.-.,-.-.---
-.--.---.,..,.-. ---.,---.
```

Interestingly, the input string has 213 characters and the output string has 589 bits. If we were storing the 14 different characters of the input with equal-length codes, we would need four bits per character, which would require 1052 bits. So Huffman coding achieved a compression ratio 1.78 times better than the best possible equal-length codes. And the ASCII encoding of the input string required 213 bytes, i.e., 1704 bits; the Huffman-encoded output required almost three times less.

Exercise 11-9: Decoding the pseudo-Morse string

For decoding efficiently the pseudo-Morse string, we need to reverse the Huffman table, i.e., create a hash in which the pseudo-Morse codes are the keys and the letters are the values. Reversing the %encode hash is straightforward:

```
my %decode = reverse %encode.kv;
```

The %encode.kv expression produces a list of keys and values, and the reverse statement transforms it into a list of values and keys. Assigning that list to a new hash produces a new hash in which keys and values are swapped. Note that this works because we know that the values are unique, so that there is no problem of duplicates when promoting them to hash keys.

Decoding the pseudo-Morse string is a bit more complicated than its encoding, because we don't know in advance how many dots and dashes will be needed to obtain a letter. So we need to look at the first character (say a dot) of the pseudo-Morse string. If this character alone constitutes an entry in the translation table, then we have found our first letter, and we can start afresh with the next character as a starting point of a new letter; if not, we need to pick up the next character and see whether the two first characters together form an entry; if yes, we have found a letter and can start from the beginning again; if not we need to see whether the first three characters together form an entry in the table, and so on.

For example, with the beginning of the pseudo-Morse string:

```
.-----..--..-.....-
```

the first dot is not an entry but the ".-" combination is an "e". The next dash is not an entry, and neither is "--", but "---" is an "a". The next dash is not an entry, and neither is "-.", but "-.." is a "s". Similarly, the next three characters, "--.", form a "t", and we can go on to decode the word "eastern".

We might implement this with two nested loops: one to go through the string and the second one to consume the necessary number of dots and dashes until the end of a letter:

```
sub decoding (Str $input, %decode) {
    my @codes = $input.comb;
    my $output;
    loop {
        last unless @codes;
        my $current = shift @codes;
        $output ~= $current and next if $current ~~ /\s/;
        $output ~= %decode{$current} and next if %decode{$current}:exists;
        loop {            # we need more characters to complete a letter
            $current ~= shift @codes;
            if %decode{$current}:exists {
                $output ~= %decode{$current};
                last;    # we're done with a letter, go back to main loop
            }
        }
    }
    return $output;
}
```

This works properly and the output is the same as the original input (except for the fact that we have folded everything to lowercase):

```
eastern tennessee anteaters ensnare and eat red ants, detest ant
antennae (a tart taste) and dread antarean anteater-eaters. rare
andean deer eat tender sea reeds, aster seeds and rats' ears. dessert?
rats' asses.
```

However, if you think about it, we don't really need two nested loops in the decoding subroutine, which can be made a bit more concise as follows:

```
sub decoding (Str $input, %decode) {
    my ($output, $current);
    for $input.comb -> $in-code {
        $output ~= $in-code and next if $in-code ~~ /\s/;
        $current ~= $in-code;
        if %decode{$current}:exists {
            $output ~= %decode{$current};
            $current = "";
        }
    }
    return $output;
}
```

Here, the $current variable accumulates the dots and dashes from the input until it is found to be an entry in the translation table, at which point it is reset to an empty string to prepare for the next letter.

The solution presented above for finding the Huffman code uses the `insert-pair` subroutine to keep ordered the `@pairs` array of pairs. This makes it easy to find the remaining least common letters or pseudo-letters. You might remember from "Binary Heaps" on page 224 that heaps are a good data structure when the aim is to rapidly access the smallest items of a collection. As a further exercise, you may want to rewrite the solution using a binary heap. David Huffman's original solution actually used a tree (called the Huffman tree) very similar to a heap.

Exercises of Chapter 13: Regexes and Grammars

Exercise 13-1: Getting the February Dates Right

We want to check if the February dates are valid.

To begin with, let's exclude February dates that are larger than 29. This can be done by just expanding the code assertion shown in the code to recognize dates:

```
my $string = "Leap day : 2016-02-29.";
my token year { \d ** 4 }
my token month {
    1 <[0..2]>                          # 10 to 12
    || 0 <[1..9]>                       # 01 to 09
};
my token day { (\d ** 2) <?{1 <= $0 <= 31 }> }
my token sep { '/' || '-' }
my rule date { [   <year> (<sep>) <month> $0 <day>
                || <day> (<sep>) <month> $0 <year>
                || <month>\s<day>',' <year>
               ] <!{ ($<day> > 30 and $<month> ==  4|6|9|11) or
                     $<day> > 29 and $<month> eq '02' }>
}

if $string ~~ /<date>/ {
    say ~$/;                            # 2016-02-29
    say "Day\t= "   , ~$/<date><day>;   # 29
    say "Month\t= " , ~$/<date><month>; # 02
    say "Year\t= "  , ~$/<date><year>;  # 2016
}
```

This is fine. February has 29 days since 2016 is a leap year. But this code would validate Feb. 29 for 2015 or 2017, which is wrong since they are not leap years.

Recognizing a leap year

In the old Julian calendar (named after Julius Caesar), leap years are years that are divisible by 4. It turned out that the Julian calendar had too many leap years to reflect the astronomical reality, so that the calendar drifted about three days for every period of four centuries.

The Gregorian calendar, introduced by Pope Gregory XIII in 1582, corrected the Julian calendar with the following additional rule: years divisible by 100 should be leap only if they are also divisible by 400. So, by the Gregorian calendar, 1700, 1800, 1900, and 2100 are not leap, but 2000 and 2400 are leap.

Depending on what kind of dates your program is going to encounter, you might decide to simplify the rules. If you are writing a module that is supposed to be accurate for any date far in the past or in the future, you probably want to implement the exact Gregorian rule. But if you know that you're going to meet only dates of the current period, you might choose a much simpler rule.

In particular, since 2000 is an exception to the exception and is leap, any year between 1901 and 2099 is leap if it is divisible by 4 and not leap otherwise. This rule is likely sufficient for any business application written in 2017. There is probably no reason to make it more complicated than it needs to be (although it may be argued that it is the same type of reasoning that led to the great fear of the "Y2K" bug).

With this simplification in mind, a subroutine to find out if a year is leap should simply return True if it is divisible by 4 and might thus look like this:

```
sub is-leap ($year) { # works for years between 1901 and 2099
    return True if $year %% 4;
    return False;
}
```

Or simpler:

```
sub is-leap ($year) { # works for years between 1901 and 2099
    return $year %% 4;
}
```

If you want to implement the full Gregorian rule, it might look like this:

```
sub is-leap ($year) { # Gregorian rule for any year
    return False if $year % 4;    # no if not divisible by 4
    return True if $year % 100;   # yes if divisible by 4 and not by 100
    return False if $year % 400;  # no if divisible by 100 and not by 400
    True;                         # yes if divisible by 400
}
```

or, if you like concision (or obfuscation):

```
sub is-leap ($y) { $y %% 400 or ($y %% 4 and not $y %% 100) }
```

The code above is given as an example on how to compute whether a year is leap, since it is an interesting and classical problem, but Perl actually provides a method for that in the Dateish role. For example:

```
> say Dateish.is-leap-year(2016)
True
> say Dateish.is-leap-year(2015)
False
```

Back to the February date validation

You *can* add the rules for Feb. 29 in the code example above if you wish, but we would suggest this is getting slightly too complicated for a code assertion within the date rule: adding a quick Boolean condition in a code assertion within a rule is fine, but when the condition becomes more complicated, it will tend to make the rule more difficult to understand. Think about the person who will have to maintain the code in a year from now (and that person might be you).

We prefer to move the code performing the validation out of the date rule into a dedicated subroutine checking all dates for February:

```
sub feb-date-not-valid ($year, $day) {
    return False if $day <= 28;
    return True if $day > 29;
    return False if Dateish.is-leap-year($year);
    True;
}
```

The date rule now looks like this:

```
my rule date { [    <year> (<sep>) <month> $0 <day>
                || <day> (<sep>) <month> $0 <year>
                || <month>\s<day>',' <year>
              ] <!{ ($<day> > 30 and $<month> ==  4|6|9|11) or
                      $<month> eq '02' and feb-date-not-valid $<year>, $<day>}>
}
```

I had originally called the new subroutine check-feb-29 but I changed it to feb-date-not-valid in order to better show that it returns a true value if the date is not valid. This may seem secondary, but choosing good names for your identifier is important because that self-documents your programs and clarifies their semantics.

Once we've introduced this minimal subroutine, we might go one step further and move the rest of the code assertion into the subroutine, so that the final code assertion would contain only a call to the new version of the subroutine. This is left as a further exercise for the reader.

Exercise: A Grammar for an Arithmetic Calculator

This is the solution to "Exercise: A Grammar for an Arithmetic Calculator" on page 294. Here's one possible way to implement an arithmetic calculator.

The grammar

Here's one way to write the grammar:

```
my grammar Calculator {
    rule TOP            { <expr> }
    rule expr           { <term> + % <plus-minus-op> }
```

```
        token plus-minus-op { [< + - >] }
        rule term              { <atom> + % <mult-div-op> }
        token mult-div-op   { [< * / >] }
        rule atom {
            | <num> { make +$<num> }
            | <paren-expr> { make $<paren-expr>.made}
        }
        rule num               { <sign> ? [\d+ | \d+\.\d+ | \.\d+ ] }
        rule paren-expr     { '(' <expr> ')' }
        token sign             { [< + - >] }
    }
```

This solution is quite simple.

An expression (expr) is made of one or several terms separated by "+" or "-" operators. A term is made of one or several atoms separated "*" or "/" operators. An atom may be a bare number or a parenthesized expression.

This guarantees that precedence rules are satisfied. Multiplications and divisions will be evaluated before additions and subtractions, since, when parsing an expression, you need to evaluate the individual terms before you can complete the expression evaluation. Similarly, since a parenthesized expression is an atom, it will have to be evaluated before the term in which it appears can be fully evaluated. Note that, in the case of a parenthesized expression, the expr rule is called recursively.

The actions

Notice that we have included two actions in the grammar (in the atom rule). One reason was for convenience: since the atom rule covers two very different named subrules, it is a bit easier to include the action just in the context of the subrules. If an action had been attached to the atom rule, it would have required finding out which subrule had been matched to know which action to perform. Nothing difficult, but doing so would have made the code slightly more complex. The other reason was for pedagogical purposes: although it often makes sense to create an actions class, it is useful to know that actions may be inserted in the grammar part. For a very simple grammar, it might be over-engineering to create an actions class with just one or two actions.

The actions class might look like this:

```
class CalcActions {
    method TOP ($/) {
        make $<expr>.made
    }
    method expr ($/) {
        $.calculate($/, $<term>, $<plus-minus-op>)
    }
    method term ($/) {
        $.calculate($/, $<atom>, $<mult-div-op>)
```

```
            }
        method paren-expr ($/) {
            make $<expr>.made;
        }
        method calculate ($/, $operands, $operators) {
            my $result = (shift $operands).made;
            while my $op = shift $operators {
                my $num = (shift $operands).made;
                given $op {
                    when '+' { $result += $num; }
                    when '-' { $result -= $num; }
                    when '*' { $result *= $num; }
                    when '/' { $result /= $num; }
                    default  { die "unknown operator "}
                }
            }
            make $result;
        }
    }
```

The `calculate` method computes expressions (terms separated by addition or sub-traction operators) and terms (atoms separated by multiplication or division opera-tors) from left to right, since these operators are left associative.

This grammar for a calculator and its associated actions class may be tested with the following code:

```
for |< 3*4 5/6 3+5 74-32 5+7/3 5*3*2 (4*5) (3*2)+5 4+3-1/5 4+(3-1)/4 >,
    "12 + 6 * 5", " 7 + 12 + 23", " 2 + (10 * 4) ", "3 * (7 + 7)" {
    my $result = Calculator.parse($_, :actions(CalcActions));
    # say $result;
    printf "%-15s %.3f\n", $/, $result.made if $result;
}
```

which will display the following results:

```
3*4             12.000
5/6             0.833
3+5             8.000
74-32           42.000
5+7/3           7.333
5*3*2           30.000
(4*5)           20.000
(3*2)+5         11.000
4+3-1/5         6.800
4+(3-1)/4       4.500
12 + 6 * 5      42.000
 7 + 12 + 23    42.000
 2 + (10 * 4)   42.000
3 * (7 + 7)     42.000
```

You might wonder whether this code works correctly with a nested parenthesized expression. I originally thought, when I wrote this code, that it might malfunction and that I might have to change or add something to get nested parenthesized expressions right and properly balanced. It turns out that it works fine out of the box. For example, consider the following test code with relatively deeply nested parenthesized expressions:

```
for "(((2+3)*(5-2))-1)*3", "2 * ((4-1)*((3*7) - (5+2)))"  {
    my $result = Calculator.parse($_, :actions(CalcActions));
    printf "%-30s %.3f\n", $/,  $result.made if $result;
}
```

The result is correct:

```
(((2+3)*(5-2))-1)*3          42.000
2 * ((4-1)*((3*7) - (5+2)))    84.000
```

As an additional exercise, you might want to add exponentiation to the list of allowed operators. Remember that exponentiation has higher precedence than multiplication and division (so you probably want to put it somewhere near the atom level). In the event that you want to handle nested exponentiation operators, also remember that they are usually right associative:

```
2**3**2 = 2**(3**2) = 2 ** 9 = 512;  # Not: (2**3)**2 or 64
```

Exercises of Chapter 14: Functional Programming

Exercise: Making a Functional Implementation of Quick Sort

This is the solution to "Exercise: Quick Sort" on page 334. Here's one way to implement the quick sort algorithm in functional programming style:

```
sub quicksort (@input) {
    return @input if @input.elems <= 1;
    my $pivot = @input[@input.elems div 2];
    return flat quicksort(grep {$_ < $pivot}, @input),
        (grep {$_ == $pivot}, @input),
        quicksort(grep {$_ > $pivot}, @input);
}
```

This functional version of the program reflects directly the approach of the quick sort algorithm:

- If the array has less than two items, it is already sorted, so return it immediately (this is the base case stopping the recursion).

- Else, choose an item as a pivot (here, we pick the middle element or one immediately near the middle).

- Partition the array into three sublists containing items respectively smaller than, greater than, and equal to the pivot.

- Sort the first two sublists by a recursive call to the `quicksort` function, but don't call `quicksort` on the sublist containing items equal to the pivot: not only is it already sorted (all elements are equal), but it would fail to meet the base case and would enter into infinite recursion.

- Return the list obtained by concatenating the three sublists.

As noted earlier, the ideal pivot would be the median of the values, but the cost of finding the median would be prohibitive.

In principle, you could choose any item as the pivot, including for example the first or the last item of the array. But for some specific input (such as arrays already almost sorted, forward or backward), this can significantly increase the runtime because the partitioning becomes totally unbalanced, thereby losing the advantage of the divide and conquer strategy. Picking an element in the middle strongly reduces the probability of such pathological behavior. Another possible way to prevent such a risk is to select the pivot at random among the array elements.

Index

Symbols

() parenthesis operator, 23
* multiplication operator, 23
** exponentiation operator, 23
++ increment operator, 20
+= augmented assignment operator, 20
-- decrement operator, 20
/ division operator, 23
:s adverb, 128
:v adverb, 113
= assignment operator, 15
== numeric equality operator, 56
⊕ operator, 309

A

abecedarian, 116, 143
Abelson, Harold, 94
abs function or method, 78, 176
abstract syntax tree (AST), 282, 289, 290, 294
abstraction, 4, 49, 237
access, 155
accessor, 241, 241, 244, 259
accumulator, 177
   histogram, 211
   list, 167, 387
   sum, 165
Ackermann function, 92, 201, 358
Ackermann, Wilhelm, 358
action
   method, 282
actions
   class, 280, 282, 284, 289, 290, 293, 295, 423
   object, 282, 284, 289, 290
add, 323

addition operator, 19
addition with carrying, 106
adverb, 113, 125, 131
   :delete, 187
   :exists, 185
   :i, 125
   :ignorecase, 125, 371
   :r, 126
   :ratchet, 126, 277
   :s, 126
   :sigspace, 126, 277
Aho, Alfred, 118
algorithm, 106, 107, 218
   Euclid's, 360, 363
   square root, 107
algorithmic complexity, 312, 333
alias, 177, 204
alphabet, 232, 234
alphabetic order, 116, 137
alphabetic sort, 172
alternation, 124, 274
alternative execution, 61
ambiguity, 10
ampersand sigil, 47, 168, 175
anagram, 179, 390
anchor, 122
   end of line, 123
   end of string, 122
   end of word, 123, 370
   left word boundary, 123, 370, 371
   right word boundary, 123, 370
   start of line, 123
   start of string, 122
   start of word, 123, 370

word boundary, 123, 370
and operator, 58
angle bracket, 186
anonymous function, 48, 50, 299
anonymous subroutine, 299, 302, 333, 383
Any special value, 44, 51
apostrophe, 18, 22, 38
append function, 381, 394
append mode, 140
approximate numeric equality, 330
argument, 32, 37, 40, 41, 51
    command-line, 411
    to the program, 411
arithmetic calculator, 283, 283, 294, 422
arithmetic operator, 6
arithmetic sequence, 319, 320
arity, 89, 243
array, 140, 153
    multidimensional, 171, 402
    of pairs, 414
artificial intelligence, 275
ASCII, 17
assertion, 122
    code, 123, 130, 279
    look after, 123
    look around, 123
    look before, 123
    negative code, 123
    negative look around, 123
assignment, 15, 19, 26, 96
    item, 156
    operator, 95
    statement, 15
assuming method, 323, 324
AST, abstract syntax tree, 282, 289, 290, 294
attribute, 264
    class, 242, 270
    immutable, 242, 260
    instance, 240, 270
    mutable, 242, 260
    object, 238
    private, 241, 260, 261
    public, 260, 261
Austen, Jane, 210
autoboxing, 238
awk, 118

B

baby Perl, 83

backtracking, 118, 134, 269, 277
backward feed operator, 304
bag, 215, 218, 408
baghash, 215, 408
base case, 68, 71, 88, 93, 328, 425
benchmarking, 222, 229
binary heap, 224
binary number, 233
binary search, 180, 394
binary tree, 224, 318
birthday paradox, 180, 392, 393
bisect, 180, 394
bisection search, 180, 218, 394, 396, 397
bisection, debugging by, 106
BisectSearch module, 398
Bison, 275
bit, 233
black box, 4, 49, 239, 259
body, 37, 51, 98
Bool type, 56
Boolean expression, 56, 71
Boolean function, 82
borrowing, subtraction with, 106
brace, 183
bracket
    curly, 37, 60, 99, 183, 402
    square, 109, 124, 154, 155
bracket operator, 109, 155
braille alphabet, 230
branch, 61, 71
breakpoint, 268
bug, 11, 12, 25, 372
BUILD submethod, 262, 263
byte, 233

C

C-style loop, 165
cache, 176, 195, 196, 321, 333
Caesar cipher, 137, 202, 268, 375
Caesar, Julius, 420
calculator, 14, 28, 294, 422
    grammar, 294, 422
call by reference, 46, 47
call graph, 196, 200
callback function, 298, 333
canid, 252
capture, 117, 125, 131, 274, 294, 371, 376
    named, 275
    numbered, 125, 275

regex, 274
capturing, 124, 275
Car Talk, 150, 202, 376, 377, 378
carnivoran, 252
carrying, addition with, 106
Cartesian coordinates, 79, 239, 243, 264
case
    kebab, 18
    lower, 17, 114, 125, 173, 211, 375, 417
    title, 17, 114
    upper, 17, 114, 125, 138, 173, 375
Cervantes, Miguel de, 256
chained conditional, 61, 72, 357
chained relational operator, 57, 63, 357
character, 109
character class, 120, 128, 135, 273, 369, 370, 370, 371
chars function, 53, 110, 111, 365
Chekhov, Anton, 256
child class, 270
child node (tree), 224
chr function, 137
Church, Alonzo, 300, 322
circular definition, 84
citizen, first-class, 297
class, 237, 238, 239, 255, 256, 270
    attribute, 242, 270
    child, 248, 250, 270
    definition, 239
    inheritance, 247
    MovablePoint, 250
    parent, 248, 250, 251
    Pixel, 248
    Point2D, 240
    Rectangle, 245
    subclass, 248, 250
closure, 101, 300, 302, 313, 333, 383, 395
cmp operator, 58, 173, 175, 176, 298
CMU Pronouncing Dictionary, 202, 404
code assertion, 123, 128, 130, 279, 280
code block, 48
code repetition, 49
code reuse, 49, 255, 398
coerce, 392
coercion, 24, 33, 57, 155, 157, 174, 216, 390
    type, 45
Collatz conjecture, 99
colon-pair syntax, 206

comb function and method, 109, 115, 116, 188, 366
comb sort, 311
comma, 9
comma operator, 153
command-line argument, 411
comment, 25, 26, 339, 365
commutativity, 24
compare function, 79, 356, 356
comparison subroutine, 175
compilation, 275
compiler, 12
complex number, 252
Complex type, 45
composition, 36, 41, 51, 81, 271, 346
    object, 245, 246
Conan Doyle, Arthur, 50
concatenate operator, 113
concatenation, 27, 41, 116
condition, 60, 72, 98
conditional
    chained, 61, 72, 357
    execution, 4, 60
    nested, 62, 72
    postfix , 63, 64
    statement, 60, 72
configuration file, 274
consistency check, 199
constant, 339
constraint, 88
    type, 45
constructor, 240
    custom, 263
    new, 262, 263
    pair, 57
contains, 120
control flow, 102
conversion
    type, 32
coordinates
    Cartesian, 79, 239, 243, 264
    polar, 243, 251, 259
    rectangular, 79, 239
    spherical, 259
corner case, 150, 361
count letters, 372, 373
count method, 135
counter, 116, 134, 187, 188, 300
counting and looping, 116

creating new operators, 214, 307, 308, 310, 407
cross operator (X), 305
crosswords, 141
cumulative sum, 178
curly brace, 37, 60
curly bracket, 37, 60, 99, 183, 286, 402
curry, 322, 323, 324, 333
Curry, Haskell, 322
cypher, 231

D

dash, 18
data compression, 233
data hiding, 382
data pipeline programming, 213
data structure, 221
data structure selection, 221
database query language, 275
date
    extraction, 127
    validation, 279, 422
date format, 278, 279
day number validation, 128
dd function, 194, 200
dead code, 78, 91, 339
debugger, 228, 229, 266, 293, 328
    accessing variables, 267
    breakpoint, 268
    debugging grammars, 293
    help, 267
    launching the, 266
    running code step by step, 267
    stepping out of subroutines, 267
    stepping over subroutines, 267
    stepping through a regex, 269, 293
    the Perl6 debugger, 266
    trace point, 268
    using a, 266
debugging, 11, 12, 25, 70, 90, 131, 149, 176, 199, 227
    by bisection, 106
    emotional response, 12
    experimental, 50
    rubber duck, 230
    the Perl 6 debugger, 266
    using a debugger, 266
declaration
    variable, 15
declarative programming, 275, 294

declarator, 99, 101
declaring variables, 16
decrement operator, 20, 97, 107
default method invocant, 65
default parameter, 207
default statement, 205
default value, 207, 229
defined, 186
definition
    circular, 84
    class, 239
    function, 37
delayed evaluation, 313
delegation, 256, 265, 270
delete adverb, 187, 385
delimiter, 113, 130
denominator method, 8
dequeue, 379, 380, 381, 383
deterministic, 208, 229
development plan
    incremental, 79
    random walk programming, 229
    reduction, 147, 148, 149
diag function (test diagnostic), 331
diagram
    call graph, 200
    object, 240, 246, 271
    stack, 42
    state, 17, 96, 133, 194, 240, 246
Dijkstra, Edsger, 149, 338, 339
dispatching methods, 243
div operator, 55, 73
divide and conquer algorithm, 326, 334, 426
divisibility, 56, 83, 342
    operator, 56
division
    floating-point, 56
    integer, 56, 72
division by zero, 71
division remainder, 55
DNA (deoxyribonucleic acid), 232, 414, 415
do-twice, 53, 347
does trait, 254
dog, 252, 253
    shepherd, 265
domain-specific language (DSL), 274, 308
Don-Carlos, 256
Don-Quijote, 256
done-testing, 408

dot notation, 238, 240, 241, 270
double letters, 150
double quote, 38, 61, 286
DRY: don't repeat yourself, 338
DSL (domain-specific language), 274, 308
duplicate, 179, 192, 201, 391, 392, 403
    checking, 190
dynamic scope, 317, 318
dynamic variable, 317

E

edge case, 150, 361
element, 153, 178
elems function or method, 156, 185, 186, 191, 391
elems method, 342
ellipsis, 255
else keyword, 61
elsif keyword, 61
embedded object, 246, 270
Emma, 210
emotional debugging, 12
empty list, 155
empty string, 134
encapsulation, 81, 116, 237, 239, 259, 266, 270, 382
end, 341
end method, 156
end of line anchor, 123
end of string anchor, 122
enqueue, 379, 380, 381, 383
epsilon, 105
eq, string equality operator, 57, 114
equality and assignment, 95
equality operator, 57, 95
equivalence operator, 157
eqv operator, 157
error
    ignoring, 340
    runtime, 26, 71
    semantic, 26
    syntax, 26
error checking, 87
error message, 14, 18, 26
Euclidean division, 55
Euclid's algorithm, 360, 363
evaluate, 19, 27
even number, 56, 61
exception, 26, 27, 381

not declared, 41
execute, 19, 27
existence
    testing for, 190
exists adverb, 185
experimental debugging, 50, 228
exponentiation, 425
expression, 19, 27
    Boolean, 56, 71
extending the language, 215, 291, 310
extracting
    dates, 127
    IP address, 128

F

factorial, 64, 66, 166, 215, 331, 407
    function, 84, 87
    operator, 215, 308, 407
    recursive function with debug statements, 91
    using a for loop, 64
    using a for pointy block , 65
    using a for statement modifier, 65
    using multi subroutines, 89
    using recursion, 85
    using the reduce function, 166
    using the reduction meta-operator, 167
    using the reduction metaoperator, 304
    with a lazy infinite list, 321
factory, function, 48, 52
False, special value, 56, 132
February, number of days, 279, 420
feed operator, 303
feral animal, 253, 254
Fermat, Pierre, 352
Fermat's Last Theorem, 73, 352
Fibonacci, 195, 353
    function, 87, 195
    function with multi subroutines, 89
    numbers, 74, 321, 353, 354
Fibonacci, Leonardo, 74
FIFO (first in / first out), 159, 160, 302, 383
file
    close statement, 139
    open statement, 139
    reading from, 139
    writing to, 139
file handle, 139
file mode

append, 140
read, 140
write, 140
file object, 149
fileparse method, 280
filter, 169
filter pattern, 167, 178
first in / first out (FIFO), 159
first-class citizen, 297, 333
first-class object, 47, 51, 53, 297, 333, 382
first-match alternation, 124
fixed-size array, 170
flag, 198, 200
flip function, 112, 359, 366, 378
floating-point, 7, 105
floating-point division, 56
flow
    control, 102
flow of execution, 39, 51, 87, 91, 98
fmt method, 346, 378
for block, 205
for loop, 64, 66, 67, 103, 115, 142, 162, 164, 244,
    300, 369, 397, 401
forest, 224
formal language, 3, 10, 12
frame, 42, 51, 67, 85, 196
French quote marks, 305
frequency, 188
    table, 231, 232, 413, 416
    word, 208
frugal quantifier, 122
fruitful function, 42, 51
fun, 221, 291, 340, 344
function, 31, 34, 37, 51
    abs, 78, 176
    ack, 93, 201
    anonymous, 48, 50, 299
    argument, 40
    call, 31, 37, 51
    chars, 53, 110
    chr, 137
    comb, 109
    compare, 79
    dd, 200
    definition, 37, 39, 51
    elems, 185
    factorial, 84
    factory, 48, 52
    Fibonacci, 87, 195

flip, 112
frame, 42, 51, 85
gamma, 88
get, 69
grep, 303
higher-order, 47, 298, 333
index, 111
join, 114, 303
lc, 175
log, 35
log10, 35
map, 302, 303
math, 34
open, 139
ord, 137
parameter, 40
pop, 159
programmer defined, 41
prompt, 69, 351
push, 159, 186
rand, 180, 209
Rat, 33
recursive, 67, 350
reduce, 303
reverse, 303
rindex, 111
round, 32
say, 6
signature, 44, 52
slurp-rest, 139
so, 125
sort, 172, 303
split, 113, 303
sqrt, 36, 80
squish, 157
Str, 33
substr, 111
trigonometric, 35
unique, 157
function composition, 81
function factory, 323, 383
function frame, 67, 196
function, fruitful, 42
function, reasons for, 49
function, void, 42
functional programming, 169, 176, 297, 318,
    383, 388, 389
    style, 325, 329, 425

G

Gadsby, 142
gamma function, 88
gather and take construct, 316
gather function, 316
GCD (greatest common divisor), 94, 360
gcd function, 94, 360, 363
generalization, 145
generic subroutine, 48
geometric sequence, 320, 320
German quote marks, 305
get function, 69, 141
getter, 259
given statement, 204, 244, 405
global variable, 198, 200
golden ratio, 17
grammar, 273, 274, 279, 281, 422, 423
    arithmetic calculator, 283, 294, 422, 424
    date, 280, 420
    debugging, 291
    FormalMessage, 282
    inheritance, 281, 291
    JSON, 284
    Message, 281, 282
    methods, 280
    mutable, 291
    subclassing, 291
grammar inheritance, 282
Grammar::Debugger, 293
Grammar::Tracer, 293
grammatical analysis, 274
grapheme, 110, 111
greatest common divisor (GCD), 94, 360
greedy quantifier, 122
Gregorian calendar, 421
Gregory XIII, Pope, 421
grep, 118, 169, 185, 298, 303, 311, 317, 333, 397
grep function, 170, 300, 385
grid, 54
grouping, 124
guardian pattern, 89, 91, 132, 354, 358
guide, 256

H

half-interval search, 180, 394
Hamlet, 256
hardcoded value, 340
has-duplicates, 179, 391
hash, 183, 200, 221, 392, 397, 400
    function, 195, 200
    invert, 193, 193
    lookup, 189
    looping with, 188
    multidimensional, 402
    reverse lookup, 189
    subtraction, 214
hash lookup, 189
hash merge operator, 309
hash slice, 341
hash table, 200
hashable, 195, 200
head, 214
head method, 214
header, 37, 52
heap, 224, 420
heap sort, 224
Hello, World, 6
hierarchical model, 252
higher-order function, 169, 297, 298, 311, 333
histogram, 188
    random choice, 210, 217, 410
    word frequencies, 210
Hoare, Charles Antony Richard, 309, 334
Holmes, Sherlock, 50
homophone, 202, 404
HTML parsing, 279
Huffman
    code, 231, 233, 234, 414, 420
    decoding, 418
    encoding, 416
    table, 233, 415, 416, 417
    tree, 420
Huffman, David A., 232
hyperoperator, 304, 305, 306
hypotenuse, 81, 356, 357

I

idiom, 340
idiomatic, 47, 59, 86, 103, 165, 184, 191, 301, 378
idiomatic Perl 6, 340
if statement, 60
immutability, 195
immutable parameter, 46, 52
implementation, 188, 200, 221, 264
increment operator, 20, 97, 107, 188
incremental development, 79, 92
incrementation, 116

indentation, 37, 60, 62, 340
index, 109, 115, 120, 132, 134, 155, 183, 337
    slice, 156
    starting at zero, 110, 111, 155, 156
index function, 111, 115, 119, 135, 372
infinite list, 313, 320
infinite loop, 98, 103, 107, 165, 342, 372, 378,
    402
infinite recursion, 68, 72, 88
infinity symbol, 320
infix, 215
information hiding, 270
inheritance, 239, 247, 252, 270
    class, 247
    grammar, 281
INIT now, 394
initialization
    variable, 107
initialization (before update), 97
input, 4
    validation, 351
instance, 240, 270
    as return value, 247
instance attribute, 240, 270
instantiate, 270
instantiation, 240
instruction, 4
Int function or method, 209
Int method, 33
Int type, 8
integer, 7, 12, 252
    even, 56, 61
    odd, 56, 61
integer division, 55, 56, 72, 73, 350
interactive mode, 21, 27, 28, 43, 81, 141
interface, 258, 260, 264
interlocking words, 181
interpolating a code block in a string, 212
interpolation, 38, 61
interpret, 13
interpreter, 5
introspection, 8
inverting a hash, 193, 193
invocant, 8, 9, 65, 120, 144, 238, 243, 244, 257,
    258, 259
invocation, 8, 34
    method, 32, 34, 37, 38, 110, 119, 158, 240,
        243, 244, 246, 386, 391
IO role, 140

IO.lines method, 140, 142
IO.slurp method, 140
IP address extraction, 128
is copy trait, 46
is divisible operator, 83
is export trait, 398
is function (testing), 330
is rw trait, 46, 242, 250
is subclassing trait, 248, 250
is-anagram, 179, 390
is-approx function (testing), 330
is-between, 357
is-leap-year function, 421
is-reverse, 131, 133, 372
is-sorted, 179, 389
isa method, 240
item, 134, 153, 178, 183
    hash, 200
item assignment, 156
iter
    grep, 314, 316
    map, 313
iter-map, 316
iteration, 97, 107, 363
iterator, 313, 316, 333

J
join, 303
join function or method, 114
JSON
    array, 284, 287
    base types, 284
    Boolean, 284
    format, 284
    grammar, 287
    number, 284, 285
    object, 284, 286
    sample, 284
    string, 284, 286
    value, 284, 286, 287
JSON grammar, 284
Julian calendar, 420

K
kebab case, 18
Kernighan, Brian, 118, 337
key, 183, 200
key-value pair, 183, 200, 286
keyboard input, 68

keys function, 218
keys function or method, 163, 187, 189, 341
keyword, 18, 27
  else, 61
  elsif, 61
  sub, 37
  unless, 63
KISS: keep it simple, stupid, 337
Knuth, Donald, 308, 339
kv function or method, 163, 187, 193, 342

L

lambda, 299, 300, 333
lambda calculus, 300
language
  formal, 10
  natural, 10
  safe, 26
  Turing complete, 83
last in / first out (LIFO), 159
last statement, 102, 372, 378
laziness, 313, 314, 316, 319, 334
lazy
  list, 319
  list processing, 313
lc function or method, 114, 175
lcm function, 306
leaf (tree), 224
leap of faith, 86
leap year, 279, 420, 421
leg operator, 58, 174
letter rotation, 137, 202, 375
lexical, 16
lexical analysis, 274
lexical scope, 41, 99, 281, 301, 317, 318
lexical subroutine, 362
lexical variable, 99, 101, 198
lexicographic sort, 172
lexing, 274, 294
LIFO (last in / first out), 159, 160
like function (testing), 330
linked list, 223, 223
Linux, 50
lipogram, 142
list, 153, 177
  element, 155
  empty, 155
  nested, 155, 386
  slice, 156

traversal, 162
list flattening, 366, 380, 381, 386
literal, 19
literal matching, 119
literalness, 10
local variable, 41, 52
log function, 35
log10 function, 35
logarithmic search, 396
logical operator, 56, 58, 62
longest-match alternation, 124
look-around assertion, 123
lookup, 189, 200
lookup, hash, 189
loop, 98, 164
  for, 64, 66, 67, 103, 115, 162
  infinite, 98, 103, 107, 165, 372, 378, 402
  keyword, 165
  statement, 165
  traversal, 115
  while, 97
looping
  with hashes, 188
  with strings, 116
looping and counting, 116
lowercase, 17, 114, 125, 375
  character class, 135
  lc function, 114, 175

M

made method, 284
magical number, 339
MAIN, 69, 332, 411
maintainable, 264
make method, 284
makefile, 275
mammal, 252, 253
mandatory attribute, 341
map, 167, 168, 169, 192, 298, 302, 303, 310, 311, 313, 316, 317, 324, 333, 401
map function, 168, 170, 299, 385
map pattern, 167, 178
mapping, 183, 201, 220
Markov analysis, 219, 220, 411, 412
mash-up, 221
match method, 119
match object, 274, 276, 282, 294
matched string, 118
matching a date, 278

math function, 34
McCloskey, Robert, 116
meaningful identifier, 338
membership
  binary search, 180, 394
  bisection search, 180, 394
  hash, 185
  set, 201
memo, 195, 196, 201
memoize, 195, 196, 401
merge sort, 311, 325
  functional implementation, 328
  nonfunctional implementation, 326, 328
merging arrays or lists, 326
metaoperator, 166, 304, 305, 306, 334, 341, 388
method, 34, 237, 238, 242, 243, 270
  abs, 176
  accessor, 241
  assuming, 323
  comb, 109
  count, 135
  denominator, 8
  dispatch, 243, 249, 254
  elems, 185
  Int, 33
  invocation, 37
  keys, 189
  lc, 175
  match, 119
  nude, 8
  numerator, 8
  overriding, 248, 250
  private, 260, 261
  public, 261
  sort, 189
  values, 185
method dispatch, 249
method invocation, 32, 34, 37, 38, 110, 119, 158, 240, 243, 244, 246, 386, 391
mix, 215
mixhash, 215
Moby Project, 141
mod, modulo operator, 73
modified quantifier, 286
modifier, 125, 131
  statement, 63, 64, 83
module, 34, 52, 397, 399
  BisectSearch, 398
  creating a module, 398

profile, 222
use, 398
using a module, 398
modulo operator, 56, 56, 72, 307, 350
month number validation, 128
Morse code, 230, 231
Morse, Samuel, 230
MovablePoint class, 250
multi
  keyword, 355
  subroutine, 89, 215, 258, 355
multi method, 249
multi subroutines, 332
multidimensional array, 171, 402
multidimensional hash, 402
multiline comment, 365
multiple inheritance, 254
multiplication tables, 70, 300
mutability, 156
mutable parameter, 46
mutator, 244, 259
my, 16, 41, 99, 101
  declarator, 281
my-grep, 311, 317
my-map, 310, 317

N

named
  capture, 275, 277, 289
  regex, 276, 277
  rule, 276, 277, 282
  token, 276, 277
named parameter, 206, 246, 250, 263
namespace, 280, 281
natural language, 10, 13
ne, string inequality operator, 57, 390
negated character class, 121
negative look-around assertion, 123
nested conditional, 62, 72
nested expressions, 425
nested list, 155, 178, 386
new constructor, 262, 263
new operators
  creating, 214, 307, 308, 310
new, object constructor, 240
newline character, 139
Newton, Isaac, 363
Newton's method, 104, 363
next statement, 102, 103

Nil, 382
node (tree), 224
nok function (testing), 330
nonregression test, 332
not operator, 58
now, 393, 394
nude method, 8
number, random, 208
numbered capture, 125, 275
numerator method, 8
numeric equality operator, 157
numeric relational operator, 57
numeric sort, 172
Numeric type, 45
numification, 127

O

object, 134, 237, 238, 256, 270, 382
    attribute, 238
    behavior, 238
    class, 239
    composition, 245, 246, 271
    constructor, 240
    embedded, 246, 270
    file, 139, 149
    first-class, 53
    instance, 240
    interface, 259
    state, 238
    type, 271
object diagram, 240, 246, 271
object, first-class, 47, 51, 297, 382
object-oriented design, 264
object-oriented programming (OOP), 237
    a tale, 264
octet, 129, 248, 249
odd number, 56, 61
odometer, 150, 377
off-by-one error, 132, 327
offset, 111
ok function (testing), 330
omitting the semicolon, 60
one-liner mode, 22, 27, 144, 209, 269, 375, 376,
    411
OOP (object-oriented programming), 237
    a tale, 264
open function, 139
open source code, 50
operand, 19, 27

operator, 13, 19
    * (multiplication), 23
    ** (exponentiation), 23
    ++ (increment), 20
    / (division), 23
    == (numeric equality), 56
    and, 58
    arithmetic, 6
    assignment, 15
    backward feed, 304
    bracket, 109, 155
    cmp, 173, 174, 175, 298
    comma, 153
    cross, 305, 305
    div, 55, 73, 350
    eq (string equality), 57
    equal, 57
    eqv, 157
    feed, 303
    gt (alphabetically after), 57
    leg, 58, 174
    logical, 56, 58
    lt (alphabetically before), 57
    mod, 73, 350
    modulo, 56, 56, 72
    ne (string inequality), 57
    not, 58
    numeric equality, 157
    or, 58
    overloading, 214
    precedence, 308, 374
    range, 64
    relational, 57
    sequence, 319
    set, 7
    set contain, 217
    set difference, 217
    set membership, 216
    slice, 156
    smart match, 58, 117, 118, 157, 273
    square bracket, 154
    string, 24
    ternary, 203
    three-way, 58
    tr, 375
    whatever, 320
    X (cross), 305
    Z (zip), 305
    zip, 305, 306, 341

– (decrement), 20
⊕, 309
operator construction, 214
operator precedence, 23, 27, 59
operator type
    circumfix, 307
    infix, 307
    postcircumfix, 307
    postfix, 307
    prefix, 307
optional parameter, 207, 213
or operator, 58
ord function, 137
order of operations, 23, 27
our, 101
out-of-range error, 132, 171
output, 4
overload operators, 214
override, 229
overriding a method, 248, 250, 263

P

pair, 223, 315, 414
pair constructor, 57, 184, 206
pairs function or method, 187
palindrome, 93, 148, 150, 331, 358, 359, 377, 378
parallelogram, 252
parameter, 40, 42, 52
    default value, 207
    immutable, 46
    mutable, 46
    named, 206, 246, 248, 250, 263
    optional, 207, 213
    positional, 206, 207, 248, 250, 263
    slurpy, 207
parameter type, 44
parent class, 271
parent node (tree), 224
parentheses, 23, 295
    argument in, 32
    empty, 37
    grouping and capturing, 124
    overriding precedence rule, 295
    parameters in, 40, 41
parse, 10, 13, 287, 295
parse method, 280, 281, 284
parse tree, 282, 289
parsing, 274, 280, 294

HTML, 279
JSON, 284
XML, 279
pattern, 117, 119, 134, 273
    filter, 167, 178
    guardian, 89, 91, 132
    map, 167, 178
    reduce, 166, 178
    search, 134, 143
PCRE (Perl Compatible Regular Expressions), 118
PEMDAS, 23
Perl 6 documentation, 344
Perl 6 grammar, 274
Perl 6 in a browser, 5
Perl 6 version, 5
Perl Compatible Regular Expressions (PCRE), 118
Perl culture, 83
pet animal, 253, 254
phi, 17
pi, 17, 23, 36, 108
    estimate, 108, 364
pick function or method, 192, 209, 217
pick method, 343
pipeline programming, 82, 298, 302, 325, 334, 413
pivot
    quick sort algorithm, 334, 426
Pixel class, 248, 249
placeholder, 164, 174, 175, 300
    parameter, 164, 300, 312
plain text, 139, 208
Poe, Edgar Allan, 231, 413
poetry, 11
point, mathematical, 239
Point2D class, 239, 240, 242
Point3D class, 258
pointy block, 66, 300, 369
    using several items, 369
polar coordinates, 243, 251, 259, 264
polymorphism, 258, 266, 271
pop function, 158, 159, 160, 379, 383, 384, 388
positional parameter, 206, 207, 248, 250, 263
postcondition, 90
postfix conditional, 63, 64
postfix notation, 65
postfix syntax, 99, 366
postmatch, 128

power, 93, 359, 360
precedence, 23, 59, 295, 308, 374, 423, 425
    operator, 23, 27
precondition, 90
prefix, 220
prefix decrement operator, 365
prematch, 128
premature optimization, 339
prepend function, 380
print statement, 6, 13
print-grid, 54, 348, 350
printf function, 346, 351, 364
private attribute, 241, 261
private method, 260, 261
problem solving, 3, 13
proceed clause, 205, 405, 407
profile module, 222
program, 3, 13
    argument, 411
    testing, 149
programmer-defined function, 41
programmer-defined type, 239, 240, 270
programming, 3
    declarative, 275, 294
    functional, 275
    logic, 275
    object-oriented, 237
programming paradigm, 297
Project Gutenberg, 208, 210, 231
prompt, 6, 13, 267, 351
prompt function, 69
prose, 11
pseudo-Morse, 233, 234, 417, 418
pseudocode, 309
pseudorandom, 208, 230
public method, 261
push function, 158, 159, 160, 180, 186, 191, 381,
    384, 393
Puzzler, 150, 202
Pythagorean theorem, 79

Q

quadrilateral, 252
quantifier, 121, 129, 274, 370, 371
    exact number of times, 122
    frugal, 122
    greedy, 122
    range, 122
queue, 159, 160, 223, 379, 381, 382

quick sort, 311, 334, 335, 425
quotation mark, 6, 9, 22
quote
    double, 38, 61
    single, 18, 38, 61
quote-word operator, 154, 186

R

radian, 35
Ramanujan, Srinivasa, 108, 364
    pi estimate, 108, 364
rand function, 180, 190, 191, 209
random number, 208, 343
random text, 220
random walk programming, 229
range, 156
    operator, 64, 154
    type, 154
range operator, 204, 320, 342, 343
range quantifier, 122
Rat function, 33
ratchet, 277, 277
rational, 13, 252
    type, 8
read mode, 140
real number, 252
Real type, 45
reassignment, 96, 107, 156
rectangle, 245, 246, 252
Rectangle class, 245
rectangular
    coordinates, 79
rectangular coordinates, 239
recursion, 66, 67, 72, 74, 84, 86, 147, 354, 358,
    387, 394, 395, 423, 426
    base case, 68, 328, 425
    infinite, 68, 88
recursive definition, 84
recursive rules, 277, 281
reduce, 169, 298, 303, 333
reduce function, 170, 299, 343
reduce pattern, 166, 178
reducible word, 202
reduction, 304, 334
    metaoperator, 304, 306, 310, 389
reduction method, 282
reduction operator, 166, 343, 388
reduction to a previously solved problem, 147,
    148, 149

redundancy, 10

regex, 109, 113, 116, 134, 143, 175, 205, 269, 273, 337, 368, 369, 376
    adverb, 125
    anchor, 122
    capture, 274, 369
    debugging, 269
    parentheses versus brackets, 124
    pattern delimiter, 119

regular expression, 113, 116, 134, 273

reinventing the wheel, 338

relational operator, 57
    numeric, 57
    string, 57

repeated method, 392

repetition, 4

REPL, 5, 20, 28, 81, 141, 154

representation, 239, 245

reserved word, 18

return, 44
    statement, 67, 77
    value, 32, 52, 77, 247

reverse, 174, 303, 418

reverse function or method, 193

reverse lookup, 189, 190, 201

reverse lookup, hash, 189

reverse word pair, 180, 396

RGB, 248, 249

rhombus, 252

right-justify, 345

rindex function, 111

role, 140, 238, 239, 252, 253, 255, 256, 271
    application, 254
    composition, 254
    type, 256

roll method, 393

root (tree), 224

rosettacode, 318

rot13, 138, 375

rotation, letter, 137, 375

rotation, letters, 202

round function, 32

rubber duck debugging, 228, 230

rule, 278, 294, 422, 423

running pace, 14, 29

runtime error, 26, 68, 71

rx regex operator, 119

S

s/// operator, 130

safe language, 26

Saint-Exupéry, Antoine de, 219

sanity check, 199

say function or method, 6, 194

scaffolding, 80, 92, 200, 339

scalar, 16, 16

scalar context, 191

Schiller, Friedrich, 256

scope, 41, 42, 383
    dynamic, 318
    lexical, 301, 302

script, 21, 27

script mode, 21, 27, 43

search, 135
    binary, 180, 394
    bisection, 180, 394, 396, 397
    pattern, 134, 143
    sequential, 185

sed, 118

self, 243

self-declared parameter, 164, 300

semantic error, 26, 27

semantics, 27

semi-predicate problem, 315

semicolon, 6, 19, 28, 402

semicolon, omitting, 60

sequence, 9, 109, 135, 153

sequence operator, 319, 321, 343
    generator, 320

sequential search, 185

set, 7, 215, 408
    contain operator, 217
    difference operator, 217
    membership, 201
    membership operator, 216
    operator, 7

sethash, 215

setter, 259

Shakespeare, William, 256

shaped array, 170

sheep dog, 265

shepherd, 265

shepherd-boy, 265

shift function, 158, 160, 381, 388

short-circuit Boolean operators, 59

short-circuit evaluation, 59, 390

sigil, 16, 18, 23, 27, 47, 154, 164, 168, 175, 183, 298
sigil, percent, 183
signature, 44, 45, 46, 52, 69, 160, 162, 164, 203, 206, 207, 215, 347, 354, 358, 361, 379, 379, 384, 398, 407, 410, 411
sigspace, 277
simplicity, 338
sin function, 35
single quote, 18, 38, 61
slang, 274
slice, 110, 135, 156, 212, 388, 389
    assignment, 160
    list, 156
    operator, 156
slurp, 394
slurp function, 140
slurpy parameters, 207, 380, 384, 384
smart match, 205
smart match operator, 58, 117, 118, 130, 157, 273
so function, 125
software metric, 332
solutions to the exercises, 345
sort, 172, 173, 176, 212, 298, 300, 303, 386, 389, 390, 391
    alphabetic, 172
    ASCIIbetical, 173
    bubble sort, 313
    case insensitive, 174, 175
    code object, 173
    comb sort, 311, 312
    comparison subroutine, 175
    function or method, 172, 189
    lexicographic, 172
    merge sort, 311, 325
    numeric, 172
    quick sort, 309, 311, 334, 425, 426
    reverse order, 174
    transformation subroutine, 175, 386
sorting, 58, 356
    advanced, 173
    data, 172
special case, 149, 150
special value
    Any, 44, 51
    False, 56
    True, 56
special variable, 64, 65

spherical coordinates, 259
splice function, 176, 384, 394
split, 303
split function or method, 113, 342
sprintf function, 151, 346, 378
spurt function, 141
    append mode, 141
sqrt function, 36, 80
square, 252
square bracket, 124
square bracket operator, 109, 124, 154
square root, 104, 107, 363
squish function, 157, 342
stack, 159, 160, 223, 382, 382
stack diagram, 42, 52, 67, 85, 92
start of line anchor, 123
start of string anchor, 122
state, 101
state diagram, 17, 28, 96, 133, 194, 240, 246
statement, 19, 28
    assignment, 15, 15, 96
    conditional, 60, 72
    for, 64, 103, 115, 162, 366
    if, 60
    last, 102
    next, 102, 103
    print, 6, 13
    return, 67, 77
    use, 52
    while, 97
statement modifier, 63, 64, 65, 72, 83, 99, 366
Str function, 33
string, 7, 13, 109, 221, 365
    concatenation, 24, 113
    length, 110
    operation, 24
    operators, 110, 112
    relational operator, 57
    type, 8
string concatenation, 24, 113
string equality, 330
string repetition, 24
string traversal, 365, 367
String type, 46
stringification, 114, 127
stringify operator, 114, 118
structure, 10
sub, 37
    keyword, 37

subclass, 251, 262, 271
subclassing, 248, 250
sublanguage, 274
submethod, 262, 262
subparse method, 281
subpattern, 128, 129, 274, 275, 278, 289
subroutine, 37
subroutine parameters, 99
subroutine signature, 160, 162, 215, 379
subrule, 276
subscript, 109, 155
subset, 249
    type, 88, 199, 361
subst method, 130
substitution, 130, 131
substitution operator, 130
substr, 337, 373
substr function, 112, 135, 324, 365, 365
substr function or method, 111
substring, 110, 111, 112
subtask, 4, 4
subtraction
    hash, 214
    with borrowing, 106
suffix, 220
sum function or method, 343
Sussman, Gerald Jay, 94
swap, 308, 309
swap operator, 309
swapping variables, 343
switch statement, 204
syntax, 10, 13, 26
    error, 26, 28
    highlighting, 21, 71
syntax error, 16, 18, 37

T

tail method, 214
take function, 316, 317
tale about OOP, 264, 265, 266
tc function, 162, 299
tc function or method, 114
temporary variable, 78, 92
term, 19, 28
ternary conditional operator, 203
ternary conditional operator, nesting, 204
ternary operator, 203
test, 339
test module, 329, 357, 374, 407

    is function, 330
    is-approx function, 330
    like function, 330
    nok function, 330
    ok function, 330
    unlike function, 330
test plan, 408
test-driven development, 332, 334
testing, 291, 407
    and absence of bugs, 149
    automated tests, 329
    incremental development, 79
    is hard, 149
    knowing the answer, 79
    leap of faith, 87
    module, 329
text
    plain, 139, 208
    random, 220
text editor
    atom, 21
    eclipse, 21
    emacs, 21
    gEdit, 21
    nano, 21
    notepad++, 21
    padre, 21
    vi, 21
    vim, 21
The Gold-Bug (Edgar Allan Poe), 231
The Little Prince (Antoine de Saint-Exupéry), 219
there is more than one way to do it, 83, 369
Thomson, Ken, 118
Three Sisters, 256
three-way comparator, 174
three-way operator, 58
tilde, 127
TIMTOWTDI, 83, 127, 192, 369
title case, 17, 114
token, 10, 13, 277, 278, 422
TOP rule, 280, 284
topic, 65
topical variable, 65, 119, 144, 154, 162, 168, 204, 244, 366
tr operator, 375
traceback, 70
trait, 46, 52, 88, 398
    does, 254

is, 254
is copy, 46
is export, 398
is rw, 46, 242
trapezoid, 252
traversal, 115, 131, 135, 147, 166, 188
    list, 162
tree, 224
    binary, 318
    leaf, 224
    node, 224
    root, 224
triangle, 73, 352
trigonometric function, 35
True, 132
    special value, 56
Turing
    complete language, 83
    thesis, 83
Turing, Alan, 83
twigil, 164, 207, 241, 246, 300
two-dimensional space, 239
type, 7, 13, 240, 243, 247, 256, 262
    -defining role, 256
    array, 153
    bag, 215, 408
    baghash, 215, 408
    Bool, 56
    building new type, 238
    built-in, 256
    checking, 87
    coercion, 24, 33, 45
    Complex, 45
    constraint, 45
    conversion, 32
    hash, 183
    Int, 8, 45, 45
    list, 153
    mix, 215
    mixhash, 215
    Numeric, 45
    parameter, 44
    programmer-defined, 239, 270
    Rat, 8
    Real, 45
    set, 215
    sethash, 215
    Str, 8
    String, 45, 46

type object, 240, 271
type subset, 88, 199, 361
typed array, 170
typographical error, 228

U

uc function or method, 114, 162
undefined value, 78
underscore character, 9, 18
Unicode, 17, 110, 111
uninitialized value, 71
unique function, 157, 192, 342, 391
uniqueness, 179
unless statement, 63
unlike function (testing), 330
unshift function, 158, 160, 180, 379, 381, 384, 393
until loop, 99
update, 96, 104, 107
uppercase, 17, 114, 125, 138, 375
use lib, 398
use module, 398
use statement, 52

V

value, 7, 13, 201
values function or method, 185, 187
variable, 15, 17, 28
    declaration, 15, 16
    dynamic, 317
    global, 198
    interpolation, 38, 61, 367
    lexical, 16, 99, 101, 198
    local, 41
    scalar, 16
    temporary, 78, 92
    updating, 96
Variable … is not declared, 41
variable interchange, 308
variable name, 25
variable-length code, 230
variadic parameters, 380, 384
variadic subroutine, 207
vertebrate, 252, 253
void function, 42, 52, 67
von Neumann, John, 326
vorpal, 84

W

Weinberger, Peter, 118
WHAT, 8, 199, 240
whatever, 190
    closure, 321, 322
    operator, 320, 321
    placeholder parameter, 321
    star parameter, 324
    term, 324, 325
whatever operator, 343
when statement, 204, 405, 406
while loop, 97, 115, 365
whitespace, 142
whitespace in regexes, 120
wildcard character, 120
word frequency, 208
word list, 141
word, reducible, 202

words function or method, 114, 342
Wright, Ernest Vincent, 142
write mode, 140

X

X cross operator, 305
XML parsing, 279

Y

Y2K bug, 421
Yacc, 275
YAGNI: you aren't gonna need it, 338

Z

Z zip operator, 306
zero, index starting at, 110, 156, 157
zip operator, 305, 341

About the Authors

Laurent Rosenfeld has been a software engineer for about 20 years, working especially as a contractor for one of the largest telecommunication operator in Europe, particularly in the field of mobile networks. Over the last few years, he has been working especially in the fields of data migration, data quality, and data munging. He has written a number of tutorials on Perl 5 and Perl 6.

Allen B. Downey is a Professor of Computer Science at Olin College of Engineering. He has taught at Wellesley College, Colby College, and UC Berkeley. He has a Ph.D. in Computer Science from UC Berkeley and Master's and Bachelor's degrees from MIT.

Colophon

The animal on the cover of *Think Perl 6* is a red admiral butterfly (*Vanessa atalanta*), which is common throughout temperate areas in North America, Europe, and Asia. It is also known as a "red admirable." These insects migrate north in spring and generally have two broods between March to October (meaning two generations are born, so it is the "grandchildren" who migrate south the following winter).

The red admiral has a vivid pattern of brown, orange, red, and black on its wings, along with white spots. They are considered medium-sized butterflies, with a wingspan of 2 inches. Caterpillars of this species feed on nettles, while adults eat fermenting fruit and flower nectar.

Many of the animals on O'Reilly covers are endangered; all of them are important to the world. To learn more about how you can help, go to *animals.oreilly.com*.

The cover image is from *Meyers Kleines Lexicon*. The cover fonts are URW Typewriter and Guardian Sans. The text font is Adobe Minion Pro; the heading font is Adobe Myriad Condensed; and the code font is Dalton Maag's Ubuntu Mono.

Learn from experts.
Find the answers you need.

Sign up for a **10-day free trial** to get **unlimited access** to all of the content on Safari, including Learning Paths, interactive tutorials, and curated playlists that draw from thousands of ebooks and training videos on a wide range of topics, including data, design, DevOps, management, business—and much more.

Start your free trial at:

oreilly.com/safari

(No credit card required.)